W

THE

PEOPLE

A Conservative Populism

Time for us to take our politics back from the political/media class that has taken it over

by
Peter Bearse

Alpha Publishers Inc.

Alpha Publishing Inc.
P.O. Box 53788
Lafayette, Louisiana 70505

PRINTED IN THE UNITED STATES OF AMERICA

Library of Congress Card Catalog Number 2004113227
ISBN 0-9717585-9-X

Dedication

To the great American majority, "the heroes of everyday life,"
especially those of:

- *9/11*
- *Operation Iraqi Freedom; and especially those who . . .*
- *Week after week manage to serve as members of local councils, boards, committees, or commissions—pillars of local government and democracy, all.*

Select Introductory Quotes

"The Congressional Library"

"Where else in all America are we so symbolized / As in this hall? / White columns polished like glass, / A dome and a dome, / A balcony and a balcony, / Stairs and the balustrades to them, / Yellow marble and red slabs of it, / All mounting, spearing, flying into colour. / Colour round the dome and up to it, / Colour curving, kite-flying, to the second dome, / Light, dropping, pitching down upon the colour, / Arrow-falling upon the glass-bright pillars, / Mingled colours spinning into the shape of white pillars, / Fusing, cooling, into balanced shafts of shrill and interthronging light.

This is America, / This vast, confused beauty, / This staring, restless speed of loveliness, / Mighty, overwhelming, crude, of all forms. / Making grandeur out of profusion, / Afraid of no incongruities, / Sublime in its audacity, / Bizarre breaker of molds, / Laughing with strength, / Charging down on the past, / Glorious and conquering, / Destroyer, building, / Invincible pith and marrow of the world, / An old world remaking, / Whirling into the no-world of all-coloured light."

……. Excerpt from a poem by Amy Lowell, in Lowell (1925), *What's O'Clock*. Boston: Houghton Mifflin Company.

Abraham Lincoln

"We cannot escape history."

"The dogmas of the quiet past are inadequate to the stormy present. The occasion is piled high with difficulty and we must rise to the occasion. As our case is new, we must think anew and act anew. We must disenthrall ourselves, and then we will save our country."

"...that from these honoured dead we take increased devotion to the cause for which they gave the last full measure of devotion.

That we here highly resolve that this nation, under God, will have a new birth of freedom…that the government of the people, by the people and for the people will not perish from the earth."

Pink Floyd: "On the Turning Away"

"On the wings of the night / As the daytime is stirring / Where the speechless unite / In a silent accord / Using words you will find are strange / And mesmerized as they light the flame / Feel the wind of change / On the wings of the night.[1]

Arianna Huffington

"Of course, there is nothing more American than ordinary people – whether dressed in high fashion pink or in coveralls – taking up the gauntlet to solve the problems and right the wrongs of our times…throughout our history, whatever the cause…it wasn't elected officials who were in the vanguard but outraged and engaged citizens demanding reform."[2]

Aristotle

"A citizen is one who participates in power."

Plato

"The penalty that goodmen pay for not being interested in politics istobe governed by men worse than themselves."

Edmund Burke

"The only thing necessary for the triumph of evil is for good men to do nothing."

Notes

1. Segment of a song from "A Momentary Lapse of Reason," copyright D.J. Gilmour / A. Moore 1986/87.

2. Arianna is author of *How to Overthrow the Government*, published in 2001, and one of the many candidates for Governor of California via the 2003 initiative referendum recall of Governor Grey Davis. The quote is from the next to last paragraph of her Internet newsletter of June 26, 2003, entitled "People Power Goes Hollywood," a review of the movie "Legally Blond 2."

Content

Acknowledgment

Thanks should go to many who shared in the process of producing this book but the greatest thanks and gratitude, by far, go to Janet Bruno, partner, lover and dearest friend, who supported the author and his work with great patience and personal sacrifice for over six years.

This book is also dedicated to Mary Perone, the leading role model for local political activism and leadership among those featured in Chapter 4 and one of the author's early political mentors who, unfortunately, passed away in the Spring of 2003 just as this book was being completed. She represented the politics of "the greatest generation."

Foreword

This is a controversial book, a book that citizens of any democracy should read and would ignore at their peril. Its Massachusetts' author is very perceptive. So, this puts the state again at the leading edge of writing on the foundations of people's liberty. The author is truly dedicated to the vision of local self government that the state has long represented. He is very concerned that the drying up of grassroots politics and local, democratic, political participation threatens our ability to govern ourselves as a Republic. He can't resist noting the irony, perhaps even the contradiction, of trying to export our democracy to Iraq while ignoring its deteriorating foundations at home. He is sounding an alarm, hoping that people will respond before it is too late. As concerned Americans have recognized for generations, the price of liberty is eternal vigilance. The author shares that view as he surveys the American political scene and marks negative trends that register "Danger Ahead."

The book's opening, bell-weather declaration, that "the political grass roots are drying up" can be demonstrated. It is not easily denied. This is indeed cause for alarm, but there are some green shoots arising from the political root system. There seems to be an increasing sophistication of citizen awareness that precludes too much manipulation, including an awareness that the power base still resides in the ballot box, with various issue combinations waiting for public judgment and direction. The author states that politics has become a "spectator sport," but this may not be true when politics really counts to the citizenry. Observe irate citizens at city council or school board meetings and large turnouts on issues such as environmental degradation. The question is: What are the trigger points to get people out and involved, to reach for pen and paper or to get their street shoes on and striding "where the rubber meets the road"?

The book states that "The political pro's have taken over," not only to the detriment of popular participation but also, it should be noted, "at their candidates' peril." The "pro's" judgment and advice are often off-base and harmful. Too many neglect certain electoral targets while indulging in campaign overkill and over-reliance upon money for interminable rounds of last-minute TV ads. Dirty campaigns often backfire. Gut issues are sometimes neglected or misread; for instance, the depth of American feeling for the 2nd Amendment and firearms' ownership. Political consultants do not fare well in this book's pages, primarily because their agenda is self-serving and their political "science" is no science at all but "spin" conjured for campaigns.

The author's diagnostic mind plumbs the implications of many key developments, behaviors, and attitudes. There is a war going on between the covers of this book as to the state in which the American body politic now finds itself. The book posits a duality of roles, as it were, that begs a crucial question: Are the American people victims or saviors of the present political system? This question suggests a moving target. They are both. They find themselves shifting from one role to the other at different times. There are many crossovers as recognitions of problems surface and political participation develops and sometimes kicks in. This is where the sweet aroma of optimism arises – the possibility that people can in fact come back into the political picture as effective participants. There is some evidence of this possibility. Political volunteers seemed to make a difference in some races during the 2000 and 2002 elections. There are some indications of a possible reawakening among political party leaders that people's help is needed in campaigns, that TV and other "media buys" are not enough. Additionally, a significant number of self-starters see the urgency of responsible citizenship. But these tendencies are fragile, and the signs are tentative.

The author's dissection of the "Y2K" Presidential campaign, including and especially the primary, is well done – a much needed civics lesson. He takes us from "pretend populists" to misleading interpretations generated by the media "commentariat." His critique, cautions, and predictions regarding campaign finance reform a la McCain-Feingold were right on target, as evidenced by the course of the bill through the U.S. Senate and judiciary.

How can one conclude a foreword as a beginning? – by returning to introduce an author who is not known to potential readers of this book but who has become well known to this writer. I see a true son of the Republic whose love for his country is reflected throughout his commentary. As I read the book, I see an author who…

- Is very perceptive and who has a special ability to be critical while also proposing constructive solutions to the problems he identifies.

- Gets to the root of problems with information and insights on why people should get involved and how they can take their democracy back.

- Has clearly examined and shown why the American people should be the key actors in the political play of *their* political system.

- Has demonstrated what is involved while knowing when to discard faulty rationales.

Thus, whether or not the book will prove to have any currency for people elsewhere, the author has written a book upon which citizens of *our* Republic should read and act. It is a book they would ignore at their peril.

—Carroll Miller
Member of the Wyoming House of Representative, 1987-1992;
State Senator, 1992-2003, Wyoming Senate District 19
(Big Horn/S. Park Counties).

Introduction

How many times have you heard politicians say they will fight "special interests" and work to "return politics and government back to the people," then return to their offices to play politics as usual"? How many times have you seen or heard political pundits bewail "apathy," "cynicism," and citizen's lack of involvement in "their" system? How often have you heard people complain about "them" versus "us"? To what extent have you been one of them, wondering why your vote and voice seem to weigh so little in the political scales and how things can be different?

Now, think back again: How many books on the market get to the root of the problem – to show why people need to be involved and how they can take "their" democracy back? NONE, and perhaps that is why you are reading this introduction, wondering whether you have finally found one. There is hope that you can help fulfill, less by reading than by acting so as to be among the citizens who will write their own distinctive chapter in the great book of American democracy. So, in the hope that some of the reading you can do here might inspire you to act, let me introduce you to this small contribution toward the greater book of political action. It is a labor of love inspired by three things: (1) my own "laboring in the vineyards" in local politics; (2) my observation that the grassroots of American politics have dried up, so the political system that is the light of the world is in trouble; and (3) a judgement, made in light of history, that the time to start to revive and rebuild the American political community from the ground up/grassroots is now. Thus, this is a book on needs and ways to revive grassroots political participation in the U.S. of A.

Read on, and you will find much that is controversial, such as:

- A core, remarkably gee-whiz, radical!(?) theme: WOW!—The American people should be the key actors of the political play in THEIR democratic system.

- That the so-called "Progressive" reforms of one-hundred years ago were actually regressive, and the same types of liberal "goo goos" are still driving the reform wagon.

- A strong case that our political system will continue to deteriorate with potentially dire but unpredictable consequences, unless "ordinary" people get involved and take "their" system back from the so-called "political class."

- That people should look to unexpected, out-of-the-way places for models and ideas of political reform, especially the business community.

- Campaign finance reform a la McCain-Feingold (et.al.) will fail because it counts only money, not the value of people's time.

- The mainstream media are a major source of our political problem and, possibly, a key to its solution.

- That "the heroes of everyday life" to whom the book is dedicated, can and do make a difference, politically, as interviews with many such people reveal.

- Our response to 9/11 can make the difference between despotism and democracy.

- The Internet is not going to save American democracy; it is helping to undermine it along with the rest of the electronic media.

There are fresh insights and new information as well as controversies in every chapter, but you do not have to read this book from cover to cover to derive some value from it. It will help to start with more of a road map for reading than you can see from just the Table of Contents. Each of us starts with more or less acquaintance or experience with what goes on in the world of politics. So, the first chapter is a short introduction to the basic weakness of American democracy today. The diagnosis is simple: THE GRASS ROOTS HAVE DRIED UP! Why, and what to do about it, especially since you are one of the roots – that's the hard part, so, many of the chapters to follow are much longer as we explore how to water and replant the grassroots.

It might not be apparent, even to the most conscientious citizen (you?), why his or her participation in politics is important, so the second chapter explains why from all angles, including intersects and conflicts between our political and personal lives. The most important intersect is along the line of personal development. None of us can become complete, well-developed human beings if we do not get out of our own skin enough to participate in the public life of our communities.

The third chapter may appeal to history buffs but perhaps may be sampled or ignored by those who simply (?) want to get on with the challenges of our political present or presence (or lack of such). The basic message of "The Context of Our Times" is twofold:

1. The roots of our current political problems run very deep, going back at least 150 years; but...

2. The past is not (necessarily) prologue. The sources of solutions to our problems go back even further and, in combination with present opportunities, imply that "The Future is Now" – this is OUR "historical moment."

Chapter 4 gives you a chance to relate to the experience of people other than the author (who had related part of his story in Chapter 3). None of these other stories are drawn from *People* magazine or from "lives of the rich and famous." They are based on interviews with two dozen people from all walks of life. All are more or less "ordinary" people. Perhaps, however, in the aftermath of 9/11, we have come to realize that the star system promoted by the media does not begin to do justice to "the heroes of everyday life," so many of whom came to our attention when we saw "ordinary" people doing extraordinary things during and in response to 9/11. The interviewees featured in Chapter 4 may differ from you and other readers in only one respect—they all have been actors in some political play at some point in their lives—"actors," not "stars." They may have been bit players, ignored by the media, but their "bit" contributions, altogether, add up to a lot. As shown in Chapter 3, they amount to a very important part of the political vitality of a living democracy. The political participation they represent puts its participants in the top 5% of the American electorate. That makes them "stars" in my book. At least as important, though, is the fact that their participation has made a positive difference to their lives and the communities in which they live; and it has enabled them to form and express views on a variety of issues that help to raise the level of debate on these issues. Perhaps their experience and their views make them "role models" for the rest of us but, unlike "stars," their good examples are ones that any of us can emulate. When these people look in the mirror, they do not say, like Pogo: "We have met the enemy and he is us."

Chapter 5 continues with insights from more of the "ordinary" people involved in politics who have made a difference at the grassroots—the volunteer chairs of local political party committees of both major parties. These insights, however, are presented via tables of numbers rather than stories because they are derived from a national survey. The chapter reveals the importance of people's participation in such committees and shows how political parties and the grassroots foundations of American democracy are weaker for a growing lack of such participation. It is this chapter more than any other that makes the book a companion to a earlier, great (1992) book by Robert Heinlein—*Take Back Your Government: A Practical Handbook for the Private Citizen Who Wants Democracy to Work.* The chapter also shows some interesting contrasts between Democratic and Republican political activists with regard to what they do and don't do at the local level. Is the Democratic party more the party of the people? From the standpoint of the reader who, like 98% of others, is not a member of a local political party committee, Chapter 5 indicates how much access and scope there is for your participation and what a difference your involvement can make in the public life of your community.

Nevertheless, even though political participation is highly accessible and important at the local level, there are "barriers and constraints" to peoples' participation that are identified and discussed in Chapter 6. This is neither a lengthy chapter nor a downer. Once they have been recognized, we can begin to see how barriers can be overcome and constraints reduced, a goal that is increasingly served by the remainder of the book as we get into how things can be changed.

The next chapter (#7) looks for "seeds, concepts, and agents of change" in the most unlikely arena, the business community, one that political reformers typically view as adverse to change. It does so because:

- the political and other parts of the public sector are backward relative to business, in many ways that the chapter reveals at the outset;
- large portions of the business sector transformed themselves during the '90s, starting with the manufacturing sector in response to Japanese competition, contributing to the long wave of '90s prosperity; and…
- the most progressive parts of the business community point the way to political reforms.

The very nature of the chapter is paradoxical. One of its most interesting (and in its author's view, most important) contributions is a detailed rundown of how politics-as-usual papers over a variety of paradoxical situations in which, especially if we want to make changes, we need to be pursuing opposites—goals that appear to contradict one another. One of the leading business writers, Charles Handy, titled one of his popular books *The Age of Paradox*. Indeed it is; except that our political "leaders" do not seem to have recognized or adapted to the fact.

It's impossible to write about any aspect of politics, especially political participation, without going into the media. As the debate on campaign finance reform has revealed, politics is being driven by an incestuous mix of money and media. Even if we are not "couch potatoes," TV watching takes up a lot of time that could be better spent by us as citizens involved in the politics of our communities. In any event, TV reinforces our roles as consumers rather than producers of anything, especially anything political. Meanwhile, people who are politically naïve but who see a technology solution to nearly every problem are saying that the Internet will save our democracy, even bring "power to the people."

Media hype suffuses so much of our lives that Chapter 8 goes into various aspects of the media's effect on politics in some detail, including that of the Internet. Overall, this chapter is highly critical of the media and concludes that changes in the media must be at the top of any political platform for reform, else political reform that would restore ownership of "our" democracy to "We, the People…" doesn't stand a chance. On a more positive note, the chapter concludes by indicating how the media can become a key part of the solution rather than a major source of the political problem.

By the time you get to it, Chapter 9 may seem dated, as it focuses on political year 2000. But this chapter is not a rehash of old news. It treats 2000 as a year which had great potential to effect political reform, starting with a bang during the primaries but ending with a whimper—fizzling and failure of reform impulses that brought volunteers from all over the country into New Hampshire for the 2000 presidential primaries. Thus, the experiences of 2000 and its aftermath are still with us as lessons to inform drives for reform into the future. As this book is undergoing final editing, the 2004 presidential campaign is already underway with debates among the Democratic contenders. We can wonder whether the potential of '00 may be realized in '04.

So, by the time you, the reader, get to the final Chapter, you are ready for a discussion of "prescriptions and possibilities" for political reforms that would "rebuild the American political community from the ground up"—from the grassroots of communities where you live. Those of you who can't stand to wait to find out "who done it" when reading a detective story may want to skip intervening chapters and leap to the conclusion. Yet, you will have missed a lot of supporting evidence, lessons, stories, and rationale for recommendations that appear in Chapter 10. But then, by the same token—of leaping to the conclusion—you may have little reason to read the book at all, for its basic conclusion is simple. If anything is to be done, then the "who" in the "done it" will be *you*. Do you want to be the figure in the mirror that Pogo saw? It's so easy to blame someone else, especially those "politicians" for whatever's wrong with a political system that is supposed to be ours. It is your participation or lack of such in our political system that makes a difference. Perhaps this book can help to show you the why and wherefore as well as the how, especially why *now is the time for the "how" of your own political participation* to begin to make a difference for yourself and for others, especially for your children and grandchildren.

Peter Bearse, Merrimac, MA, democracyanddevelopment@msn.com, 5/7/03

1.

What's the Problem?—
The Grass Roots Have Dried Up

Outline
- People Don't Count
- Money Matters
- The "Pro's" Count Us Out, Too
- Preliminary Signs of Hope?

People Don't Count

Ever since the founding of our nation, we have thought of ourselves as being a young country, yet the United States of America is now the oldest constitutional democracy in the world. Our uniquely American democracy is the light of the world. It is our finest and most valuable export in terms of beneficial national influence. Yet, even as the torch of liberty is lit and relit in countries around the world, the grass roots of our democracy have been drying up in our own backyards. As we export our democracy abroad, it is deteriorating here at home.

Ever since the founding, we have been an optimistic people—labeled as brashly optimistic by many, especially cynics soured by history. Yet, our own recent political history should give us pause. Evidence of disease in the body politic has been turning up all around us for years. The symptoms have been getting worse; negative trends have not yet turned the other way. We see them in declining voter turnouts, low participation in the political process, rising apathy and cynicism regarding both politics and government. Not least is decreasing faith in the ability of our elected officials to solve problems, even those currently "in the news," let alone those that have nagged in the background for years. Inability of "the system" to deal with important issues is the prime reason political pundit E.J. Dionne attributes to *Why Americans Hate Politics*, the title of one of his books.[1]

Yet, the underlying factors behind the symptoms run much deeper than lack of action on the issues or problems of the day. The latter come and go. Some of the more cynical commentators even go so far as to say that the political system doesn't solve problems; it just recycles them. The causes of the cancers afflicting American politics run very deep. Historical roots going back at least 150 years were revealed many years ago by Richard Sennett in *The Fall of Public Man*.[2] Even though Sennett was writing as a social psychologist and historian, not a political forecaster, much of what he had to say foresaw our current predicament. His book reminds us of an old advisory that this book will honor: that we need to select from the best of the past in order to build a better future. We start to do this in the next chapter.

When we or our doctors try to diagnose a physical disease, certain questions are asked and answered, such as: How do we feel? What is our temperature? Blood pressure? Heart rate? Carry this analogy over to politics. How do we feel about it? Is it an object of hate? Not really. Hate is also a verb. It suggests that someone may act. At this point, what prevails is arguably more dangerous for the present and future of our Republic—passivity, apathy, and indifference. At least at election times, most people feel politics is important and do their best to pay some attention to political activity. What really bothers us, however, is that it's not *our* game; it's somebody else's. It's not "us"; it's "them." We're not taken seriously, except as consumers of the propaganda that political actors euphemistically call "literature" or that congressmen reference as "newsletters" if it's on paper, and "media buys" if it's on TV.

Does this mean that "the system" is to blame and that, individually, we have no responsibility? No. As Pogo once said: "We have met the enemy, and he is us." But doesn't Pogo go too far, appearing to "blame the victim"? No again, because citizens in a democracy have the ultimate responsibility for its survival. As Abraham Lincoln said in his Annual Message to Congress of 1862: "We—even we here—hold the power and bear the responsibility." But the truth of responsibility is somewhere between a set of mirrors reflecting "us" vis a vis (not vs.) "the system." In this book, we need to break into the space between the mirrors to see what we can do to exercise our portion of responsibility as prime political actors to change the system so that it can work better for everyone.[3] As Sierra Club Executive Director Carl Pope urged in an editorial in the club's magazine, *Sierra*: What is needed is a "New Patriotism," for "the antidote to cynicism is participation… Most important,…we all need to re-engage in politics, blending the new volunteerism (as called for by President Bush's State of the Union address, which Pope references) and a renewed patriotism into a new democracy."[4] *Harper's Magazine*, writer Lewis Lapham observed that "The successful operation of a democracy relies on acts…by no means easy to perform, and for the last twenty years, we have been unwilling to do the work…a shared work of the political imagination." The implication?—There is a very real danger that we will continue to be victimized by those whose "press releases count on an audience that thinks of politics as being trivial entertainment…who take for granted the stupefaction of an electorate too lazy to open its mail."[5]

Those of us who haven't tuned out politics completely may still read or watch. We can hardly help ourselves if we turn on the television news or glance at a newspaper, with lurid, attention-getting headlines and sharp sound bites hardly failing to get our attention even in spite of ourselves. We may even listen; some of us may even vote, albeit reluctantly, faced as we so often are by what Dionne has described as "false choices" in terms of issues and/or "the lesser of two evils" with respect to candidates. But does our participation count for anything in terms of either time or money without a "new patriotism" that brings forth a "new volunteerism"—NO. Even on a patriotic national holiday, "participation" has "degenerated into a day where only token nods toward our honored dead are given, if at all."[6]

Money Matters

Note the inclusion of money in the paragraph above. But for the single-digit percentage of us who have been lucky enough to be involved in a political committee or campaign in situations where our time commitment counted for something, we know how lightly the value of our time is weighed. But money? Yes, money, too. Except for a tiny percentage of an already minuscule proportion, those who have served on candidates' finance committees know that their opinions and participation, too, count for little. The politicians and their handlers take the money and run. The political pro's have taken over. The flowering of the professionals' approach to politics and their commanding presence in political campaigns is a major part of the problem. The "pro's" may be destroying the system that feeds them; but they are filling a void left by the absence of us as participants in what, after all, should be our politics, not theirs.[7]

The latter can be seen in high relief in debates on campaign finance reform. Commentators and analysts across the political and media spectrum agree that "the system is broke."[8] One major reason has already been implied: Politics is a spectator sport observed by an "audience that thinks of politics as trivial entertainment."[9] It is no longer a "sport" in which citizen players count. This is part and parcel of rising reliance upon expensive media, especially TV advertising. The latter feeds, and is fed by, increasing reliance upon professionals in campaigns and political committees. It is a vicious cycle (VC), one of a set of such cycles infecting and affecting our politics. The fact that there are several VC's where negatives feed on each other is what makes the decline of political participation so very worrisome. There's no automatic or built-in antidote or corrective if people don't recognize what's happening and deliberately, decisively act to counter the negative trends.

The connection between escalating campaign costs and the media is documented by a report of the Committee for the Study of the American Electorate (CSAE) entitled "Use of Media Principal Reason Campaign Costs Skyrocket." Political "pros" are partly compensated by pulling down a percentage of each media "buy." Their role continues to increase as increasingly sophisticated target marketing techniques borrowed from business are applied to marketing candidates like detergents and other commodities. One candidate for statewide office in Massachusetts who is also a cable TV consultant even goes so far as to say: "It's not TV; it's the paid consultants!" (who are the main source of campaign cost inflation). This claim wouldn't hold water, however, but for the fact that campaigns are increasingly dependent upon costly media to get candidates' messages out to an increasingly inattentive electorate. One of the interviewees for Chapter 4, Mike Lynch, remarked (with regard to political campaigns): "It's all communications media."

A simple, startling fact about the debate on campaign finance reform highlights our basic problem—the issue of reform has been defined entirely in terms of money! No stronger indicator of the irrelevance of political participation can be found when it is practically ignored by those most concerned about "reform." Isn't it ironic that those overwrought about the increasing dominance of money in politics define the issue of reform entirely in terms of money?

Apparently, the only political commentator who argues differently is former Iowa Congressman Mickey Edwards, now at Princeton's Woodrow Wilson School. He stated that "participation" should be a prime goal of reform efforts. Yet, even he has failed to observe that a basic weakness of *all* the many versions of campaign finance reform put before the Congress is that they place no value on people's time—*even though time is all that the overwhelming majority of the American electorate have to contribute.* The "atrophy" of the system observed earlier is evidenced by the mere 3% who volunteered to help during the 1996 election cycle—even less than the 4% who contributed money.[10]

One can read article after article on campaign finance reform and find no mention of people's participation as a factor to be considered, let alone as a goal to be honored. A quote from one of them suggests that analysts and commentators are making an implicit assumption—that political volunteerism has declined to the point where it does not merit even honorable mention, it has become such a negligible factor:

> As money becomes the resource of choice in campaigns, the parties depend less and less on the vanishing volunteers of the grass roots and more and more on the organizational capacity to raise large sums of money.[11]

The role of local political party volunteers in a general election campaign for the U.S. president was last featured by national media in the 1992 presidential campaign. A network TV news item at the time showed precinct workers in Chicago going door-to-door for Bill Clinton. During the 1996 campaign, no such vignette was featured, yet another sign of the decline of local political participation. During the 2000 and 2004 election seasons, some network news programs showed volunteers "laboring in the vineyards" of New Hampshire, but these were featured as individuals working for individual presidential candidates during the primary season, not as political party committee members or volunteers at work after the primaries.

Claims have been made by some involved in state-level "Clean Money" campaigns that public financing of campaigns, by reducing the importance of large, private contributions, should induce more citizen participation. As yet, however, such claims have not been substantiated. One cannot point to voting statistics for presidential elections—the one Federal example of public financing—for any inkling of support in this regard. It certainly has been heartening to see significant numbers of volunteers helping to get Clean Money initiatives on state ballots. It remains to be seen, however, whether such campaign finance reforms in Maine and other states can be associated with increases in political volunteerism, political turnouts, and other reversals of trends affecting political campaigns that elect people to office. Chapter 9 turns to this and other reform issues.

So, again, we seem to have gotten ourselves caught in a vicious circle. As the influence of money in politics increases, people's participation is less important. As participation is less important, more and more services that have been provided by volunteers need to be purchased. So campaign costs and the importance of money continue to go one way—UP. Curtis Gans, Director of CSAE, stated:

> If more than 50 percent of the campaign budget goes to media and an average of 30 percent goes to fund raising, and the rest goes to candidate travel and staff, there is nothing left for any activities involving people. It is little wonder that American politics is withering at the grass roots.[12]

Similar testimony has been heard from the California Voter Foundation: "A vicious cycle is now going on *even at the local level* for local elections: Political consultant involvement increases the money to be raised. The more money is raised, the more likely consultants are used. They go up and up." [as reported by National Public Radio (NPR) News, Sacramento, 2/16/98 (my emphasis in italics)].

The "Pro's" Count Us Out, Too

Another reason why political volunteerism has been overlooked may lie in the backgrounds of the authors of reform articles, studies, and reports. The reform literature has been produced by another variety of "pro's"—political scientists, writers, journalists and commentators, many of whom are otherwise known as political "pundits." Many have made fine contributions. Some of these will be acknowledged in later chapters. One is hard put to identify authors of any significant contributions to the political science or reform literature, however, who have any experience "laboring in the vineyards of politics," especially who have invested significant amounts of time working on campaigns, running for office themselves and serving in elected office. One exception was mentioned earlier, Mickey Edwards.

Lack of direct political experience can easily limit or color one's perspective on political reform. As Don Shea remarks in *Transforming Democracy*, "those in the political vineyards see things differently." An analogy from the arena of reforms in business practices may help. Relying on professionals with no experience of politics to diagnose and prescribe reforms in politics is analogous to American manufacturers, pressed to respond to the Japanese challenge of the '80s, at first failing to elicit suggestions for improvement from those on the shop floor. In contrast to other books on political reform, this relies upon the author's political experience and that of others "laboring in the vineyards" as prime sources of intelligence. The perspectives to be offered, therefore, may provide inputs into the political reform debates that are at least as refreshing and, hopefully, as significant as inputs "from the shop floor" were to business reforms and the renaissance of American manufacturing. See Chapter 7 for much more on the relevance of "the business revolution" to political reform.

Preliminary Signs of Hope?

The chapters to follow will reference, complement, and reinforce some encouraging developments arising from non-political quarters. Among the most important are:

- Increasing attention to the quality of our "civic life," primarily via community-based initiatives supported by several major foundations;

- The "public journalism" movement, promoted by the Kettering Foundation and others;

- "National Issues Forums" and reports reflecting how or why people get involved or fail to get involved in politics, also supported by the Kettering Foundation.[13]

Add to these some nascent political signs of hope arising from the influence of volunteers in some congressional mid-term elections via door-to-door, person-to-person politics.

Seeing the promise of these, one can only hope that over the long term they will help to reverse the negative trends noted earlier. Even a sympathetic monitor of these initiatives like the author, however, might be struck by a curious limitation or blindness among them. With rare exceptions, they do not directly come to grips directly with the political process or proposals for political reform.[14] Papers on "reviving civic culture" in *The Kettering Review*, for example, discuss a variety of "intermediary" organizations or community-based initiatives without mentioning political committees or their activities. The League of Women Voters (LWV) counts as its "coalition partners" a similar variety of local organizations without ever citing local party committees, who have traditionally carried out voter registration and "get out the vote" (GOTV) activities.[15] One can cite example after example of the same sort.

Thus, inadvertently and ironically, the approaches to "reform" stemming from other, "non-political" quarters help to underline the importance of the explicitly political thrust of this book—to rebuild the American political community from the ground up. Like the non-political types, the reforms featured herein seek to re-engage people in public life but, unlike the non-political types, they would do so by discarding the disingenuous, emasculating and ultimately self-defeating assumption that there is an effective "public life" without participation in electoral politics. Such an assumption appears to underlie what one commentator calls the "Goo-Goos" approach to campaign finance reform. [16] Arthur Lipow indicts this approach more strongly and convincingly. He shows that the "Goo-Goos" approach is a direct legacy of the "Progressive" movement, which "debased (the) American political system" and led to "undemocratic" reforms, including those "post-Watergate."[17] Lipow goes on to claim that current efforts at reform, especially those advocating public financing of electoral politics, will further undermine the American democratic system.

The latter, in turn, suggests there may be a dangerous dynamic at work whereby efforts at reform may have unintended, counterproductive consequences. They could even be one of the causes of one of several "vicious cycles" affecting American politics. Intellectuals, foundations, not-for-profit organizations and others concerned with the quality of public life in the U.S.A. lament the major, negative, long-term trends in political participation cited earlier. Then they proceed to support projects that shy away from any involvement in electoral politics, be it the activities of parties, political committees, campaigns, or candidates. Thus, they further reduce the capability and repute of these basic parts of our political "infrastructure." These parts thereby are less likely to receive support, and so forth—negatives feed negatives. This is analogous to "lemons" behavior observed by economists. If a system has acquired a reputation for producing "lemons" it is less likely to attract talent to turn things around, so the negative reputation is enhanced and things get worse.

It would be tragic if we were to let the flower of American democracy continue to wither and die even while seeds we had planted abroad grow and flourish. As noted in the next chapter, economists, management gurus, futurists, and others say we are in the midst of a great transformation even greater than that characterizing the age of industrialization. Indeed we are. The forces of science, technology and business are transforming our lives. Compared to the progressive dynamics of these, our politics and government seem locked in limbo and lagging, hopelessly unable to keep pace. Yet, no one would deny that we are in an era of rapid, unsettling change and increasing complexity.

An era of complex change has implications for the life of a great democracy that will need to be drawn out in many ways. This book, however, honors the desire for simplicity. It starts from some simple premises, cites many "ordinary" examples, and ends with some simple conclusions. The freedoms we have won can never be taken for granted. The roots of democracy need to be watered and cultivated by each generation. Lincoln's words at Gettysburg need to be honored in action: "That a nation of the people, by the people and for the people shall not perish from the earth." That means a system OF and BY, not only FOR. With rights go responsibilities.

The basic premise of this book is that neither "technology," nor "professionals," nor trying to "make a difference" only through community-based, non-political activities will improve our politics and enable better government. Only a broad cross section of the American people, "ordinary" citizens, getting involved in politics themselves will suffice to reclaim the process as their own, for *US*, not *THEM*. As "Granny D" (aka Doris Haddock), who walked the country at age 89 to arouse support for campaign finance reform has said: "We must take our country back." [18] But do we want it?

We do, and we can. The tasks before us are urgent, important, and hard to accomplish, but the efforts would be both personally satisfying and politically transforming. The concluding chapter indicates how. Try it, you'll like it. The appendices add a wealth of resources and linkages to help you. You're not alone.

Notes

1. Dionne, E.J. (1991), *Why Americans Hate Politics*. New York: Simon and Shuster, Touchstone Edition.

2. Sennett, Richard (1977), *The Fall of Public Man: On the Social Psychology of Capitalism*. New York: Vintage Books.

3. A 1992 article used the image of the "Man in the Mirror" in a song by Michael Jackson to characterize a "citizen leader for a new politics." See my article with the latter title in *Public Leadership Education: The Role of Citizen Leaders*, Dayton, OH: The Kettering Foundation in partnership with the Council on Public Policy Education (Vol. VI, November, 1992).

4. In the May/June, 2002 issue of the magazine, p.14-15.

5. Lapham, Lewis (2003), "Cause for Dissent," *Harper's Magazine* (April, pp.38 and 40).

6. The quote continues: "The blame belongs to those of us who know what the true meaning is but fail to observe the day...," from www.usmemorialday.org (May 20, 2002).

7. Mike Lynch, one of those interviewed for this book (See Chapter 4), remarked on this paragraph that it's "our own fault." This seems to me to have a little too much flavor of "blaming the victim," but we all need to reflect on the matter of both individual and collective responsibility for the decline of grassroots political participation that led to this book.

8. The quote is from Bill Bradley, who made the claim in one of his speeches.

9. Quoted phrase from the Lapham article cited earlier in footnote 5 (p.38).

10. Reference is made here to 1996 rather than 2000 or 2004 because of upticks in political volunteerism during the past two Spring presidential primary seasons. It remains to be seen whether these are transient blips or harbingers of something more. See chapter 9.

11. Citizens Research Foundation (1997), "New Realities, New Thinking." Los Angeles, CA: University of Southern California (March). [This is the only explicit reference to "volunteers" in dozens of articles on this issue reviewed by this author.]

12. Committee for the Study of the American Electorate (CSAE, 1997), "Use of Media Principal Reason Campaign Costs Skyrocket." Washington. D.C.: CSAE.

13. For a critical review of the Foundation's work on this topic, however, see my "Review Essay: Meaningless Chaos: Understanding How People Fail to Form Relationships with *Political* Concerns," The *Good Society* (Fall, 1995).

14. One exception is the Pew Charitable Trust, which has provided support for some papers on campaign finance reform. Yet, these suffer from shortcomings already noted in this vein of literature. In addition, they make no connections with "civic culture," also a concern at Pew—as if "campaign finance reform" were in one box and "civic culture" were in another, with no possible relationship between them.

15. See, for example, the 1996 end of year (December/January) issue of the LWV's magazine *The National Voter* on "Who Voted and Why." The LWV writes: "Imagine a grassroots organization that is effective in every community, from a small rural town to a large, inner-city neighborhood, and at every level, from the local school board to the U.S. Congress." One doesn't have to "imagine"; it exists in the form of local political party committees (LPCCs). The LWV, however, completely overlooks LPCCs while expressing great concern over how "effective" are "grassroots organizations" in the political process.

16. See Judis, John (1997), "Below the Beltway: Goo-Goos Versus Populists," *The American Prospect*, no. 30 (January-February, 1997).

17. Lipow, Arthur (1996), *Political Parties & Democracy* Chicago and London: Pluto Press.

18. Quoted in "Pilgrim's Progress," *People* Magazine, 5/10/99 (page 251). She also remarked: "I've got 11 great-grandchildren and I don't want them to be brought up without a democracy." Note that Doris Haddock is a long-time political activist. She was one of the hardest working volunteers for Bruce Babbitt in New Hampshire during his brief campaign for the presidency in 1988. See: Duncan, Dayton (1990), *Grassroots: One Year in the Life of the New Hampshire Presidential Primary*. New York: Viking.

2.

The Context of Our Times and The Historical Moment
The Future Is Now

Outline

Executive Summary

The future is now. Many signs and signals from past history point to now as the historical moment when, simply by virtue of becoming part of the political process using whatever time we can afford to contribute, we can reverse long-term negative trends threatening our democracy and begin to take our republic back from the political class that has taken it over. The "signs and signals" include the transformation of our economy in ways unmatched since the industrial revolution. Socially and politically, the similarities of our time with the last great "Progressive" wave of reform make us sit up and take notice that another one has begun that we can influence if we don't continue to be AWOL from politics. The difficulties of a political transformation to accompany that of the "new economy," however, are underlined by the deep historical roots of our lack of participation, especially narcissistic behavior and the depreciation of public life. Nevertheless, the historical moment to begin to reverse past trends is indeed now. The "new" politics also has deep roots going back to the beginnings of our scientific age. Notwithstanding its long-term depreciation, the public is now poised to come into its own.

Introduction

They say that, in politics as in life and sex, "timing is everything." The thesis of this book and its opening chapter can be simply stated: now is the time to start to reverse the negative trends that both reflect and effect citizens' declining political participation and threaten our democracy. Trends of several decades are typically labeled "long term" in the United States, where historical memories and trends tend to be short. The historical roots of the trends affecting citizens' political participation, however, run long and deep. If we understand these, we will be better able to confront their recurring symptoms in the here and now and be better prepared to change things for the better. That is, we will be better prepared to make history (fulfill our destiny) rather than just to suffer it (fulfill a fate determined by others). If we ignore history, then we indeed fulfill fate, as the old saw goes, by living to repeat the worst of it rather than shape it in light of the best.

The roots of both the problems and the promise of democracy go back, like so much in our "modern" time, to the Renaissance, as exemplified by Machiavelli, Bacon, Montaigne, and Shakespeare. A crucial part of the promise is a heritage of "open-mindedness and skeptical tolerance" that began with the Renaissance (Toulmin, p.25). The Renaissance is the first of three great transformations, transitions, or passages in human history that this chapter will feature because they presage the great historical opportunity that is the focus of this book. We are living in the third. This is a chapter that focuses on historical parallels and similarities with our own time so that we can better see how, living in the context of another great era of change, we can make a difference by being active historical agents rather than bystanders or victims of change.

Deep Roots of "The Past is Prologue"

The roots of promise can be found in the writing of two of the most famous figures of Renaissance history—Francis Bacon and Niccolo Machiavelli. One is regarded as the father of science, the other, the father of modern politics. The major common denominator to both is a scientific approach, one to the natural world, the other to the human, usually unnatural world of politics. Both were true Renaissance men—that is, men of many parts. Both looked to discover the ways things really are in order to be able to influence, shape, or control them, not to the way men have imagined them to be or hoped to make them via myth, magic, ideology, religion, or other forms of wishful thinking. Another shared characteristic is that they were both very public men experienced through active, long-term, and high-level participation in the political and governmental affairs of their countries and their time. Bacon was a lawyer and parliamentarian elected to the House of Commons who rose to become Lord Chancellor of England.

Machiavelli was an active participant in the political life of his native Florence. He served as Secretary to the Second Chancery of the Republic of Florence, successfully concluded many diplomatic missions, and was commissioned to write *The History of Florence*. The primary difference with Bacon is that Machiavelli's writing dealt with human nature, not purely physical nature.

Thus, he emphasized, even though "there is no truth…other than what is actual…," that—

- "representing things as they actually are is insufficient" (Althusser, 1999, p.33).
- "what is involved is not the natural order of things…but…a political under-taking and innovation…" (Ibid., p.43).
- (there is a need to) "*transform this consciousness into a political force* capable of producing this event, or *participating* in its production…" (Ibid., p.28) [NOT a utopia].[1] [emphasis mine]

The "event" to which Machiavelli referred, the object of his desire, was the unification of Italy—its becoming a nation. In the case of this book, it is a big jump in political participation among the great majority of ordinary Americans who are now non-participants—those not in the game or part of the picture except when they vote, usually against something or someone. In both cases, observation of what is real and actual points to "the imaginary character of the reigning ideology in political matters" when observed from the standpoint of the people rather than "The Prince."[2] There is the American myth that local government is "closer to the people," for instance. We shall see more of the "imaginary" in the form of media "un-reality" in Chapter 8.

Perez Zagorin's study of Francis Bacon attributes "a significant effect" of Bacon's political career on his thought, giving to it "its extreme wordliness."[3] Yet, Bacon is known for setting forth the vision for a new age of scientific discovery, not for a political career long forgotten and hardly memorialized except in biographies read by few. Bacon wrote:

"There is no hope except in a new birth of science…raising it regularly up from experience…Men have made numerous discoveries by accident, so imagine what they will discover when they apply themselves to seek and make this their business."[4]

Imagine, indeed! Only now, after it has influenced 400 years of scientific discovery, do we see the remarkable fulfillment of this vision, as scientists and entrepreneurs, together, now make science their business. Indeed, as Bacon warned in 1608: "Knowledge is power." Except that we now add money to the equation.

Indeed, "Machiavelli was…Bacon's type."[5] Bacon refers to Machiavelli numerous times, almost always approvingly." Bacon's essays are almost as Machiavellian as people tend to think of Machiavelli himself—akin to the political self help advisories that Machiavelli provided to his Prince, such as advisories on "cunning," "ambition," "riches," "reputation," &c. Both men were writing "for those who want to move the world."[6]

In the hip parlance of our own day, we would call Bacon and Machiavelli soul brothers. At the dawn of a new, modern era, both pointed the way, set the tone and provided the basic methods, indeed, the ethos of a new era. Bacon's natural science has revolutionized human life and will continue to do so, at least for the rest of the 21st century. Machiavelli's political science was bastardized by succeeding generations of power-hungry politicians of all stripes as "Machiavellism."[7] Bacon defended Machiavelli from biased mis-interpretations during his own time. "Bastardized" is not too strong an adjective. For most of the politicians who have read *The Prince* and benefited from its advisories have lacked its author's devotion to a republic and its people.

Political science after Machiavelli, and the human or social sciences more generally, have not made nearly the same progress, nor has their work been nearly as beneficial as that accomplished by the physical and biological sciences. Some claim that it has mostly served to aid and abet the "will to power" of nation states, politicians, dictators, and bureaucrats who have sought to rule, manipulate, and control rather than "empower" the rest of us.[8] Thus, the major bequest of Bacon and Machiavelli to us, altogether, is the challenge of how to apply our science to our politics and public lives in ways that will truly empower us (free us), as democratic citizens of the world's greatest republic, to fulfill the American dream for ourselves and for others, worldwide. This is the major challenge of the historical moment we now face.

"The Great Transformation"—A New Politics to go with the New Economy?

It has been obvious for several years that our 21st century economy and society are in the midst of a sea-change comparable only to the great trans-formation driven by the Industrial Revolution of the 19th century.[9] It is now so obvious to so many that even the media caught on, especially during their millenial …Y2K hype. We do not need to devote space in this book to specifying all the shifts in progress nor speculate on their implications except as they relate to people's political participation. These larger changes in economy and society have been, and will continue to be, discussed at length by others.[10] However brief the treatments of historical context in this chapter may be, it is important to realize that "We are now at the end of an era, not just in the calendar sense of leaving behind a thousand years starting with a "1" and entering a thousand years that…start with "2"—but in a deeper, historical sense" (Toulmin, 1990).

A quick take on our time is this: the 21st century transformations are driven by technology, which is driven by science. People and organizations of all types, at all levels, are struggling to adapt. The byline of our time, especially in business, may be: Innovate and change, or die! Meanwhile, politics and government, notwithstanding all the P.R. about "reinvention," is predomi-nantly "same old, same old" and, thus, a fundamental impediment to transformative progress in the society at large.

So, do we need a "new politics?" Damn right we do. To recap: the thesis of the book is simple (that is, easy to state; achievement of a transformative political vision is quite another matter)—We can't have a better government without a better politics. We can't have a better politics without a better democracy. American history demonstrates that the only answer to the problems of our democracy is more democracy, not less.[11] And we can't have a better democracy without the direct, active participation of greater numbers, a broader base and higher percentages of the American people.

The essential lines of influence are illustrated by Fig. 1, a path diagram, below:

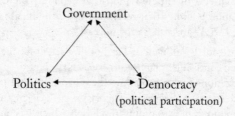

Fig. 1

The arrows represent lines of influence running both ways between all paired categories. So the figure is the political counterpart of the kind of illustration we might find in a book on the environment, where "everything relates to everything else." Another counterpart is the so-called "chicken and egg problem"—which comes first? In fact, the diagram represents the *political* environment. Government affects politics and political participation through laws and regulations that are directly and indirectly influential—for example, campaign finance laws and ballot-access regulations. Political participation influences politics, what some often refer to as "politics as usual," if enough people take part and turn out to make a difference, as, for example, hordes of volunteers from all over the country made a difference for McCain and Bradley in New Hampshire during the Y2K presidential primary season.[12] Politics obviously influences government in myriad ways, at least as practiced by big money contributors or well-heeled interest groups represented by lobbyists who have access to elected officials.

It helps to distinguish "politics" from "democracy" because there is nothing necessarily democratic about politics. Neither democracy nor the "free market" are free, even though (and partly because) most actors in either sphere would rather have a free ride or the deck(s) stacked in their favor.[13] Most prefer non-competition to competition. It is only political entrepreneurs like McCain and Bradley, together with the fresh energies of people wanting to see political reform and real political competition that, at least for awhile, turned the Y2K and 2004 presidential primary seasons into real, interesting political horse races (see Chapter 9). For all their talk of "competition has made me a better candidate," G.W. Bush, John Kerry, and Al Gore would rather have coasted to receive preordained blessings of their party establishments.

Before getting down to political reform in the U.S. of A., let us recall highlights from the last great transformation in order to get some perspectives

on our own. Here, we draw from Karl Polanyi's classic book on the subject.[14]
The process of change that he describes reveals some remarkable parallels
with our own time. He saw:

- Established powers (the English "squirearchy" of the late 18th
  century) initiate a radically miscast "reform" (of "poor relief"; what
  we call welfare) in an ultimately futile effort to forestall destructive effects of the new industrial economy on English society.
  Chapter 9 argues that recent, so-called political reforms here in
  the U.S.A. are also, sadly, miscast"

- Intellectuals, influenced far more by scientific theories than the
  often confusing or contradictory facts of their time, provide rationalizations for an economic theory to drive and preempt public
  and social policy—the theory of a "self-regulating market
  economy...an astounding revelation which hastened greatly the
  transformation of society." The "new economy" theorists of the
  late '90s hypnotized us with a similar vision to rationalize
  "downsizing," "outsourcing," and "globalization."

- Politicians and policy makers in the newly industrialized societies,
  reacting to facts—the obviously destructive consequences of a
  self-regulating market economy at later stages of the industrial
  revolution (1840-1940)—and with only flawed theories to guide
  them, tried as best they could to adapt public policy to ameliorate
  those consequences. So, they tried to re-establish some small
  degree of public control over the new economy, often in response
  to emerging interest groups created by that economy. These were
  primarily the new middle class and organized labor trying to
  deploy political and government regulatory powers for their own
  benefit. Nevertheless, acts to ameliorate negative effects of the
  self-regulating market reflected "a variety of local conditions...the
  most varied slogans (and) very different motivations of a multi-
  tude of parties and social strata..." (p.147). Not unlike this piece
  of a distant past, there has arisen a variety of state and local
  responses to economic and political problems that arose from the
  bust following the '90s boom.

- Those who provided the main rationalizations for the "institutional degeneration" of society and the "degradation" and "de-
  moralization" of the working class rested their case upon a crude
  "naturalism"—a biological model best known as "Malthusian,"
  which influenced Darwin and, after Darwin, Social Darwinism.
  The latter, in turn, further rationalized the new economy as a
  mechanism that evolved "naturally" via the "natural selection" of
  unregulated "laissez faire" competition based upon unbridled
  individualism. We now see descendants of this way of thinking
  among Libertarians and others.

Not only apologists but also prophetic critics of the last great transformation have counterparts in our own time. Polanyi favors two from the 19th century, Harriet Martineau and Robert Owen:

- "Only a woman, Harriet Martineau...understood and clearly expressed the need of society for a new class of "independent laborers..." (p.100).

- "One man alone perceived the meaning of the ordeal...*he alone possessed intimate practical knowledge of industry*....Robert Owen...looked to the state... for helpful intervention designed to avert harm of the community..." (p.127, emphasis mine).

Owen, not unlike others noted further on, strongly criticized the trend toward "individualization" in light of "his insistence on the social origin of human motives" (p.127). To him, according to Polanyi, "the most obvious effect of the new institutional system was the destruction of the traditional character of settled populations (i.e., communities) and their transmutation into a new type of people, migratory, nomadic lacking in self-respect and discipline – crude, callous beings..." (p.128).

Another historical figure, Jeremy Bentham, receives mixed reviews, perhaps because he was more influential than the latter two. On the one hand, Bentham advocated a science of society via his "principal of utility." On the other, he was an inveterate social engineer right up to his death in 1832, ever trying to invent institutional innovations and set up social experiments to solve socio-economic problems. We still have Benthamites among us who believe that they can use social engineering to do "the greatest good for the greatest number." But Polanyi (along with this author) admires his empirical approach and laments its demise. According to Polanyi, "Once the market organization of industrial life had become dominant, all other institutional fields were subordinated to this pattern (and) the genius for social artifacts (i.e., social/political/institutional experiments) was homeless" (p.121). Doesn't this seem remarkably similar to what we see in the present, the increasing dominance of the market economy in all spheres of life?

R.M. McIver, an early President of the New School for Social Research (now New School University, with former Sen. Bob Kerrey as its President), wrote the foreword to Polanyi's book. His remarks not only highlight the significance of Polanyi's historical perspectives; they are also evocative of the main concern of this book—to define a politics sufficient to the challenge of change in a new economy. McIver writes, in light of Polanyi's rendering of the last great transformation:

- The tremendous problem of the social control of a revolutionary change was unappreciated; optimistic philosophers obscured it, shortsighted philanthropies conspired with power interests to conceal it, and the wisdom of time was still unborn (p.x).

- What our age needs is the reaffirmation...of the essential values of human life...we must rebuild society for ourselves, learning from the past what lessons and what warnings we are capable of learning...trust(ing) our values in action (p.v)...to rebuild the institutional fabric so that it may better withstand the shocks of change...the institutional fabric must maintain and control the economic scheme of things (p.xi)... learn to look beyond the inadequate alternatives that are usually offered...discover the primacy of society, the inclusive, coherent unity of human interdependence...to transcend the perplexities and the contra-dictions of our times (p.xii).

- As Aristotle said, we can learn the nature of anything only when it has reached—and passed—its maturation (p.ix).

All of these are challenges to us lest we learn the nature of our own time too late. Currently fashionable theories and philosophies, like those of the 19th century, are more likely to dangerously dissuade or mislead than help us to meet the challenges. As Polanyi noted of the 19th and early 20th centuries: "Nowhere has liberal philosophy failed so conspicuously as in its understand-ing of the problem of change...the pace of which...should be slowed down...to safeguard the welfare of the community" (p.33). Ditto for the 21st century which, as Gleick documents, is already moving along much, much *faster* at an accelerating pace—like a 3rd wave or a tsunami (tidal wave).[15]

Which Wave of Change are We Surfing Now?

Alan Toffler refers to the transformation that Polanyi described as "the second wave," what many others have called the industrial revolution. This is the predecessor of the "third wave" transformation that Toffler says we are now in the midst of.[16] Unfortunately, neither Toffler nor unnamed others have Polanyi's depth of insight or historical understanding. As we have just seen, the great transformation that Polanyi describes set the foundation for the industrial revolution; it was not the revolution itself. Toffler's insights are more telling of the present time even though his book was advertised shortly after its publication as "The book that makes sense of the exploding eighties." Since then, the only thing that people recall as "exploding" during the '80s was the greed of the "me generation."

Perhaps more to the main point of this book is the fact that Toffler sets its reason for being in terms of all three dimensions of time—past, present and future:

The time has come for us to imagine completely novel alternatives, to discuss, dissent, debate and design, from the ground up, the democratic architecture of tomorrow. (p.417)

Who is or will be the 21st century Bentham, a source of institutional innovation to help save our democratic republic?

Toffler advocates an agenda that is avowedly radical in terms of both diagnosis and prescription. Unfortunately, his bestseller, though widely read over the past twenty years, does not appear to have influenced current debates on reform initiatives. One can only wonder: did most of his readers ever reach the final Chapter, #28 of his voluminous *Third Wave?*[17] He puts forth some penetrating insights grounded in readings of history, then uses these to propose major features of what he imagines to be a better future. The question we need to ask with regard to any such futurology, however, is whether the author's writing provides rationalizations for the presumptions of power by new elites or helps to empower the rest of us, the great majority. The answer in Toffler's case is both, so it is up to the reader to read carefully, cull, and select.

Toffler writes:

Majority rule...is increasingly obsolete. It is not majorities but minorities that count. (p.419)

It will require a protracted battle to radically overhaul—or even scrap—the United States Congress...(and create) wholly new institutions and constitutions...(p.441) (that)...focus on the problem of structural political obsolescence... (p.442)

Much depends on the flexibility and intelligence of today's elites, sub-elites and super-elites (whether they can "flow with the Third Wave")...never in history have there been so many...educated people, collectively armed with so incredible a range of knowledge. Never have so many enjoyed so high a level of affluence ...ample enough to allow them time and energy for civic concern and action. (p.441)

Via such remarks and many others, Toffler provides ample ammunition for elites, especially young pretenders, ambitious "wannabe's," to selectively pick up parts of his technocratic, futurist agenda and run with them. And Toffler, not unlike many other intellectuals, would feel swell, and perhaps even be somewhat swelled, if a charismatic political leader were to bless his thinking by picking up some of his ideas and running with them.[18] Yet, other remarks in his Chapter 28 reveal Toffler to be a thoroughgoing small "d" democrat at heart, one devoted to "We, the People."

The responsibility for change...lies with us... (we should) launch the widest possible debate...to generate the broadest array of imaginative proposals... think...of thousands of conscious, decentralized experiments...by launching a vast process of social learning....(with) tremendous pressure from below. (p.442)

Using advanced computers...an educated citizenry can...begin making many of its own political decisions. (p.430)

Combine elements of direct and representative democracy by allowing "our elected representatives...to cast only 50% of the votes on any one issue, while turning the other 50%...over to a random sample of the public... (p.426)

So long as the decision load of the social system expands...democracy becomes...a evolutionary necessity (with) exciting prospects for a radical expansion of political participation. (p.436)

So we have the same dilemma confronting Toffler (who is still alive) that confronted Machiavelli and other intellectuals with political messages ever since: Which side of my thinking will be the dominant side in terms of influence and effect—the side oriented to an elite or the side pitched to a wider public, the citizens of a Republic? As we have seen, in Machiavelli's case, the question answered itself because the modern "public" had not yet been born; so he addressed his message principally to "The Prince."

In Toffler's case, the question answers itself, too, for if "We, the People," do nothing, the process of change will be dominated by elites by default. Thus, only the public can answer the question for Toffler as well as itself in an age in which the public has, at least potentially, come into its own.[19] Toffler has at least put a challenge before us, along with a menu of options, many of which hope or assume that "We, the people" are willing to come back into the foreground of the political picture as active players.

In fact, several of Toffler's propositions resonate with some of the major themes of this book, such as "decentralization" (again, with page references to chapter 28 of his book):

we are witnessing a fundamental decentralization of production and economic activity (p.433) (and) of communications, as the power of the central networks wanes... (and so we are) being compelled to decentralize government decision-making as well. (p.434)

Nowhere...is obsolescence more advanced or more dangerous than in our political life. So frightening is the prospect of deep political change . . . The creation of new political structures...will...come...as a consequence of a thousand innovations...at many levels in many places over a period of decades...(p.440)

too few decisions are left for the subnational level...novel proposals warrant careful local experimentation... (p.431)

The first of the above quotes opens with Tofflerian perspective on the "great transformation." In other sections, he reveals himself as one of the first to recognize the revolutionary impacts of new computer and telecommunications technologies. His 1980 observation that "Today the stakes are much higher, the time shorter, the acceleration faster, the dangers even greater" (p.440) could have been drawn from a recent issue of *Wired* magazine or from a recent book by a Silicon Valley seer.[20] The quote is also a good lead-in to this book's chapter 8, which includes some discussion of the effects of the Internet.

His cheers for decentralization and local initiative are attended by a wise reminder: "Political decentralization is no guarantee of democracy...quite vicious local tyrannies are possible" (p.433). Those of us who have served in local government appreciate this all too well.

Nevertheless, this brief turn to Toffler also begins to reveal the limits of the intellectual in politics and to suggest other reasons to be wary. No intellectual would deny that ideas have consequences. Any such denial would undercut his or her reason for writing. To the extent that political ideas are put forth, however, with little or no political judgement as to how they can be made effective or what their consequences might be given the actual political forces at work, then no intellectual should be surprised to find, many years later, that the "law of unintended consequences," "Murphy's Law" or some other untoward, unexpected, undesirable result has taken root.

A major problem with Toffler and others is that they are not sufficiently, self-critically wary of how their ideas may be picked up and used by those in positions of power and influence, including "the people" in times of revolutionary change. Lacking experience with politics and/or that of living or working with and among "the people" for whom they presume to advocate, they cannot imagine either how their ideas can be moved from thought to action to benefit the majority, or the consequences of so doing.

A good antidote to intellectuals' political presumptions is provided by Eric Hoffer, an intellectual longshoreman who wrote about the matter with Machiavellian detachment.

> In almost every civilization we know of, the intellectuals have been either allied with those in power or members of a governing elite, and consequently indifferent to the fate of the masses...There is also the remarkable fact that where the intellectuals are in full charge they do not usually create a milieu conducive to genuine creativeness...when the intellectuals come into their own, it is usually the pseudo-meagerness on every phase of cultural activity.[21]

Machiavelli, an intellectual who could ground his political ideas upon considerable political experience, probably would have been pleased.

So to return once again to Toffler: In the same chapter where we have seen prescriptions that would empower ordinary Americans, we also see some that could well serve to dis-empower them, such as the following "We shall almost certainly have to discard our obsolete party structures...and invent...plug-in/plug-out parties of the future" (p.423-424). ...(and adopt) a variation of the National Plebescite proposal..." (p.430).

We shouldn't get too far ahead of ourselves here. Party and related reform considerations arise primarily in Chapters 4, 5, 7 and 9. Suffice to say, as others have said long since, that recommendations to undercut political parties and employ plebescite techniques can easily be manipulated to weaken rather than strengthen the role of ordinary people in a so-called democracy. It would not be the first time that those who advocate changes for the people end up favoring mainly themselves and/or the powers that be among the advocates' supporters.

One must not only be wary of prescriptions but also of the diagnostics that intellectuals put forth as their basis. One reason some of Toffler's nostrums are questionable is because he mistakes (as Machiavelli did not) the nature of the political struggle that would have to be won for his goals to be realized. He writes: "The decisive struggle today is between those who try to prop up…industrial society and those who are ready to advance beyond it" (p.436). Toffler recognizes that "The advocates of the 3rd Wave are more difficult to characterize" (p.438); e.g., "the fast-expanding millions in the self-help movement (even though) all of them share a radical disillusionment with the old institutions…" (p.439). He fails, however, to recognize that there is no straightforward correlation or connection between 2nd and 3rd wave forces and political parties or organized groups. If the political implications of this were recognized, "radical disillusionment" might find effective expression in concrete political proposals with some chance of being realized. Perhaps because he is trying to write for and sell to (that is, trying to please) both elite and popular audiences, he either misses or does not want to face the true focus of "the decisive struggle." Ironically, for one who had read broadly and deeply in American history before writing *The Third Wave*, Toffler overlooked the tension between elite and populist forces during the last major wave of political reform, the so-called "Progressive" era.

"The Age of Reform" (II? to be continued?)

The last significant wave of "reform" in the U.S. was known as the Progressive movement. It arose from tripartite protest—*against:*

1. Falling agricultural prices and the decline of the family farm,

2. Corruption in city governments, and

3. The growing size, power, and social costs of corporations.

These are not prioritized, nor were they independent factors. Big business, growing bigger in the age of the "Robber Barons," fed the corruption of city governments and favored declining agricultural prices so that they could pay less to largely immigrant laborers in city-centered manufactories. Corporate contributions to city-centered political candidacies became an important political factor, starting in the 1890s. Labor was still largely unorganized.

The Progressive movement was driven by an alliance between municipal reformers based in big cities and farmers in rural states. This may seem like "politics makes strange bedfellows" writ large. The degradation of American democracy was their shared concern. The rural pressures for change were far more populist in nature. The urban pressures were focused on changes in laws and improvements in representative democracy. The two strands thus adapted and reinforced the fundamental, long-standing debate between Madisonian and Jeffersonian versions of democracy that figured among the founders and that has continued with variations on the themes ever since, including those in this book (Chapter 3, &c).

Theodore Roosevelt became known as a "trust buster" for pushing anti-trust, labor reform, and other laws that honored major portions of the Progressive agenda. Woodrow Wilson's stirring restatements of Progressive themes during the campaign of 1912 helped to win him the presidency. The beginning of World War I, however, effectively marked the end of the movement even though there was another Progressive uptick during the LaFollette 3^d party candidacy for president in 1924 that won 16.6% of the vote. The populist, mainly agrarian, wing of progressivism had long since been defeated by McKinley, with corporate money financing his victorious 1896 campaign for the presidency. Unfortunately, because we need to move fast forward to confront the political problems of our own time, we cannot dwell at length on the history of the Progressive era. Interested readers will find many histories and biographies that cover these and the key actors involved. Hofstadter's *Age of Reform* is one upon which this chapter relies heavily.

Again, there are many fascinating parallels between present and past; here, between the situation we face now and that faced (and changed) by reformers around 100 years ago. These are highlighted below with brief annotations highlighting the nature and possible relevance of the parallels indicated. With reference to Hofstadter (1955; pages indicated in parentheses), the Progressive era saw:

- "The emergence of great contrasts of wealth and poverty...a jump in the number of millionaires...9% of families owned 71% of wealth" (p.63).

There has been a repeated and rising chorus of references in both the popular, economics, and business media to growing economic inequality evidenced by increasing disparities of income and wealth. Now, 5% of families own 55% of wealth.[22] We have seen, not only a big jump in the number of millionaires, but an increase in the number of *billionaires,* symbolized by Bill Gates.

- A "minority in the highest places of power..." (p.64).

"Minority" here does not refer to an ethnic or racial group; it means, as in Webster's Dictionary definition #1, "the smaller in number of two groups that form a whole." More specifically, in the context of the Progressive era, it meant a very small minority commanding the heights of power. Many feared that a "secret conspiratorial plutocracy" would "put an end to traditional American democracy." Similarly, now, there are many who believe that our politics and government are dominated by a small minority of people supported by big corporate contributors.

- the emergence of "professional reformers—men who had much experience in agitation but little or no experience with responsibility or power" (p.101).

Hofstadter here pointed to a great and ultimately destructive divide in the political world of 100 years ago—that between the reformers, mostly professionals, including lawyers, clergy, editors and professors, and the political "bosses" controlling urban political "machines."[23] Although not quite such a yawning chasm, there is a similar divide that weakens reform efforts now— between the advocates of an improved civil society, a very small portion of whom have any political experience or responsibility, and mainstream political parties, elected officials, and partisan political activists. There are long standing, overlapping divides in American politics between intellectuals and practitioners and between reformers and politicians. There is little chance of reforms that would significantly revive grass roots political participation if we do not find ways to bridge these divides. So, we introduced this "divide" issue in chapter 1 and return to it later.

- A "Progressive revolt (that) took place almost entirely during a period of sustained and general prosperity..." (p.135).

Even the agricultural part of the economy turned around and upward after 1898. 100 years later, we were in the midst of what became the longest sustained period of national economic expansion up to about February, 2000. During this period, a number of proposed political reforms started to receive serious attention.

- "upheaval in status...changed...the distribution of deference and power... transformed...and revolutionized the distribution of power and prestige..." (p.136).

It appears as though, due to the great transformation of our own time, that our society is also undergoing "status upheaval," as entrepreneurs are held in higher regard than professors, doctors, lawyers and other high-prestige professionals; as the new Internet/IPO-rich got (for awhile) more media play than conventional corporate chieftains, as unconventional "geeks" become more popular than go along/get along types, and as knowledge embodied in knowledgeable human resources is valued more highly than bricks and mortar or machinery.[24] Hofstadter cited "The newly rich...bypassing the old gentry..."(p.137).

- reformers characterized by, "distaste for machine politics...(who preferred) the cultural ideals and traditions of New England...(&) positions (in the economy) in which the initiative was not their own ..." (p.139).

Most of today's reputed or self-styled reformers can be similarly characterized, especially "civil society"advocates. Positions ... in which the initiative was not their own ..." means that they were neither entrepreneurs nor business leaders. Reference to "the cultural ideals and traditions of New England" primarily points to the town meeting model of citizen deliberation and decision making via direct democracy. Progressives' "movement for a direct primary," for instance, derives "from the town meeting model..." (p.264). It also connotes an "appeal to universal personal responsibility and (to an) ethos of mass participation…(and) civic conscienciousness …not unlike the pathetic proletarianism that swept over many American intellects in the 1930s" (p.205).

• politics "dissociated from the world of morals and ideals" (p.201).

In part, this refers back to the "divide" identified earlier. One hundred years ago, when machine politicians were focused on representing the interests of their constituents, politics was corrupt, and any good intentions were increasingly corrupted by money. By contrast, reformers were concerned about ethics and morals. One is tempted to ask: So what else is new? But the quote takes us even further back in historical memory to Machiavelli. Recall his attempt to put politics on a foundation of (scientific) fact without it becoming an "ideology of morality." A major question underlying the divide between politics and morals, even now, is: how can the twain ever meet?

• "a mild and judicious movement (for reform) whose goal was not a sharp change in the social structure but…the formation of a responsible elite to take change of the popular impulse toward change" (p.163).

Some of the lines written by reformers of our own time resonate with this quote, often including pejorative remarks about populism. Thus, it appears that some even now fancy themselves to be latter day exemplars of a "responsible elite."[25] Another version of this is the Progressives' view that all we need is to get the "right men" in positions of power and all will be well with the (political) world.

• "a disposition among the middle classes to put aside…discontents and grievances until the time should come when it seemed safe to air them" (165).

There is a parallel "disposition" now and a corresponding concern. Do the American middle classes have any more gumption now, any more than 100 years ago, to work and fight for what was once the most revolutionary democratic system in the world? Will this book help to pull people away from their TV's and PC's and rouse them from their undemocratic lethargy? Will the great American majority, whom some say have been put to sleep by prosperity, continue to play it "safe"? Will the new political energies that arose during the last three presidential primary campaigns rise again, even stronger?

• the impulse for reform "passed into the hands of youth (the generation that came of age in the '90s with…) "a quickening sense of the inequities, injustices and fundamental wrongs of American society…who felt need of…a new politics (for) returning government to the people" (167).

We see similar signs of hope, that the reform banner will be picked up by "youth" even now, in spite of past low voter turnouts among the 18-35s and putdowns of "Gen X" and "Gen Y" by many in the media. A surge of youthful volunteerism as well as voter turnout was seen during the early stages of the 2000 and 2004 presidential primary seasons. Hopefully, these will not be transient blips. See Chapters 4 and 9 plus Mitchell (1998) for more, plus turnout stat's for the 2002 Congressional elections.

- "discovery of the essentially undemocratic nature of the federal Constitution" (p.201).

This discovery was apparent about one hundred years ago yet, for all the calls for a new Constitutional Convention over the past 25 years,[26] the put downs of "judicial activism" and efforts to effect "strict construction" of the Constitution, the 225 year debate between Jeffersonian democracy and a Federalist Constitution continues even now, much as it did among the Progressives, between them and the Populists, and between both and their mutual enemies. The "discovery" was also made again quite recently by many who did not favor the role of the Supreme Court in the election of George W. Bush. The case has been made most authoritatively, however, by Yale professor Robert A. Dahl.[27]

- "muckraking" (vs.) "the more smiling aspects of life (that are) more characteristically American" (p.201).

Compared to the "muckraking" carried on by firebrand journalists and writers for newspapers and magazines over the period 1880-1910, investigative journalism and political polemics among U.S. media now are weak tea and/or in short supply—not that there is any lack of topics to muckrake. Instead, we have muckraking on personalities rather than public issues and a surfeit in representations of "the more smiling aspects of life (that are) more characteristically American." It may still have been "morning in America" as marked by the extreme wake-up call that came at 8:45 a.m. on September 11, 2001, but the day passed very quickly into evening. There is much further on in this book on the media as "part of the problem" rather than solution. See Chapter 8, especially.

- "generic reform—the education of public opinion" (p.202)

Again, what else is new? So often, during American history, when there is a serious problem to be confronted, "education" is trotted out as the cure all. But the kinds of education earlier generations came to know as "civics" do not appear to be receiving much serious attention these days, for all the talk of educational reform. To the extent that any attention is paid to this at all, it is far less than math, science, the 3 Rs and, above all, test taking. The emphasis given to education in the Progressive era was far more general than schooling and closer to what civil society advocates are trying to accomplish now—preparation for responsible citizenship. As for "education of public opinion," what does this represent now more than patriotic propaganda and the results of political polling?

- A "view of reality (promoted via the media of the time) that corruption is found on every side (but that) the mischief could be interpreted simply as a...breaking of the law (so) If the laws are the right laws...enforced by the right men...everything would be better (and) "evils...can be remedied by a reorganization of government" (p.265).

The parallel with one hundred years ago evident now is the focus on campaign finance reform and "reinvention" of government, as though enacting new laws and rules would suffice to revive democratic politics and renew political participation.

- Reformers: "prosperous and respectable figure(s) needed...a **feeling** that action was taking place...(involving) **ceremonial** (PR-type) solutions" to basic problems (and) popular reforms...to institutionalize a **mood**...(driven by) a negative goal rather than to give positive momentum and direction to popular rule" (p.267).

The temper of the Progressives' time, as characterized above with keywords marked in bold, seems hardly unlike our own, judging from characterizations of politics now as "feel good spectacles" put on for citizens as "consumers," "PR" with "spin," and "small change" with no big ideas.

- Reformers..." trying...to keep the benefits of the emerging organization of life and yet to retain the scheme of individualistic values...," e.g., periodicals "full of little individualistic ads...to tell clerks how (to) get ahead" (p.219). (and) "a system intended to stimulate and reward certain traits of personal character..." (p.225). (and) Assumptions "that the people were capable of acting effectively as individuals" (p.263).

Paradoxically, the above "Assumptions" were wrong, as this book will point out throughout (especially in Chapters 3,4 and 7), but it is amazing how long it takes a myth to die, even though the facts of American politics have been contradicting it for much more than 100 years. The myth that people are "capable of acting effectively as individuals" in the political arena still burns bright. Internet folklore has given it new currency, even though most people know that it is not true (see Chapter 8). Another force giving it new life is the rise of the new, entrepreneurial economy, which is renewing the Horatio Alger myth in an electronic age. The current counterpart of the Progressive era's "little individualistic ads" are countless notices on the Internet as to how one can make "big money" working alone at one's home computer. The "emerging organization of life" faced by Progressive reformers was the growing size and power of the large corporation," against which they felt they had to fight "to retain the scheme of individualistic values..." This seems to be a significant difference between then and now. But is it really? We may soon have to ask again, what with the AOL/Time Warner merger and giant consolidations of banks and other large corporations. After all, what were the protests in Seattle all about?

A prominent leader during the Progressive era advocated a strategy of counter-organization, writing that:

> A simple and poor society can exist as a democracy on a basis of sheer individualism. But a rich and complex industrial society cannot so exist...It...becomes necessary for these ordinary individuals to combine...to act in their collective capacity...(p.247) This is as true now as then.

- A "fear...that the great business combinations...would be able to lord it over (us) to put an end to traditional American democracy...(though) the central fear was fear of power...(and) distrust of authority" (pp.227, 229 and 241).

Fear of power and distrust of authority is also deeply rooted in the American public. It is still prevalent and justifiably so. This fear cannot be characterized as a myth because facts continue to substantiate and reinforce it.[28] Since even the largest corporations have been vulnerable to competition in the new economy, the fear that "great business combinations" might "put an end to traditional American democracy" is not prevalent but it does exist. Many, perhaps most, of the protesters against the WTO in Seattle seem to believe that it is true now. The Progressives' apprehensions were borne out in 1896, when corporate money effectively defeated the populist wing of the Progressive movement. So, if "traditional" is defined as many Progressives defined it, as "widespread participation of the citizen," then American democracy was indeed defeated. We must be wary. When Steve Case says: "I want to play a role in the transformation of America," who remembers Charlie Wilson, Chairman of GM during the '50s, when he said: "What's good for General Motors is good for the country"?

- Gap between words and action with regard to anti-trust issues: "disparity between the two...and the material results...so marginal." Reformers (e.g., Theodore Roosevelt) accepted money contributions from the same "interests" they railed against (p.252).

This harkens back to earlier remarks about middle class Progressives being primarily satisfied with "mood" and "feeling" rather than the substance of significant change. Although the press made a lot of noise about efforts to enforce the then new Sherman Antitrust Act, the "material results (were) so marginal." Will we look back, some years from now and make a similar remark about the handling of Microsoft, AOL, Bank of America, et. al. by the antitrust division of "our" Department of Justice? Indeed, self-styled reformers now, too, are accepting big-money contributions from the same interests they railed against. See Chapters 8 and 9 for more on this, especially regarding the soft-peddling of anti-trust issues regarding media ownership.

- "240 volumes on business management published" (between 1900 and 1910, p.243).

Here is another remarkable parallel. We, too, have seen a splurge of books and articles on every aspect of business management, especially on "leadership," over the past 15 years or so. This tidal wave of books on business began to surge, first, as a response to the competitive challenges of the '80s (remember "Japan, Inc."?). It has mounted and continued, more generally, in response to the "great transformation" of the new economy. Contrary to the main thrust of the business literature of 100 years ago, now labeled "Fordism," however, the business literature of today is much more democratic; that is, less in service to old business elites and their pecking orders. The best of the new wave of business literature provides some "best practices" and valuable lessons for those of us interested in reforming politics and government. See Chapter 7.

- The extension of the market or market institutions into non-market arenas… (primarily in pp.138 and 46-59).

This tendency, which became apparent during the Progressive era, has now come upon us full force. Polanyi had recognized its beginnings much earlier, as extension of the market in the 17th and 18th centuries turned labor and land into commodities. Its implications for politics, community, and other aspects of public life here in the U.S.A., however, are only now coming fully into view as the insinuation of private market values into every sphere of life diminishes public values and the "space" that we have for their expression.[29] It used to be said that, "The best things of life are free." This is hardly the case anymore in a world in which all of the things advertised as "best" are hardly "free"; they carry premium prices. What appears to be free is the "social capital" built up by previous generations that we are consuming as free riders. Putnam warns that the cost of such behavior may be high.[30]

- A movement that "put a new premium on publicity and promotion…and thus introduced another entering wedge for the power of money…designed to facilitate minority rule" (p.268).

The use of paid "publicity and promotion" first became a significant factor in political campaigns during the Progressive era. Indeed, this "introduced another entering wedge for the power of money" which has come to dominate campaigns. This, in turn, led to campaign finance reform becoming, for the first time in a quarter century, a major issue in presidential campaigns. See Chapter 9 for a discussion of how current reform proposals fall far short of what is needed to encourage a renewal of grassroots, volunteer political participation, short of which we will continue to have "minority rule."

- "pressure for civic participation…followed by widespread apathy…" (p.282).

The Progressive era ended with a political whimper marked by the bang of the beginning of World War I. A lot of Progressive rhetoric helped to mobilize popular support for the war, but both reaction (the first "red scare") and apathy (giggling through the boom of the '20s before the bust of '29) followed.

Compared to this long list of similarities, the set of major differences between 100 years ago and now is a short list of two:

1. There is now no "crusade for municipal reform" (p.164)—a prime driver of the Progressive movement; and...

2. Arguably, there appears to be no counterpart now to the "class of substantial property-owning citizens whose powers of economic decision had been expropriated by...corporate organization."—another prime driver of the movement.

How significant are these differences?—quite, but not so significant as to suggest the lack of any sufficient basis for a reform movement at this time that could be at least as influential as the Progressive movement. Difference #1 refers to local government. The comparative lack of municipal corruption speaks in favor of reforms that would revive grassroots political participation. Reformers oriented to national government as the focal point of political action may believe otherwise, on the basis of assumptions that the federal government is more professional, ethical, representative, and lacking in corruption than most state or local governments. Those oriented to decentralization and/ or devolution can make a strong case to the contrary (as in Chapters 7 and 10). In government as in business, smaller-scale organizations are leading the way, especially those that "think globally, act locally."

As for difference #2, in spite of current complaints about the lack of a "traditional business elite,"[31] which sound curiously like complaints of "new money" elbowing aside the "old gentry" during the Progressive era, the socio-economic shifts now going on are more favorable to reform, not less. The robber barons of the Progressive era transformed themselves into today's representatives of old money and a traditional business elite; e.g., John D. Rockefeller via the Rockefeller Foundation. But new entrepreneurial energies are both supplanting and transforming old, well-established, big-name corporations and corporate leadership. This may favor reform, but not assuredly so and not in conventional terms (see Chapter 7). The new entrepreneurial force could take us back to an "*earlier tradition* of political protest (that) had been (in part) a response to the needs of entrepreneurial classes..." to clear the way for new enterprises and new men..." (italics mine)

Thus, it should be no surprise that current debates on political reform issues are eerily similar to those of the Progressive era (1890-1914). Tension between the Madisonian and Jeffersonian versions of American democracy is with us still. The reformers who favor "top down" vs. those who favor "bottom up" approaches are at loggerheads even now. Those who hope to mount a new populist movement are still running against the grain of those who would favor the establishment of a new, "traditional" elite with "noblesse oblige"—those who would condescend to improve and manage our representative democracy for "our" (their?) best ("public"?) interest.[32]

For those of us wrestling with similar issues one hundred years or so later, the Progressive movement represents a host of historical problems still unsolved. The claim can even be made that the so-called "reforms" of American politics produced by the Progressives were rather more regressive than progressive. Lipow's (1996) critique of political reform efforts in fact makes such a claim on the basis of much evidence and a political science standpoint oriented to empowering people rather than established elites. Of the Progressive reforms, Lipow writes:

> these…far from being instruments of democratic participation, made citizens into tools used by an elite…Progressive reformers did not aim at, nor did they accomplish to any degree, the 'democratization' of the American political system…The Progressives… system…gave the appearance of increased participation while taking away its necessary substance…Progressive reforms (were) the structural sources of the debased existing American political system in which money and celebrity replace issues…and responsible, democratically organized parties are non-existent…[33] (Lipow, 1996, pp.15-17)

Of course, if "We, the People," have been so infected by a "Culture of Narcissism" that we cannot tell our public parts from our private parts, then the pretenders to an elite, both old and new, may be right. "Public Man," like the prodigal son, may have fallen, irretrievably, his/her virtue never to be revived. Signs of the times are not reassuring in this regard. A leading political commentator, Fareed Zakaria, for example, seems to be advocating an "illiberal democracy" for the U.S.A. as well as for apocryphal "emerging democracies" abroad. "Our best hope, he concludes, is to delegate more power to impartial experts, insulated from the democratic fray," a view quite contrary to what this book is all about.[34]

"The Culture of Narcissus" and "The Fall of Public Man"
(to be continued?)

Remember Narcissus—the Greek god so in love with himself that he spent hours admiring his own reflections—in mirrors, puddles, ponds and others? Thus, ever after, "narcissism" has been synonymous with self absorption and a host of other near-synonymous behaviors such as vanity, self-satisfaction, selfishness, and asocial individualism. Yet, as Christopher Lasch, whose book indicted American life in the '70s as "The Culture of Narcissus" pointed out, it hardly helps our understanding of people's behavior to simply string together a host of supposed synonyms suggesting a number of casual associations. The social scientist would like to replace "casual" with "causal." So would we if we really want to understand where we stand, how we got here, and where we're going, both individually and politically.

The history of how we got to where we are today raises a number of cause and effect questions. How these questions get answered is crucial for how we act now and henceforth, at least to the extent that action may be more effective if grounded on understanding. We need to be able to identify what is public and what is private in our lives and strike some reasonable balance between them. The most important question to try to answer is of the "chicken and egg" variety. Which came first?—

- Narcissistic behavior, so that the decline in political participation and public life is a reflection of individualism?, or...

- The breakdown of politics and other forms of public life, so that people's retreat into themselves and narrowly private worlds is a reaction, not a cause?

The truth is somewhere in between; each of these is both cause and effect. Each has been generated and maintained by overlapping sets of historical factors with deep roots. Unfortunately, they feed on each other so that, together, they represent the broadest of the vicious cycles that appear in this book. Their historical roots and interactions have been set forth and analyzed in two books that appeared within two years of each other.[35]

Richard Sennett, a distinguished social psychologist at New York University, defined narcissism as "self absorption which prevents one from understanding what belongs within the domain of the self...and what belongs outside it (usually designated "the other").[36] Notice how either half of this definition, "self" or "other" determines the scope of the other half. So, if the requirements of "self" are overriding or consuming, then the "other," more public side is necessarily quite small or narrow, by definition (and vice versa). This feature of Sennett's definition alone opens it to serious question for two reasons:

1. A person's personality is seen as comprising two separate boxes, self and other, such that...

2. the two sides seem to be playing an either/or, zero-sum or trade-off game such that more of one means less of the other. Sennett writes, for example, "There is a trade-off between greater psychic absorbtion and lessened social participation..."[37]

Lasch criticizes Sennett and others for using definitions of narcissism that are not grounded in clinical psychological facts, and that are insufficiently precise or just plain wrong. Sennett's specification is close to what psychotherapists have called "primary narcissism"—that exhibited by infants, who cannot distinguish their own well-being from that of surrounding objects. Lasch defines narcissism as a "psychic (character) disorder" manifest among those who...[38]

- Complain of "vague, diffuse dissatisfactions with life;"

- Gain "a sense of heightened self esteem only by attaching (themselves) to strong, admired figures..."

- "act out their conflicts" (but) "avoid close involvements..."

- "depend on others for constant infusions of approval and admiration..."

- are "chronically bored, restlessly in search...of emotional titillation..."

- "dread old age and death..."

The "who" implicated by these diagnostics are not characters in Dr. Seuss. One reason Lasch titled his book *The Culture of Narcissism* is because the character disorders he observed seemed so pervasive in the '70s. Read back over the set. Do they seem any less pervasive now? They still seem to be with us and among us, even if any individual reader may say "hey, that's not really me!" The narcissism that Lasch pointed to in the '70s seems to be on exhibit more publicly and blatantly now than ever, brought out of the closet and off the couch by *People magazine*, Bill Clinton, *MTV*, and many other representative types of politics, sports, and pop culture.[39]

The trouble is, in order to get a handle on the diagnosis in some way that might help us to find a prescription, we come up against another "chicken and egg" question (get used to it; the book is full of them): Do we blame "the system" for narcissism (like '60s lefty leftovers might do) or narcissism for the system? Enter Sennett again, for he delves deeper into the historical roots to help us to understand how we got to the state we're in. The prevalence of narcissism as a social "character disorder" gave rise to the title of his book, *The Fall of Public Man*. He saw narcissism displayed over the broad canvas of American society, exhibited by people's retreat into private pursuits from public activities. Along with Lasch, he documents and analyses shifts in popular culture, sports, family life and other factors that constitute context and causes of the declines in political participation, voting turnout and other aspects of public life that animate this book. He writes in a way that resonates with the late Roman Empire appearance of present day Washington (DC):

> There is a rough parallel between the crisis of Roman society...and present day life...the Roman participated more and more in a passive (way)...investing less and less passion in his acts of conformity...he sought in private a new focus for his emotional energies. (op.cit., p.3)

Sennett saw the roots of these trends in the last great transformation from agrarian village societies to urban industrial societies. Over an earlier one hundred year span following the "ancien regime" of 18th century Europe, this transition led to the evolution of:

- *Intimacy* as an exchange relationship (perhaps the most insidious aspect of what American Progressives perceived as the insinuation of the market into non-market aspects of life) and as "an attempt to solve the public problem by denying that the public exists," leading to "an intimate domain overburdened with tasks it cannot fulfill" (pp.10, 27 and 30).

- *"a new kind of society"* characterized by people concentrated on "authenticity"—a need of "feeling genuinely," as in "Look at me feel;" (let me) "show you my attempts to feel…" while, simultaneously, being less willing to express their own feelings to others, finding themselves at "the lonely, inexpressive end of individualism (via) less and less emotional risk taking…" (p.24). Who's been our very own new kind of leader/representative of our own time in this regard? Would any "Friends of Bill" care to make a nomination?

- *science* as "radical objectivity" facilitating "radical subjectivity" as a counter-force or reaction (p.30).[40]

- *the self and selfhood*—from an assumption that "experience gained in the company of strangers (was) a matter of urgent necessity in the formation of personality…" (to) "self absorption" and a "Romantic search for self-realization" (pp.24 and 6).

- *Public behavior*—becoming "a matter of observation, of passive participation, of a certain kind of voyeurism," leading to "the paradox of isolation in the midst of visibility…blatant signs of an unbalanced personal life and empty public life…a long time in the making…" (pp.15,16).

- *secularism*…based on a code of the immanent (here and now, as in "immediate sensation") rather than the transcendant (after death or long-term) (p.21).

- *the psyche*…"more privatized…obsession with persons at the expense of more impersonal social relations…psychic life seen as so precious and so delicate that it will wither if exposed to the harsh realities of the social world" (p.4).

- *community groups*…"people feel(ing) they need to get to know each other as persons in order to act together (and so) social action…being devalued…placing more weight on psychological matters…in terms of what it shows of…personalities" (p.11).

- *character disorder*…"because a new kind of society encourages the growth of its psychic components and erases a sense of meaningful social encounter…" (p.8).

- *performers*—"elevate(d)…to the special status of public figures they occupy today…" because people come to fear acting in public and project their desires for recognition, glamor, success,etc., onto stars of the stage, screen, sports, et. al. (p.26).

- *family*—"withdrawal into…" as it came to be viewed as the epitome of the private realm wherein people "realized" their true "nature"(s) (p.18 and 20)…and, with reference to D'Tocqueville's *Democracy In America* (vol.2)…

- *citizens*…"trusting the state, would abandon their concern for what was occurring outside the intimate realm…" (p.31).

Lasch and Sennett, insightful colleagues of the '70s, still speak to us now with their similarly important, overlapping, reinforcing messages, even though Lasch is dead and Sennett has somewhat shifted focus. Their differences, as expressed in Lasch's critique of Sennett, take us back to the "chicken and egg" question that introduced this section. Lasch says:

> Reversing cause and effect, Sennett blames the contemporary mal-aise on the invasion of the public realm by the ideology of intimacy...In fact, the cult of intimacy originates, not in the asser-tion of personality but in its collapse.[41]

Lasch says that the breakdown of public life is to blame for narcissism, given that "public life" has been dominated by "ruling classes" whose interest has been to turn democratic politics into a spectator sport that serves as what Karl Marx might call another "opiate of the masses." Sennett suggests that narcissism is to blame for the breakdown of public life. So, "which came first, the chicken or the egg?" The earlier reference to this implied what we should now recognize: *It's the wrong question.* Besides, no one wants to get caught up in debates on such a question between two intellectuals. It takes us nowhere.

As chickens and eggs both realize, neither one takes priority in sequence. But pecking order may be another matter. The important point to realize, indicated earlier, is that the two major historical influences have been feeding and reinforcing each other in a vicious cycle that continues. Thus, the key question is: where do efforts to break the cycle stand in the pecking order(s)— of media, politics, powers, and forces at work now? The real difference between the two lies far less in their diagnoses of "causes," which largely overlap, than in the implications of these that we might draw out in the form of prescriptions for reform as in Chapter 10.

The set of factors that influenced both narcissism and the decline of public life need to be highlighted because, under the influences of the third great transformation now going on, "the times, they are a changin'" As diagnosed by both Sennett and Lasch, these changes include:

- The rise of corporate bureaucracy;
- The rise of the nation-state, primarily as a means of building a national economy based on the extension of markets (even as the nation state is undermined by trans-national corporations);
- The growth of national government power and bureaucracies due to the above, to world wars and to the need to offset the influences of corporate power and bureaucracy;
- The destruction of community or life centered on relatively stable, small town cultures;
- The rise of a consumer rather than a producer society.

- The growing power of media, including advertising, that promote image, perception, "pseudo events," consumption, spectatorship and spectacles.

If Lasch were still alive, he might reword his critique to say that Sennett's thinking is akin to "blaming the victim" and then emasculating the victim's ability to take action to remedy his situation. Lasch accuses Sennett of providing an elaborate rationalization of conventional interest group politics and discounting "the validity of many radical goals" and "the entire revolutionary tradition" (p.28). He also accuses him of overlooking the "irrationality" of human behavior at all levels. The main criticism of Sennett, which Lasch does not explicitly recognize, however, is that Sennett puts "public" and "private" in boxes while, to Lasch, they are "always intertwined" (as via loops in the path diagram of Fig.1, p.28).

The key to reconciliation and integration of the views of Lasch and Sennett lies in the concept of self or personality, the influences thereupon and its/their development. Sufficiently broaden the concept of "self" to include various levels and categories of "other" and the differences disappear. If more Americans get involved as direct participants in the political process, as more than just voters, then they will confront their interests vis a vis those of others. The search for common ground may lead to views that broaden selfhood. If the politics of the past generation is any indication, many so-called "interests" will be infused, indeed, even highly charged, with values and conflicts over values. Many that seem just "local" will implicate higher level, even federal constitutional concerns, etc.

Thus, the search for common ground between Sennett and Lasch leads to a shared concern for our politics and our selves. The two historical views are much closer than intellectual nitpicking would lead one to believe. The main common denominator can be expressed just so: Our political selves are limited ("cabined, cribbed and confined" as Shakespeare might say) by the constraints of our everyday lives. These are largely dictated by the evolving structure of the economy (the jobs we have; the opportunities we face, etc.) and the ideas (some would say "ideology" or "propaganda") promoted by media "opinion leaders" to support that structure. On the other hand, as citizens having varying degrees of discretionary time, "free will," awareness, thoughtfulness, choice, degrees of freedom, latitude for discretionary decision, and influence with/over others, we can, to varying degrees, overcome the constraints on the power of our political selves by individual actions in concert with others (what "political" means, after all).

The attention that both authors paid to the politics of the '60s provides an illustrative application of their ideas that also underlines basic similarities in their diagnosis of our political situation. Both Sennett and Lasch view '60s "politics" as a serious downgrade in American politics, to be distinguished from, or hardly confused with, effective, meaningful or serious democratic political activity. Their shared view is that '60s radicalism was tantamount to "play acting" or "street theater," reinforcing politics as "government crisis management" and TV "spectacle."

In contrast to an earlier generation of radical politics in the '30s, '60s radicalism was "a mode of self-dramatization" (Lasch, p.83). The political activity of young '60s activists resonated with creations of the more aesthetic pretenders to the self-appointed avant garde of the time, whose works expressed the idea that reality itself was an illusion. Characters in "avant garde" plays were filled with uncertainty with regard to "what is real." These tendences were part and parcel of an "escalating self-consciousness" expressed through "playing," as though one's own "life becomes a work of art" (Lasch, p.88-90).

Not surprisingly, '60s politics did nothing to change the structure of "the system" that '60s radicals railed against. Thus, in its own terms as well as that of analysts, it must be viewed as the bankrupt, pretend politics of a failed political generation. As a new generation confronts the political problem (=opportunity) of our time, it may sobering to realize that politics can indeed fail for (at least) an entire generation, even in an open, democratic system. As Lasch acidly remarked: "Acting out fantasies does not end repression." Or as another writer commented: "Democracy and demonstration aren't the same."[42]

So we are all, each of us, both chickens and eggs. Even "immanent" (immediate or short-term) influences upon us, or choices we make, may have "transcendent" (longer-term, higher order, community-wide or life-changing) implications. The self comes in here almost day to day—the need to be constantly self-aware and self-critical regarding the potential "irrationality" of our behavior as we interact with others over matters that, just by virtue of any such interaction, take us beyond the narrow boundaries of "self" to "other," or from the familiar over to the stranger. Much of the behavior being promoted through the media is irrational. Much of what any of us would vote to support in our own seeming self-interest is irrational from the standpoint of non-voters, such as our children, future generations, the underclass and other communities not represented.

Thus, the genuine and most important reconciliations to be sought among the deeply rooted historical tensions documented by Sennett and Lasch are those that we ourselves can effect as actors responsible for the history of our own lives, families, and communities. And, ironically, the narcissism that both Sennett and Lasch deplore as a major symptom of a poor politics, once refocused on self-development in the large rather than the small, can be part of the solution rather than part of the problem. Self-development is more than "making it" individually, treatments at a health spa, or reading the latest from "Oprah's List." It is the maturation of individual lives in context—to become fuller, richer, more influential, more in control, and more empowered by interacting or working with others and learning from others at some level of community. It is individuals striving to make a difference in the only way that most of us can outside of our family circle—together. Then we begin to see how our qualities and expectations as individuals can be fulfilled and recognized. Otherwise, as Bill Maher so aptly expressed in the title of his recent book, *When You Ride ALONE You Ride with Bin Laden.*

The Historical Moment: Now?; The People, Yes?

Many people, having seen the famous Robin Williams' movie *The Dead Poets Society,* remember the cry "carpe diem"—"seize the day." This is akin to the '60s call to "seize the time." All the historical evidence that we have seen signals that the historical moment is now. Both the need and time to create a better politics for the sake of a better future is now, not another generation from now. As others often say: "the future is now",[43] at least as of the moment we determine to make it so.

As many of the Progressives realized, the best of the future could be realized if we would reclaim the heritage of the past—to fulfill the promise of our democratic tradition in a new time. This promise was well stated in the 1960 Walter E. Edge Lectures in Public and International Affairs at Princeton by one of our Republic's great men—just before the quality of our public life was downgraded by the subsequent politics of the '60s. The "substance" of the lectures was "political only in an older, deeper sense of the word than is now common."[44] Former Supreme Court Justice, William O. Douglas, speaking from his own deep reading and reflections on American history, declared:

> This default of ours begins at home. It involves not one but many influences… long in making. They have robbed us of imaginative plans and bold action. We move more and more with the crowd and are infected with mediocrity…the struggle of this century is between…two forces—for submission, subservience and conformity on one hand, and for independence, individuality and dissent on the other…individual freedom and initiative…(in light of)…the growing tendency of American democracy to become polarized in four large bureaucracies…each tends to breed conformists…(while) the financial rewards go to those…that Madison Avenue promotes (by) manipulating response and behavior patterns… television… captive of Madison Avenue…makes millions our of our capacity to endure mediocrity. (Douglas, 1960, pp.4-19)

There is still much truth and inspiration in what Douglas had to say even now, a generation later. The 3[d] great transformation now underway, however, indicates that Douglas's remarks marked the end of an era—call it the age of bureaucracy—that is now being supplanted by the "age of the entrepreneur."[45] Also, it is clear from Lasch's analysis of our narcissistic consumer society in the decade following Douglas's lecture that Douglas did not fully understand the nature of the "Madison Avenue" influences he criticized. The modern advertiser promotes consumption, not by emphasis on achieving confidence in conformity, but by accenting difference, distinctiveness, self-doubt, change, shifts in fashion, instability—the need to be "up to the minute" (not just up to date) and personally distinctive in virtually every arena (including now, virtual arenas). The fact that the differences being promoted are quite superficial and beg the question of whether any of us, individually, by ourselves, can achieve "the American Dream"—well, that's no concern of the ad writers.

One reason it may not be a concern is that creative advertising, "the propaganda of consumption," also "turns alienation (rather than conformity) itself into a commodity" according to Lasch's more sophisticated analysis. One way it does so says a lot about our political culture—by "disguising the freedom to consume as genuine autonomy (and inducing) consumption as an alternative to protest"(Lasch, 1979, p.73). In other words, if we can express ourselves and "empower" our individuality through our clothes, cars, houses, books, "do it yourself" activities, et. al.—what else do we need?

The answer is that, after "The Fall of Public Man" documented by Sennett and Lasch in the '70s,"We, the People" need to first imagine and then bring about the rise of Public Man. This would be a first in human history, but history has brought us to a point where this is now both desirable and possible. There was a lot of idealist romanticism and naivete in previous Progressives' allusion to the renewal of an American "tradition" in their calls for reform. Both that tradition and Progressive reforms represented highly elitist forms of "democracy." "Public Man" is not "the gentry" of the early American Republic. It is not the leaders of the Progressive movement of one hundred years ago or any other more currently self-styled progressive movement for that matter. It is most certainly not another self-styled "political class," including the media "commentariat" of the present time. Public Man is us and, like Pogo, "we have met the enemy, and he is us, too." For "if we are not for ourselves, who will be for us?"—no one, including those we like to think of as leaders.

The New Politics—
Machiavellism for the Majority, "We, the People"

Sorry to use history, starting with the Renaissance, as a stick to beat romantic idealists and revolutionaries over the head, but the implications are unmistakable. The new politics is not romantic; it is not vaguely idealistic; it is not revolutionary in the sense of the last two centuries and their ideologies. The new politics is Machiavellian. Its keyword is "hard." It is scientific, based on an understanding of human nature derived from lessons of life learned the hard way, through history revealing the hard facts of human behavior and its consequences. So the new politics is hard-nosed and realistic, a politics for real, down to earth people in real places who struggle to make their living, raise families and build communities the hard way—they work hard for it. Nonetheless, it will be progressive without being Progressive. That is, we will learn from our own distinctively American political history.

The new politics will be of, by, and for those people, the great majorities of every country and society, who struggle to make their way while also wanting to "make a difference" in service to some larger community. It will not be a politics of, by, and for an elite who claim they are working for us. The age of the entrepreneur, individuals, families and small producers is in. The age of the bureaucrat, elitist noblesse oblige, "avant garde" ideologues advocating "dictatorship of the proletariat" or "service to you" as a cover for their own pretensions to power—these politics are out, or will be, to the extent that the rest of us are "in" as producers of our own politics rather than consumers of others.

The major lessons of history are sufficient to the last paragraph. These are many, but there are three that need to be highlighted in the starkest possible terms so that the lessons hit home, specifically, that:

1. The greatest force of progress for the past five hundred years has been science and the values of openness, tolerance, truth-seeking, and respect for evidence upon which science is based.[46]

2. The greatest source of backwardness and stagnation, even unto evil, has been politics grounded upon egos, elites, special interests, and ideologies or religions that honor neither human life nor science.

3. A major source of—more than just ill-defined complicity in—the evils of the 20th century has been people's willingness to sit and watch, not get involved, let somebody else do it, defer to charisma, media and symbols of authority and not even pay attention when public issues are at stake.

Thus, the new politics should be Machiavellism for the majority—a matter of fact, broad-based, scientific and humane politics that we can share and use as part of our everyday lives in order to:

- empower ourselves and others among the non-powerful;
- have a more effective voice in politics and governmental decisions; and...
- make a difference in the qualities of life in our communities in at least one of those communities—local, state, national and/or world—of which we are all a part.

The implications of lesson #3 can be stated simply by paraphrasing an old saw from our experience with wars: "War is too important to be left to the Generals." So, too, with politics. It's too important to be left to the political counterparts of the Generals—professionals, media, and others among the politically self-interested. Arguably, the latter have already taken over politics as a competitive game. The problem is that, if we continue to let "them" dominate, then we lose. The great American majority will count less and less in the "us" vs. "them" game that has already taken shape. In addition, just in case our precious democracy still means something, we will also have foresworn a heritage that is a light for much of the rest of the world even if we have come to take it for granted here at home.

"Machiavellian" as it is used here does not carry the negative baggage that commentators more interested in ideology than the facts of political life have attached to Machiavelli over the centuries. Here, it means what it meant to Machiavelli originally: before subsequent overlays distorted the meaning:

1. Politics as a source and means of power;

2. A scientific approach to politics; and

3. A focus on the means and mechanics of politics—the *how to* of politics in terms of behavior, tactics, tools, methods, and the like.

Because of the power structure of his time and the political purpose he wanted to serve, Machiavelli's famous political "how to" was written primarily as a memo to *The Prince,* with a side glance in the direction of the Italian public of his day, the Prince's subjects. Many parts of this book also amount to a "how to" guide but they are addressed to "We, the people" because now, nearly five hundred years later, the people of a democratic republic are the proper focus of attention, not their presumed princes. By seeing how crucial their political involvement is to the future of their own republic, and by seeing how to make that involvement both feasible and effective, a democratic people can take their political system back from the minority who have assumed power, presumably on the people's behalf. Lacking such taking back, "presumptuously and by default" would increasingly substitute for "presumably" in the last sentence.

This book complements what is by far the best book on the ways and means of grass roots politics that I have yet found. It is: *Take Back Your Government!: A Practical Handbook for the Private Citizen Who Wants Democracy to Work* . This book is a great resource for all of us one which we should tap into as we move forward. Unfortunately, its author, Robert A. Heinlein, has passed on. No one who has read his book, however, can doubt that he would agree to label the grass roots approach to politics he describes as "Machiavellism for the Majority...We, the people." In a most readable and entertaining way, as in so many of his best selling science fiction books, Heinlein makes the ways and means of politics immediately accessible to any citizen who is concerned about public issues, the health of our democratic republic and how to make a difference with regard to issues and politics in the U.S. of A. Heinlein writes as a true member of what Tom Brokaw has called The Greatest Generation, the generation that provided the foot soldiers for democracy, both domestically and abroad, at home, as neighborhood, ward and precinct political workers, as well as the fighters for democracy in foreign wars. Some of the "workers...laboring in the vineyards" interviewed for this book, along with this author, reflect on grassroots political experience in ways that resonate with Heinlein's words (see Chapter 4).[47]

Notes

1. In contrast to Dante's *De Monarchia*, Machiavelli's *The Prince* is most definitely not a utopian treatise. See Burnham (1943) for a useful contrast. Some of Burnham's other insights on "Machiavellism" may come into play later.

2. Much of this section on Machiavelli is drawn from the publication of Louis Althusser's lectures on Machiavelli (Althusser, 1999, p.8, et. al.) Althusser claims that Machiavelli, as an advocate of a Florentine republic, was addressing the political lessons of *The Prince*, not only to Lorenzo Medici (the actual Prince of Machiavelli's time) but also to the people over whom "The Prince" ruled.

3. Quoted by Valiunas (2000) in his article "Modern Times: Science, Religion and Francis Bacon."

4. Valiunas, op.cit., p.34.

5. Valiunas, op.cit., p.33.

6. Valiunas made this remark about Bacon (on p.33) but it applies to both.

7. See Burnham (1943), *The Machiavellians* and Toulmin (1990), *Cosmopolis*

8. See Scott (1999), *Seeing Like A State*.

9. "Great Transformation" is in quotes because it is the title of a book by Karl Polanyi (1957) about the massive changes brought about by the industrial revolution. This section relies greatly on Polanyi's rendering.

10. See, for example: Kelly, Kevin (1994), *Out of Control*. Reading, MA: Addison-Wesley Publishing Company; and Gordon, Robert J. (2000), "Does the "New Economy" Measure up to the Great Inventions of the Past?" NBER Working Paper No. W7833. Washington, D.C.: National Bureau of Economic Research (August).

11. As stated originally by Thomas Jefferson.

12. The author was one who, paired with a volunteer from Alexandria, Virginia, Bob Smith, walked door-to-door for Bradley in New Hampshire and (at other times and in other ways) also tried to help McCain.

13. According to one of those interviewed for this book, Mike Lynch, this remark applies to ordinary citizens as well as candidates. He remarked: "Many synonymize "democracy" as freedom without responsibility. More democracy…almost implies more freedom with less responsibility." See chapter 4 for more.

14. Polanyi, Karl (1957), *The Great Transformation: the political and economic origins of our time*. Boston, MA: Beacon Press. The book was written during the Second World War.

15. Gleick, James (1999), *Faster*. As I write this paragraph, I am reminded of Henry Adams' characterization of the last great transformation as a period of "acceleration," too, symbolized by the dynamo, in *The Education of Henry Adams*.

16. Toffler, Alvin (1980), *The Third Wave*. New York, N.Y.: William Morrow. This discussion of Toffler's views that follow relies upon his Chapter 28 on "Twenty-First Century Democracy" (pp.416-443).

17. It is possible that we are not being fair to Toffler here. Some of the ideas that he advocated, such as selecting some officials by "drawing lots," closely resemble some reform initiatives, such as "citizen juries." It is by no means clear, however, whether the ideas inspiring certain reforms came from Toffler or some other source. See Chapter 9 on "Reform Initiatives..."

18. This happened for example during the 2000 presidential primary season in which Toffler came out for John McCain, the "reform" candidate, even though it was not apparent from newscasts that McCain was advocating any specific part of Toffler's agenda.

19. One indication that "the public has come into its own" is the complaint voiced by several political commentators (a.ka. "pundits") that the public has *too much influence* because politicians have turned into poll readers. Responding to polls, however, does not count as a form of political participation. Toffler advocated "a variation of the National Plebiscite..." (p.430). More recently, so has Barber (1984, p.281-289).

20. E.g., Stewart Brand's (2000) book on *The Clock of the Long Now*, to which we will return later, or Bob Davis' (2001) book: *Speed Is Life*.

21. Hoffer (1963, pp. 36 and 47). A more recent rendering in the same vein is that of Stephen Hunter in the Washington Post (4/6/00): "The academics write their mighty histories...the intellectuals record their ironic epiphanies. And in all this hubbub...the key man is forgotten—the lonely figure crouched in the bushes..."

22. Guadrini, Vineanzo, and J.V. Rios-Rull (1997), "Understanding the U.S. Distribution of Wealth," *Federal Reserve Bank of Minneapolis Quarterly Review* (Spring, 1997), pg. 22-36.

23. This divide is apparent in writings from those on both sides. N.Y. State Senator George Washington Plunkitt ("Plunkitt of Tammany Hall"), for example, "a believer in thorough political organization," referred contemptuously to those in "the reform movement of 1894" as "mornin' glories" who "did the talkin' and the posin', and the politicians in the movement got all the plums." [Riordan (1963), p.18]

24. A recent article by a friend and colleague also appears to recognize that there is also now going on what Hofstadter called an "upheaval in status," in the following terms: "People who are successful at making money often were not particularly intellectual at school. By contrast, those who did well at school

often gravitate to the liberal professions, in which they make less money than their more financially successful counterparts...No wonder they adopt an anti-rich stance, one no doubt born of self-hate and envy." [Kruger, Eric (2001), "The Conflict of Values Between the New Republicanism and Neo-Liberalism," in Goodall, Douglas K., et.al. (2002), *The American Culture Civil War*. New York: The Pacific Institute, pp. 25-60.

25. David Matthews, President of the Kettering Foundation appears to be one example, by far the best of the lot. His book *Politics for People* is an important contribution to any debate regarding political reforms. Note he uses the word "for" rather than "by." Also note remarks in his book implying that a reform movement should be led by a "responsible elite." For example: "Change can happen, people can have a voice, but the effort has to be well orchestrated and organized. The effects of popularization...can be destructive...or the effects can be constructive if more and more people come to politics as a responsible public." [Mathews (1994), pp.31 and 1] Who is the judge of who or what is "responsible"?

26. Including calls by myself and Gore Vidal in separate articles on the same editorial page in the *Hunterdon County Democrat* of August 24, 1987.

27. See his (2002) book, How Democratic Is the U.S. Constitution? (New Haven, CT: Yale University Press).

28. For better or for worse, this fear and distrust, as perceived by the majority of the electorate, centers more on government and less on large corporations. See Gary Wills (1999), *A Necessary Evil: A History of American Distrust of Government*.

29. For one good slant on this, see Margaret Kohn's "The Mauling of Public Space" in *Dissent* (Spring, 2001).

30. Putnam, Robert (2000), *Bowling Alone*.

31. See Judis' article "Top Down: Whatever happened to noblesse oblige," in the *New Republic* (March 27, 2000)

32. Judis laments the decline of the old "business elite" with its "noblesse oblige." Why is this not surprising? Judis's magazine was founded by one of the leading Progressives, Herbert Croly. Are we seeing here a direct line of descent from Croly? Judis's elitist stance reminds one of the classic condescending line of Marie Antoinette: "Let them eat cake!" But what are we less favored, the great American majority, to eat, politically? Does Judis recall what he had to say in his review of Lasch's *Revolt of the Elites and The Betrayal of American Democracy*?

33. Lipow goes on to quote from a book about Progressive reforms in Wisconsin that comments on the impact of the direct primary: "The overthrow of parties through the ascendancy of the individual destroys party principles, and individuals take their places with organized personal followings bearing

the motto 'Anything to Win' as their most sacred principle. The discussion of real principles is lost in the public exchange of bitter personalities."(Phillip, 1910). 1910?, or McCain v. Bush, 2000?

34. Quote from Niall Ferguson (2003), "Overdoing Democracy," a review of Zakaria's *The Future of Freedom: Illiberal Democracy at Home and Abroad* in The New York Times Book Review (June 1, 2003).

35. Lasch (1979) and Sennett (1977).

36. Sennett, op.cit., p. 8. Sennett continues to shed light on the social psychology of our time. His latest (1998) book is on *The Corrosion of Character: The Personal Consequences of Work in the New Capitalism.*

37. Sennett, op.cit., p.11.

38. Lasch, op.cit., p.37.

39. National Public Radio reported that the spread of American culture via TV and the Internet throughout Iraq has been described, in part, as The Spread of American "Racism."

40. The attitude of science as representing "radical objectivity" denies the values-based nature of the scientific enterprise, as best set forth by the scientist/humanist Jacob Bronowski (1956) in his little gem of a book *Science and Human Values.* These values are the same as those that animate democracy, as we saw earlier in this chapter.

41. Lasch, op.cit., p.30.

42. In "Stop Marching," an article in the *Wall Street Journal Europe* on anti-globalisation protests (April 25, 2002).

43. This was the apparently original byline of the author's campaign for Congress in 1984 (12 C.D., NJ: see Chapter 3). The line has since been coined and employed by others.

44. Douglas, William O. (1960), *America Challenged.* Princeton, NJ: Princeton University Press; quoted from the foreword by Robert F. Goheen, President of the University (p.vii).

45. As announced by Ronald Reagan in the early '80s, even though statistical evidence of the beginning of the age began to emerge in the mid '70s. The use of "3ᵈ" here, and the significance attributed to it, is similar to Alvin Toffler's use and attribution of "Third Wave" (Toffler, 1980).

46. Note the distinctive characterization of science here as fundamentally representing a set of human values—and the most progressive force because it is so grounded—rather than the usual confusion of science with technology—valued as a source of "whiz bang" things. See the works of Jacob Bronowski, including *Science and Human Values, A Sense of the Future,* and *The Ascent of Man* for more on this fundamental, critically important feature of science.

46. There is ample support in the rest of the book for statements made here that may seem opinionated and arguable at this point in the reading. An editor of a leading academic press described this book as "a Jeremiad"—damn right, and thank God for Jeremiah.

47. Another handbook entitled *Politics for Dummies* is also useful but it is not nearly as entertaining, interesting and inspirational as Heinlein's. Heinlein does not view any citizens as "dummies," nor do I. See *The Handy Politics Answer Book* by Gina Misiroglu, too, for a good deal of useful information to support this book, as well as Bzdek, Jim (1999), *How to Participate in Politics effectively: A Step-by-Step Guide Every Citizen Can use.*

3.

WHY IS PEOPLE'S POLITICAL PARTICIPATION IMPORTANT??

Outline

- Introduction
- Reasons for People's Voluntary Political Participation
- Representative vs.(?) Direct Democracy
- A New(?) Politics (1)
- The Challenge to Political Science
- The Politics of Everyday Life: Some Perspectives on the Intersect of the Personal and the Political
- The Politics of Everyday Life: Some More Personal Notes
- Various Forms of Participation: Why are some more important than others?
- Frequencies of Participation: What are the odds? Why are they important?
- Extent or Amount of participation: Why is this important?
- The Significance of Intermediaries
- Seeds of Political Leadership
- A New Politics? (2)
- The Paradox of Politics and the Politics of Paradox

Executive Summary

Why do people become political volunteers? —Two major reasons, as those interviewed for the next chapter attest: (1) Because they have come to realize that such involvement is an important part of adulthood and citizenship in a democratic society—taking responsibility for some things that affect others as well as one's family and oneself; and (2) they want to make a difference as members of some political community. The trouble is, there are so many good causes out there, parties are weak and the media give politics a bad rap and a poor rep. Then some political scientists tell us that a "new politics" is coming on that emphasizes issues and individual involvement. But such a politics dis-empowers people and, along with the decline of parties, TV and media hype, hands what can and should be our politics over to a small, professional political class. We are deflected away from becoming fully mature individuals—responsible citizens of a once revolutionary Republic that is now the oldest constitutional democracy in the world. The media provide major, but only one of several, "barriers and constraints" to political participation—reviewed in Chapter 6.

Introduction:

Why is people's political participation important? There is an unavoidable conflict in this question—between real and ideal, actual and potential. On the one hand, our founding fathers, leading political philosophers and leading lights all say that we SHOULD be involved. They rest their case on claims that our democracy cannot long survive without active political participation by citizens from all walks of life—that, in fact, it is our responsibility as citizens to be involved. In other words, our founding fathers sometimes speak to us like Jewish mothers. They lay the guilt on us. Their words imply that we are to blame to the extent that we choose to spend our time doing other things to the exclusion of fulfilling our responsibilities as active citizens of **our** Republic. These responsibilities extend to thought as well as action. Lapham emphasizes that the very "survival of the American democracy depends… on the capacity of its individual citizens to rely… on the strength of their own thought" (to which I would add: our own actions, too).[1]

On the other hand, many current and past students and practitioners of politics say that citizen participation is not requisite to a healthy, functioning democracy because our democracy is representative. Some apply this view up and down the line. Only those sufficiently motivated, concerned, and informed come out to vote. Others have a right not to vote, i.e., to vote with their feet. Still others, similarly motivated, concerned, and informed, will participate in other ways according to their time, lights, and resources. The official representatives that these more responsible citizens elect can represent us because they are listening to the voices that count, even if loudness of some of the voices is measured only in money.

According to Verba (1995), however, real and potential aspects go together, for the self-selectivity of people's participation has significant adverse impacts on the ability of our political system to be adequately representative or to honor equal opportunity, equal access, and related goals of a truly democratic system. Those who participate are significantly more likely to be the higher income, better educated classes of the American population.

Janet Bruno, Selectman in the Town of Merrimac (MA), believes that citizens' participation is important over and above voting because elected representatives need to hear from diverse cross sections of their constituents in order to be able to make well-founded decisions on public issues. Thus, significant portions of various constituencies *at least* need to: (1) pay attention to what is going on in government and (2) make their opinions known to their representatives. In local communities, at least one additional element of participation is also called for: either attendance at city council meetings or at town meeting, where new ordinances, budget decisions, and other matters are decided.

Yet, there's still something missing here, isn't there, in response to the lead question, "why?" The foregoing reasons are what academics call normative; why people *ought* to participate. What about the more personal side—what people feel they *want* to do, in their own interest? The next chapter sheds some light on this from people who have been involved as political volunteers. They want to out of self interest—because they came to see how politics could make a difference to their own lives as well as make a difference to the lives of their communities. Their lives demonstrate that the "self" in self-interest can be larger or smaller, depending on the extent and nature of their involvement.

Reasons for People's Voluntary Political Participation

Others say that citizens do get involved—when they really need to – when some important concern has been neglected or badly handled by the powers that be. Such involvement, however, is too often the product of what may be called the politics of crisis—of reaction, resentment, accumulated grievance(s), and the like—what one political scientist has referred to as "political responses to pain and loss" or of fear and wrong. This was highlighted by a line made famous by the movie *Network*: "I'm mad as hell and I'm not going to take it anymore." The rights and needs of citizens to seek redress should never be denied, whether via the ballot box, demonstrations or other actions. Yet, one is mistaken to see such involvement as sufficient to the maintenance of a healthy democracy even though it is sometimes necessary. The degree of insufficiency depends on the degree to which the political system is challenged to deal with a variety of deep-rooted, emerging or longer-term issues, i.e., with the degree to which "politics as usual" or political "conventional wisdom" is NOT up to the challenge(s) of our times. This degree is now higher than at any time in recent memory and, perhaps arguably, than at any time in a century.

The fact of the matter is that volunteerism positively animated by good causes is alive and well. This form of volunteerism has been on the rise. It's that on behalf of political and other public organizations which has been dying out. For example, the most familiar type of volunteer for a public organization has been the volunteer fireman. A feature article focused on a town in upstate New York headlined, however, that "As Volunteers Dwindle, Firehouse Tradition Gives Way" and "Professionals Move In…," adding:

> No one can fault the volunteer firefighters here for not trying. With their corps dwindling, the department in this Dutchess County town put billboards on Route 55, built a gymnasium to attract young members, tried a pension plan for old-timers and set up an 800 number for new recruits. None of it made a difference.

One example does not a case make; however, this example fits nicely within the broad swath of evidence gathered by Robert Putnam for his *Bowling Alone*, which we'll pick up in chapter 8. The evidence from original interviews and a national survey done for this book helps to drive the point home—volunteerism to help serve the positive purposes of many sorts of public organizations, not just firehouses, has dried up along with grassroots political involvement, (see Chapters 4 and 5 for evidence that would sway a jury if there were enough public-spirited people to form a jury).

For lack of a better term or phrase, let us refer to the other brand of political volunteerism—citizens getting involved only "when they really need to" as "reactive politics."[2] One basic problem with this is the flip side of its success. Reactive politics often succeeds in getting media attention and motivating politicians to take action. But it usually does not succeed and, perhaps by its very nature, cannot succeed in improving the political system itself—that is, in removing the barriers and constraints that led to the system being unresponsive in the first place. Sometimes, the immediate or direct effects of such involvement can even be negative. Reactive hyperactivity can generate undesirable results. Fear is a two-sided coin whose bad influence can multiply by powers of two or more. People might fear injury or disadvantage by political decisions made by others. But they might also fear participating, even in their own interests. The latter fear is significant. It might even be the greater fear, so we will turn to it in a later section.

To the extent that people are reacting to abuses in the political process itself instead of to other issues, reactive politics may also have long-term effects contrary to those intended or desired. Lipow (1995), for example, argues convincingly that this has been the case with the political "reforms" brought about by the Progressive era of a century ago and, more recently, by Watergate. All the protests and demonstrations around Vietnam effectively brought down a president and had other even more significant impacts but they did not succeed in effecting salutary changes in our political system. As Chapter 9 indicates, this already appears to be the case with recent reforms.

Reactions to a more recent crisis, that of September 11th, 2001, could have impacts on domestic politics that are more negative than positive. Already, only a month after the terrorist acts had killed thousands, the media had concluded that big government was back. Even as incredible, spontaneous outpourings of volunteerism and public giving, plus demonstrations of fine local leadership were featured in local newspapers nationwide, the *Wall Street Journal* declared that the attacks "brought an end to the trend toward less expansive government" and "Washington is erupting with proposals to give existing agencies new powers."[3] Another view expressed by the cartoon that follows but also confirmed by some surveys, is that the "volunteerism" that seemed to promise a renewal of public-spiritedness was short-lived.

The war in Iraq, "Operation Iraqi Freedom," a direct consequence of 9/11, had a similarly beneficial but seemingly short-lived political impact. It also brought people together. For awhile, it seemed to bridge the political chasm revealed by the 2000 presidential election. "Reds" and "blues," blue collar and white collar, liberals and conservatives, et.al., came together in support of the troops.[4] As of this writing, old political divides seem to have returned, sometimes with even more spitefulness and partisan heat, but the signs of hope that we saw have not disappeared. These included broad mixes of citizens coming together for both pro- and anti-war demonstrations (see Chapter 6 for more on the implications of 9/11).

At times of crisis, it often helps to do what referees do during a hard-fought athletic contest—call a "time out" and try to get some perspective on the situation. So, let us take a moment to note perspectives provided by one of the few political "scientists" who appreciates the true science of politics—"politics as an art:"

> ...the worse the trouble, the *easier* for most men; the blacker the fear, the more the inner eye is blinded by desperation, the more likely that crude sleight of hand can pass for a miracle (but)...If sudden increases in participation during crises were associated with the totalitarian rise to power, might that not indicate the desirability of a more general participation *before* crisis...?[5] (emphasis added)

There is a danger that needs to be noted here and now before we venture any further remarks on reactive politics. This is the danger of rendering superficial judgments of the sort that often serve to discredit populism. Language pejorative to populism has often been, and continues to be, employed by political pundits or scientists whom Bell (1992) and others would properly label elitist. Such language is often found, even in publications reflecting the best of democratic political intentions, e.g., those that aim to show how we can generate a more "deliberative" politics. In an article on the potential of Internet/

Web technologies to enable "strong democracy," for example, Benjamin Barber observes:

> the new technology...can facilitate participation in deliberative political processes...(but) In order to be something more than the government of mass prejudice (reflecting "unthinking prejudices"), democracy must escape the tyranny of opinion (and) sustain rational discourse and citizen education. (Barber, 1999b)

Note that the latter is drawn from Barber's discussion of his so-called Jeffersonian Scenario, the most populist among three, presented by a political scientist whose concept of a "strong democracy" is one of the more populist slants advocated by a leading political scientist.

This is not the place to get sidetracked on a discussion of the political implications of the new technology. This is one of the focal points of chapter 8. The point here is that we should not let any discussion of the desirability of citizen involvement in politics be deflected or infected by anti-populist biases or language. Reactive politics could easily be misconstrued or taken out of context as representing knee jerk reactions or unthinking prejudices. Through guilt by association with anti-populist rhetoric, it could then be used to oppose citizen involvement in our political system. There are too many needs, desires, and unfulfilled opportunities for citizens to be positively, proactively involved to allow the latter voices to prevail. You need other reasons to get involved? The tragic lessons of indifference noted in Chapter 6 may be the most important of all.

Representative vs.(?) Direct Democracy

The concern for citizens' involvement in what is supposed to be **their** political system is part and parcel of a debate that has been going on ever since the founders of our democracy debated its foundations over two hundred years ago—representative vs. direct democracy. Although the founders were revolutionary within the context of the British political system of their time, they were actually quite conservative. They feared direct democracy, as many have ever since. As they convened in Philadelphia during the Spring of 1787, the founders may have been deeply shaken by Shays Rebellion just a few months earlier.[6] So the founders constructed a political system with many checks and balances, so much so that political commentators now wonder whether we have inherited a political system afflicted by gridlock. Yet, the fear persists, as revealed by the quote from Barber noted earlier. A century ago, this fear was reflected by the equation of direct democracy with mob-ocracy.

The divide between representative and direct democracy is overdrawn and the fears exaggerated, even though direct democracy now seems technologically more feasible, as indicated by instant polls and electronic voting. Even if they desire to do so, a majority of citizens will never have enough time to indulge in the sort of deliberation that the advocates of a far more deliberative politics would like to see, especially in an era of two-income families and an increasing variety of activities demanding or attracting their attention. There are too many, increasingly complex issues to deliberate about. Even if an era of one-income families were to return as in the '50s and '60s, it is hardly imaginable that husbands would defer to the political judgments of more deliberative wives, or vice versa. Thus, there always will be need and scope for political representation. We will always need to defer to the pro's to some extent—those whom we, as sovereign voters, can hire and fire to do the homework on issues that we lack time to properly address. The problem is that by withdrawing from the system, even in the role of informed voters, most of us are leaving it to a small minority whose arrogation of power cannot substitute for our lack of responsibility. "Leave it to Beaver" is a good line only as a comment upon childish ways, even though it may sometimes be pleasant to think of professional political beavers being busy on our behalf.

One basic conclusion of this book, therefore, is that elements of a more conservative populism need to be introduced, adapted, and widely adopted in order for our representative democracy to be able to:

- Address the problems of our times and ensure a better future for our children;
- Ensure accountability to voters, non-voters, and history;
- Learn from its own experience in order to adapt and adjust;
- Grow in health and stature, or even...
- Survive.

It will become apparent from the chapters to follow that conservative populism is not an oxymoron, nor a contradiction in terms. It is conservative in its grounding on two propositions, namely that:

1. The basic assumptions of American liberalism, as set forth by George McGovern, for example, are either arguable or just plain wrong[7] and that...
2. We should adapt, strengthen, reform, and extend existing organizations and the best practices of the past devoted to electoral politics, especially local political party organizations.

And, above all, it is populist in putting people first as producers of their politics rather than consumers of someone else's. What is not? A more conservative populism would **not** be a populism of the sort that "beyond the fringe" political characters on the right like Pat Buchanan represent, nor the leftist variety that media pundits typically discredit, nor the faux versions that Al Gore, et.al., have put forth as opportunistic campaign lines (see Chapter 9).

What changes are desirable to bring people back into the political picture? This question will not be answered until the final chapter. What are the MINIMUM REQUIREMENTS for improvement? Three of the latter were noted earlier — paying attention, becoming informed, getting involved, and voting. No democracy worthy of the label can long survive if a majority of people eligible to vote don't pay attention to what their representatives are doing, try to keep informed on major issues that cry out for resolution, and get out to vote.[8] Too many people may not survive, either, if the horrific tragedy of September 11th, 2001, is any indication. For we cannot avoid the implication that, but for local fire and police department heroes in New York City, our government failed in its most fundamental, public responsibility – provision of safety and security for its citizens – and that we citizens will have to attend far more to the public's business than we have in the recent past, if only to help ensure our own survival.[9] Which one of the figures featured below is the real patriot, the responsible citizen?

There is an old saying whose truth has been demonstrated time and again, especially over the past century (here paraphrased): "If good people stand aside, the fools, thieves, or turkeys take over." Even in terms of minimum requirements, the functioning of our political system leaves much to be desired, as implied by the phrase "political participation." More direct forms of participation need to be undertaken by more people if we are to have a healthy, problem solving, and hopefully vibrant American political community. More voices heard, ideas adopted and changes implemented, and more trust in the processes of both politics and governing are the core causes and effects of a participatory democracy.

People typically focus on the what of politics, as in the question: "What have you done for me today?" What about the "how"? The old cliché is (to paraphrase) that "politics is like making sausage, and once you've seen what goes into it, you wouldn't want to eat it, let alone be part of the making." This old saw needs to be turned around to say: "If you're not part of the making, how can you be sure that the product is of good quality, even edible?" How can our political system be accountable? How can it be improved, if not on the basis of a greater proportion of people involved as participants? Everyone needs to see "the system" at work. Most important, our democratic system cannot "work" without the active, direct participation of a significant proportion of its citizens. The foundation of democracy is the idea that the collective wisdom of an informed majority is superior to that of any one person or minority of the citizenry, no matter how bright, well brought up, well informed, or otherwise "elite" they might be.[10] "The best and the brightest"? – Didn't we learn from the tragic debacle of Vietnam how little we can rely on them?

A New Politics? (1)

Bennett (1998) suggests that there is a new "lifestyle politics" that doesn't spell *dis*engagement, but rather, a shift from "group" political activities to more individualistic modes of political engagement that he labels "politics by other means." The latter includes petition signing, boycotts, demonstrations, and other forms of direct action." Curiously, some of these are "group" actions. He goes on, however, to remark on features of the new politics that seem suspiciously akin to what was labeled earlier as "reaction politics." That is the fragmentation of political orientations around lifestyle issues akin to causes that arouse deeply conflicting views, e.g., abortion, affirmative action, and homosexual rights. So we have people on both sides of such issues reacting to each other rather than deliberating together.[11] The "impossibility of compromise" on such issues "has undermined support for...institutional remedies" (Bennett, 1998, p. 749). The latter, in turn, undermines political parties, traditional vehicles for what political scientists call "issue aggregation" that is, bringing diverse people together to compromise, identify shared concerns, and hammer out shared positions on major issues.

So here is another one of the "vicious circles" undermining our democratic system: A more personalized, divisive, "issue advocacy" politics undermines political parties and their role of bringing people together, which then reinforces the divisive politics, and so on. This points to the need to revitalize the grassroots, local organizations of political parties in order to help break the circle. Thus, the argument that Bennett (1998) and others are trying to make —that there is no decline in political "interest" or "engagement," only a shift in the style or composition of political activity—is an inadequate response to the concerns that animate this book, even if it were true. No matter what label we attach to the "new politics"—"lifestyle politics," "reactive politics," "issue advocacy," or what have you, it is not an adequate substitute for the decline of participation in organized political groups, especially local party committees or partisan political clubs. As Ed Schlossberg observed: "The more chances we have to work collaboratively, the less chance we'll be manipulated by people in power."[12]

The Challenge to Political "Science"

One of the problems in evaluating the danger felt by the contra-populists is lack of evidence from the field of political science. It is also partly a failure of the science to enable participant-observer roles in political action arenas so that more and more relevant evidence could be collected. Two questions arise here on which the field has little to say:

- Whether populist positions advocated on behalf of the people are substantially different in nature from those advocated by special interest groups. The obvious difference is simply one of numbers—large vs. small. Yet, really, how can special interest group positions be distinguished from populist prejudices if the thinking of educated groups or professionals fails to consider what economists call the externalities of their positions—the more general, public, unanticipated, longer-term consequences or spread effects of their recommendations. The failure to consider such consequences is remarkable, for example, among American political reform initiatives over the past century (Lipow, 1996).

- How much deliberative simmering may have taken place in advance of any populist pots boiling over, especially in the form of informal discussions and debates among people in the contexts of families, circles of friends and/or colleagues, and communities?

Political science, if it is to become truly a science, will need to pay much more attention to informal mechanisms influencing how people form opinions on public issues, discuss them and, ultimately, act on them. This is especially the case given the emerging evidence that people are increasingly disengaged from formal political organizations and their procedures, especially from political parties (Shea, 1999). Political scientists need to adapt some of the methods of anthropology in order to delve more finely, deeply, and closely into the factors that affect the creation, maintenance or deterioration of political communities.[13] A good start in this direction came from a pollster rather than a political scientist.[14]

In order to do so, the field of political science will have to confront alienation. People's alienation from politics is a major concern of this book. So, perhaps it's OK for political scientists to treat alienation as a disease. But alienation is paradoxical. It's a positive virtue for scientists. Alienation from the subjects of their study enables them to maintain some critical distance. So "alienation...is associated with great science." Ironically, what political scientists believe to be their objectivity represents little more than their alienation from their own subject matter, people, and politics. According to McWilliams, it reflects their fear of human nature – "what is subjective, fleshly and private in man...and...(of) fact allied with value, of fact as value."[15] This may be one reason why they treat political alienation as a sort of sickness, not unlike children's attention deficit disorder.

A very different view was expressed by Martin Pawley: people prefer to live private lives—"at the heart of political apathy lies the mainspring of consumer desire."[16] This implies, by the way, that fear of a populist mob is passé. Much of what Pawley wrote about the dire "private future" state of politics and government has unfortunately come true with a vengeance, but political scientists have not followed up on his insights – after 20 years!

Part of the danger that Pawley foresaw is being fed by the fact that advanced cognitive (not political) science and technology are being placed in the hands of media and advertising to maintain "the mainspring of consumer desire" and keep it taut. One student of the marketing industry writes:

> marketing and advertising are beginning to guide the way scholars investigate brain function, perception, and language. Cognitive science course catalogs are studded with classes on branding, marketing and advertising. Faculty lounges from MIT to the University of Indiana are filling up with profs who specialize in the psychology of acquisition and the science of material desire.[17]

We will see again and again in this book that the greater danger is the misuse of science and technology by the media and political professionals to manipulate and disempower us in ways that are so subtle or entertaining that they may count, too, as scarcely perceptible, informal ways to influence our perceptions and choices.

The nature, substance, and influence of informal mechanisms are directly related to two other concerns that surface in this book, especially in Chapters 4, 6 and 7:

- How electoral politics connects with a variety of organizations that are addressing a variety of people's concerns at the level of community in non-political ways; and...

- How electoral politics connects with people's lives most directly; i.e., through what we can call the politics of everyday life.

For what is the value, let alone the import, of people getting involved in electoral politics if they feel that it is irrelevant to their lives? In 1999, political scientist Daniel Shea reported that:

> In 1996... a whopping 82% thought both parties are pretty much out of touch with the American people... Whether the 2000 elections will change this view remains to be seen. The trend is clear: fewer respondents see elections as important and their role in the political process as meaningful.[18]

Yet, as the cartoon which follows below illustrates, there is the danger of another vicious circle here: to the extent that people view the political process as meaningless, the more people become irrelevant to the electoral process, the less their democracy is theirs and the more meaningless the process becomes. In Chapter 9, we will see to what extent the events of 2000 and 9/11 made a difference. The trend seems to have worsened as a result with, at least, little "change (in) this view through 2002."

Mike Lane, Baltimore, Maryland, The Baltimore Sun

Bennett (1998) further expresses a fear, along with many others, that the break-up of the American electorate into semi-private subcultures means that there is no public, an essential basis for a democratic system that works. Thus, his individualistic, brand of new politics does not bode well for the future of American democracy. There is a real danger that the "Fall of Public Man" will continue with a thud.

The Politics of Everyday Life: Some Perspectives on Intersects of the Personal and the Political

Politics is important to everyone because life is paramount and politics is part of life. An essential part of life is choice, so, too, of politics. Everyday, we choose to live or die to some degree. Who was it that said "We live a thousand deaths before we die." Likewise, we are making choices that affect the healthy life or perhaps lingering death of our political system even if we are completely alienated from it and decline to participate at any time in any way. Whether by decision or default, doing nothing is no less a choice than doing something. McWilliams wrote of political participation: Its "relevance is a fact, not a choice; abstinence is action...."[19]

Some political scientists view non-voting, for example, as essentially no different from voting because a choice has been made — that none of the candidates on the ballot are worthy of support. They are only partly right since, unlike Russia and some other countries, our ballots do not provide an explicit "none of the above" voting option. Non-voters are making a choice, indeed, but it is a choice of proxy—to allow others to make their choices for them. This is only the most obvious example. Our political system also dies in thousands of ways through the micro-decisions of individuals, families, and communities not to participate. Barber has made this point most strongly: For lack of political participation, "Citizens become subject to laws they did not truly participate in making; they become the passive constituents of representatives who…usurp their civic functions and deflect their civic energies."[20] What an apt description of our political situation now, though published in 1984! So far, we are lucky that George Orwell's vision of 1984 has not come to pass.

In at least a thousand and one ways, choices affecting political participation get made almost continuously between and outside of elections. Before turning to these, later in this book, let us mark the many ways politics is part of life, i.e., politics mirrors life and life mirrors politics. First, it is almost a cliché' that there is politics in virtually every sphere of life. There is politics in marriage, family, workplace, church, union, club, business, non-profit organization, other membership organization, and practically any group(ing) or interaction involving more than one person. Perhaps the only places where one does not encounter politics are bathroom and bed if one is living and sleeping alone.

In virtually all of these micro-settings where two or more people interact, practically all of the problems that one typically ascribes to politics are to be found. These include problems of:

- Communication and Language (even between twosomes, as in "Women are from Venus; Men are from Mars;"
- Political correctness (being acerbic or outspoken may earn adverse reactions);
- Negotiation (trying to win at any cost may be counterproductive);
- Winner Take All (the star system does not work well outside of Hollywood);
- Cooperation and/or collaboration or competition (some say "Coopetition" is the way);
- Winning people's confidence;
- Building/earning trust;
- Building or maintaining some sort of community (even a marriage of two);
- Organizing efforts and/or allocating resources involving two or more people; and…

· Formulating shared goals, objectives, and understandings that represent what is at stake, today and for the future.

In his comments upon an early draft of this chapter, Mike Lynch provided a perspective that helps to crosscut several of these problems:

If politics is the mechanism by which society resolves conflict, our society fails the test because it no longer teaches that (1) majority rules and (2) not everyone can win <u>all</u> the time. The lack of willingness to concede has led to increased polarization instead of resolution.

These are political problems at all levels and sizes of human congregation, from two to 2 billion and up. In other words, politics is a fractal phenomenon. A fractal is a pattern that reveals and results from two basic features:

• <u>Self-similarity</u>, that is, the pattern is basically the same at all scales, from the very small to the very large, e.g., the legislative/executive pattern exhibited at all levels of government from the local to the national and...

• <u>Branching</u>, the patterns grow like trees or branch like the system of blood vessels in our bodies.[21]

Therefore, the "us" vs. "them" attitude that underlies political antipathy or cynicism has no basis in fact. We are all politicians. **To the extent that we are not, we have trouble making our way in the world**. As Pogo said: "We have met the enemy and he is us." The oft-heard statement: "Politics is not relevant to my life" is false. There are politics and political problems to be faced and resolved in all spheres of life.[22]

Failure to recognize this simple fact leads to some self-defeating separations and hypocritical carryings-on. Many organizations self-consciously and somewhat hypocritically advertise their non-political character. Unfortunately, some of these exhibit distinctly undemocratic features. They would benefit from some greater self-awareness of their own political nature(s), both within and without, and from adaptation to their own use of the more democratic, self-governing procedures borrowed from organizational models that are unashamedly political. Common Cause, for example, is not an internally democratic organization. Nor are many churches, unions, businesses, and other organizations. The U.S. Catholic Church, for example, is under pressure to become more open and democratic in response to its widespread sex-abuse scandal. It is a rather strange, built-in contradiction to a democratic society, to find a number of significant, basic organizations that are not democratic. As indicated by the phrase "small town politics," there are also many small communities who think they are democratic but really are not due to lack of participation and/or the dominance of small "in groups."

Failure to recognize politics as an integral, inevitable, unavoidable part of life also leads to a destructive "us vs. them" attitude—politics is a game for "them," not for "us." "They" are the "pro's." Who are we to get in the way or tell them how to do their "job"? We are just "ordinary" people, trying to make a living, raise kids, minimize the time we have to spend dealing with government over taxes and regulation, have some fun, and live our lives. Especially now, in an era of emphasis on personal expression and development, stop and think of just how incredibly self-defeating this attitude is. If we adopted the same stance with regard to other basic aspects of life, we'd be labeled irresponsible fools or put away. Correction: In a time that has featured de-institutionalization of mental illness, we'd walk the streets doing damage to ourselves, others and/or our communities, as many are already doing unconsciously. Perhaps we'd even be elected to office. "We the People," not "They," are most important and without "we" in the political process, all else will fail.[23]

Yet, we hand the game over to many self-interested, egocentric, sometimes psychotic and/or well-intentioned others under the illusion, utterly incredible in a democratic system, that we can blithely proceed to successfully pursue our private lives while the public system degrades. This situation is like the auto lemons example featured earlier.

There is an analogy here with our political system. The attitudes that people reveal in response to polls and media queries indicate that they think that either our political system is full of lemons or that it leads to the production of much more in the way of lemons than lemonade. This gives them an excuse to avoid politics. Thus, the percentage of lemons rises, leading to the onset of another vicious cycle: Lemons lead to less non-lemons entering the system, which leads to increasing dominance of the system by lemons (etc.). But this dealership cannot go out of business. It can only go from not-so-bad to bad to worse and increasingly worse, with adverse consequences to us all. The U.S. democratic political system is *our* business (US), whether we like it or not.

It's interesting to observe here that political cynics, hardly any of whom would identify with radicals, actually have something essentially in common with them. They both believe that the last paragraph is baloney. One excuse to avoid politics is cynical negativity. The other is that the forces against people's political participation are so deeply rooted that the political system can only get worse. *The private future* describes a system in which people don't need an excuse to avoid politics. They're such willing slaves to a media-driven dream world of private consumption that public life, community, and politics simply don't matter. They don't want the political system to be US; they want it to be THEM so that they can blame someone else when politics and government fail to solve problems, as they often do.[24] What was once set forth as a "private future" now prevails to an extent that is very troubling. Nevertheless, the great American majority can prove both radicals and the cynics wrong, as this book shows.

An important part of an answer to growing political alienation is the realization that politics and life are self-similar. Politics is like life; life is like politics. Politics is not out or over there or above us. Life without politics is not complete; politics disconnected from the rest of life is tyranny. The similarity is most apparent to those who run for office or manage a political campaign. Then, politics is like life only more so—life when the tape is run at four times normal speed, life at its most intense. Decisions are made, large and small. The path(s) branch and divide. Paths not taken become the source of later speculations of the *what if* or *what went wrong* variety. The inner circle, the confidants of a candidate, become like family. One learns who one's friends truly are. There are disappointments and betrayals. There are triumphs and victories. Most of all, there is the growing realization of adult life—that most of what one does has consequences that affect others and that the personal politics, even of our most intimate, "private" interactions in family, business and other settings, are essentially similar to those in larger, "public" world(s).

Another analogy was suggested earlier from the business world. Relying on professionals with no experience of politics to diagnose and prescribe reforms in politics is analogous to American manufacturers, pressed to respond to the Japanese challenge of the '80s, at first failing to elicit suggestions for improvement from those on the shop floor. Once they did so and also took related steps to "flatten the hierarchy" of business organization and "democratize the workplace," productivity in U.S. manufacturing grew apace, manufacturing exports recovered and the U.S. economy once again became the wonder of the world in the '90s. If the U.S. political system brings the American people back into the workplace of the political system, the exports of our political system will benefit the rest of the world as well as ourselves. See Chapter 7 for more on business innovations that are relevant to political and governmental reform.

The fact that politics has become stereotyped as a game played by them, not us, is not only a basis for the antipathy and alienation that most people feel toward politics, it is also a basis for artificial, discriminatory, and counterproductive separations between political and non-political organizations. These separations are detrimental to both. Non-political organizations, often devoted to certain issues or causes, have less influence to the extent that they cannot mobilize political groups and forces. Political party organizations, serving political electoral and campaign roles increasingly divorced from issues and causes, suffer reduced capacity to the extent that they cannot mobilize people devoted to issues or causes, nor can they make effective common cause with other organizations that are devoted to improving the quality of life in their communities. The latter is personal as well as political-organizational, as many adults form personal attachments to community-based organizations, their causes and their goals. We return to this problem via interviews in the next chapter.

The Politics of Everyday Life: Some Personal Notes

The author and others laboring in the political vineyards can speak from personal experience of how their volunteer participation in politics has played a significant role in their lives and made a difference in their communities, not without difficulties (as with the rest of life) but, on balance, most definitely for the better. Interviewees' recollections of most of their political experience is a source of great personal satisfaction. Those of the political volunteers interviewed for this book are presented in the next chapter. Some of the author's memories follow, recounted in the first person, a more personal voice.

The purpose of these semi-autobiographical notes is not to copy the Culture of Narcissism but to draw out lessons of value to others. Home, family, and community are microcosms. The basic lessons of politics, good, bad, and indifferent, are first learned there. Politics first began to dawn on me as an important topic of interest and concern as a teenager, though my first strong, relevant memory goes back to the age of twelve in the 6th grade. I was asked to review a biography of Abraham Lincoln and give an oral presentation of my review. I shook in my shoes; I was so nervous, trying to give my first oral presentation before an audience. Abraham Lincoln has been my greatest political hero ever since. His words provide inspiration and foundation for this book.[25]

There may have been some nascent prior influences but one would be hard put to label them political. The ambience, the context, of growing up on the fringe of a small, independent, New England community with a distinctive history was somehow significant, but this became a consciously important feature only much later. Likewise, the influence of growing up in a community where neighbors were close and neighborly relationships were important. Similarly, the influence of a father who was a very neighborly person who went out of his way to help others and took me with him on his frequent visits to neighbors—this was influential, too. My own experience confirms the importance of the reality of place and community as emphasized by Kemmis (1990) while it runs against the grain of a virtual digital democracy. The virtual place is often without reality or virtue (see Chapter 8). My earliest memory of public events, however, comes from Houston, Texas, rather than Gloucester, Mass. While staying there with my aunt for six months for my health, I recall seeing maps of Korean military campaigns and reading about them in the Houston newspapers.

Not that my father was political at all. If anything, he had attitudes toward politics that would now place him among the politically alienated. He might feel right at home today. I never knew him to attend any local city council, board, or commission meeting. With reference to state legislators and congressmen, he would occasionally say: "We just ought to take the bastards out and shoot them." He thought Harry Truman was a lightweight and would mock the pictures of Truman on our new TV, especially those featuring the President on vacation in Florida wearing flowered sport shirts. It took many years for me to overcome the prejudice and find that Truman was a remarkable president. Suffice it to say that I never heard one political word come from the mouth of my mother.

My father's bias against politicians seemed to have been influenced by his work experience at Sylvania Electric Company, where he was employed as an electrical engineer throughout his whole professional life. He was a fine engineer and an extremely conscientious worker. Besides serving as a manufacturing engineer in a plant devoted to the production of fluorescent lamps, he was also very much involved in R&D to develop what came to be known as Sylvania's "grow lamp"—to grow plants bigger and more rapidly with the help of fluorescent light. He pursued this line of R&D with enthusiasm and devotion for many years, perhaps because he was also an amateur gardener. I recall test beds in our basement with experimental lamps growing begonias with huge leaves, like elephant ears. Yet, he was denied promotions, and he ascribed the promotion of others to their having the same gift of gab that he ascribed, pejoratively, to politicians. So, if anything, my father's political influence should have been negative.

The reason such influence was largely for naught was that once I became a teenager, like all teenagers, I began to construct my own world. Since, in those days I was a shy, bookish, somewhat sickly nerd, geek or wonk (the inverse of "know"), such construction owed mostly to my reading. I began to be influenced by books rather than parents. The most influential of these was Whyte's *The Organization Man*. Then there was Max Lerner's *America as a Civilization*. Another was *Man and the State* by Jacques Maritain, a Catholic theologian. For all the isolation I experienced in an attic room, surrounded by books, my world began to widen. The isolation was a motivator, to reach out, break out, reach beyond, and nurture a nascent social awareness.

A corresponding curiosity had already been at work for years. As a young boy going around Gloucester with my father, I'd ask all sorts of questions, to learn more about what might change the place where I was trying to grow up, questions like…

- Who owns these woods?

- What if too many people dig the clams?

- Why is Julian (a local property owner) filling the marsh? – an incremental nibbling away that continues today with city fathers looking the other way.

- What do you think of what's going on? In town? In the country?

- Why are there so many (public) beaches?

I was sensitized to women's rights, not by the women's movement, which anyway came much later, but by my father's treatment of my mother and younger sisters. He was not a physically violent man at all, but he would put them down with words. I was sensitized to the issue of child abuse, widely recognized as a public issue only much later, by my father's treatment of both me and my sisters.

My awareness of environmental issues, which also rose to the forefront of the public agenda later, began with my childhood experiences in West Gloucester, still the most rural part of the city even now—planting gardens, digging clams, fishing, building walls, chopping down trees, skating, and swimming on the reservoir across the street, collecting shells, pressing seaweed, camping with the Boy Scouts, et. al. These influences were later crystallized by reading Edwin Way Teale's wonderful book *North with the Spring* and Rachel Carson's *Silent Spring* while in high school.

My father's influence, however, cannot be marked simply as negative or neutral. It was through him that my basic political values were acquired. The combination and interaction of books and family influences was telling, not one or the other strand separately or much greater than the other. It was the combination of my reading of *The Organization Man* and my reaction to my father's constraints of a corporate bureaucratic environment that led me later to seek to go into business for myself and make promotion of entrepreneurship one of the kernels of my approach to politics and government. It was my father as a good neighbor, helping many, plus the context of growing up in a real place and reading *The Maximus Poems* focused on that place that imbued a strong sense of the meaning and value of community.[26] So community and entrepreneurship became basic political values. Fortunately, they have become increasingly important values for others, too, notwithstanding the claims of many on the left that community has been destroyed by consumer values, the media, and big corporations.

There was also the politics of everyday life at school. Since I liked to write and wanted to be liked, I joined the book reviewers' club and school newspaper. So I got to write a review of *The Organization Man* that was published in the school magazine. I also got to edit the school newspaper. Another fatherly influence came into play in the form of a love for science and math transmitted by the 1929 alumnus of MIT. I had fine chemistry and physics teachers whom I was able to talk into letting me use their class labs. The high school also had a vocational track. For some reason I can't fully explain, "voc-Ed" kids were among my best friends. They still are. Perhaps my father's influence was beneficial here, too, because he showed me how to make things with my hands and he imbued a reverence for craftsmanship. And Gloucester was a very mixed, predominantly blue collar community. The school environment was probably important. The academic and shop kids were mixed up in corridors, cafeteria, and classes. They weren't kept apart in separate wings or isolated sections. Compulsory ROTC was a great mixer and leveler, like the influence of the U.S. Army when young people were subject to the draft. It was very special growing up in a community of mixed classes and cultures with a strong, distinctive historical identity, rather than in one of the homogeneous suburbs that were being developed at the time.

These are retrospectives of early experience. A full awareness of politics and its importance, and how it rears its head at virtually every turn in nearly all parts of life—these came later. The lessons of experience were often hard, more so because, they were avoidable if I had grown up in a political household... Key experiences and lessons included:

- <u>Jobs</u>: The lessons of the pecking order, office, and academic politics. My first real job provided encounters with Hugh Adonnizio, Mayor of Newark, and my first, firsthand negative image of a politician. I gained an appreciation of how local government, with better leadership, could make a difference. Through later jobs, I learned that:

  —working hard is no substitute for working (politically) smart.

  —political cliques can block your advancement. I should have learned this in high school but I had to learn it the hard way in state government.

  —academic politics is the lowest form of political life because academics have little to lose but their egos.

- <u>First loves</u>: Confrontations with the tensions and challenge of mixing electoral politics, marriage, jobs, and family. (And I blew it! then and later.)

- <u>First higher level responsibilities</u>: The challenge of mixed agendas and inadequate resources—a continuing struggle, as indicated further on in this chapter.

- <u>Own first campaign for elected office</u>: A premature, losing effort driven more by opportunism and vainglory rather than calculation or judgment. The lesson? —If you are interested in running for office, plan ahead: Locate in a place where there's good political opportunities, get involved locally and build a political base before you become a candidate.

- <u>Big issues of the day</u>: What's remarkable is how little influence these had on me, politically, compared to many others of my generation; e.g., Watergate, the energy crisis, et. al. Vietnam was the most crucial of these. I was classified as "4F" in the early '60s because of my long history of bad asthma; I would have gone to Vietnam if I had been drafted, but I was not called. The exception among issues of the day influences, however, was Ronald Reagan. He succeeded in changing my (party) politics by (1) helping to defeat my candidacy for Congress in '84 and (2) by way of an early member of the "Reagan Brigade" who influenced me as a close friend in the '80s.[27] The lessons? —Pick your issues and become knowledgeable in a few, select your friends, and remember: In politics as in sex and business, timing is important.

What were the leading lessons learned, overall? Let's cut to the quick. The envelope, please! They are that:

- <u>Politics is important to all our lives</u>: For me, it has been a primary concern ever since my first real job, which was also my first opportunity to work for an elected official. I started working for the City of Newark two days after the infamous Newark riots of

1967. Most of the problems I encountered and grappled with then continued to fester for many years, aggravated by self-serving political representation and poor leadership.[28]

- Politics is a responsibility, not a profession: My most satisfying political experiences were (and still are) from collaborating with a variety of people from many walks of life, not from working with the pro's. Politics is interesting and fun to the extent that a variety of people take part. To the extent that it's dominated by so-called professionals, it's more of a grind dominated by the need to raise money.

- Politics can be taken in small doses: The pro's view politics as a way of life. They're like surfers, politically, ever in search of the perfect wave. Every year there's a campaign and preparations for the next. Political activity is never ending. So the great majority of non-political others have the impression that, to participate in politics, one must either dedicate one's life or budget far more time to it than is feasible or even imaginable. My own experience as well as that of the many interviewees featured in Chapter 4, however, indicates that small amounts of people's time can be well-spent in satisfying ways on political activities. Those small doses, moreover, add up to a broader-based, more representative and more democratic political system as well as to winning campaigns. People need to say to professional politicos: Get a Life. The latter should respond, Come help. For politics is comprised of many levels, each with greater risks, requirements and potential impacts. Start by being involved at the grassroots, in your local community, pick a degree and level of involvement that's right for you and your family and see what a difference it makes!

- Politics is long-term: Ibid, as per above (and the footnote below). The frequent admonition of the late Barbara Boggs Sigmund, former Mayor of Princeton, NJ, that "politics is played in the present tense," may be more of an indictment than an acknowledgement.[29] Most leading issues, such as tax reform, budget balancing, abortion, school finance and educational reform, etc., etc., have been with us for decades. This raises a key question that any political reform movement must be prepared to address—why does our political system handle long-term issues so poorly? We will return to this key question further on. The lesson here, however, is paradoxically twofold. Barbara was right, too, as I had to learn the hard way after losing many races. I was focused on the future while voters too often fixated on the present. The key is to pay attention to long-term consequences while addressing urgent public issues.

- Time trumps money: The pro's say that money is the mother's milk of politics but commitments of time by increasing numbers and proportions of people over the long pull makes an increasing difference with regard to the long-term political concerns that matter most, especially that of improving the political system itself.[30] Waiting for the pro's to reform the system that feeds them would be like waiting for foxes to secure the chicken coop. Ironically, what the pro's don't seem to understand is that their emphasis on big money and negligence of the grass roots is undermining the very system that feeds them.[31]

- Community is important, and political participation helps to build community: My prime, best, and most direct experience of politics has been in real communities where people had a sense of place—Greenwich Village in New York City, Princeton, New Jersey, Gloucester, and Merrimac, Massachusetts. Most people are yearning for the sense of community that those living in these places have experienced. Political participation helps people to recover or experience a sense of community with others, primarily because it enables them to do work together on something that is worth doing—a campaign, voter registration drive, issue, referendum, community project(s), et. al. Politics is better done together with others. It can and should be fun.

- Everybody, bar none, has something of value to offer in the political process: In my experience, people from all walks of life, colors and creeds would work together politically for/through a party committee, political club and campaign. We would lick stamps, stuff envelopes, canvass the neighborhood, assist candidates, make calls, distribute literature, put up and hold signs, get out the vote, debate issues, et. al. Any talent could be matched with a task. Largely routine tasks were more fun by virtue of doing them with others. The sharing of tasks by everyone further developed the comraderie needed to maintain cohesion and build a sense of community.

- People appreciate person-to-person contact(s): I found people always appreciated personal contact—usually via the door to door approach—more than other, less direct approaches. Indeed, the pro's have begun to find that their costly, more indirect approaches to the electorate—direct mail, TV, and telephone—have reached diminishing returns or even become counterproductive.[32] Many people, for example, are averse to telemarketing calls of any type, as well as to negative TV advertising. They also discard political fundraising solicitations through the mail, many of which come in the misleading guise of surveys soliciting opinions on issues. They ignore these sooner than they would click to tune out a mattress commercial.[33] People are smarter than the pol's think, knowing that their opinions count for far less than their dollars, if at all.

- <u>Channels and tools through which people can make a difference in politics:</u> These are readily available to anyone who cares to take an interest and occasionally commit small amounts of time. The most promising vehicles are local, political party committees. Most of these are ripe for revitalization. Most are weak, with numbers of active members far less than the numbers allowed by law. Many have fallen into limbo and exist only on the books. An enthusiastic group of political amateurs could take over many such committees and revive them as a political force in their communities. Good examples can be found in this book.[34] See Chapters 4 and 5 for more.

These are prime lessons for the majority of people who simply want to be better citizens or who would like to take back the political system from the pro's and make it what it is supposed to be—their own.[35] Political participation offers a great two-fer: Personal growth plus collaboration with others in a larger undertaking. The lessons may not hold much water, however, for political careerists.

The lessons for the latter are mostly different. Politics...

- Corrupts those who see politics as a career or profession (as illustrated by the cartoon below)—

- Threatens to consume one's life and undermine marriage and family—

- Cares little or nothing about building community—

- Is corrupted by money—

- Has little regard for truthfulness or ways to search for truth, including science except as it's (mistakenly) viewed as little more than a source of whiz-bang technologies—

- Looks for politically correct answers without first asking the right questions or testing alternative potential solutions—

- Expends and wastes rather than saves—

- Focuses on *what* instead of *how* and proceeds as though the end justifies the means—

- Puts people and issues in boxes while ignoring their interrelationships—

- Focuses on personalities rather than issues, or style over substance—

- Is a winner take all game—

- Fails to give credit to the non-politically self-interested who help in the process, while taking credit for anything significant that happens on an elected officials' watch—

- Is risk averse or go-along; get along—

- Has little appreciation for the innovator, muckraker, iconoclast or whistle-blower (as revealed by another cartoon to follow)—

- Uses basic values as grist for the mill of political speechifying but seldom works to find ways to honor them.

"If elected, I promise to do my darndest to get re-elected!"

Jeff Stahler, The Cincinnati Post, Ohio

The irony is that the negatives are mostly the other side of the coin of positives. Both sides indicate the importance of broadening and deepening the base of political participation. The negativity of the negatives noted above would at least be diminished if a greater number and variety of people were to participate in the political process to pursue some of their shared goals as responsible public (not just private) citizens.[36] This is especially apparent with respect to three of the negatives, for example, that politics—

- Consumes one's life and undermines marriages and families—

- Cares little or nothing about building community—

- Is corrupted by money, especially given the lack of the only significant antidote to money—people's contributions of time.

A greater number and variety of people helping out would make campaigns at least a little less consuming and more satisfying for candidates, involve people who care about community, and substitute volunteers' time for money.[37] Here, political scientists could help us out. Even though some of them have done good studies to identify the characteristics of those who are political volunteers, we know too little about the dynamics of political volunteering—what induces people to drop in or drop out and why some become political junkies or pro's.

One of the most painful lessons of my own experience, however—mixed agendas and inadequate resources—will always be a problem for those interested in campaigning for higher office unless the candidate is supported by a rich family or a rich, politically well-connected spouse who shares the candidate's devotion to politics. Call this the conflicted mix problem along with the challenge of mixing politics and marriage. In my case, there was a chronic, four-way tension between politics, business, writing, and family. The stress was aggravated by the fact that I possessed a strong desire, some ability, and lots of illusion that I could pursue all four goals together, if not always simultaneously. Foolish me! What an illusion! Bob Meyner, former Governor of New Jersey, knew better. After losing my race for congress in New Jersey's 12th C.D. in 1984, he advised me to focus on my business to make a lot of money before running again. I was outspent in that race 4:1 in spite of raising more money for a campaign than I had ever raised before. He might as well have advised me to focus on my marriage and family, for my wife and I separated in 1986 and divorced in 1989.

There is great irony or paradox in the mix of the personal and the political. There is no avoiding the mix even though many political commentators and activists bewail personality politics a la *People* magazine. The demands of politics on someone who runs for any office above the local level in a small town are so nearly all-consuming that the personal and political are constantly bumping into each other. During a campaign, the candidate will be sacrificing personal time with his family as well as personal money to keep his or her campaign going.[38]

In the public sphere, contrary to Sennett (1977), the increasing attention on politician's personalities is not all bad. Style and substance are not readily separated. Voters look to see how a candidate handles various situations; e.g., to see whether he or she is ascerbic, temperamental, diplomatic, calm under pressure, etc. Also, so-called private behavior usually implicates public values of legitimate concern to the electorate; e.g., whether a candidate advocating family values is faithful to his wife, whether one talking of truthfulness has lied to customers or vendors in business dealings, etc. A candidate for public office finds that there is no clear boundary between public and private nor, perhaps, should there be. The candidate's private behavior must be able to withstand scrutiny in light of values that, because they are shared and deeply rooted, are fundamentally public in nature.

The question at all levels, however, from individual choices to national and international media attention, is one of balance. More of the individuals who have been active in politics should share memoirs of how they balanced the personal and political sides of their lives. The lessons would inform all of us. The media should focus more on the intersect between personal style and political substance rather than on aspects of politicians' personalities that may titillate the private fantasies of readers without informing their roles as public citizens.

How to strike a balance, moreover, is not just a personal, individual matter. It is a matter of sharing the load. To the extent that volunteers help with campaigns, candidates can be more relaxed and able to devote more time with their families, and volunteers may have the satisfaction of helping to elect someone who will listen to them.

Various forms of participation: Why are some more important than others?

Participation and Voluntarism are catch-all labels that obscure more than they reveal. They cover a wide variety of activities, some of which are far more relevant to political effectiveness or people's empowerment than others. Verba's (1995) comprehensive study distinguishes eight activities among forms of participation in the political process: voting, campaign work, contributions, contact, protest, informal community activity, board membership, and affiliation with political organizations.[39] The latter primarily refers to political parties; that is, partisan affiliations.

Verba's large sample study, contrary to some others, does not find a significant fall-off in political participation, broadly defined. It does, however, find a significant shift among the activities under his participation umbrella —from those where volunteers are more directly and interpersonally involved with others to those that are far more indirect, such as writing checks, writing letters, and becoming nominal members of politically oriented groups. This shift is consistent with the observations of others, especially Putnam and the NCCR,[40] that there has been a significant decline in people-to-people political involvement that appears to be part and parcel of a more general decline of involvement in public life or civic affairs. These trends are reviewed in Chapters 4-6 and 8 of this book.

Thus, the issue is not just one of participation but, indeed, the specific forms that participation takes or lacks. Simply put, there have been declines in the forms of participation through which people of ordinary means can be politically empowered or effective, and we have not yet seen the end of these negative trends.[41] In this book, the (renewed) local political party committee (LPPC) is held to be a model of voluntary political participation open to people in all walks of life.[42] This model still exists in many places even though it has been gradually heading towards extinction. It is a model that the author has experienced over many years of activity known to participants as laboring in the vineyards.[43] The traditional LPCC enabled volunteers to do the following:

- Get to know one's neighbors;
- Register people to vote;
- Get acquainted with candidates and issues;
- Educate others with respect to candidates and issues;
- Help people get out to vote on election day (especially the elderly and disabled);[44]
- Help identify and recruit people to be candidates for local and other offices;
- Participate in political debates, formal and informal;
- Make their views known to candidates, political parties and elected officials; and
- Otherwise participate effectively in electoral politics.

Our survey of LPPC's, however, reveals that most committees are in limbo or decline, with activities falling far short of potential (see Chapter 5). Thus, a venue that, arguably, has been the most effective vehicle for the man (or woman) in the street's effective political participation is far less so and diminishing.

Not that local partisan political activities are the only venue for participation. There are local charitable organizations, churches, fraternal organizations and others. *Voice and Equality* also shows that these non-political organizations, especially churches, serve to convey and develop political skills. "Citizens who are active in voluntary associations are also more politically active."[45]

The findings of the lengthy study by Verba and his colleagues' highlight what may be the most important reason why some forms of political participation are more important than others—some provide a basis for a democracy that is representative; some for one that is not. Contributions of money, the form of participation that has become increasingly important, points to a system that is un-representative, one dominated by wealthy, high income and well-educated people. Those that involve commitments of time enable a system that is more representative, i.e., more democratic. Thus, the shift documented by the study is a major piece of evidence pointing to both decline and displacement of American democracy.

Verba's study also puts the influence of another basic shift into perspective—that of women into the workforce. This factor had often been featured as a prime reason for both the decline of community and political participation because stay-at-home moms typically volunteered time for community activities. This is only one factor of several, however, and there are now countervailing demographic trends at work such as reduced participation of men in the workforce. To the extent that public policy can be more supportive of families, especially enabling couples to share and afford the burden of adequate child care, married men and women with children might be able to afford more time to participate in the politics of the future.

People's commitments of time, or lack thereof, also have to do with the quality of American democracy in other terms that have been addressed by those concerned with the quality of our public or civic lives more generally. The root concern in this regard is a worry over the quality of our deliberation as citizens. Deliberation is not an indirect form of political participation, nor is it one that is exercised by writing checks. It is also not necessarily a way that is formal. Verba and others point to the importance of non-political as well as political settings; e.g., churches, workplaces, and associations, as well as political parties, as venues where people of varied status and backgrounds can talk informally about issues and politics.

Forms of participation that enable direct interaction among people are important to the extent that they...

- Bring people from varied walks of life together around shared goals and concerns;

- Enable continuing conversations around shared concerns over public issues;

- Help to inform people with regard to their objectives and concerns for public issues; and

- Help to elect good people to public office.

Thus, the decline of forms of direct political participation involving contributions of time rather than money is detrimental to the quality of American democracy. Concern over this decline is one that is shared by partisan political, non-partisan political, and non-political types. Perhaps it is a concern that can bring these sets of people together, sets that have been too often or too long apart. These two concerns—reviving the direct forms and bringing the three sets together—occupy subsequent chapters of this book.

Frequencies of Participation: What are the odds? Why are they important?

Frequencies of participation are important for two main reasons:

1. To spread and democratize the burdens and pleasures of fulfillment of our responsibilities as citizens; and...

2. To see to it that the views of a broad-based majority of citizens are more influential than those of the small minority of the politically self-interested—the lobbyists, big money contributors, political careerists and professionals, political junkies, et. al.

These two very much go together as part and parcel of the same overall direct participation problem. Each of us should seek to participate with some frequency, however small or infrequent that might be, if we are to reclaim our birthright from those who see politics as a profession instead of a responsibility.

In other words, if each of us doesn't commit small amounts of time from time to time, the political system will continue to be taken over and dominated by those whose interest is in politics as a full-time or overtime job, or who see that politics is best left to the experts.

At the same time, those of us who get a life in the real world need to help spread the load, else too few are bearing the burdens of too many. This bears on the possible pleasures of fulfillment from being involved, because if too much of the political work falls on too few then, indeed, political activity, like any other, becomes too much like onerous work-work, a load or a burden instead of the pleasure that it is or can be like other voluntary work for good causes. This is too often the case now, as too few are carrying the responsibilities of too many. We economists refer to the latter as *free riders*. The more popular term is *free oaders*. How many of you readers who are not participants in the political process resent being called freeloaders? Sorry; truth often hurts. No American likes to think of himself this way. We all like to be thought of as carrying our share of any load.

Note the positive: If you are involved at a time different from me, then you complement, supplement, or build upon my efforts and the sum value of our participation adds up. If you are involved with me at the same time, the satisfaction that I can derive from my participation is greater from being able to work with you. Those who have been so involved testified to the satisfactions of their involvement during our interviews, featured in the next chapter.

Spreading the load is also important to take the edge off the feeling of sacrifice that many in public life come to feel if, as most do, they feel that running for and serving in political office demands so much that they have to sacrifice family, private and community aspects of their lives. As Peter Berger showed many years ago, it's no good if too few come to feel that they are sacrificing for too many.[46] Why? Because even if politicians are not egomaniacal or solely power-driven, the siren call of power comes to be a satisfying offset to sacrifice. It is especially easy for the powerful to forget where they came from or who put them there if there were no people there in the political picture when they were needed.

So the frequencies, likelihood or odds of people's participation in the political process are a serious issue somewhat distinguishable from the forms of involvement. People should be at least as concerned about the odds of political participation as those of winning a state lottery. The benefits of playing politics are win-win benefits—I win, you win, we all win. The chance of benefiting is far, far greater than that of winning a lottery. Political scientists like Verba have approached this issue from the standpoint of the representativeness of our democracy. Our concern here is also for shared responsibility and citizens' effectiveness.

As noted earlier, citizens' likelihood of political participation (volunteering time to campaigns) is even less than that of their contributing money—3% vs. 7% of the electorate.[47] As is well known from studies of campaign finance, the money contributions are dominated by big money contributions in excess of $200 (contributed by only about ¼ of one percent). So the need to redress the imbalance between time and money is clear if a broadly representative base of citizens' voices is to be heard.

Extent or Amount of participation: Why is this important?

The extent, amount, scale and scalability of political participation are important because it is either very difficult or impossible to make any significant political difference without political organization; that is, without engaging or joining with others. There are obvious connections here with form and frequency—

> FORM: Forms of participation whose frequencies are increasing, such as writing checks, e-mails and letters, are individualistic contributions. Those whose frequencies have been decreasing, such as participation in party politics, are more group-wise, collective efforts that are larger scale and scalable to even greater magnitudes.

> FREQUENCY: A host of small contributions can add up to an amount or scale of involvement that, either individually or overall, as an aggregate set of individual contributions, is quite significant. Thus, individual frequencies of political participation are indeed scalable in that they can add up to a lot, especially when candidates, campaign managers or chairs of political committees match talents to tasks, provide some how-to instruction, and employ volunteers' precious time effectively.[48]

The problem here is that the American myth of individualism is anti-scale; that is, prone to shy away from large-scale group or collective efforts. The corresponding irony or paradox is that major political changes are needed in order to fulfill the individualism of the American Dream, but such changes will not occur on individualistic basis. Prevailing shifts in the forms and frequencies of political participation are self-defeating. The reality of the contributions needed to fulfill the myth is political organization—individuals participating group-wise rather than individually. The exception proves the rule. Unless I am rich like Steve Forbes, Ross Perot, or Jon Corzine, I need to make common cause with others, to multiply and magnify my individual efforts, in order to have any realistic hope that, politically, I can really make a difference.

The Significance of Intermediaries

Most of us who simply yearn for a better politics and government, let alone fulfillment of the American dream, also need to affiliate with some appropriate organizations to multiply and magnify or leverage our individual efforts. These are sometimes referred to as intermediaries because they stand somewhere, often as go-betweens, between the individual and government.

Intermediaries usually fall under the general heading of voluntary associations. Ever since d'Tocqueville, the vitality of American democracy has been known for its great variety of associations inhabiting every nook and cranny of the American political landscape. They are self-organizing forms.[49] For all the individualism of the American myth, it seems that whenever Americans share a concern, they gather together into a group to advocate and effect that concern.

Insofar as political participation is concerned, there are two basic questions concerning intermediaries:

1. What are the overlaps or relationships between political and non-political intermediaries?

2. How do mainly non-political intermediaries representing various facets of civic society orient their members toward politics or enable them to participate in political activities more effectively?

As noted earlier, Verba's study largely answered the latter question by showing that voluntary organizations convey civic skills as well as involve members in discussions of politically relevant issues. These influences suggest an answer to question # 1 as well—that there may be politically relevant overlaps or relationships. Such an implication cannot be drawn, however, and whether such connections as exist are politically relevant is really an important question.

Rather than effective linkages, overlaps, or relationships, there are significant gaps between voluntary associations and organizations that are devoted to electoral politics. Organizations representing civic society exist in a sphere that is largely divorced from the world of politics per se. Their orientation to politically relevant issues is usually limited to those that fall into their specific areas of concern that have been the basis for their formation. Health associations are concerned about health issues; environmental organizations about environmental issues, etc. Large, well-organized associations of long-standing support political lobbyists. Rather than supplying political volunteers, their members participate indirectly, by writing checks. But issue-advocacy via these organizations does not begin to fulfill the traditional issues' aggregating and cross-cutting roles of political parties or make up for parties' increasing inability or unwillingness to play such important roles.

The gaps are primarily of three types:

- Little overlap in memberships or leadership between political and non-political groups;[50]

- Little sharing of politically relevant information except via lobbying or candidate support to try to influence the views of candidates and elected officials with respect to some specific issue (rather than the larger issue of political reform);

- Little inter-organizational collaboration on shared concerns.

In his book, *Democracy Realized*, R.M. Unger, a professor at Harvard Law School, makes some very trenchant observations on "the independent organization of civil society" that put these "gaps" into a larger perspective. He writes:

> We find the idea (all too prevalent, in this author's view)...that the spontaneous self-organization of civil society... can make it unnecessary to win and use governmental power (even though) politics and government are driving toward a future that...civil society may despise and narrowing the terrain... (for political transformation or major reforms). [Yet,] "voluntary association (is)...impotent to create its own conditions (for playing effective roles in any process of political transformation) unless it...joins forces with a different style of politics... **Voluntary associations with a message for society at large...remain detached from the everyday world [of politics**, et. al.] (Unger 1998, pp. 220-228; emphasis mine).

In other words, the prevalent, conventional form of voluntary association...

- focuses upon narrow gains rather than larger issues, akin to the what's-in-it-for-me attitude that seems so prevalent; and...

- is reluctant or, in some cases like charitable foundations, unable under a private law (tax exempt) charter, to get its hands dirty with involvement in politics.

A good, new but rather typical example is provided by the AOL Foundation and its "Helping.org" site. This promotes "e-philanthropy," including volunteerism. Click on the AOL web site's "Volunteer Match." However, if you are looking for a political organization to match your interest in volunteering —to get involved in something, anything, political—you will come up dry. I followed the AOL directions and did a quick search for volunteering opportunities in the Gloucester, MA 01930 area and got several leads—to "library help," "homework assistance," "United Way," "community garden," "childcare provider," et.al. None were in Gloucester; none hinted at even a taint of politics or political organizations where volunteers are needed and could serve.[51]

Thus, we mark another paradox to explore in later chapters of this book. On the one hand, even now, somewhat as observed by d'Tocqueville when our democracy was still young, the voluntary sector is a major contributor to the vitality of our political system, i.e., intermediaries are important. On the other hand, this sector is increasingly divorced from politics except for an aspect that citizens increasingly deplore—the politics of special interests. It is even more distant from the pursuit of larger issues of political reform except via indirection—via non-political channels of civil society that lack linkages, overlaps, or relationships with political organizations.

We have seen an increasing proliferation of political think tanks and lobbying organizations, but these are part and parcel of the professionalization of politics, not organizations activating or empowering political voluntarism.[52] It is ironic that the only parts of the latter that have succeeded in bringing large numbers of people back into the political process through grassroots involvement are those that are devoted to a cause or single issue, e.g., the Christian Coalition and pro-life or pro-labor organizations.

There is a warning here with respect to voluntary political involvement, especially that oriented to political reform. Unger expresses it best: The danger is that "the spirit will tire because the institutions fail to sustain it." Only a few of us self-identify as public entrepreneurs who are self-starters. Like even most business entrepreneurs, we need a support system to sustain our spirit, indeed, to revive the spirit of popular democracy.[53]

Seeds of Political Leadership

Where do political candidates and leaders come from? Traditionally, candidates for public office have arisen from the pool of participants in the political process. This is another reason why people's participation is important. If the pool of participants dries up, it is just a matter of time before the supply of candidates competing for public office dries up as well. We can already see this happening in many states, apparent through another negative but developing trend—growing numbers of uncontested seats and non-competitive elections where no candidates or only incumbents are on the ballot, or they have only token opposition.

The lack of effective links between the political and non-political sides of our civic society, as indicated in the last section, is an issue here, too. There is an essential similarity between public (civic) and private entrepreneurship. Those with entrepreneurial qualities are the true leaders in either sphere. We are seeing increasing numbers and proportions of citizens with leadership qualities at all levels avoid politics to devote their time to good causes in the non-political sphere. The most prominent such citizen is former Gen. Colin Powell. He is many people's ideal vision of a presidential candidate, yet he has chosen to stay out of electoral politics. Before becoming Secretary of State, he chose to lead a nationwide voluntary campaign on behalf of children called America's Promise. He is literally the tip of the iceberg, exemplifying millions of Americans who, alienated from politics, nevertheless volunteer to do all kinds of good works in their communities.

Recall the remarks about lemons made earlier. If good, community-spirited people avoid politics, leaving it to the lemons, then our political system will turn into a lemon, too. There is a great need to recruit more political candidates from among the non-political public entrepreneurs. Which means, first of all, that there is a great need to get non-political volunteers to cross over the non-political/political divide to become political volunteers, too. Then some of these will see how they can make an even greater difference in the political sphere, become candidates for public office, and develop into the political leaders we need in our future.[54]

One of the questions raised earlier in this chapter, however, is: At what personal cost do volunteers make such a transition? Political scientists make note: We don't have studies to help answer the question, only anecdotes. One thing is clear. People of ordinary means will need some support systems to help sustain their political initiative. Without training, many political ingenues will be exploited a la "Mr. Smith goes to Washington." Party committees at all levels will need to be prepared to provide local and entry-level support, not just big-ticket financing for federal level star candidacies. Do you think Colin Powell would have been able to mount America's Promise or been so successful if corporations and foundations had not come through with big bucks of support?[55]

A New Politics? (2)

Since the old politics apparently has turned so many away, it appears that we need a new politics. Or do we? What's really old and what's really new in the politics of what is now the oldest constitutional democracy in the world? The question is primarily not one of vintage but of value. We need some of both—old wine in new bottles and new wine in old bottles. We may also want to throw out or alter some of each—some that is new as well as some of the old—without watering the full-bodied wine of politics.

Traditionally, until recently, the local committees of political parties (hereafter, labelled LPPC's) have been among the pillars of American democracy —doing those things that most need to be done to keep the grassroots of American political life watered—registering voters, getting out the vote (GOTV), distributing political literature, talking issues with neighbors, recruiting candidates, campaigning for candidates, et. al. Such committees were the foundations of political life. They provided the foot soldiers of the parties, the "seed corn," the "farm team," the "activists" of democratic communities that, in turn, made up a vibrant national political life.

This is the old model of the author's experience.[56] It is still relevant in ways that would be attractive to many people if they would come to know it. The model local committee man or woman was, and in some communities still is, the person who:

- knows his or her neighbors, including when their children are coming of age;
- canvasses (visits) neighbors, wards and precincts door-to-door at least twice a year;
- registers people to vote at their door, in front of markets, at their places of work, in schools, at events, on the street or during public gatherings;
- talks up candidates and issues with friends and neighbors;
- listens to what people from all walks of life have to say and passes their views on to candidates, party officers, and elected officials;[57]

- helps to set up public forums to air candidates and issues;
- distributes flyers, brochures and other political literature on candidates and issues;
- helps his or her party and candidates get out the vote via canvassing, door knockers, phone calls, rides to the polls, et. al.;
- helps people who need help to get to the polls; e.g., the elderly and disabled;
- strengthens the campaign teams of select candidates;
- contributes to the production as well as the distribution of newsletters, brochures, and other political-informational materials;
- beats the bushes to encourage others to get involved and to help recruit candidates for public office; and...
- puts up political signs or stands out with signs to alert others as to elections and candidates.

Notice that these are all direct, hands-on, grassroots, people-to-people activities. The increasingly indirect, couch potato forms of political participation, such as writing checks and letters are not included. Not that local committee people don't do such things; in fact, they are more likely to do so because of their direct involvement. The people-to-people emphasis of their activities, however, is most important because politics, by definition, is an undertaking of, by and for people. Perhaps what we need is a new/old model via new and renewed LPPC's, especially in order to bring back to politics the closeness, neighborliness, warmth, and community spirit that the new consultant polling and computer-driven politics lacks.

The old model is exemplified by Mary Perone, long-time committeewoman and Chair of the Princeton (NJ) Borough Democratic Committee. A sketch of Mary and her involvement introduces the interview of her featured in the next chapter. Take a look. She's an inspiration, one of many to be discovered, not only in the chapter but in your own cities and towns.[58]

The Paradox of Politics and the Politics of Paradox

This introductory focus on the importance of everyman's (and woman's) political participation has uncovered several troublesome contradictions that are paradoxical. Paradox, the root of paradoxical, is a keyword throughout this book. What does it mean? It means that the same thing has opposite qualities. They generate tension because they are opposites. One quality may be emphasized or viewed positively by someone; the other emphasized or viewed negatively by someone else. The pluses and the minuses debate and do battle. They may even form opposite parties or factions within parties. Such is the nature of politics today. To some, it is an exhilarating activity; to others, it is a pox upon us. To those with the deepest insight as to the nature of American democracy, the political fray or battle is essential. This was as true for de Tocqueville in 1835 as for Lapham in 2003. The latter wrote: "Defined as a ceaseless process of change, democracy assumes the pain of contradiction…as the necessary condition of existence."[59]

The centerpiece of our politics, our democracy, is also a paradox. Some believe that, via instant polls and the Internet, we are on the verge of a new, far more democratic democracy in which every adult person is empowered. Others say that this vision would be the death of democracy. The nature of paradox is revealed by the simple claim we often heard in the early '90s, especially from environmentalists: "Less is more" and "more is less."

Several more specific paradoxes have arisen without being identified as such. Lacking a new and better politics, these are the basis of several vicious cycles. Let's recall some of them:

- More people participating in res publica—public activities; less participating in res politica—political activities that are the foundation of a democratic system of governance;

- People, feeling that politics is for *them*, not for *us*, are staying away from politics, thereby leaving it to *them*.

- People, complaining that politics has become a money game, are neglecting to contribute any time, thereby making it even more of a money game.

- Public-spirited people, complaining that politics has become the province of the pro's, political careerists, lobbyists, and others among the politically self-interested, stay away from politics, thus confirming their negative opinion and making it even more the province of the pro's.

- People participate in community-based organizations (CBO's) hoping to make a difference in the quality of life in their communities while ignoring or deprecating local politics which, for better or for worse, does indeed make a difference; indeed, it affects the ability of CBO's and their members to be effective in fulfilling their own goals.[60]

- The paradox of time in a so-called service and leisure society is that we have less of it.

The key to political development or transformation in an age of paradox is creative management of the tensions that result. The tensions arise or become apparent primarily in the lives of individuals, families, and communities. Thus, there is no way that they can be resolved without people's political participation. Since the tension is public and political, it is not resolvable by doctors of psychology applying therapy one-on-one to us as patients on a couch. The therapy is group-wise and new balances need to be struck via a new and better politics in which we are the essential actors and in which the pro's are resources serving us, not them(selves).

You'll find more on the Politics of Paradox in Chapter 7.

Notes

1. Lapham (2003), op.cit. (p.35).

2. Another, even more negative view is that of Mike Lynch, which one could label "self-interest politics." In response to an early draft of this chapter, he wrote: "We are still a me society; that is, so long as I am OK and my issues are OK, then I don't care…! Parties are intended to collect everyone with a similar agenda to them. Hence, if I'm OK, let them fight it out; but please keep the (partisan) volume down; you're interrupting the game or Martha Stewart!" His insights from an interview are provided in Chapter 4.

3. Quotes drawn from Saletan, William (2001), "Reinventing Trust in Government," *Slate* (Oct.4), who concludes that the big blips in polls showing increased "trust in government" in the immediate aftermath of Sept.11 will turn out to be temporary. Gary Wills views our chronic distrust in government as "a necessary evil." See Wills (1999). Anyway, the big up-blips were ironic, for Sept.11th was evidence of government failure to fulfill the most fundamental of its responsibilities – public safety and security.

4. Recall that the media colored red the states that went for Bush and blue those that went for Gore. See Chapter 9 on the 2000 presidential election.

5. McWilliams, Wilson Carey (1969), "Political Arts and Political Sciences," in Green, Philip, and S. Levinson (1970), pp.360 and 364.

6. The view of Daniel Kemmis (1990). For a more recent rendering of influences on the founders in the making of our Constitution, see Wills (1999).

7. As set forth in "The Case for Liberalism," *Harper's Magazine* (December, 2002, pp.37-42, especially page 38). The points will not be argued here, as they have been treated ad nauseum by political commentators and ideologues representing both sides. McGovern cites Webster's dictionary's definition of liberalism as "a political philosophy based on belief in progress…goodness of man…autonomy of the individual and…protection of political and civil liberties." In this author's opinion, only the last (1 of 4) is indisputable.

8. A bumper sticker spotted on a car reads: "If you're not outraged, you're not paying attention!" (June 13, 2003).

9. The evidence of government failure is substantial. It was amply reported in the aftermath of the tragedy and has been confirmed and/or elaborated by the investigation of the tragedy by Congress and the 9/11 Commission. It includes the failure of intelligence agencies, government agencies' ignoring many signs and signals and failing to follow-through on previous recommendations to act; members of Congress commissioning and then ignoring GAO studies of airport security; and lax security at Logan Airport, Boston, managed by the state agency, MASSPORT, which had earned a reputation as a haven for political appointees. At the time, MASSPORT's Executive Director and Director of Security, were formerly Gov. Weld's driver and PR person, respectively. For more on this point, see my October, 2002 article, "We Have Met the Enemy. He is Us," in *The Ethical Spectacle* (www.spectacle.org).

10. "Distributed intelligence" enabled by the new "wired world" of people on the 'Net and 'Web gives this democratic assumption a new and more powerful credibility. See Pamela LiCalzi O'Connell's article "Mining the Minds of the Masses," *New York Times* (March 6, 2001). Also see Potier, Beth (2003), "Groups, like people, can be intelligent…," *Harvard University Gazette* (July 17). Chapter 8 addresses the potential of "digital democracy."

11. In an excellent book, *Republic.com*, University of Chicago law professor Cass Sunstein claims that this tendency of "fragmentation" is being aggravated by growing use of the Internet. We return to this issue in Chapter 8.

12. In Weiners, Brad (2002), "Making Headlines in 10,000 Point Type," *Wired* (December, p.114). Founder/head of his own highly regarded design firm in Manhattan, ESI Design, Ed is better known as the husband of Caroline Kennedy Schlossberg.

13. As in Asef Bayat's (1997) *Street Politics*: Poor People's Movements In Iran. New York: Columbia University Press.

14. See Yankelovitch, Daniel (1991), *Coming to Public Judgment*.

15. McWilliams, Wilson Carey (1969), op.cit., p.372.

16. Pawley, Martin (1974), *The Private Future*. New York: Random House, p. 125.

17. Quart, Alissa (2002), "A Smarter Way to Sell Ketchup," *Wired* (December). Quart (alissa_quart@yahoo.com) is the author of *Branded: The Buying and Selling of Teenagers*.

18. Shea, Daniel (1999), "The Passing of Realignment and the Advent of the Baseless Party System," American Quarterly, V. 27.1 (January)

19. McWilliams, Wilson Carey (1969), op.cit., p.359.

20. Barber, Benjamin (1984), *Strong Democracy: Participatory Politics for a New Age*. Berkeley: University of California Press.

21. See Bearse (1999) on "The Fractal Revolution" for more.

22. Even in church. See Bearse and Bruno (1998), "Church and Politics: Thoughts on building community-based politics," Marlboro, MA: *Main Street Journal* (February 28).

23. "We the people" are the opening words of our Constitution. A recent contestant on "Who Wants to be a Millionaire" could not identify the source. Note the importance of the words by contrast with an undemocratic society, China. On Public Radio International (July 11, 2000), women from a non-governmental organization (NGO) were commenting on why the NGO assumed a neutral stance towards China's bid for Beijing to be the 2008 Olympic site: "We make a distinction between the Chinese people and the Chinese government." Aren't we in danger of approaching such a state, when many Americans are making such a distinction about their own country?

24. Pawley, M. (1974), op.cit.

25. These are the words narrated during Aaron Copland's "Lincoln Portrait," primarily those from the "Gettysburg Address." Listen to Carl Sandburg's great rendering on the CD: Sony Music Entertainment (2000), *A Copland Celebration* (Vol.2).

26. Olson, Charles (1963), *Maximus Poems*. New York: Jargon. Note especially Letter 5: "Polis is eyes." Also see Maud, Ralph (2000), *What Does Not Change...*

27. My age may also be a factor. Born in 1941 and a college graduate in 1963, I can't be called either a boomer or a child of the '60s. I was on the cusp of both groups. My father's age was a factor, too, because the great historical event shaping his life (and, indirectly, mine) was the Depression, not World War II (WWII). He was married, in his thirties with a child, and an electrical engineer working for a defense contractor when WWII started, so he was not drafted, either.

28. With the benefit of large state and federal projects and public investments, Newark started to make a significant comeback thirty years later; however, neighborhoods that gave people a sense of place and community to those growing up there are in the process of being destroyed by gentrifiers and developers.

29. I served on Borough Council while Ms. Sigmund, also a resident of Princeton and daughter of Hale and Lindy Boggs, former Members of Congress, was serving as a County Freeholder. Later, before tragically passing away of eye cancer, she was Mayor of the Borough.

30. Good examples of this are provided by the histories of the civil rights and environmental movements.

31. As noted in the final chapters, there are signs that the pro's are coming to recognize the value of people's participation. But it remains to be seen whether they will help to empower the latter or themselves.

32. The first draft of this chapter, written several years ago, in fact predicted this finding.

33. One example of direct mail solicitations from political parties that are especially annoying because they are so deliberately misleading is the letter soliciting money from a national party committee that pretends to be a grassroots solicitation to support local political activities. The money so collected does not go to local political committees.

34. Mike Lynch reported that the Christian Right succeeded in taking control of many local political committees in the South after their views were ignored by committees' leaders. See Chapter 4.

35. Mike Lynch's comment on this was: "Hence, the struggling Reform Party, but lack of patience and Perot's money pushed it too far, too soon."

36. Mike Lynch also commented: "Shared goals must be defined for them (people)." Unfortunately, he is right. The overwhelming majority of the American people have long since ceased to be self-starters in the public arena even though (or partly because?) we live in an age of private initiative and entrepreneurship. So there is a role for political leadership in defining shared goals; but that's largely missing, too. It's now considered political suicide for politicians to get out front on controversial issues.

37. My most fond memories of my campaign for congress, for example, focus on various volunteers, including Steve Weinberg, campaign manager, and Paul, an environmental activist who drove me crazy insisting that environmental issues should be the prime focus of the campaign, plus a number of local political committee workers of the old school like those featured in Heinlein's book cited earlier.

38. For example, see Vivian Marino's article: "A Run for Office Can Mean a Run on Your Money," *New York Times* (Jan. 23, 2000). She wrote: "While the finances of high...officeholders...get the attention, it is a different story on the local front...some individuals must make serious financial sacrifices..." (as I did, even for local campaigns).

39. Verba, Sidney, Kay Lehman Schlozman & Henry E. Brady (1995), *Voice and Equality: Civic Voluntarism in American Politics*. Cambridge: Harvard University Press.

40. Putnam, S. (1995), *Bowling Alone* and its book sequel. NCCR refers to the National Commission on Civic Renewal and its 1998 Report. See also Kemmis (1990).

41. Notwithstanding the numbers and enthusiasm of political volunteers during the 2000 Presidential primaries, especially in New Hampshire, which were heartening.

42. The openness and vitality of this model, however, are subjected to some strict scrutiny and skepticism by some of the interviewees whose views are featured in the next chapter. There is a danger that even party committees, like other segments of the political universe, will fall to the like-minded, turning away people who challenge old school, single-issue or ideological members already in place.

43. This experience is reflected far more in Heinlein's book, referenced at the end of the last chapter, and in Chapters 4 and 5, based on the interviews and survey conducted for this book.

44. On this, Mike Lynch remarked: "You need the machine to affect this," perhaps having in mind the old Daley machine in Chicago. Indeed. Political party machines, maligned and undermined by the Progressives, need to be revived and strengthened —via broader bases of popular participation.

45. Verba, et. al. (1995), p. 335. Mike Lynch's take on this is skeptical even to the point of being cynical (Mike would say "realistic"): "Why (are citizens active)? – because their self interests are not being embraced by the public at-large or their self interests are being threatened by the system or larger society." No mention of "the public interest" or public spiritedness here, but as indicated earlier, some self-definitions of "self" are broader than others.

46. See Berger, Peter (1976), *Pyramids of Sacrifice*. New York: Anchor Books.

47. Source: Putnam (2000), op.cit. As indicated earlier, we employ '96 presidential stat's because of the NH and IA blips during the Spring of '00 and '04.

48. This was best demonstrated by the leading "populist" campaign of the 2004 presidential primary season—that of Howard Dean.

49. A troubling set of exceptions, typically **not** a product of citizens' self-organizing, has grown up in response to both the increasing need of politicians to raise money

and the efforts of reformers to limit the role of money in politics. This is the set of organizations established by both corporate interests and issues' advocates to finance both issue-advocacy and political campaigns-related media. Included are section 527 organizations permitted under the tax code, which now need to report their sources to the IRS.

50. Exceptions can be found among many local political party committees, as revealed in Chapter 5.

51. This has also been the experience of Jim Bzolekm author of *How to Participate in Politics Effectively* in Chicago and Denver (as reported by phone on 4/21/04).

52. One example of this, an excellent source of information for state legislators and others, is the Heartland Institute, a conservative political think tank founded by Joe Bast and his wife Diane in Chicago.

53. This is the major reason why this book is supplemented by a website: www.politicalcommunity.us.

54. One example among the interviewees featured in Chapter 4 is Amy Handlin, an elected official in Monmouth County, NJ.

55. Here again, thanks are due to Mike Lynch in his role of reviewer of an early draft of this chapter.

56. It is also the model of political participation of the "Greatest Generation," so well set forth in detail by Heinlein (1992).

57. This is the core of the "bottom up" approach that political parties need to effect, as emphasized by Mike Lynch during his interview featured in the next chapter.

58. It was with great sadness that I learned of Mary's passing as this book went to press. she was my inspiration, and I wanted to present her with a signed copy in person, with many thanks.

59. Lapham, Lewis H. (April, 2003), op.cit. (p.40). As for de Tocqueville, see Gannett, Robert T., Jr., (2003), "Bowling Ninepins in Tocqueville's Township." 97 *American Political Science Review* 1 (February), pp.1-15.

60. Here again, the remarks of Mike Lynch provide a sobering additional perspective, more realistic than idealistic: "People usually participate on their own terms and then fall out when they don't get their way… Politics is not (and should not be viewed as) a moment. It is instead an ongoing, give and take, day after day process! When people refused to become temporary losers, they dropped out, and parties had nothing to offer." Look for more of his insights in the next chapter.

4.

Role Models & Views from the Political Vineyards:
The Old Politics vs. the New

Executive Summary

Two dozen people were interviewed for this book. With the exception of one wealthy political fund-raiser, the interviewees represent a diverse cross-section of middle-class America—a variety of occupations, life styles, ages, and political affiliations. What makes them exceptional is that political participation has been a significant and satisfying aspect of their lives. Thus, their views on the variety of factors that affect the extent and nature of political participation by themselves and others are interesting and insightful. These are highlighted below and labeled by chapter sub-titles that headline interviewees' observations on a number of important issues including:

• *Volunteerism, The Value of People's Time, and Person-to-Person (P2P) Contacts:* The best and most effective politics is that which involves people volunteering time to approach others on a person-to-person basis. Unfortunately, the increasing value of people's time, and their feeling that any time devoted to political participation would be wasted, work against "P2P" politics.

• *Media:* The media's negativity, as well as other media features, makes them a major source of the problem of declining political participation. With some exceptions, like use of the Internet to bring people together around some campaign or issue, there is little sign of the media becoming part of the solution.

• *Political Parties:* The local organizational foundations of the major parties have wasted away for lack of participation and neglect by the parties themselves. The major parties are now dominated by their big money donors.

• *Community-Based Organizations (CBO's):* There is a disconnect between politics and CBO's. Those involved in community activism should become the political candidates and leaders of the future. Some interviewees represent models for linking community and political activism.

• *Voting:* Voting needs to be made easier, though not compulsory, but there is no substitute for local people getting their neighbors out to vote via "P2P" contacts. Does declining voter turnout represent a protest vote?

• *The New (?) Politics:* The new politics of now is all about money and media. Political reforms have not overcome apathy and alienation. They may provide the public with excuses not to participate.

• *Campaign Finance Reform (CFR):* Although most interviewees believe that something needs to be done to reduce the dominance of politics by money, there is disagreement as to what should be done via CFR. The role of public money is an especially contentious issue. Recent reforms are likely to fail.

• *Decentralization:* The common denominator among most interviewees is a positive attitude toward decentralization, but there are differing views on its importance, the capacity of local governments to assume greater roles and the connection of decentralization to political participation.

• *Power:* Ironically, this primary political concern earned the fewest responses; however, a minority of those interviewed understood that politics is power and that those who are unable or unwilling to face this fact (the majority) are effectively disempowered.

• *The Business Community:* Though big business contributions may turn many people off of politics, the business community is not all of a piece. It has been a source of pressure for CFR, local political support, models of good practices, and entrepreneurial candidates.

• *Youth Involvement and Civics Education:* The non-involvement by youth is a major concern. Many interviewees, however, saw signs of hope and advocated more and better civics education, with emphasis on students gaining practical political experience in their communities.

• *Elections:* There is no crosscut here. Interviewees spoke to many aspects of elections, including referenda, primaries and political competition. Their remarks are quite provocative.

• *Local Political Party Committees (LPPC's) and Political Participation:* LPPC's are important vehicles for involving people in politics, improving voter turnout, and nurturing potential candidates for public office; but they need to reach out to and welcome a broader spectrum of people, diversify their activities, and get more involved with community and other public issues.

Introduction: The Old Politics of P2P

There are two key abbreviations in some of the earlier headings: "vs." (versus) and "P2P" (person-to-person). Is P2P "vs." the new media-driven politics, or vice-versa? This is the major question running between the lines of this chapter as well as Chapter 8. The answer that emerges is yes, unless we can change American politics so as to bring the best of the old into the new or adapt the best of the new to the old—a challenge that we will address in the final chapter. A quick way to characterize the conflict between the old and new is to note that it's a lot like the choice of knowing your neighbors and having a party vs. spending time with your TV and PC. The severely critical might translate this as a conflict between the real and the unreal, or between people-dominated politics and money and media-dominated politics. We could run on in this vein, but let us move on to recognize real people doing real politics before we leap to too many cliché-ridden conclusions about where the conflicts lie or how to resolve them. Another major question that will arise here, although it will mainly be put off until Chapters 8 and 10, is to what extent certain substitutes of new for old are actually desirable and beneficial. This chapter is based on interviews with people who have been active in politics at the grass roots level, some of whom provide role models of citizen participation.

What do those laboring in the political vineyards have to tell us about the "old politics," especially on motivations for getting involved. Political participation in the past was motivated by:

- The rootedness of politics in participants' daily lives due to:

  —Their feelings, derived from growing up in earlier periods, that politics was relevant and worthwhile;

  —Their strong roots in the communities in which they lived, corollary desires to help their neighbors and their ability to do so in ways that often were small but appreciated;

  —Respect and recognition accorded active participants by party and elected officials, candidates, and neighbors;

  —Recruitment into political activity by friends, neighbors, or work-life colleagues whom potential participants held in high regard.

- Significant dependence of political campaigns at all levels upon volunteer efforts.

- Candidates' dependence upon political parties and parties' relevance to people's lives.

- Political parties' interest in building and nurturing their local political infrastructures to effect outreach to the electorate (recruit members from all walks of life), register people to vote, and get out the vote (GOTV).

- Exciting or charismatic candidates for office who spoke to large public issues and inspired past generations to get involved—e.g., John F. Kennedy and Ronald Reagan.

Simply to list these factors, many of which have already received some mention in earlier chapters, immediately suggests why political participation is now problematic. So few of them pertain now as in the past, many have atrophied; and others are depreciated, discounted, or denied. Most people now view politics as hardly relevant to their lives. Except at the local level, candidates and their campaigns place little reliance on volunteers to get their message out or to "GOTV"—Get Out the Vote. Political parties see their main function as mobilizing money rather than people. Politics is held in such low repute that few people urge their friends and relatives to get involved or run for office. The "new politics," featuring mass media, personalities, candidate-centered campaigns, and "winner take all" behavior, makes candidates much less dependent upon parties and their local committees than in the past.

Yet, as shown in this chapter, the personal political histories of real people, ordinary citizens in real places, testify to the importance and value of political participation by people committed to playing a citizen's role, one that makes more of a difference than the tiny iota they can contribute by just voting. These histories provide the best evidence from past experience, from people from all walks of life who are hardly different from you and me, even if not just like either one of us. Then, too, as the great social psychologist Erik Erikson showed through his life's work, it is not enough to simply trace individual histories as though they had only "personal" import, or as though it were sufficient to distill only the lessons of their lives at a personal level.[1]

There are at least two other veins among lessons from the past that need to be mined in order to understand:

- The intersect and mutuality of influence between individuals and the larger historical context that Erikson refers to as "the historical moment." For example, the defining moment for my father was the Great Depression; for others, it was World War II; for many younger men, it was and continues to be Vietnam. For some others, it may be the death of JFK or Watergate.

- The influence of larger historical, governmental and social forces on people's participation in the political process.

Some of these have gotten honorable mention or suggestive allusions in earlier chapters. Now we need to turn to personal histories more specifically. Perhaps these will help us to:

- Identify the best of the past that provides models we can adapt for our purposes now and in the future.

- Transform personal fate (which will afflict us if we learn little and do nothing) into destiny (which can affect us if we take charge of our private and public lives).

Since, as Abraham Lincoln said, "We cannot escape history," let us at least try to put it to good use, personally and otherwise. It is remarkable how the experience and observations of those who have been laboring in the political vineyards interweave to provide a consistent, coherent picture of the politics of the past that contrasts in many ways with the politics of now.

Personal Histories Extending…

The most varied features to emerge from the interviews conducted for this book were those of the early personal histories of the men and women

I interviewed. There's no one or typical personal trajectory that led most of them to get involved. Only a few of them had parents or very close relatives who were involved in politics, relatives who could serve as role models.[2] Some were drawn to political activity almost by accident because they were involved with issues in their community that needed some political resolution, or because they were angered at their City Fathers' failure to solve a problem that directly affected their lives. Others got involved as young people through encounters in school, first jobs, or in their communities. A few got hooked through ethnic politics. It's rare for the hook to be a book, as in my case, but an author can still hope…

In an age of narcissism, personal vignettes of others may not be compelling if they are not the stuff of *People* magazine. But such glimpses of others are never boring. There is a "My intro" for each person interviewed, then they introduce themselves before we turn to catch their views on the issues involved in political participation.

Mary Perone

My intro.: Mary is one of my all-time favorite people. It is from her that I learned the methods, flavor, challenges, and pleasures of grass roots politics. For many years, she was the Chairman of the Democratic Committee of the Borough of Princeton, New Jersey (NJ). We would canvass our neighborhood (Election District #6) together. She is the best representative of the old school of politics that I have ever met, somewhat like those characterized by Tom Friedman's book, *The Inheritance*—but not one of those who has lost the Democratic (big "d") faith, or ever will. It is worth noting that Princeton Borough, even though it is a small, exclusive town with a tony rep, has partisan local elections, so the work of local political party committees meant something.

Mary in her own words:

"Democrat" was a big word in the Perone family. It was a big family, all Democrats. But none ran for office. My younger brother, Joe, and his wife worked at Borough Hall. He became Assistant Postmaster and then Postmaster before he retired. I was employed by Thorne Lord, former Chairman of the Mercer County Democratic Committee. He hired me as a buyer of sundries for Thorne Pharmacy. When Lord became a Freeholder, he relied on me to run the store, too, and that's how I became well known.

I started with the Princeton Borough Democratic Committee when I was 18, as soon as I could vote. I canvassed neighborhoods door-to-door, people-to-people. It was great; that was the way you learned about people's politics, how they felt about local politics and why. My district was very supportive. We won local elections and put good people in office. Those are the facts. Door-to-door campaigning is good experience.

Amy Handlin

My intro: I never met Amy in person. One of my New Jersey political contacts said she had seen a neat piece by her in a New Jersey policy mag, *New Jersey Reporter,* that resonated with the concerns of this book. This brought back memories. I used to write for them myself. Anyway, her article, "Too Much Money, Not Enough People" is a great short piece that indeed resonated, with vibratto, with the song of this book. She wasn't going to be around during my last swing through New Jersey for interviews, so the interview with her was conducted by phone via two calls, supplemented by some e-mail exchanges. The "Freeholder" position referenced below is that of an elected member of the legislature of a county government in New Jersey, the Board of Freeholders of Monmouth County.

Amy in her own words:

> I have been a Freeholder since 1989. Before that, I was Deputy Mayor of Freehold. I got into politics only after being active in a variety of grass roots activities, e.g., the League for Women Voters and battles for open space. Following years of such involvement, I became frustrated after finding that I could recommend, suggest, and pressure but that local officials held the decision-making power. There was nothing in my family background to excite political participation.

Gary Todd

My intro: Gary is an example of those I call "heroes of everyday life," so-called "ordinary" people who do extraordinary things. He is one of the more recent acquaintances among the interviewees, but one who has become a friend even though we see each other very seldom. From being somebody who was quite apolitical, Gary made a rapid transformation into being a candidate for the U.S. Senate. I met him through Ron Mills, another interviewee, who was our political consultant; first, for me when I ran for Mayor of Gloucester and later, for Gary after Ron talked him into running for the Senate. Gary is a person of solid values and great integrity with no hidden agendas. See for yourself.

Gary in his own words:

> No one I ever knew was politically involved. Two things got me started: One, I was asked by my church pastor to work with teenagers. I looked to a book by Arthur Moss, *Rebirth of America,* which was highly influential in getting Christians involved. I was also influenced by David Barton, a Christian political historian. Barton's organization is Wallbuilders. I always felt patriotism. My brother and uncle were in the Marines. My family always voted, and they were heavily involved in the community. I was periodi-

cally asked to run for mayor. I had three brothers and a sister. None were even remotely involved in politics, and none became involved in my campaign.

Second, while working with teens, I was led to go back to a TV taping titled "America, You're Too Young to Die," on America's Christian Heritage. I got the book based on the TV show and used it as a foundation for teaching kids. Later, I started "Hope for America" with two co-founders, Nancy Sutton, founder of Family First and a church pastor. I tried to create pamphlets for churches. Their basic message was to promote honesty and morality in Church, family, and government. I also hoped to get Christians involved in the political process. One problem is that Christians are conservative in all respects, with respect to time, money, &c, so nothing gets done. This became a real problem during my Senate campaign when I had to ask myself almost daily: How do I get donations of time and money?

As regional sales director for Christian radio, I met Ron Mills through Peter Blute during an airplane ride with former Mayor and State Rep. Burke of Fitchburg, my home city. Blute was a former Republican Member of Congress for my area whose winning congressional campaigns Ron had engineered. Burke urged me to run for mayor. He also pledged mentorship and support. Thus, I was somewhat prepped to be receptive to Mills' profile and entreaties.

News stories followed around my becoming a Fitchburg delegate to the Republican National Committee (RNC) convention in San Diego in '96, but it's easy to become a delegate. All you need is a nomination plus a three minute speech plus enough votes plus growing up Catholic with a conservative, Christian, patriotic father.

I have been little involved since my (U.S.) Senate race.[3] I have attended some Christian Coalition meetings. Such attendance is wonderfully educational. The Coalition's focus is good and their teaching aids are helpful. I became a '96 RNC delegate alternate as a Christian, pro-life conservative with Coalition activists' support. The wife of a former judge helped get the Coalition off the ground in Massachusetts. I listened to Coalition tapes on the political process. Ralph Reed is young and articulate, but he still couldn't rally a large enough membership. The latter numbers 1.8 million, but how many are active?

Patricia Anderson

My intro: I met Pat via an Internet match factory called DreamMates. After corresponding for awhile, we met and became friends. She was then washing dishes at a student cafeteria at the University of Rhode Island. She is a creative soul and quite a good artist. She used to have a craft shop where she sold wooden creations featuring hand-painted decorative patterns. Pat is a loyal Democrat and a strong supporter of union labor organization. Many of her remarks amounted to a strong indictment of government's treatment of the poor. The most troubling and provocative of these to me was: "Government is removing any incentive for poor people to get ahead."

Pat in her own words:

> My father was a truck driver; my grandfather was an iceman in one of the New England centers of the old urban, labor-dominated politics, Providence, Rhode Island. They would hang out on street corners with other men. Sometimes local politicians would join in. I got involved in politics while a teenager because a local pol got me a summer job. The local pol's would take kids to baseball games, and buy them ice cream, and organize local hot-dogs and beer block parties for adults. Local politicians also belonged to my church. My family was involved in other community-based organizations, too. The American Legion had things going all the time. I started my political activity at age 14 or 15 by getting involved with other activists advocating lower electric rates through an organization called CHICK. I can't remember exactly what this stands for. Our neighborhood was an important focal point for all kinds of activities. Everyone knew everyone else. We'd mount a neighborhood watch to keep an eye on vacant housing—with refreshments brought 'round to the watchers.

Steve Weinberg

My intro: Steve is a warm, big-hearted person whose personal philosophy, behavior, and livelihood all fit together, rooted in community, ecology and, "small is beautiful." Steve is a mensch. He was also the able campaign manager for my 1984 race for Congress in New Jersey's 12th C.D. The campaign provided mixed blessings, one of which was a definite plus for Steve—he ended up living with the then-wife of one of my major contributors. Dorna and Steve are still happily together.

Steve in his own words:

> I was influenced while very young by my Hebrew school and camp. Civics education? You need practice as well as classroom training. Examples: A Labor-Zionist self-governing youth camp; a U.S. Chamber of Commerce sponsored, community-based civics course. I had this course in 5th grade in Scranton, PA in 1955, but it was then part of a national curriculum.

> In 1967, I worked for McCarthy for president, and I got to know something about how elections work. Not many others of my generation got to know this. This may explain why I have a relatively optimistic view of how to get involved and how the political game is played. Few people seem to have this sense. It

needs to be imbued from a young age as, for example, in the unit leaders' elections for youth in my synagogue. Candidates presented themselves before the entire congregation. Kids in school classes are not elected to anything. In Hebrew camp, real money allocations were provided and treasurers elected.

As far as participation in public life is concerned, what difference does it make whether I'm Mayor of East Brunswick or Chairman of the Board of a Synagogue?

Mike Angarone

My intro: Mike is another fine role model from the old school but one who, still very much involved, is adapting the old ways to the new to rebuild a local political organization and base that suffered a major defeat during the 1999 election cycle—loss of the Mayor's seat in his town. Notice how, politically, he seems to be coming full circle. Politically, he grew up in and through his community; now, he turns back to it.

Mike in his own words:

I have been Municipal Chair for 3 years, after serving as a Town Committeeman for 11 years and a Freeholder for 3 years. I believe that good politics is a prerequisite of good government and that it is important to do try to do the right thing(s) for the community. These were hallmarks of the administration of former Mayor Jack Rafferty. Jack's example helped to build the Republican Party, not only in Hamilton Township, but in other parts of Mercer County.

My family was Democratic. My college education included a political science minor. Ernie Hubscher got both Jack and me involved. He urged me to run for the state legislature fresh out of college as a sacrificial lamb. So I ran my first campaign on a $2,000 budget. My running mate was plucked from the convention floor. Hubscher was a local businessman who was involved in the GOP and sponsored local sports teams, including a semi-pro team.

Later, I became Mercer County Chair for Reagan's 1980 campaign. Then I ran for Town Council and was elected. My cousin Phil was Hamilton Township Republican Committee Chair at the time. When I ran as a Republican, my father said my Democratic uncle would roll over in his grave. My wife's family was politically involved but not my father's. My wife's uncle was Mayor prior to Jack. Phil was Deputy Chief of Staff for Gov. Whitman (former head of the EPA in the Bush administration) and Phil, Jr., has been the GOP Chair of Mercer County.

The old politics was not personal. You could hug afterwards. There's no "honor among thieves" anymore—though politicians aren't thieves.

Kathryn McMichael

My intro: Kathy is a very old, very dear friend. She was the major influence on my shift from the Democratic to Republican Party in 1986. She has been an active, conservative Republican since early high school. After serving in the Reagan White House (where the following narrative ends), she worked in a number of positions, including senior staff for Ray Donovan, former Secretary of Labor, the National Commission on Employment Policy and the National School Boards Association. She loved to have parties at her condo in Alexandria. I often said that she could be the Perle Mesta of Republican politics as hostess of a conservative political salon. But she eventually tired of D.C. and moved back to her hometown in NJ in 1999. In my last letter to her, I ventured the opinion that, if we had been working together for Bob Franks, then people politics might have won over money politics in the race of Franks v. Corzine for U.S. Senate.

Kathy in her own words:

It all started when I was 15. My history teacher was into politics. We started a Political Problems Club. I was elected president. My parents were active in Republican politics. I recall helping them carry "I like Ike" signs. The most important early influence, however, was Andy Seamans. He was an officer of the Young Republicans at the time of the Rat Finks, a group of renegade young Republican's in NJ. He got me to form a Teenage Republican Club in High School. My boyfriend was elected president; I was elected Secretary. We'd meet at the Y. The Rat Finks included Andy. He worked many years for the Heritage Foundation and now works for Grover Norquist. The teenage club grew; we did grunt work for the Young Republican's—mailing, stuffing, lit drops, stamping, signs, etc. Bob Franks was a Young Republican.[4]

I recall the Goldwater for President campaign of 1964—a campaign picnic, a Teenage Republicans booth. I met my future husband there. We sold cans of "goldwater" (AuH2O); really, ginger ale + kisses. After starting college at Mary Washington, I started a Young Americans for Freedom (YAF) chapter. I attended the 1968 Republican convention in Miami as a YAFer. During 1969-70; I organized counter demonstrations vs. the anti-war liberals on campus. I was frequently involved in local and congressional races in VA during this period, too. I also attended Republican conventions throughout the '70s.

After marrying, I became an election challenger and then an election board worker. After moving to Hamilton in 1975, I helped Jack Rafferty, then mounting his first bid to be mayor. My husband became President of the Republican Municipal Committee, and

I became President of the Hamilton Republican Club and a County Committee member.

In 1978, Jeff Bell ran vs. Clifford Case. I was heavily involved with the campaign from the start. My husband was involved with me. We would hold and attend many political functions. I was still a school teacher, and I would go to Trenton every day after school to help for about three hours. Susie Dean was the scheduler. We began our long friendship at that time. The campaign vs. Case was a classic. Case looked down on Jeff and would scarcely deign to speak to him. Richard Vigurie did our direct mail campaign which, at that time, was a first for NJ. We had GOTV efforts by conservatives organized all over the state. The primary victory was decisive but Bell was defeated by Bill Bradley. Jeff was too stiff.[5]

I was asked to work for Bell as his administrative assistant, primarily to work down his campaign debt. At the same time, I was Executive Director of the Mercer County Republican Party and scheduler for Bill Mathesius' campaign for County Executive vs. Sypek, the candidate of Dick Coffee's County Democratic organization. Bill was reluctant to get out and press the flesh and still acknowledges how I constantly "whipped him" to get out. We won with Bill via an old fashioned campaign—DTD, meet and greet, stuffing and stamping, etc. We went after "Wild Bill" to recruit him as a candidate because he had earned a reputation as a flamboyant prosecutor. It didn't hurt that he was so good looking. Billboards and campaign literature featuring his photo were largely responsible for winning the women's vote.

Then it was on to the Reagan campaign even though Bill offered me a position in county government. I became an alternate delegate to the Republican convention and active in the Reagan campaign. Jeff Bell had formed "Project 80" to recruit conservative candidates for Congress. Chris Smith was one. He won after Thompson was discredited.[6]

It may be worth noting that I ran for the school board of Hamilton in 1977 and won. I ran on a platform of "Don't build a 3rd high school." I served one three year term and the high school was not built.

Bob Smith

My intro: Bob was a help and support to me when I ran for Congress in NJ's 12th C.D. in 1984. At the time, he was a member of Piscataway Town Council and Chair of the Town's Democratic Municipal Committee. Later, he became mayor and then state rep. He was serving in the latter position at the time of our interview. I remember being impressed by the vitality of his

Committee as well as by Bob's own energy, enthusiasm, and commitment. Some of its members would walk door-to-door with me and for me and the rest of the Democratic ticket. I wish that I could remember their names; they were true, dedicated laborers in the political vineyards, down-to-earth, diverse representatives of the grassroots. As for Bob, though he makes his living primarily through his law practice, he is a political "pro" and a "pol" in the best sense, not anyone's political stereotype.

Bob in his own words:

I was always interested in politics, starting in high school. My first job was that of newspaper delivery boy, so each day I would read the paper. One key event in my young political life was the day that I saw JFK and asked him to sign my paper. This was in 1960, when I was 13 years old. It was a magic moment. Later, in 1968, I was active for McCarthy as his local coordinator. I voted five times in the primary, once for myself and four times for the elderly and disabled. My father said he had run for tax collector and that his supporters were beaten up at the polls.

I went to the DMC (Democratic Municipal Committee) and started helping. I successfully challenged the organization in Piscataway. I registered students to vote because student housing was a factor in voter turnout. The contest was McGovern vs. Nixon. The youth vote was crucial to the local contest. I have relied upon it since. I have pushed aggressive voter registration to build a student power base in the community. In my first contest for City Council, I lost by only 50 votes; I won next time and in subsequent races. But I lost a race for Congress in 1992. A roll of the dice by a new Republican Clerk gave me a bad ballot position.

Walter Orcutt

My intro: I began to get acquainted with Walter Orcutt through the survey of LPPC's conducted for this book (reported in the next chapter). Walter was one of only 7 of 21 County Chairs in NJ to respond to the survey, and he thoughtfully included his e-mail address for follow-up. So we exchanged a few e-mails, and I tried to arrange an interview during my first swing through NJ for interviews. We did not make contact then, but we did so the second time, just before the 2000 presidential election. As Warren County GOP Chairman, Walter was extremely busy then, fielding calls from the press and local Committee Chairs, plus knee deep in political signs and other paraphernalia. Yet, he generously and patiently committed time for a thorough interview. Shortly thereafter, he not only suffered through the presidential recount in Florida but also with another squeaker in his own backyard. Warren County is part of NJ's 12th C.D. Right after the election, there was a gap of only 56 votes between Rich Holt, the Democratic incumbent, and

Dick Zimmer, the Republican challenger. The recount awarded the seat to Holt.

Walter in his own words:

> I moved back home, five miles from where I grew up, after discharge from the Navy. I went into business for myself. My landlord and businessman friend saw networking benefits for a new businessman and so invited me to a local club meeting in 1980. He also thought that I had a gift for politics. The club was looking for fresh blood and so they put me right to work as Treasurer. Six years later, I ran for city council and won and, subsequently, for mayor and won again. I was aiming to run for county Freeholder, but I did not have a large enough base in a small town. So I went to Trenton for four years to work for Chuck Haytaian, Chairman of the State Committee (SC), as his Chief of Staff. I was his protégé. My grandfather, a dairy farmer, was Mayor of my home town, but my parents were not involved in politics and grandpa was not a significant influence.

Ron Mills

My intro: Ron Mills was the political consultant for my first campaign for mayor in my hometown of Gloucester, Massachusetts—the second best campaign I have ever run, thanks to Ron's political intelligence, my hard work and many fine volunteers from within the Gloucester community. Ron was positioned to be the #1 GOP consulting guru in Massachusetts when he got tired and disgusted with the state's politics and its lackluster Republican leadership and moved to New Hampshire to concentrate on private business. Ron is not only creatively adept at marketing; he's also one of the most insightfully outspoken political analysts that I know, more so than any of the political pundits on TV, as you will see in due course. First, let him introduce himself through his thinking, which will also be a good introduction to some of the reform and "Y2K" issues treated in later chapters. Ron didn't share his bio., so there's nothing particularly personal to highlight here.

Ron in his own words:

> You can't look at the political process objectively; it's like talking about religion. There is nothing inherently wrong with patronage: a job for campaign work. Contrast this with graft: a job for which someone is unqualified or there is no need. Now, we not only trade off jobs but accountability and performance. Patronage also implies the power to get things done. There is a symbiotic relationship between elected officials and public employment. Our society— led by the LWV, reformers, media, dilettante wives of the upper middle class, and the insipidly stupid (e.g., McCain)—has stripped parties of the power to fulfill their purpose. This implies the nega-

tive trends with regard to turnout, domination by single issue groups, campaigns by single issue candidates and cashiers' checks. Remedies?—We need institutions other than political parties (e.g., Heritage, Cato) to begin (a la the NAACP in the '40s) a program of legal actions, suits and articles aimed at demonstrating to the judiciary that previous Supreme Court decisions with regard to (a) ballot access and (b) free speech are essentially flawed, counter-productive and in violation of the Constitution.

Chris Wilder

My intro: I found my way to Chris via Kathy. Chris is a proven, experienced, savvy grassroots political operative who became an equally savvy municipal clerk and President of the International Institute of Municipal Clerks. The clerk's office in municipal government is the nerve center of local politics, so I was very pleased when Chris consented to be interviewed. The man she helped get elected Mayor, Jack Rafferty, is a friend from NJ politics whom I also tried to interview but, frankly, I believe that it is more important that I was able to interview Chris. We met in Atlantic City at one of the annual meetings of the NJ League of Municipalities.

Chris in her own words:

I came from a large, Polish-American family of hard workers in Lawrence. My grandfather built their local church. Several family members were involved in the American Legion. One of my uncles ran for office and served several years. There always seemed to be an awareness of politics as something outside of self and family. I recall helping my uncle with his campaigns as a teenager. The young man who eventually became my husband was a roommate of Jack Rafferty. He helped Jack and felt that Jack was an honorable guy so I, too, came to feel that a Republican in the mayor's office wouldn't be bad. My husband ran for school board. I gradually got increasingly involved with the Republican Party. In 1975, I was involved as a proponent of a charter change initiative for Hamilton. I was working in private industry when Rafferty was first elected mayor. He offered me the deputy clerkship. I once ran for county Freeholder but lost.

Ingrid Reed

My intro: Ingrid is someone I first got to know in the late '70s when we were both involved with local politics along with Mary Perone and many others in the Princeton Community Democratic Organization and the Princeton Borough Democratic Committee. Ingrid was not only one of the most sensible members; she was and remains a true local leader of long standing, providing essential continuity and community sensibility as well as political leadership through her involvement. She now works at the Eagleton

Institute of Politics at Rutgers. Her husband Marvin, part of the same large set of concerned Princeton Democrats that grew up together politically, is Mayor of the Borough and a worthy successor to the previous mayor, the late Barbara Boggs Sigmund who, along with Mary, was an inspiration to us all. The interview with Ingrid helped to highlight the importance of political competition at the local level and of non-political types being involved. Like Ron Mills, one of the interviewees from another state, she did not dwell on the personal but rather provided much food for thought by public citizens.

> *Ingrid in her own words:*
>
> Politics is out of step with the ways we live our lives; for example, with respect to time for voting, leadership training, recognition of excellence and information sharing. Politics doesn't match up with the rest of modern experience. Newspapers seldom show photos of candidates, for instance, while the share of visual images in the media has been rising. Sample ballots in New Jersey, unlike those in California, include no phone number or web-site address so voters can find polling places The California League of Women Voters' voter information page includes photos and bios of candidates.
>
> Political parties provide no rewards for, nor recognition of, organizations within their structures. There is no investment in organizations' development or growth; no rethinking of their strategic mission. Even the National Junior League has done the latter. Jon Corzine (now U.S. Senator) put money into county and local committees. He is applying marketing principles to GOTV (see a recent issue of the NJ Reporter). He hired people one month before the election so that relationships of trust could be developed in advance, rather than relying on late, 1-shot calls. Higher level party organizations should be putting money into local political party committees.

Dick Woodbridge

My intro: Dick and I were in opposite parties when we served together on the Princeton Borough Council, but we became good friends and colleagues. Unlike myself, Dick had an invariably friendly and affable demeanor that appealed to everybody. I never found anyone who didn't like Dick. Memory can play strange tricks, but I don't recall having a serious disagreement with Dick at any time. When I visited with him to do the interview, it was like old times, as if I had never left Princeton.

Besides getting back in touch, one reason I wanted to interview Dick is because, like me, he had an independent professional practice, and I was curious as to how he managed to balance the demands of politics and business. This was always a problem for me. Dick was a patent attorney. At the time, this was not the type of law practice of a typical politician and the overlap with politics appeared to be slight. Like me, Dick took his politics seriously and aspired to higher office. He ran for state rep. His wife was also involved. She served on the school committee. They were both dedicated to community service and deeply rooted in the Princeton community, a community graced by a great deal of civic involvement and political participation. Dick was also a member of the Borough's volunteer fire department.

Dick in his own words:

> People need to feel that they have a stake. They have gotten too used to others doing things for them. Yet, they have so little time, with two people working, man and wife, plus other commitments. Volunteerism is a general problem. It's harder to find volunteers for anything, even fire volunteers. People don't want to get their hands dirty. Let someone else do it—the free rider problem.

> Person-to-person (P2P) politics works best, especially in smaller places. Ads in local newspapers are not as effective. P2P gets amplified by neighbor-to-neighbor. The media, no matter what, are no substitute for P2P contacts. Politics is not only local but personal. Negative messages don't work except for higher level, broader-scope campaigns, where the impact is limited to dissuading some potential supporters of an opponent to stay away from the polls on election day. Negative messages in local contests boomerang.

John LoCicero

My intro: I first got to know John starting in 1967, when I became an active member of one of New York City's renowned political reform clubs, the Village Independent Democrats, known affectionately as VID and featured in James Q. Wilson's classic on political clubs, *The Amateur Democrat*.[7] I'll never forget him striding up and down the isles between the seats, plying our ears with his political passion, during a particularly contentious meeting about whether or not VID should support one candidate over another for president. He is another role model of activism and commitment over many years. He became Chief of Staff for Ed Koch when he was Mayor of New York City, and he is still very much involved in the political affairs of the city as a consultant through the firm Locicero and Tan.

John in his own words:

> I was encouraged by my wife while going to school at night. I liked history and politics. I worked for JFK's election. My wife urged me to join the VID. I got involved and found politics to be fun. I got involved with Koch, who was goal oriented. I am the child of a generation of younger people who, following World War II, created a middle-class based on the GI Bill. We were idealistic. Things happened even during the Eisenhower years. There were

always issues. The main issue now is that government is being sold—lock, stock and barrel. The rich and the corporations are buying government. Fewer and fewer people are having input. Government is for sale.

Alan Everett

My intro: I didn't know Alan at all before visiting friends in Sedona, Arizona. I called him out of the blue with the red rocks of Sedona in the background. He kindly consented to be interviewed even though he then had a busy schedule as mayor, and he was preparing for local elections.

Alan in his own words:

The mayor's job takes 30-40 hours a week. The early years of town development set a precedent. I get lots of calls from constituents. My goal is to be very accessible. But some situations absorb inordinate amounts of time; for example, the case of a neighborhood water company and one neighbor complaining about the height of a company building that serves the neighborhood.

I agree that decentralization and renewal of grassroots politics are linked per Reagan's legacy. I like your emphasis on time vs. money on the CFR issue. My re-election campaign is budgeted at only $5,000. I spend two hours a day meeting people door-to-door (downtown) but not in their neighborhoods because they are seldom home.

Nadine Bonnie Hack

My intro: I first met Nadine in D.C. at a National Alliance of Business conference on employment and training in 1983, just before I began my campaign to run for Congress. She was, then and now, a passionate advocate for liberal causes as well as a major fund-raiser for Democratic candidates, especially minority and women candidates. At that time, she was also active in the Democratic party, trying to shape the party's platform as a delegate to the 1984 National Democratic Convention. More recently, her public passions have been embodied in her own private consulting firm named, most appropriately, "BeCause." After many years of no contact, I got back in touch with Nadine, and she kindly consented to be interviewed for this book.

Nadine in her own words:

My first campaign was in 1964, when I was just a teenager. Since then, I have constantly flipped back and forth between two sides of a coin—between feeling that politics is corrupt and influenced by forces I don't want to have anything to do with, and thinking that if people like me are not involved in politics then, by default, we cede the process to forces whose controlling influences are so questionable. So, I've gone back and forth more times than I can recall, yet it's essential for people like me to be involved in order to enfranchise others and to press for a more egalitarian and inclusive system. So, then, I get re-involved in politics until I get disgusted again, etc. I don't know whether I will ever come to a resolution of where I should be.

Bill Batson

My intro: I was led to Bill and his wife Alissa by Nadine, who described them as dynamic young political activists. She was right. Though, at first, I interviewed Bill by telephone, I soon thereafter met him on more than one occasion in New York City. We first met in his office in Harlem when he served as chief of staff for New York State Senator Patterson.

Bill in his own words:

I grew up in Teaneck, NJ, a progressive community, and attended an alternative high school. I was active in the arts, but I can recall only two front-line political activities during high school. I was involved in student council, but there were no hearings or forums. I recall two demonstrations—No Nukes and Anti-Klan—but I somewhat begged off both. I got involved in politics when someone knocked on my door asking for help to establish a local tenants' organization. I was impressed by the fact that someone thought it important enough to organize others, and that the issue affected me. For awhile, I headed the tenants' organization and then did projects involved in the arts with the NYC Housing Authority. After that, I got involved with a labor union, Local 1119. The union had a long political history and was known for its "bread and roses" program. So I got some experience organizing large demonstrations and getting out the vote (GOTV). I acted as press secretary to the head of the union, Dennis Rivera. In unions, there is a close connection between political participation and results to the participants in terms of benefits.

I recently (2001) ran Norm Siegel's campaign for Public Advocate in New York City. He came in second. Norm is head of the Civil Liberties Union in the city. My goal now is to work in an environment that takes a longer-run view. I am not at the union anymore. There, I was involved with cyclical and short-term issues and events. Now and for the foreseeable future, I would like to pursue a long-term, progressive agenda.

Alissa Batson

My intro: I also first got acquainted with Alissa by telephone, reaching her at her home number in Brooklyn where she lives with her husband, Bill. She is a young woman whose political coming of age benefited from involvement in community-based organizations, as she herself relates below. Our interview was conducted by telephone, but I subsequently met Alissa in person along with Bill at a bar near city hall in Manhattan.

Alissa in her own words:

My father was an elected official, the city attorney in Los Angeles who served under Mayor Bradley. I was not interested in politics as a youngster, but my father always talked about public service and its importance. I attended alternate schools. Most of my teachers were dedicated '60s activists, and I was influenced by them. So I began to challenge my parents' mainstream views even though they were both Democrats. I attended Wesleyan College, one of the last bastions of progressive, left-leaning ideology, but I was not much involved in political issues there—involved some, but not a lot. I was a Latin American studies major focusing on colonialism and indigenous cultures. I would have liked to study American history more. Following graduation, I wanted to be involved in some progressive activity, especially after participating in the AFL-CIO's union summer immediately after graduating. My peers wanted to make money, but I was not concerned with money. I considered teaching in under-privileged communities but chose a union option instead. I put on union organizing campaigns and protests. Later on, in '96, I did voter registration and tried to educate workers on issues of concern to labor, such as California referenda issues. This period ended with me becoming leader of a group and serving in Sacramento for three weeks on a Justice for Janitors campaign. I volunteered to work with the Hotel and Restaurant Workers Union for awhile. Then I got a job with the UFW and was sent to New York City. I organized literature handouts in supermarkets and community organizing, meeting with clergy and community groups—very grass roots. My parents helped with the rent, which was $1,000 a month.

I met my husband, Bill Batson, when he was working with Local 1199. I got more involved with New York City-based issues and looked for a new job in '98. I landed one working for City Councilwoman Marguerita Lopez, a lesbian activist from the Lower East Side. I worked in her district office on labor and education issues and constituent services. People were being screwed by the city with respect to problems of benefits, housing, welfare and homelessness. With respect to housing, for example: There was a big stink in '98 when Guiliani proposed to create "Alphabet City." This involved neglecting or removing affordable housing via gentrification and displacement. The mayor was helping the gentrifiers by privatizing public housing. He also wanted to build power plants in poor communities.

Now, after 2½ years with Lopez and some brief health care-related activity, I work for another city council member, Gifford Miller, who represents the Upper East Side. As a legislative aide, my work differs from its prior social work orientation. The council has been weak under Guiliani. He vetoed a lot of council legislation. Miller was running to be Speaker of the Council, so she helped other candidates in all five boroughs. With volunteers, we did door-to-door campaigning, voter registration and GOTV. I phone banked for 30 hours, did mailings, and also assisted two other candidates in Queens for two weeks. Both of them won and Gifford became the Council Speaker.

Interview Highlights

The only way to catch the full flavor of what these and some others shared with us during their interviews is to read the interview transcripts, which are available from the author on request. For those like most of us who are too much in a hurry to go back to the sources, the remainder of this chapter will highlight choice insights and observations on a number of topics that arose during the interviews by design, association, or accident.[8] The most important concern cross-cutting the interviews is the contrast between the old politics and the new. The branches of the book's thematic tree, however, are many. The interviewees had much to say about many things, but they amount to variations on the theme of this book. Some of what they had to say is scattered throughout other chapters, to reinforce or qualify insights from other sources.

Volunteerism, the Value of People's Time, and P2P Politics

Political volunteerism has been dying, but it's not yet stone-cold dead. According to Alissa Batson, "the spirit of volunteerism" is the defining quality of political activists. Even those who recognize that the old politics must change to adapt to new circumstances (e.g., Reed) and/or who have mastered use of the new politics with a vengeance (e.g., Smith and Orcutt) call for continuation or renewal of reliance upon person-to-person (P2P) politics. As Dick Woodbridge remarked: "Person-to-person gets amplified by neighbor-to-neighbor." For a dyed-in-the-wool Republican, Dick was also remarkable for evoking the late, great Democratic Speaker of the House of Representatives, Tip O'Neill, with regard to both the fundamentally local and personal nature of politics. Many interviewees besides Dick see our democracy in danger if people don't come back into the participatory picture. The personal side of politics, however, is paradoxical, as we saw in the contrasting observation reported earlier from Mike Angerone: "the old politics was not personal. You could hug afterwards."

The contrast between old and new politics was sharply drawn by several of the interviewees, with no disagreement from those who did not remark on the contrast so sharply. The remarks of Chris Wilder are not atypical: " People's attitudes towards politics have changed significantly for the worst, especially with respect to people's willingness to volunteer. I recall rooms being packed with volunteers to help campaigns. Now, we have to beg people to show up, and I'm not sure why. A much greater proportion of volunteers now than in the past seems to be people whose jobs depend on politics." This observation was underscored by remarks of Alissa Batson: "Others only get involved if there's something in it for them. There's a lot of selfishness in the culture right now."

Recognition of the value of people's time and the lack of it is also a key common denominator among interviewees. This recognition was best expressed by Mike Lynch. He first recognized that the root of the increased value lay in increased productivity: [9]

> As U.S. industry has pushed for higher levels of productivity, even where people may have more time available to do other stuff in their personal lives, they still don't have the time they need to give to others and they don't want to participate in organizations that don't use their time productively…So when you now look at volunteer organizations, (you see that) they're not well organized or well managed…If you offer time to a local party committee, you don't want to go into a building and be told: We don't know what you can do…A volunteer who shows up in high gear says: If you don't need me, I'm leaving. Once they've left, you don't get them back. The same is true of charitable organizations. Unless you have a vested interest…if you don't feel that your time is well spent, you'll walk. (Thus) volunteerism…is a dead duck.

Pat Anderson simply observed that voluntary contributions of time have been decreasing because everybody's working. Anybody can confirm this by trying to canvas a neighborhood for votes or sales during a workday. Few people will be found at home.

Most interviewees commented in some way or other on the increasing difficulty of getting people involved and what it takes to get them to participate in political activities. Such remarks were strongly reinforced by the entries of 199 respondents to a special survey done for this book, reported in the next chapter. John Locicero remarked, for example: "It's hard to get people involved unless there is an urgent issue at stake in some local district, such as over-development in Scottsdale, so that upper middle-class citizens form a group, then elect members to city council. An area-localized issue is what it takes. For example, my wife organized a women's group forum for female candidates on 'How to Be a City Council Member.' It's a City-wide women's group, but it takes a local issue to do it. Local leadership is a basic factor." Somewhat similarly, Pat Anderson succeeded in getting local women involved via craft projects, followed by "beer and 'dog parties." Nearly all of them were women who hadn't been out of their houses before—not the upper middle-class group referred to by LoCicero.

John then wondered: "What issues will be catalysts for political participation in the future?—campaign finance reform? Environment? Globalization? as, for instance, with the WTO protesters? People must go back to their own neighborhoods and lives and organize their neighbors. Examples? Note the charette process for PS (public school)#3 to make an independent school (even though) the union was adverse. Note the Parkland, anti-growth movement in Staten Island plus local organization to stop the landfill…We hear the claim: "It's the economy, stupid." Don't believe it. It's not the poor who are activists; it's average people who are working through their churches and other community-based organizations. There are lots of people doing things such as soup kitchens and saving people's lives that are not momentous." Not momentous! John's remark underlines the power and meaning of volunteerism.

The word "momentous" also provides a good lead into the next section, on "media," for we more and more have the impression that media coverage has become the standard of whether something is even worthy of our attention, not to mention worth doing. But John clearly thinks his and his wife's involvement in politics was momentous, and people doing things such as soup kitchens and saving people's lives is an inspiration to us all, whether it's covered in the nightly news or not (mainly not; see below and Chapter 8).

Yet, can volunteers still be an influential factor in political races? Bill Batson provided an example from the 2002 political season in New York City that says definitely 'yes' to this question. Bill remarked: "political volunteers…are important…The 8,000 volunteers for Ferrer were not there for Green and Green lost by less than 30,000 votes…The effort to collect over 30,000 signatures to put Siegel on the ballot…was an all unpaid volunteer effort."

Media

The media are such an important influence on politics that an entire chapter to follow (#8) is devoted to it. Observations made by the interviewees were pretty much all of a piece in noting negative influences. They remind me of what we all heard about money when we were kids: "Money is the root of all evil." Money and media?—the roots of evil in the new politics? John Locicero remarked: "The media has taken over everything."

Also recall Mike Angerone. He said that: "The media are turning people off of politics. There is too much media play on polls. Most political reporting is negative. You need to call your opponent an asshole to get your name in the papers. I am surprised that we can get any good people to run these days…"

Steve Weinberg noted: "The media and news are entertainment businesses. Why should they report the news?…It's more fun to be in the power game. It's hard to do investigative journalism…Do you want to step on a lot of toes; say, of an old boys' network, trying to get something done?" In a similar vein, Bill Batson remarked: "The media are driven by consumerism and fads."

With the perspective of local political experience in a very different state, out West, Alan Everett's view is that: "The media are part of the problem. Note, for example, a recent (2000) article in the *Arizona Republic* saying McCain had an affair with an actress. The claim was unfounded but the correction was small and not printed until more than a week later. (Partly as a result), we have a problem getting people to run for local offices, those from city council to county supervisor…One local activist was approached who attends city council meetings frequently, a retired engineer who we recruited for over a year. His wife said: "I don't want to see your name in the paper plus letters to the editor." From out East in New York City, Alissa Batson noted that "the media don't pay enough attention to local politics or to issues in communities that are fundamental."

In a somewhat more positive vein, however, Alan went on to say: "The main barriers to people's political participation are hostile and negative feelings plus time commitment. But the press could also be part of a solution to the problem. I try feeding them positive stories; for example, one about mayor and council painting over graffitti."[10] Back East, Alissa Batson cited another positive role of the media: "When the New York City Council considered passing a bill to penalize landlords with lead paint in their buildings, a newspaper wrote that it would show pictures of those who voted against the bill. The bill passed." Query to the reader: When did you last see a positive story in the media reflecting people's political participation locally, or even a positive reflection on politics?

Nadine Hack answered the question with questions of her own: "Why are good works not news? Why are there not more public service advertisements?"

Nadine went on to contrast the generally negative stance of the media toward politics with the media outpourings immediately following 9/11. Her remarks were so telling that they are quoted in full:

> It's been a wonderful thing to see—people being exhorted and praised for being compassionate, generous, public-minded, responsive, engaged and involved. Why cannot similar messages be put forth with regard to politics, and not just at a moment of darkest horror?

Pat Anderson's remarks reinforce those of Nadine. She remarked:

> The media make a big difference with regard to political participation. Media people can get people fired up; they are experts in getting people fired up or not. Most people are basically lazy but will follow if others are involved. After 9/11, people were fired up with patriotism because of media propaganda—similar to the way evangelists get people to participate.

TV is reputed to be a major cause in the negative trends affecting people's political participation, from Putnam's *Bowling Alone* thesis on down.[11] Locicero provided some insight on the effects of TV from the perspective of political experience in New York City, national media center: "We need free TV. Similar to Chicago, we have seen a decreasing reliance upon volunteer workers. In 1977, there were still powerful organizations in the Bronx, Queens and Brooklyn supporting the Mayor (Abe Beam), but Koch won with TV ads featuring Bess Myerson. My wife said at the time that "this is the end of grassroots politics."[11]

But Mike Lynch's remarks bring us back to a focus on the more local newspaper media as a continuing problem: "I have seen for decades that newspaper reporting is an oxymoron. Every article is written after an editor makes a decision to cut and run. Reporters seldom have all the information they need, so articles are snippets to lead the reader to a conclusion…As a result, and as the public has less time available and is fed news with shorter snippets, the public is more easily swayed by the media rather than being helped to draw their own conclusion."

Parties

Some political scientists say that political parties are now stronger.[12] But, like most self-styled (otherwise, non-) "reformers," they are simply following the money. This reminds me of a period in the late '80s when the *Wall Street Journal* was reporting cartons of cash being brought into Miami banks for deposit. Were the banks stronger as a result? Or were they candidates for industrial re-classification—as laundries? Most polls and journalists indicate that parties are weaker in those terms that most count, those that reflect people's affiliations, loyalties, political activities or membership(s). Our interviewees didn't label parties "strong"(er) or "weak"(er). Together with some of the survey results that are reported in the next chapter, however, their remarks point to growing party weakness in people terms, either directly (their inability to engage people) or indirectly (what they need to do to engage people in active participation).

For example, Kathy McMichael remarked: "The local party structure is very important. The local party organization(s) controlled outreach, recruitment, phoning, GOTV, etc. Hamilton Township provides a great example. Follow up with Chris Wilder. She says the party structure has fallen apart—that now local committees are unable to fill slots or get people to come into a committee or campaign headquarters to canvas or make calls." Her judgment is seconded by someone on the opposite side of the political spectrum, Nadine Hack, in terms of a far more sweeping indictment: "The local bases of parties have been depreciated, discounted and abandoned." The next chapter provides much more on the local bases.

Continuing in a similar vein, Pat Anderson remarked that party organizations now seem to have "little or no outreach…They don't want others to know what they're doing. There are too many little Caesars." Although she is an outspoken Democrat and union member, she wasn't aware of any local democratic organization in her town.

From her standpoint as both community activist and elected official, Amy Handlin observed that: "Parties need to be friendlier and to play more community and grass roots organizational roles. Party stalwarts are too financially dependent on government and the political process. When you're a person in a neighborhood concerned with better lighting for a local soccer field, you're not comfortable or confident going into a political meeting where they all know each other as political buddies. Parties must reach out to those who have no connection to government and politics—just regular people who may come to see a party as a route to change." Other interviewees identify two perspectives on Handlin's point of view:

1. Bill Batson: "There is a huge divide between the worlds of community-based organizations and the world of politics."

2. Alissa Batson: "There is little or no political participation because people are disenchanted with the whole political process and the difficulty of electing people who can change things."

Mike Lynch would agree with Handlin but his own experience leads to a broader, deeper diagnosis of the weakness of parties at the local level: "As a result of national parties… putting more dollars into media buys, undercutting the viability of parties, they have robbed local parties of competent management. Without competent management, they are unable to provide volunteers with a sense of value for the time they contribute. So people who would join an organization and move up are discouraged from doing so. People who might provide leadership are discouraged because local political party committees lack money. This is because the party is not getting money to provide management to engender participation by volunteers. The problem feeds on itself like a vicious circle…Unless party building activities are handled so as to invest in local parties, then parties may become extinct."

Again, it is remarkable how views here converge from opposite sides of the political spectrum. Nadine Hack, liberal Democrat, would agree with Mike Lynch, Republican. Nadine doesn't see a shift of political party focus from the national to the local or from the top to the bottom. Why? Because "There has been more and more emphasis on media buys. They have replaced face-to-face contact…the entire system has shifted its thrust. We've seen the disappearance of buttons, bumper stickers, people canvassing door-to-door and handing out literature…this trend means that there are 10 million less people involved (and) that a whole generation has been disengaged."

Mike Lynch went on to describe how there's now "a generation missing in the membership" because parties, unable to deal with the new situation of people having "a need to express themselves through organization," turned people off and away…" Note the case of the Republican Party in Iowa, for example. It had traditional party managers that, in the '80s, began seeing anti-abortion crews surface and hearing conservative Christians saying 'we want to be heard.' Party bosses said 'you're too extreme; this is what we support, over here.' So, the conservative Christians had a choice: form their own organization or take over the party. They took over because the party bosses didn't provide a forum for these new members to present and discuss their views. They forced them to create a coup…So now the Iowa GOP is very conservative and losing races because the Party is viewed as extreme, with leaders not listening—like the old farts in the VFW who turned Vietnam vet's away."

As a bridge between the old and the new politics, Bob Smith noted: "County party chairs can award the ballot line and County Committee members decide whom the party will support. This is an aspect of the democratization of parties that arose via contenders for party leadership competing on 'democratization'—a trend in New Jersey. Having candidates selected by the County Committee, however, is a mixed blessing. It's a big deal to become a County Committee member, but sometimes bosses do a better job. Statewide, bosses still rule. It's a tough balance on a lot of this stuff… It remains to be seen whether there will be any differences in political participation as a result."

Ingrid Reed added a perspective seldom seen or heard but one that is very important because it points to parties' backwardness in terms that contrast sharply with the best practices of business highlighted in Chapter 7. "Political parties provide no rewards for, nor recognition of, organizations within their structures. There is no investment in organizations' development or growth; no rethinking of their strategic mission."

And so we recall Kathy again, who concluded: "What needs to be done to revitalize local party committees; indeed parties overall?—I don't know. The stock answer is to restore people's faith in the system—as if we could just restore people's faith in the goodness of government and the integrity of most public officials. Get more dedicated people to run for office." Note here we have run into another of the "vicious circles" noted earlier—If we can restore people's faith in the system, then parties would revive, but if parties don't revive and reform, how can we expect to "restore people's faith in the system"? (and vice-versa)

Community-Based Organizations (CBO's)

As we noted earlier, lack of participation in matters public seems to afflict political organizations much more than others. Other CBO's have less of a problem attracting volunteers. Related concerns for outreach into the community by political party organizations, and the community relevance of party activities, surfaced via responses to both interview and survey questions. Thus, we explored actual, potential, or desirable interconnections between local political committees and presumably non-political CBO's during the interviews.

Piscataway, New Jersey, provides something of a model in this regard. According to Bob Smith, former mayor: "The Mayor, City Councilors and Committee members have cross memberships with CBO's in Piscataway; e.g., church, seniors group, Lions, Italian-American Club, firemen. The Democratic Party makes sure there is a diverse group on City Council with roots in CBO's. If local politicians are smart, they will do that so they don't make stupid decisions—so that they know what the community wants."

Mike Smith, head of a true CBO in Chicago, the Institute for Community Empowerment (ICE), offered a very different perspective. "From the community-organizing standpoint, politics is a necessary evil. There is a big gulf between two sides of a community—the community interest(s) and the political interest(s). If we get these together, perhaps some local pol's would realize that there's benefit to working for the community rather than spending 30-40 years on the public payroll." Yet, as Bill Batson observed in New York City: "Participation in political clubs is now much less important than participation in (issue-oriented) affinity groups which attract the majority of political activists." This view was seconded by Pat Anderson, who observed that most "volunteers get political only if the political activity coincided with a cause they're interested in."

As usual, the truth may lie somewhere in between, or perhaps it should, because if the pol's don't address the gap to which Mike Smith so eloquently speaks on the basis of hard community organizing experience over many years, then the politics they practice and represent has no meaningful future. Several other interviewees testified to this gap, as indicated by Bill Batson's remark on the huge divide, quoted earlier. Besides the kind of cross memberships mentioned by Bob Smith, other ways that some local political party committees have bridged the gap are revealed in the next chapter. As Alissa Batson advocated, it would help if political candidates emerge "out of a community matrix" so that they "stand for something...Political and community activism should go together hand in hand...The best political leaders emerge from community activism." Unfortunately, they seldom do and increasingly do not, and even exceptions may turn out to be contrary. Nadine Hack observed that "you can see it (the gap) even within politics itself, looking at the Wellstone's and Mikulski's of the political world."

Nadine also helped to explain why so seldom the twain do meet:

> Political party committees give lip service to GOTV, but they're concerned their influence could be usurped if the constituency base is broadened. Their political positions are of greater import than broadening the political base. Parties' political organizing structures...are an entire world unto itself, and people who tend to be involved in that world find it to be so time consuming, in order

to stay active and play any sort of significant roles, that their involvement eliminates the possibility of getting involved in civil-society (CBO) types of activities. Conversely, people involved in civil society activities on issues or causes such as health, women, environment or children are so consumed by their causes that they can't find time for conventional politics even if they wanted to…Each is so involved in their own issue, pursuing it with zealous purity, that they are unwilling to make compromises, recognize trade-offs, and give up something in order to get part of what they want. Too often, it's all or nothing. This is one reason they are suspicious of politicians…they would need to compromise…

Pat Anderson, however, recalled there was no such divide afflicting the old neighborhood politics she grew up with. "The local pol's would help with jobs. They knew the poor and would help to prepare food buckets for them. They got a community health center and a youth center built. They were involved with United Way projects."

Note how two recurring, interrelated problems stand out here: (1) the consuming nature of political involvement as electoral politics is now structured; and (2) the lack of time to be both politically involved and devoted to good causes. A major point of this book, however, is that it doesn't have to be this way.

Voting:

Even though voting is the lowest common denominator and the least-effort form of political participation, no one should doubt its enormous importance after the 2000 presidential election. Many reforms in voting systems will continue to be debated as a result (see Chapter 9). Bob Smith noted: " We need a less onerous voting process because of the great time constraints that people face; e.g., voting by mail as in Oregon. There exist so many other priorities in people's lives, plus a belief that politics is irrelevant to them. Compulsory voting?—Why not? In Oregon, the process is tracked and information is sent to the parties, so that they know who has voted and who not. So GOTV (Get Out the Vote) activity can take place over more than two weeks. Oregon has a 80-90% turnout."

As for GOTV, Mary Perone and many others pointed to the importance of the role of the local party committee man or woman. Mary: "You need strong people to take charge and follow up with people, else voters won't come out….Some turn out; some don't. The latter group won't without follow-up by someone telling them who's running and picking them up (to take them to the polls). If you don't work at it, you won't get the turnout. The 6th Election District, especially, needs extra effort. If you don't keep after them, people don't bother." [Note: At the time of Mary's most intensive activity with the author as the District's Committee woman and man, the 6th election district in Princeton was largely a black minority district.]

Mary's experience and views have been confirmed by many others; e.g., the *hustle* among Piscataway (NJ) Democratic Committee people cited by Rep. Bob Smith, which continues to this day. As for voter turnout, Mike Angerone remarked: "People now shrug and say: 'I don't make a difference.' Voter turnouts are horrible, but Gov. (Christie Todd) Whitman's winning margin was one vote per election district." Former Gov. Whitman became head of the Environmental Protection Agency in the Bush administration.

Voting is compulsory in Australia. According to Ron Mills, however, such a proposition would be a non-starter here in the U.S. of A. He was seconded by Priscilla Ruzzo: "I say no to compulsory voting. Voting by mail is okay along with other moves to make voting easier."

In contrast even to a relatively undemocratic country like Russia, American ballots lack a "none of the above" option so that voters can explicitly express their dissatisfaction with the choices that the system provides to them. The only way that they can do so is by not voting or by leaving ballots blank. The latter leads to the undervotes that caused so much controversy in Florida, as members of local election boards tried to decipher the intent of the voter if a vote for one of the presidential candidates was not counted by machine but there was a bare impression of perhaps an attempt to punch a hole, or a hanging chad, in some ballots (see Chapters 9 & 10 for more on this). As for voter turnout, it is possible that part of the decline reflects an increasing protest vote by those whose only option is to vote by their feet. This should be the focus of a study now that voting systems are receiving attention that they haven't received since the civil rights movement led to the Voting Rights Act. The way the political system works today, one can justifiably claim that we're nearly all disadvantaged.

The New (?) Politics:

According to Steve Roche: "Politics is all media now. Some say volunteers are unnecessary. Is your book going backward? It's not retail politics anymore…People don't get involved unless they're angry. They don't have time, given the need for two-income families and all. Also, politics is a fishbowl and the media turn everything into soap operas. There are definite disincentives to run. Recall the old saying: 'Ten people will watch a house being built; ten thousand will watch one burning.'"

"Retail politics" is a phrase to remember. We will encounter it again. It resonates with person-to-person (P2P), neighbor-to-neighbor, door-to-door, or one-on-one. That's retail, in contrast to the wholesale new politics, featuring advertising, bulk mailings, polls, and phone banks—all indirect approaches to large numbers of people simultaneously. The closest that the new politics comes to P2P or personal approaches is niche marketing, personal attacks, or other personality slants via media.

Mike Smith, the community activist, is a world apart from Steve Roche, the political consultant, but they are brothers under the contrasting skins of their roles. Mike: "The biggest shift I have seen over 30 years is people increasingly disengaged from the process. This is worrisome and should be a concern for everybody. The implications are not positive. People used to see being involved as a part of their value system. Now, and in more recent years past, it's as if they had been visited by Narcissus, as if they were navel gazing…[13] Now, they ask: If I do this, what do I get out of it? Thirty years ago, that's not what people asked or felt. Rather, they asked: If there is a problem in the community, what do I have to do? They had been brought up to help and to pitch in if there was a problem."

Bob Smith observed that: "Overall, there is now less participation, more alienation and more apathy than when we were involved in politics together here in New Jersey in the early '80's. Handlers, polling and money win elections, which are less about leadership and more about fundraising, money and media… Not that the old model was necessarily good, either, even though the character of parties has changed so that they are now money laundries in support of star candidacies. We must remove the perception that it's all money. Then we will see increasing popular participation."

Another political pro, Walter Orcutt, reinforced Roche's remark on retail, but with an odd, new political twist on the old: "There is still a need for retail politics. People still like to be involved with others. But it's tough to get candidates to do retail politics even though it's most effective. Technology now enables us to pinpoint whom to talk to, those most likely to vote. Door-to-door (DtD) politics is not dead, but it's more effective if you go DtD and people are not home. It's also more effective when you call people and leave a message rather than find them in. No bad impressions!; you don't have a chance to get into issues. When making calls to GOTV, hang up if someone answers. People will think the candidate is making calls if someone leaves a message."

Now see the new politics vs. the old through the eyes of another political pro, Ron Mills, a man whose political experience puts him closer to Steve Roche and Bob Smith than to Mike Smith. Ron says: "the priests are back in business, contra Luther.[14] Political pro's are one of the modern priesthoods. Goal #1 is survival of the priesthood. As political parties get weaker, people's ability to fight the priesthoods is taken away. A key question is: Are we better off politically after all the political reforms of the past century? What percentage of the electorate voted 100 years ago; e.g., for the McKinley race? Information, knowledge and level of political campaign language were much higher and more substantive 100 years ago than now. More recent politics hit a high water mark in '84 with Reagan vs. Mondale, a race showing passion, ideas and quality of information on issues. Since then, the quality of candidates and political discourse has gone down and down."…

Since the new politics is basically a money game rather than a people participation process, and latter day reformers are claiming that campaign finance reform (CFR) will bring people back into the picture, it helps to note something that Mike Lynch had to say:

> The volunteerism of the '40's and the '50's is a dead duck (and) Unless an individual is truly enlightened with regard to the need to participate in the political process via money contributions, he and most others will be unwilling to give ten cents to politicians. Society has become more selfish. Most give to United Way only because of employers' subscriptions.

Since the new politics is basically also a media game, also mark what another old hand, John Locicero had to say: "Do people pay attention to anything else but TV? I knew every Democrat in those (old) days—whether they were married, other characteristics—it was all on cards. Putnam is right."[15]

A key question to emerge here is whether the kinds of political reforms now being debated will give us a new new politics that is significantly better than the old, or even the old-old, politics. Ron Mills says no. So does Mike Lynch: "As they try to position themselves on the (campaign finance reform) issue, politicians and the media are providing the public with excuses not to participate." We turn to this issue below and try to resolve it in Chapter 9.

Campaign Finance Reform (CFR):

CFR is the overriding focus of the political reform movement today. This is ironic, for reformers wanting to get money out of politics ignore the value of people's time. In the reform movement, political volunteers only count if they come in buses from out of state to help get referendum items on the ballot or to help candidates that are usually losers. We will turn in earnest to CFR in the "Reform" chapters (9 & 10). Our interviewees help to frame the issue and its major options. As a prelude to Chapter 9, we can see one reason why CFR is so controversial. It is not just an issue of the pro's vs. the people. There are serious disagreements on CFR among those highly involved and politically sophisticated.

Though Mills is vehemently opposed to the CFR reformers and views McCain with disdain,[16] he states the crux of the CFR problem better than most: "You need to be independently wealthy to finance the political way of life, which requires as much time as money. One can't afford the time even if one can afford the money. Note the example of a State Senate race in New Hampshire. The job pays $100; each candidate spent $40-50,000. This is a problem at the local level, too, where in fact local running and serving is even more time-consumptive. This implies that there are now only three types of people who can hold public office—the very wealthy, the retired, and women who work at home. In New Hampshire, for example, we have a woman governor, speaker and majority leader, none of whom have economic careers outside of government."

Bob Smith adds another perspective: "As long as dollars dominate, people will be more frustrated. Money wins. Parties won't accept candidates if they don't have (or can't raise) enough money.[17] For high political office—major offices making decisions on public finance—no campaign contributions should be allowed; campaign financing should be all public money. Wealthy individuals shouldn't be able to use their own money to become a Governor or a Senator. Candidates would have to prove themselves. There should be limits on both contributions and expenditures. These points have tremendous implications; they imply great changes." Bob is right about the latter. One surprising feature of his remarks on CFR is his advocacy of public financing. This is surprising, given his concern for the health and strength of the Democratic Party and serious claims that CFR as currently advocated would undermine parties (see below). Though correct, his reference to "great changes" is also surprising. Prohibition of wealthy individuals from spending their own money to run for office would require a constitutional amendment. The danger—of high office being reserved for the rich—is already clear. Mike Lynch noted: "The Senate Club of 100 is increasingly being occupied by those whose races are self-funded."[18]

Another active and significant purveyor of campaign finance also testifies to the growing dominance of big money and its iniquitous implications for our political process. Nadine Hack: "I have seen greater and greater attention paid to…high-level donors. People in the parties' select circles…the big donors' groups, have access…This would have been my characterization of the Republican Party thirty years ago but it applies to all parties now... We see similar developments at the state and local levels…(and thus) CFR is critical…to bring people back into politics whose participation has been negatively affected by the influence of money in politics."

The attitude of another political pro, Republican County Committee Chairman Walter Orcutt, is quite different towards CFR: "The issue didn't ring; it's not an issue even though McCain rang the bell. There is disclosure; regarding Corzine, for example, of his own dollars. Most people in Warren County don't care where the dollars come from. The fact that there are gobs of dollars involved is not on their radar screen. The exception is Corzine; that's obscene, but in most such cases, the big dollar people don't win."[19]

Another Republican perspective is provided by Gary Todd, a distinctly non-rich former candidate for the U.S. Senate: "Unless you can reach people, there's no way to motivate them to action. Public Campaign [the title of the main vehicle for advocating public financing of campaigns] seems to fly in the face of democracy, as if we want to engineer people getting involved. Even if we limit dollars, if only the politically astute are involved, the result would be the same." A political opposite, Alissa Batson, agrees with Gary on the role of money in political campaigns but disagrees with him on the role of public money. "Money buys the ability to reach voters. TV helps a lot but, at the end of the day, it's the number of people you can involve that makes a difference—but this takes money, too."

Gary's reference to "Public Campaign" denotes one of four major efforts to enact a form of CFR using public money at the state level. The other three were in Maine, Vermont and Arizona. The counterpart of Public Campaign in Massachusetts was a very similar CFR ballot initiative in Arizona called "Clean Elections." Remember Alan Everett, Mayor of Sedona, AZ? He remarked: "The Clean Elections initiative was not well written. It raised many questions, so there are two or three lawsuits challenging it. I am against the McCain-Feingold campaign finance reform (CFR) initiative. I favor instant electronic disclosure over the Internet." Two of the state initiatives earned negative comments from interviewees. Another has failed (see chapter 9). Alissa Batson, however, stated that: "It's good to have public money in campaigns...(it) helps those who could not afford to run otherwise (and) it's so expensive to run that candidates spend too much time chasing people with money instead of spending time with constituents." She pointed to a local CFR initiative involving public money—that of New York City on a 4:1 matching private to public basis—as a good system.

Here as elsewhere, the perspectives of those deeply involved in the raising and giving of big bucks for political campaigns should not be overlooked. Fundraiser Priscilla Ruzzo added: "There's no point to CFR if there's continued use of soft money by issue advocacy, union and other non-profit groups." A dispenser of PAC funds, Mike Lynch, adds: "I'm for full, 100% disclosure, particularly now with access to elections data on the Web. Full disclosure, including contributions from 3^d parties, takes the whole process into the sunshine. There should be no loopholes. But the CFR debate jumps over the (reform) issue into banning soft money."

For now, Ron Mills gets to have the final as well as opening shot on the issue. His remarks amount to a frontal attack on the history of reform—a direct challenge that will whet your appetitite for Chapter 9:

> Reform always achieves results opposite to what's intended. The Progressive Movement, for example, was destructive of American politics.[20] People touting reform don't understand the institution they are trying to change. It's like putting a homeowner in charge of the MWRA (Massachusetts Water Resources Authority) because he knows how to flush the toilet. The political system is complex beyond the appreciation of reformers. [We should] adopt the same rules and regulations applied to campaign finance in other countries, where the only entities to raise and spend are political parties. This implies only soft money, no "Committee to Elect Peter Bearse." Ban soft money and you eliminate parties....There should be no regulation of how parties use money... Eliminate public financing of campaigns and/or parties. Public financing implies increased regulation."

Decentralization:

Recall one of the conjectures underlying this book: that moving far more power, money, and responsibility down to the local, municipal and community levels from the higher levels of politics and government would spur grassroots political participation because more people could see that their political involvement would make a difference. A scientist would call such a statement a hypothesis and ask: Is it testable? How do we find out whether it's true? A sample of interviews doesn't suffice to make a case, especially when the interviewees are not all of the same mind, as the paragraphs to follow indicate. The only way to test is to try, and see what happens.

Someone may ask: Haven't we already done this, starting with Nixon's "New Federalism" and Reagan's actions to move power and money out of Washington? The answer is both Yes and No. We have, but only part way—down to the states. Limited movements of power and money down to localities mostly exemplify devolution rather than decentralization. Devolution either moves money to lower levels while reserving power to those at higher levels—there are strings attached—or else it moves responsibility down without sufficient money to cover the costs. The latter is referred to as the imposition of "unfunded mandates."

Anyway, decentralization down to states has not provided a full test of the hypothesis. State governments are scarcely closer to most people than the national, and they reserve their powers just as jealously. Let's see what interviewees have to say on the subject.

Chris Wilder was very skeptical about decentralization. She said: "Small municipalities wouldn't be up to the challenge. We need more regionalization, perhaps via select inter-municipal service agreements. More burdens would fall on counties." [Note: Some county governments, e.g., Miami/Dade County, are larger and more powerful than some state governments. In some other states like Massachusetts, county government counts for very little but, in either case, counties are more local than the state.] A bit of Wilder's skepticism was echoed by her NJ friend, Kathy McMichael, who is otherwise quite supportive of decentralization as a central feature of her hero's and former employer's (Reagan) legacy: "It would help to devolve more power and responsibility for problem solving to the local level. But then a question arises: Is there enough talent at the local level?"

The latter is like a parent asking whether a child is able to handle some task when it has not yet been provided the opportunity to assume responsibility for the task. In New York City (and most other municipalities of all sizes), "community boards composed of volunteers decide on land-use and zoning matters (and)…The involvement of volunteers on such boards encourages political participation. Those involved get to know their elected officials, and *many candidates for elected office arise from these boards*" (emphasis mine). In another more positive vein, Amy Handlin remarked: "The experience with block grants, in big, unallocated chunks, has been good—a legacy of Reagan and devolution. So we should continue down that path. General revenue sharing is not now being discussed on the political agenda but it could be; the concept still has currency."

With Mike Angerone, we begin to catch a view of a possible downside to decentralization, (but note that he appears to be confusing it with devolution):

> With greater decentralization of government, people would take more interest, but we depend too much on government even at the local level. There are too many mandates, as in education, putting too much of a burden on the system. A recent Hamilton Township ordinance, for example, would allow cops to go into private property to arrest under-age drinkers. Another intrusive ordinance is under debate with regard to smoking. Government interventions are getting out of hand. Unfunded mandates are also an issue. With greater decentralization or devolution, we'd need a different type of local tax system that does not rely on the property tax. I would like a certain percentage of revenues collected at higher levels coming back to the local level.

Similarly, Nadine Hack observed, with reference to the education issue, for example:

> This is a complex issue. There may be some empowerment of people if decentralization is extended but there is also a danger of different standards and great disparities of resources between localities...There are a lot of weaknesses in any thrust towards greater decentralization without supports from the state or federal level to help create more level playing fields.[21]

Is it possible that rich and poor could come together against decentralization? This question is suggested by responses from Anderson similar to those from Hack on the issue: "Decentralization is against poor people. What about them?—as with welfare reform, for example?" She went on to say that the elite drive centralization.

Steve Weinberg provided some wise words from the standpoint of community politics in the spirit of the popular aphorism "Think globally; act locally!" He advised: "The guideline here should be to get problems solved at the lowest level at which they exist. You can't deal with the Firestone tire problem at the local level, nor air pollution. See a recent edition of *Co-Evolution Quarterly* that recommends an inventory of species on our planet. This is an undertaking that would require mobilizing local resources all over the planet.[22] There is a movement on the 'Net called 'community-based research.' Why can't communities take on a goal to advance knowledge in certain areas as a global goal? Politics is power and don't hide it!"

Other remarks from Steve seemed to suggest a more radical approach to decentralization. Judge for yourself: "There should be a check off on our federal tax return for neighborhood purposes. As per a report card: If a locality were to aggregate federal and state tax obligations, the reporting would knock people's socks off. Payments to higher levels should be somewhat discretionary. This implies we should give powers back to local level as much as possible. Here, he agrees with Handlin—The experience of CDBG and other block grants has been good."

Another seemingly "radical" view of decentralization was provided by Mike Smith:

> Citizens should take away the power of the centralized government...(and) construct a community which they believe is more fulfilling...we have socialized our citizenry to run to 'daddy'— the mayor or governor, etc...to get the money. We sell our votes to get crumbs... this is not the way towards a reinvigorated democracy...Jefferson's local, precinct-oriented, day-in-day-out interaction, debate and decision-making amongst the local people was the only true indicator of the health of American democracy[23]

Walter Orcutt raised his own question regarding our "hypothesis" and followed it with a counterpoint. He asked: "Is your premise correct—that greater decentralization will induce greater participation? Recall how school systems work, on basis of home rule—but where's the least participation?— in school board elections. And the most participation on school issues occurs when people feel that too much is being spent on schools. School Board elections typically earn a 10-15% turnout. He was seconded on this point by Kathy McMichael: "Local school board members are more 'local' than other elected officials because they are closer to voters via their involvement with parents. But turnout is horrible."

Here's another possible downside seen by Priscilla Ruzzo: "There's a possible danger in increasing decentralization. We could have lots of graft at the local level. There are possibilities of abuse and mismanagement at the local level." [Note: After all the identifications and discussions of fraud and waste at state and federal levels over the years, one could also wonder: What's the difference, except that abuse and mismanagement may be more visible and more liable to remediation at the local level.]

In favor of the conjecture, Alan Everett simply remarked, at the end of his interview: "I agree that decentralization and renewal of grassroots politics are linked per Reagan's legacy." Now there's a fellow Republican for you!

Mike Lynch was the only one who made a direct connection between this issue and how political parties operate. He said: "In concept, I agree with your conjecture, but my agreement is based upon a separate premise—that a party has established core areas of agreement and provides (decentralized) forums for discussion among its members. Instead, you face a platform that is very stringent at the national level, which is then pushed down to state and local levels." This is a key insight to which we will return in the final chapter.

The largely common denominator among most interviewees is a positive attitude toward decentralization, whether the connection was made to political participation or not. But every group needs a good curmudgeon or contrarian. Ron Mills played this role with regard to the decentralization theme as well as some others, saying: "I would eliminate municipal/local government. Note that there is a great difference between Gloucester (MA) and Hampton (NH) with respect to their local governments, even given many similarities. A new arrival from Gloucester would be at the bottom of a learning curve." Good thing you aren't running for local office, Ron!

Power

What's perhaps most remarkable about the interviews is how few of those interviewed said anything about politics as a competition for power. It's almost as though it's taboo or un-kosher to talk about power—as if we've fooled ourselves into thinking that politics is about something else. Perhaps, subconsciously, or as a result of media brain-washing, we've come to associate power, like politics overall, with low-life ambitions, with self-seeking (in the narrowest sense of "self"), with grubbing for gain, and with dirt. Machiavelli knew better; so did a few of the interviewees.

Recall Amy Handlin. For years, she was active in a variety of grass roots activities, e.g., LWV and battles for open space, but she became frustrated. Why? Because that's not where the power lies. Her experience out of power taught her that she could "recommend, suggest and pressure, but that local officials held the decision-making power." Amy has been seconded by Alissa, who stated bluntly, in remarks directed to her CBO friends, "Politics is power..." It "controls the ability to put forth legislation and put money into certain programs"(and not others).

Ron Mills, ever the master of realpolitik, reminds us of what political parties are about and how our children are being dis-empowered:

> The purpose of a political party is to enable people to obtain political power, which can't be done in any other way. But political power is quite diverse. It may mean policy, employment, running for or serving in office, etc....kids are being disempowered, perniciously—being taught they can't, as well as not taught how to. Children are taught that power is bad—an effect of the media, too. Power brokers, politicians and other symbols of power are portrayed in a negative light.

We will return to the latter concern when we focus on civics education later in this chapter and elsewhere in the book.

The Business Community

How the business community figures in the picture of political participation and reform is a puzzle. Many so-called reformers harp on only one—big corporate contributions to parties or powerful politicians—as though the business community was one-dimensional or had only one relationship to any political community. The interviews, however, elicited views reflecting on more than one aspect, three major features in fact, reflecting the role of business community in:

1. Campaign finance and CFR;

2. Local communities; and

3. Individual political histories.

On #1 itself, some remarks are bipolar. On the one hand, politically active members of local business communities have inspired and helped some of our interviewees to go into politics and run for office (e.g., Orcutt, Angerone). On the other, there's a concern for how big money may be corrupting our political system and turning people off of politics.

The local community aspect is not without tension and paradox, too. This is perhaps most apparent in the interview with Steve Weinberg. On the one hand, he speaks of the positive influence of local business elites who are both committed to their communities and able to get things done. On the other, he is concerned about non-elite people's power and their ability to play effective roles. The tension between these poles was felt by the interviewer. Steve did not point to it. Some of the tension also seemed to be felt by Amy Handlin in light of her mix of experience as both community activist and elected official.

#3 is an aspect that needs a lot more attention than it has received, especially if we want to continue to live in the Age of the Entrepreneur. Dick Woodbridge indicates that his involvement in politics has helped his business activity. But this positive connection may owe more to the nature of his business (law) and/or the nature of the person (Dick's unusually amiable personality). My own experience, some of it side-by-side with Dick in Princeton, speaks otherwise. As related in chapter 3, the experience involved direct conflict between my entrepreneurial and political aspirations.

What is the basic issue here?—a serious one on the supply side of politics—the ability of the small businessman or entrepreneur to actively participate in electoral politics. Even though the NFIB (National Federation of Independent Business) has enjoyed a resurgence of influence lobbying for small business in Washington, D.C., we need to be concerned about the ability of the small business man or woman to run for office with a reasonable chance to win and serve. Small businesses are more likely to be community-based. Most small business entrepreneurs are not likely to make it big or have either the interest or the ability to buy an election. If we don't want America to turn into a plutocracy dominated by big business, then people of all political persuasions – right, left and in-between—should be concerned about the vitality of small business. Yet, another insight from the interviews is that it is a mistake to have an us vs. them attitude about business involvement in politics. The business community is at least as varied as any other. Some businessmen, including CEO's of some of the largest, are quite altruistic; others are narrowly self-interested, with all points in between.

Now note what our interviewees have to say on the matter.

Dick Woodbridge on his involvement in local politics: "In relation to my own legal practice, 14 years of involvement in Borough politics hasn't helped to bring business in the door, but it has helped to develop people skills that have helped my practice. I recall not only Tip O'Neill's famous phrase but his personal touch—how Tip knew people and knew how to deal with and motivate them. I've distilled lessons of local campaigning from my experience and set them down as a set of guidelines for others."

Weinberg speaks from a small town community perspective when he says: "One positive role of business in politics is apparent, primarily via the role of power elites in communities that want to undertake community improvements." Handlin, too: "Community harmony and stability are business interests, too. Political leaders should be on the same page as their business counterparts. Grass roots groups can bring development projects to a screeching halt. [Note the tension implied here.] The business community is mainly interested in economic development or planning activities. But I don't see business people as different from others. The business community would benefit greatly from a more open and inclusive politics."

By contrast, Ingrid Reed spoke to the relevance of something that is featured in a later chapter on political reform—the relevance of business-inspired models: "Politics doesn't match up with the rest of modern experience… Political parties provide no rewards for, nor recognition of, organizations within their structures. There is no investment in organizations' development or growth; no rethinking of their strategic mission."

Gary Todd's remarks related both to the business community as a source of candidate recruitment and to the tension between business and political life: "As regional sales director for Christian radio, I met Ron Mills… Right now, my focus is on business development. It's a sales business. Later, I hope to be able to segment part of any given day, say, morning, for other activities; e.g., City Council or School Committee meetings. The problem is that these are evening activities. Still later, if I can multiply my business effort via others, I might free up more of my own time. Who can do this?—a very small percentage of people." [Note: This was but one segment of remarks by Gary that point to the tension between political participation and all other aspects of life.]

Priscilla Ruzzo spoke to businesses' possible connection with campaign finance concerns: "As for business influence, I don't see it in political reform except via a tiredness of being approached for money.[24] Efficiency of fundraising (FR) is bewildering to contributors in the business community. There is much more awareness because of the reporting of contributions. Many businessmen contribute for altruistic reasons. These are the ones bewildered by the efficiency of fund raising. They contribute and then find 4-5 more solicitations arriving in the mail. They become overwhelmed, angry and disgusted by stages of giving." [Note: This anger found expression in debates on campaign finance reform, as the Chapter 9 on reform reveals.]

Recent corporate scandals a la Enron and WorldCom, however, have brought to the forefront of political discussion other reform issues of the business sector in relation to the other sectors of our society. This is where Nadine Hack spoke with a broader perspective that, for now, deserves the last word on the business community:

> Corporations...I am trying to move them beyond the narrow 'bottom-line' focus...community-based organizations should look for corporate partners rather than view corporate dollars as dirty...Reebok, for example, is trying to help reduce breast cancer. We need a thrust for corporate citizenship.

Chapter 7 reveals how more progressive parts of the business community have already moved far beyond solely bottom line concerns in ways that can and should inform political reform.

Youth Involvement & Civics Education:

Americans typically invest a lot in their kids. They invest their hopes for a better future in young generations. Sometimes, politically, this hope is misplaced, as when American voters make a facile association between youth and new ideas or innovation. Many young, aspiring politicians I know are old before their time. They are careerists who use rhetorical public service goals as a gloss for their own ambition.

The hope seems misplaced even in terms of the lowest common denominator of citizenship—voting. The low turnouts of young adults 18-35 is even more shameful than those of their parents—the lowest of any age group and hardly better than the typically low turnouts of African-Americans.

Yet, the hope remains undiminished. Similarly, we invest great hopes in education, even though some of the naively hopeful bloom seems to have come off the educational rose. To the extent that the latter is true in a political vein, it is justified by the virtual collapse or serious deterioration of what used to be called civics education. This is usually associated with youth, even though civics education is as badly needed for adults as for their children. Much of the two-sided optimism and even more of the urgency is reflected in our interviewees' remarks on these themes. A major question that Bob Smith answers below with optimism is whether the young coming of age will bolster the body politic and turn things around.

Bob is bullish on the youth role and sees a coming resurgence of interest in politics: "Demographics implies that replacements are coming. Young people are coming up and being groomed. There is new energy coming up in Piscataway. A problem lies in the fact that there are fewer numbers because our generation represents a population bulge. There are always people with our genetic defect coming up and stepping forth. The political participation issue is partly a life cycle issue. As kids get older, their views and political participation will change."

Bob's optimism is seconded by Locicero: "We must get young people involved. People's lack of involvement runs in cycles…Are there positive signs? McCain stirred the pot. It will happen again. It takes someone to provide the leadership plus a new crop of people. Look at the demographics, the young, for example, the influx of new people into teaching. It takes leadership plus an issue. You got to press the right button."[25]

Nadine Hack also saw some positive signs…

> of revitalization on campuses (and in) feminism's new Third Wave. A whole new generation of activists is coming alive as shown, for example, by the WTO demonstrators…But do they, will they, find their way into politics?…Amy Richards, one of the founders of the Third Wave (says that) unless women translate this (the benefits of feminism) into political action, their causes will fail…We can't say off politics. Get involved![26]

Positive signs more specific to electoral politics were cited by Bill Batson, who is himself evidence for Nadine's optimism, along with his wife, Alissa. Bill pointed to "some younger people running for and elected to (New York) City Council…Another positive sign is the resurgence of involvement by young people around the Green Party and Ralph Nader…The model is the Civil Rights Movement…When the young are involved politically, you can see some of the old '60s zeal once again, but the numbers are small." His wife sees "a rising level of social consciousness among teenagers…as, for example, in the anti-sweatshop campaign."

Does this mean we can expect to see more Kathy McMichaels arising from the younger generation? Remember, "It all started when I was 15. My history teacher was into politics. We started a Political Problems Club." But also recall: Her parents were into politics. How many parents of today's youth even pay attention to politics except to bitch and moan over the evening news? How typical is the childhood of Bill or Alissa Batson?

Weinberg's recollections of his civics education as a youth also may also provide reason to pause. Remember, he said: "You need practice as well as classroom training," and one of the examples he gave was his experience in a Labor-Zionist self-governing youth camp… Kids in (today's) school classes are not elected to anything. In Hebrew camp, real money allocations were provided and treasurers elected." Another example was a U.S. Chamber of Commerce sponsored, community-based civics course that he had in 5th grade in Scranton, PA in 1955. It was part of a national curriculum.

Steve went on to say (partly as a result of his youthful experiences up through young manhood), "I have a relatively optimistic view of how to get involved and how the political game is played. Few people seem to have this sense. It needs to be imbued from a young age as, for example, in the unit leaders' elections for youth in a synagogue (his 3rd example). Candidates presented themselves before the entire congregation…This area of concern goes back to education….there are very low hurdles (to political participation). But we need to go through a paradigm shift to recognize this."

If we grant Weinberg's word about the importance of practice in civics education, then the Hamilton Township (NJ) school system may be on the right track. Mike Angarone reported that, "Kids in the High School get credit for working on campaigns. Schools moved away from this (civics education) for awhile but are now shifting back, e.g., by holding mock elections in schools."

Angarone was seconded by his municipal colleague, Christine Wilder:[27] "We are building bridges with the school system and engaging young volunteers. There are government and law-related courses in the high school, attended by about 20 kids each. One of the assignments is to invite somebody from the government to come speak to the classes. Another is to attend school board, town council or other local government meetings, or volunteer to help with political campaigns or other local political activities. Students get credit for these. Some kids show up at local political committee meetings. This set of courses has been going on for several years. One former student became a candidate for town council. He lost, but he was endorsed by newspapers and is still involved."

Alissa Batson sees "trying to build up younger candidates who attract younger voters" as one of the defining features of political leadership. Reinforcing others on civics education, she added: "High schools and colleges should encourage political participation and political clubs…modest stipends…should be provided to encourage political participation in campaigns or community organizing." Yet, she complained about County Committee "workers (who were) not volunteers; they were paid teenagers."

Another illustration of the value of civics learning-by-doing was provided by Ingrid Reed at the college level—Rutgers University's New Leadership Program for Young Women in High Schools: "This programs works with a rotating set of colleges and college advisors. We ask: What does it mean to be in politics, and how? The participants do senior year projects. They return a year later to review and think about what they've done. So much of what we see going on to encourage young people to get involved is divorced from politics. If we want people to be involved in solving community problems, they must know that much depends on politics and government—how we choose our rep's, etc. We help young people to see the connection and see that they can make a difference shaping solutions."

Amy Handlin, whose views are based upon a good blend of involvement in public life, has the last word on our youth and civics theme: "Civics education, such as it is, is not enough. There needs to be a fundamental understanding of how our system works. Unfortunately, among young people,

I see no great encouragement or interest even though I have been a college professor for many years."

We will pick up these concerns in Chapter 9 on reform as well as via some recommendations at the end.

Elections:

The 2000 Presidential elections woke up even the most apathetic as to the importance of elections (see the Y2K chapter). The great count, however, was pleasing only to the devotees of Sesame Street, and the press treatments and Florida hearings in its aftermath focused only on the narrow technical and procedural aspects of elections. Remarks of our interviewees reveal a richer fabric of elections issues to examine. Several emerged:

- The role of electoral party politics and partisan elections at the local level;
- Both fruitful intersects and debilitating conflicts between elections and the personal side of life;
- The role of primary elections;
- The importance of political competition;
- The possibility of great change via elections; and
- The role of initiative and referendum (I&R) or public ballot issue elections.

As one who has run for office in Massachusetts, I have been struck by the overwhelming tendency of localities in that state to establish non-partisan municipal elections, notwithstanding substantial, long-standing evidence of how non-partisan arrangements depress political participation and voter turn-out. A couple of the interviewees spoke to the matter of the partisan/non-partisan choice. Weinberg's remarks, derived from local political participation in another state (NJ) reinforce the political science evidence, my own experience in Massachusetts and the observations of Ron Mills to follow.

Mills's companion recommendations on primaries are controversial but deserving of serious consideration. The lack of local inter-party political competition is a depressant pointed out by some, most pointedly by Reed. Contrary to popular opinion about "what difference does it (elections and voting) make," Mills notes the radical change brought about by a recent election in Canada. Other remarks, on initiate and referemdum, resonate with a growing debate of whether, paradoxically, such a "Progressive" initiative may be more undemocratic than democratic.

Without explicit reference to the partisan/non-partisan debate, but speaking from experience living and working in non-partisan towns, Steve Weinberg observed: "Party has little influence with regard to the politics of most towns, where relatively small groups of the 'same old/same old' people are running things. If people are concerned, they could end up with two local parties—the ins and the outs."

On national electoral systems, Steve had this to say: "Note that, in Israel, people vote for a party, not individuals, in a proportional representation (PR) system. This is no good, even though the system politicizes life so much that a high percentage of people are involved. (With such a system) we'd get greens, pinks and browns, all fighting over prizes. There is a trade-off here with serenity in government." [Note how Weinberg's remarks jibe with Mills's, below, and see Chapter 9 for more on the pros and cons of PR.]

McMichael and Todd, each in their own way, spoke to the impact of their involvement in electoral politics on their personal lives, one positive, the other bittersweet. Paradoxically, both are true. [Note: the latter is not unusual. See sections on "The Paradox of Politics (and vice-versa) in Chapters 8 and 9.] Kathy: "I recall the Goldwater for President campaign of 1964—a campaign picnic, a Teenage Repubican booth. I met my future husband there. We sold cans of "Goldwater" (AuH2O)—really just ginger ale + kisses... In 1978, Jeff Bell ran vs. Clifford Case. I was heavily involved with the campaign from the start. My husband was involved with me. We would hold and attend many political functions (together)."

In contrast, Gary remarked: "...at any level, running for election means that your life is not your own...When you get involved, it doesn't just affect you but others, too—family, business, profession, etc. There are tensions. The implied cost/benefit calculus comes out with cost so much higher than benefit. You need to put family, church, business (&c) on the back burner to run...(but) My Senate run was eye-opening, fun and worth the process."

On primary elections, Ron Mills said, without hesitation or qualification: "Do away with primary elections. Unfortunately, they can only be done away with by negating previous decisions that did away with or illegitimized prior methods and thereby undercut political parties, who lost control. [Note: Here, he is alluding to the Progressive Movement and its follow-on impacts over the past 100 years.] Without primaries, the Reform Party method is better. Primaries are the single most important factor raising elections' costs, as well as undercutting parties' control...Bearing the cost of primaries is analogous to taxpayers paying for the conduct of the Elks Club. They are not elections; they are nominations. We should deregulate and privatize political parties. They should be able to discriminate as they see fit."

Mills went on to point out an example of radical change through elections: "The second most profound political event of the '90s (next to the collapse of the Soviet Union) was the unparalleled defeat of the Progressive Conservative Party (PCP) in Canada. It fell down to 2 seats; now, 16. The Opposition Party in Canada is now the Reform Party, which inspired formation of the Reform Party in the U.S. So, Canada was able to effect fundamental change in its politics in one election—because political parties in Canada are privatized and can control who will run. The PCP's nomination of Kim Campbell was disastrous—a sign that the PCP had lost its mooring, purpose and raison d'etre." [One cannot help noting here that this is the way many people feel about both major political parties in the U.S.]

Ron's blast against conventional political wisdom continued: "Eliminate non-partisan elections. In Massachusetts, the choice is a local decision, so we would need lots of local charter changes. Non-partisanship is trendy, as in 'it's for the children' trendy. Its image is everything; its substance is nothing but negative. Under state law, towns can have caucuses (in town meetings, to elect local officials, not elections). Read the election laws. Brockton, for example, changed from partisan to non-partisan local elections. The latter lead to personality politics and/or a banana republic featuring continued control by local juntas because people lack the tools to marshall opposition. Proportional Representation (PR), on the other hand, is designed to represent cultural minorities. It's idiotic, something only a Ph.D. in political science would come up with. PR to politics is what Esperanto is to language." [Note: Do references to PR seem academic to the reader? They aren't. Many of those favoring political reform are advocating its adoption here in the U.S. See Chapter 9.]

Initiative and Referendum (I&R) is another Progressive elections' reform, advocated by Mike Smith in Illinois. The difference in his case is that he pushed it forward as a way to empower localities and neighborhoods vis a vis higher powers—not, as some have advocated, as a national or statewide plebiscitary device that could be taken over by powerful entrenched interests. Smith told an interesting story of how his community-based organization worked to get a home equity issue on the ballot in the face of opposition from Illinois Democratic legislators: "Most legislators resisted. One or two pushed a precinct-level I&R bill. This passed the State Senate. Then Mike Madigan (Democratic leader) changed it to say that the bill pertained for one time and one time only, for the home equity initiative. On the last day of the legislative session, during the veto session, one Republican freshman called in, checked on the bill and threatened to kill it even though (or because?) Madigan wanted it his own (compromised) way. Madigan gave in, and the legislative I&R enabling has since been used several times in Chicago."

The importance of even more modest reforms like those under discussion in many states and now, nationally in the aftermath of Florida was highlighted by Alan Everett: "Allowing early voting up to 30 days in advance of election day raises turnout. About 30% of voters cast their votes in advance…This changes campaign dynamics, too."

More than anyone else, Ingrid Reed reminded us of the importance of competition in electoral politics: "The (Princeton Borough Democratic) Committee collaborates with campaign committees.[28] We're still doing voter registration. But there isn't enough competition and there's not a lot of energy. The Mercer County Democratic Committee is coasting along. Party organizations are using up political capital from the past." Her view from Princeton was reinforced by Todd's from Fitchburg: "No local seats have been contested except for one Ward seat and one State Committee seat. This lack of contests has been true for several elections. In fact, there has been no contest for Mayor over several elections. There has been only a 16% turnout."

LPPC's & Political Participation:

As the good book says, the first shall be last. All of those interviewed had some experience with local political party committees (LPPC's) and political participation other than just voting. Thus, it is both interesting and important to observe what they had to say on these interrelated aspects of our political system.

Amy Handlin: "Local political leaders need to constantly remind themselves that job #1 is to make their activities relevant to residents – not just to call people to put up signs before an election. Politics should be a force for betterment and change year-round. One local Republican club activity, for example, is to have programs with speakers to highlight local issues."

Walter Orcutt: "Local Committees would do little if not kicked in the butt by the County Committee. There are some spirited races in towns with no local committees but the majority of towns are not engaged. There are 50-60 active people, but we must shine a light down the path to show them the way. In Blairstown, for example, membership of the Republican Municipal Committee decreased from 180 to 150 until there was wholesale outreach via direct mail with County Committee help in the form of money for stamps."

The importance of an active local political party and the positive potential of committee members as community leaders, however, is pointed up by Alan Everett: "A high percentage, about 85%, of the Precinct Committee positions are filled in Yavapai County even though they are getting harder and harder to fill. When controversies and issues rise to the fore, Yavapai County and local Republican Committee leaders say 'get involved,' and some people are more likely to respond and do so. State Committee positions are pro-rated to Precinct Committee slots that are filled. This implies that Yavapai County has greater influence in the state party than many others. Some Republican Committee percentages are less than 15%... Strong voter turnout in the precinct is attributable to the Precinct Committee."

Alan went on to indicate just how easy it is for people to get involved: "Precinct Committee members can be appointed by the County Supervisor or Committee candidates can get 15 signatures to run. There are five slots filled in my Precinct Committee, plus two in my neighborhood who don't go to meetings but provide proxies."

Alan's additional remarks reinforce what was said by partisan counterparts of the opposite party out East (Locicero, et. al.): "If you get people involved, they start liking it. Don't lay on guilt; ease them into process. Most didn't know there was a process."

Ron Mills again plays the curmudgeon's role, pointing out a conflict that may be uncomfortable to some when he says: "Note the contradiction between LPPC municipal and ward committees enabled by law while local governments are non-partisan." [Note: some years ago I first recognized this contradiction when the Trenton (NJ) City Democratic Committee invited me to review the relevant research from the field of political science in order to advise them on the partisan/non-partisan option for local elections.]

But the last word on this last-is-first topic belongs to Mary Perone: "You need to get people together. Interest is a big word. You can't do a campaign without interest and people. You've got to give them something to come for. That's tough. There isn't enough County Committee and Local Committee attention to issues that concern people. How do you get the message out and across?... Becoming and being a local leader is important because you need to find out what people really do, think and feel... You've not to get out to hear from people directly. I believed...in people...My opinions were influenced by theirs, and vice-versa."

The counterpart of the decline of politics in the tradition of Mary Perone is the rise of politics dominated by big money and costly media, a politics which doesn't seem to have any room for ordinary people to play any significant roles. Mary's role, however, was significant. She embodied a major source of political vitality in her community. Politics was not something out there, a game played by them that was not for us. For Mary, it was part of the on-going life of her community as well as an essential part of her own life. Without adapting the best features of the old school that Mary Perone and others among those interviewed for this book represent, any so-called new politics won't represent much, if any, improvement over the current version which, according to Washington Post columnist E.J. Dionne, most Americans have come to "hate."[29]

Notes

1. Erikson, Eric (1994), *Life History and the Historical Moment* N.Y.: W.W. Norton & Co.

2. Note, by contrast, the increasing number of political family "dynasties" following the Kennedy's.

3. No one who has endured a race for Congress would be surprised by this remark.

4. Grover Norquist is President of Americans for Tax Reform; Bob Franks was a Member of Congress but he had to give up his seat to run for U.S. Senate in 2000, losing to Jon Corzine, who spent $70 + million to get elected.

5. More recently, another establishment Republican was defeated by a conservative, Bret Shundler, an innovative, colorful former Mayor of Jersey City.

6. Chris Smith is still a Member of Congress. He has been one of the more conservative Republican members for 24 years. His predecessor, Frank Thompson, had become a powerful member representing the Trenton-based C.D. Bill Mathesius stepped down as Mercer County Executive in 1998 after having been re-elected several times.

7. Wilson, James Q. (1962), *The Amateur Democrat*. Chicago: University of Chicago Press.

8. I love doing interviews because of their open-endedness, No matter how one structures an "interview protocol" such as that employed for this book, the dynamics of a good interview always allow interviewer and interviewee, interactively, to chase some bunnies through the bush—to explore unexpected remarks as they arise.

9. Although Lynch is not an economist, his diagnosis jibes with that of leading economists.

10. My personal experience resonates with Everett's remarks: When I was running for local office in Gloucester, MA, I felt that I had three opponents: whoever was running against me plus the local paper. Any "corrections" of paper misstatements were always belated, small and placed on some high numbered inside page. Could the fact that I was a Republican and the publisher was a liberal Democrat have something to do with this, even in a legally non-partisan local election set up?

11. See Putnam, Robert (2000), *Bowling Alone*. His thesis of "civil disengagement" has earned him critical responses from other leading political scientists, but the voluminous pieces of supportive evidence in his book are reinforced by the evidence in this one, especially in Chapter 5. See highlights of Putnam's analysis in Chapter 8.

12. For example, Green, John C. and D.M. Shea (eds., 1999), *The State of the Parties: The Changing Role of Contemporary American Parties*. Oxford, England: Rowman and Littlefield.

13. Mike had read Lasch's book, *Age of Narcissus*, referenced in Chapter I.

14. Ron's a good historian here. He alludes to Luther's fight against the Catholic hierarchy of his time and his battle for a more democratic church in which every man could be his own priest, not dependent on the priesthood to interpret scripture for him.

15. The reference being made here is to Putnam's *Bowling Alone* thesis about civic disengagement.

16. Recall that in another segment of the interview, Ron characterized reformers as "led by the League of Women Voters…media, dilettante wives of the upper middle class, and the insipidly stupid; e.g., McCain."

17. This reminded me of my '84 run for Congress. Major county organizations backed me in the primary because they thought that I could raise a lot of money for the race vs. a Republic incumbent.

18. Here, Mike made specific reference to Jon Corzine, a former executive of Morgan Stanley who spent over $60 million, most of it his own money, to win a U.S. Senate seat from New Jersey. Mike went on to say: "The $60 million

he (Corzine) put into the campaign could have been put into social service programs and done more good than he could as a U.S. Senator."

19. Orcutt's reference here is also to Corzine. He defeated Bob Franks, a politician who had risen through the ranks, starting from the grassroots.

20. Among other sources that support this claim, see "Shutting the Public Out of Politics," An Occasional Paper of the Kettering Foundation by R. Claire Snyder (1999).

21. This issue has been highlighted by "Bagehot" in *The Economist* of May 3ᵈ, 2003, as "The devolutionist's dilemma… There is a real choice to be made and the new localists should admit it: does democracy, or…fairness, matter most" (p.60). This insightful article, however, confuses "localism" or decentralization with devolution.

22. A more limited but nevertheless ambitious version of this proposal is now being implemented with support from major foundations as "The Global Census of Marine Life." The project involves scientists from 40 countries but there is no indication of any involvement by localities. [*Science*, December 28, 2002].

23. Via e-mail of 5/29/02 from mcsmith@excite.com.

24. The Campaign Reform Project, started by Jerome Kohlberg, is one example of a campaign finance reform group representing mainly big business executives, in part because they got tired of being hit up for money by pol's. Priscilla did not mention it but I happen to be involved with it, partly as a representative of the small business community. See Chapter 9.

25. John went on to fondly recall young political leaders from our shared past in New York politics: "Look at Kennedy and Koch, for example. Recall Jerry Kretchmer and Allard Lowenstein, too. Lowenstein was charismatic. Political competition was severe…" I fondly remember another Jerry, too, with whom we all worked at VID. Jerry was the club member famous for taking care of the precious card files that were built up from door-to-door voter outreach, files that guided GOTV efforts on election day.

26. See her 2002 *Manifesta*, written with Jennifer Baumgartner (Farrar, Strauss and Girroux publishers).

27. The interviews were totally independent and occurred many months apart. In fact, the interview with Wilder took place long in advance of that with Angarone.

28. Note that this matter of "coordination" between party committees and campaigns has become a major issue in the debate on campaign finance reform and before the Federal Election Commission (FEC). Reformers would prohibit coordination even though it is a traditional, common sense activity of party politics. Ironically, FEC rulings may support party practice rather than reformers' desires.

29. This paragraph is paraphrased from an op-ed piece published by the *Gloucester Daily Times* entitled: "Return to Mary Perone's old school" (March 10, 1997). Dionne's book is entitled *Why Americans Hate Politics*.

5.

More from the Political "Vineyards"
Findings from a National Survey

RESPONSES FROM CHAIRS OF
LOCAL POLITICAL PARTY COMMITTEES (LPPCs)

Executive Summary

The ten most important factors affecting people's political involvement and their Committees were reported by nearly 200 respondent LPPC Chairs to be:

Questionnaire Rank Item	Rank Score
1. People increasingly apathetic or cynical	534
2. Apathy and Cynicism	532
3. Exciting political campaigns	519
4. Neighbor-to-neighbor outreach and recruitment	496
5. Charismatic political leaders	480
6. Change in attitudes towards politics overall	455
7. Politics increasingly money and media driven	432
8. Campaigns increasingly dependent upon money rather than people	330
9. People working longer hours	292
10. More and better political leadership	271
Changes in attitudes towards parties	270

Overall, these summary scores reflect a troubling negativity in attitudes toward politics, political parties, campaigns, and political participation. Other major survey findings follow.

- LPPC Chairs are middle-aged and older; their Committees do not appear to be attracting young people as in the past.

- The Chairs and their Committee members are deeply rooted and involved in their communities—long-time residents with many years of involvement in their Committees PLUS participation in many other, non-political community activities.

- Significant proportions of Committee memberships appear to be nominal or inactive because statistics representing Committee activity are significantly lower than percentages of membership slots filled. Even though overall LPPC activity scores were not computed, significant percentages of reporting Committees are inactive in traditionally key areas of LPPC endeavor. LPPCs' voter registration and GOTV activities are weak relative to what they can and should be doing in these major areas.

- Door-to-door activities and others involving person-to-person (P2P) outreach and contact are especially weak, reported by only small minorities of Chairs.

- Contrary to one of the myths of American democracy, LPPC campaign activity tends to rise with campaign level from local to federal. It also increases with the degree of indirection of campaign methods, from personal to impersonal.

- Committees' involvement with public issues is not bad but there is a lot of room for improvement and opportunities to do more that, if exploited, would increase LPPCs' relevance and memberships.

- LPPCs lack dependable sources of financial support. State Committees' (SC) support of local Committees is inadequate, especially financial. The latter is miniscule even among the very small percentage of LPPCs that receive any at all; the extent of such support, moreover, has been trending downward.

As for major party contrasts, there are no significant differences in the responses regarding reasons for people's non-involvement, but there are some with respect to barriers and constraints to involvement and how to get people (re)involved.

Characteristics of Survey Respondents

Nearly all (96.6%) of the survey respondents were the survey's target group: Chairs of Local Political Party Committees (LPPCs). They are predominantly older Americans. Their median age is 54. Three quarters of them are older than 45. In the past, LPPCs have attracted young people interested in politics. For the most part, this does not appear to be the case today. Refer to Table 1, below, for characteristic statistics.

About two-thirds of the Chairs (67%) are men; one-third, women. Most are very well educated. 92% of respondents completed high school. The median number of years of education completed is 17 – one more than a four-year college education. A majority (52.4%) have completed a master's degree or better. Over one-fifth (21.4%) of respondents have a law or higher degree. It is somewhat surprising to find, however, that lawyers are not the most numerous reported occupation. Entrepreneurial or retired categories were the ones most frequently checked.[1] They each amounted to 12.1%. Lawyers and educators were the #2 most frequently reported occupations, at 10.7% each. Thus, these four categories occupied nearly half of the sample.

Table 1
Characteristics of Respondents

DATA LABEL	DATA ITEM	NOTES [MV = # of Missing Values]
Age	54 years (median)	MVs=50; ¾ > 45 years
Sex	67.3% male	MVs=46; Most of missing Female?
Education	17 years (median)	MVs=54; 92% above High School
Occupation	24.2% Entrepreneur or Retired (modes of 18, or 12.1% each)	MVs=50; next largest #: educators, lawyers=16, or 10.7% each
Member of Association?	34.9% YES	MVs=72
Married?	83.1% YES	MVs=44
No. of children	2 (median)	MVs=61; 12.4% with no child.
Homeowner?	97.3% YES	MVs=49
Years of active membership	12 years (median)	MVs=47; 31.8% < 10 years.
Committee Chair?	96.6%	MVs=52; Current, Co- or past chair.
Years resident in community	25 years (median)	MVs=49; 9.4% < 10 years.
Active in a church?	66.9% YES	48 missing values
Member of fraternal/sisterhood?	34.6% YES	72 " "
Political club or civic assoc'n?	69.2% YES	56 " "
Sports team or youth coaching?	26.7% YES	68 " "
Run for public office?	57.1% YES	44 " "
Served in public office?	58.2% YES	45 " "
Ever elected to public office?	59.6% YES	99 " " ;. LPPC included

In some key respects, the Chairs seem like average Americans – married (83% of them), homeowners (97%) with two children (50%) and active in a church (67%). In other key respects including education, however, the Chairs seem quite atypical, especially in light of how Putnam and others have characterized the average American's civic and political non-involvement.[2] Most respondent Chairs are significantly rooted and highly involved in their communities, in addition to being active in their local churches. Most have resided in their communities at least 25 years. 69% belong to a civic association other than their local political committee. 57% report having run for public office. 58% say that they have served in public office, either elected or appointed. Half or more of the respondents have been active members of their local political committees for at least 12 years. Significant minorities report that they are members of fraternal associations or sisterhoods and/or that they are involved with local sports teams or coaching.

Community Involvement

The high degree of community involvement just noted is reinforced by what responding Chairs report to be the community involvement of their Committees and members. Half of the Committees are "sometimes" involved with other community-based organizations (CBO's) relative to public issues or other community concerns. The median number of members' involvements with CBO's other than their LPCC embraces five (5) different types. The actual number of other organizational involvements could be greater. See Table 2 for details.

The table reveals that at least half of responding Chairs report that LPCC members are involved in local churches or religious organizations (90%), business organizations (81%), civic associations (64%), social service organizations (63%), veterans organizations (61%), fraternal or sisterhood organizations (51%), and arts or cultural organizations (50%). Those who report members being involved with "other, politically-related" organizations are a minority (42.5%). Half (50%) of respondents report that they "work with" CBO's with some frequency on shared concerns for "public issues." Nearly one-quarter (23.3)% of the committees represented through the survey make contributions to non-political "good causes" in their communities. More than one-quarter of them (29.3%) "collaborate" with CBO's.[3]

Extent to which LPPCs are active

One of the interesting aspects of the statistics just presented is that LPPCs are not established to "get involved" in communities at large or commissioned to collaborate with other, non-political CBO's on a wide range of issues of community concern. LPPCs are established by political parties and enabled by state election laws to hoe a much narrower row; that is, to help their parties win elections. Thus, the extent to which LPPCs and their members are involved in non-political aspects of community life is surprising. The goal to win elections, however, does require that a number of tasks be undertaken and objectives fulfilled, none of which can be done if an LPCC is not up to strength and active. These features begin to be reflected by the survey responses shown in Table 3.

The number of slots that an LPPC has to fill, that is, the number that represents a Committee's full, formal membership, is established on the basis of state laws governing elections and the organization of local governments,

Table2
Community Involvement of Committees and their Members

DATA LABEL	DATA ITEM	NOTES
Extent Committee works with CBO's	50 % "sometimes"	Only 9% "frequently"
No. of member CBO involvemnts	5 (median)	5 is also the mode at 19%
Local business organization memberships	80.5%	Only 4 non-responses
Social service " "	63.1%	Individual membership
Church/religious " "	89.7%	" "
Fraternal organizations or sisterhoods	51.3%	" "
Veterans organizations	61.0%	" "
Other politically-related	42.5%	" "
Civic associations	63.6%	" "
Arts or cultural organizations	50.3%	" "
Sports	45.1%	" "
Attractiveness of non-political activity	32.2%	Responses ranked 1-4
Collaboration with CBO's	29.3%	One of "ways Commitee involved..."
Contributions to "good causes"	23.3%	One of "purposes" ... devoted to
Committee Chair residency	25 years (median)	Rounded to nearest year
Chairs active in churches	66.9%	48 missing values
" " " frat.or sister societies	34.6%	72 " "
" " " civic association	69.2%	56 " "
" " " sports or coaching	26.7%	68 " "

often with some reference to the sizes of local population(s) to be served. The author's hometown, for example, the City of Gloucester, has five wards. Massachusetts' state election laws specify 35 members per Ward Committee, for a total of 175 members for the overall City Committee. The Gloucester Republican City Committee has about 50 slots filled; however, there are not more than 15 active members citywide. In percentage terms that correspond

	Table 3 Extent to which LPPCs are active	
DATA LABEL	DATA ITEM	TREND (%=Up) or NOTES
Committee slots filled	89.9% (median)	26.5%
Members actively involved	50.0% (median)	25.8%
Attendance at meetings	57.1% (median)	27.8%
Competition for Committee slots	21.9% (=Yes)	Yes = code 1
Competition for officer positions	30.7% (=Yes)	Yes = code 1
Efforts to recruit new members	80.2% (=Yes)	Yes = code 1
Recruiting candidates —State & Local —Always or often	87.7.3% 41.5%	Local & state legislative candidates Extent to which Committee involved
Annual dinner?	51.0%	Same % report significant revenues earned
Forums	41.1%	Sponsorship of or particip'n in
Involvement with public issues	36.8% (-)	(-)=NOT involved with issues...

to the reporting of Table 3, therefore, there are only 28.6% of "Committee slots filled" and 8.6% "Members actively involved."[4] The adjective "only" is appropriate in light of the nearly 90% median shown in the first two rows of Table 3. Given the legal limits on LPCC memberships, some Committees have established a category of "associate," non-voting members to provide places for people who would like to be involved with the Committee and its roles in electoral politics. Such "members" are not counted in the statistics reported by Table 3.

Table 3 shows significant downdrafts from the baseline median percentage (90%) of "Committee slots filled." Much lesser proportions are reported for members "actively involved" (50%), "Attendance at meetings" (57%), "Competition for Committee slots" (22%), "Recruiting" of candidates (35%) and other indications of the "Extent to which" LPPC's are "active." Note that only 41% of respondents report "Forums," that is, "sponsorship of, or partici-pation in, forums, presentations or other public meetings in which issues are discussed or debated;" while 37% mark "NOT involved with issues in any way outside of elections or campaigns." Also, only about half (51%) now hold an "annual dinner," which used to be a tradition among a great majority of political committees. What about many more specific Committee activities –

	Table 4 Voter Registration	
DATA LABEL	DATA ITEM	TREND
Voter Registration campaign?	56.6% yes	16.4% up
Door-to-door	13.9% "	
DATA LABEL	26.2% "	
Tables in public places	32.8% "	
Assisting efforts of others	21.1% "	
In schools or colleges	23.7% "	
Effect of "motor voter" registration	20.7% report effect negative	
No. of new voters registered per LPPC member	0 (median)	72% stable or declining; i.e. trend not up.

those that represent their major roles in electoral politics? These are shown in Tables 4–8.

Major LPPC activities include voter registration, get out the vote, political "literature" distribution and various tasks in, around, and for campaigns and elections. From the standpoint of one who has been "laboring in the vine-yards" as an active member of more than one strong, active LPPC, the activity statistics that have emerged from the survey are quite disappointing. Look first, for instance, at respondent LPPC Chairs reporting of their Committees' activities in one of the most traditional, fundamental roles of LPPC's — Voter Registration (VR).

Voter Registration

Only 56.6% of Committees conduct VR campaigns. "Only" is the right word here because every LPCC (100%) should conduct one or more VR campaigns per year. In the author's experience working as a member of LPCCs in both parties, these campaigns were often conducted in concert with other organizations, especially the League of Women Voters or local high schools. Table 4, however, shows that only 21% of LPPC Chairs reported "assisting efforts of others" with VR and only 24% indicated that their Committees conducted VR "in schools or colleges." The door-to-door personal touch of direct contact with the unregistered is especially lacking at 14%. The next best alternative in terms of person-to-person contacts is VR via "Tables in public places," but this is reported by only 33%. The minimal type of VR campaign is represented by "Notices or advertising" that tell people where to go to register, usually the office of a local town or city clerk. This is shown for only 26%. In view of these "only" stat's, it is perhaps no surprise to notice that the median "No.of new voters registered," overall and per LPPC member is 0 – zero, zilch – one big goose egg like any bowler would have to mark on his sheet from throwing nothing but gutter balls, whether bowling alone or not.

What might explain these results? One possibility is that the national "Motor Voter" law requiring states to register people to vote when they register their cars or obtain auto licenses might be effectively pre-empting or supplanting local Committees' traditional VR role. This does not appear to be the case given another "only" percentage — 21% who believe that the law has had a "negative" impact on "Committee VR efforts." It is possible, however, that this percentage may understate the negative impact because respondents who did not pay special attention to the word "Committee" in the question may have confused LPPC "impact" with the overall change which has been positive in terms of numbers of new registrants. A likely negative impact on voter turnout will be considered further on.

No matter what the cause of the low stat's for VR may be, the negative consequences for LPPCs and political parties should be understood. Traditionally, VR efforts have been the first point of contact between political parties, their committee members, and potential voters. Direct person-to-person contact by friends and neighbors, especially, helps to elicit voter interest in the political process. To the extent that LPPC members are not motivated to conduct VR campaigns themselves, the process is further de-person-alized. Voter turnout and other forms of political participation suffer.

Getting Out the Vote

Another basic role of LPPCs is to "Get Out the Vote." This is such a familiar role that it is usually referred to by the shorthand "GOTV." The pertinent stat's on this role can be found in Table 5. Note that the percentage of LPPCs that mount GOTV campaigns, at 82%, is significantly higher than the 57% that mount VR campaigns. Nevertheless, the extent of direct personal outreach of door-to-door politicking and mobilization of volunteers to GOTV are both quite low. About 27% of Committees do GOTV door-to-door, which is low even though nearly twice the 14% DtD activity observed for VR. The "Election day volunteers" ratio of 0.44 per member means that, among at least half of reporting LPPCs, less than half of their members turn out to work on election day when the major GOTV press usually occurs.

The main method appears to be calling. This is reported by 76% of respondents. This method, though, is also likely to be least liked by voters, who are annoyed by telemarketing. The second most frequently reported GOTV method, at 64%, is "stand-outs," with signs, usually at key intersections or traffic circles, waving to traffic and passersby with or without candidates also being present. "Driving voters to the polls," has also been a standard part of Committees' GOTV repertoire, yet it is reported by only a small majority of 58%.

No GOTV campaign is complete or truly effective without "Checking at the polls" to identify who has voted during any election day. The check-off sheets are then supposed to be forwarded periodically during the latter part of the day to volunteers manning a phone bank, calling to remind those who have not voted to get out and vote, and/or volunteers knocking on the doors of registered non-voters, usually in targeted neighborhoods. Yet, only half of respondents say their Committees do "Checking." Somewhat greater proportions, 57% and 55%, employ "Mailings" and "Campaign headquarters," but these are known to be less effective. A lot depends on whether enough volunteers are available to man the headquarters, yet we have already seen some evidence of the difficulty LPPCs have in mobilizing volunteers and we will see more as we run through the rest of our survey data. 78% of respondents say their campaign headquarters are "manned" but half of the Committee Chairs surveyed did not respond to the question. How many readers have seen campaign headquarters that look like settings for an Edward Hopper painting, they seem like such empty or lonesome places, lacking in activity?

Table 5 Get Out the Vote (GOTV)		
DATA LABEL	DATA ITEM	TREND (% up)
GOTV campaign?	82.0% yes	
Campaign headquarters established	55.1% "	
Calling	76.1 % "	
Driving voters to the polls	58.2% "	
Door to door	26.6% "	
Checking at the polls	50.5% "	
Standouts/signs	64.1% "	
Mailings	57.1% "	
Election day volunteers	0.44 (median, per member)	

Distribution of Campaign and Other Political Materials

"Literature Distribution" is another basic Committee function. Now, referring to political flyers, brochures and other handouts as "literature" may seem quite a reach to most readers but, in fact, that's how those "laboring in the vineyards" refer to them. Others call the stuff "propaganda," but let's allow some benefit of the doubt. After all, among the variety of printed materials we can choose to read or not these days, there's true literature, like Shakespeare or Melville. There's also literature from Danielle Steele or Tom Clancy. Table 6 reports the incidence of Committees' "Literature Distribution" activities from their Chairs' responses to our survey. Perhaps the most interesting stat's, in light of the American myth of local democracy, is how percentages of Committees doing distributions rise with the level of campaigns, that is, with distance of campaign level or scope from locality.

Note that the percentages move higher as the eye on Table 6 moves from strictly local races to county to state and federal campaigns. The numbers increase steadily except for mayor and president. The very low percentage for "Mayoral race" is due to the fact that many such races are non-partisan; thus, there is little or no incentive for LPPCs to get involved. The dampening effect that non-partisanship has on political participation deserves more attention than we can give it here.[5] As for the presidential level, the fall-off of nine percentage points, from the 61.7% for "U.S. Congress" to the 52.6% for "President" is not surprising, given the increasing reliance of presidential campaigns upon TV and decreasing reliance upon political volunteers. The latter has been noticed even in Chicago.[6] LPPC Chairs have complained about lack of literature from well-funded Presidential campaigns because so much of campaign finance is devoted to expensive non-print media.[7] The flurry of volunteer activity during the Spring 2000 and 2004 Presidential primary seasons provided indications that Presidential politics could be otherwise. Will these turn out to be transient upward blips in an otherwise downward trend? See Chapter 9.

The low numbers for three indicators — volunteers for "lit distribution" (0.37 per LPPC member), percentage (40%) of Committees distributing door-to-door, and "Number of lit. drops before election (median = 2) coupled with the high (more than two-thirds) percentage reporting "Increasing difficulty of mobilizing enough volunteers;" all reinforce earlier observations of the declining "person-to-person" nature of political activity. Other reasons marked by respondents as "major trends affecting their Committees' ability to serve as a distributor of political literature and campaign materials" include:

- Increasing reliance upon non-print media
  to deliver political messages 31.4%
- Small or decreasing supply of materials 19.5%
- Decreasing reliance upon party committees
  by candidates or campaigns ....:................ 39.5%
- Little or no State Committee support 32.4%

In the future, the past person-to-person quality of political participation may be further diminished by use of the Internet or it may not, depending on how the technology is utilized (see Chapter 8). Over two-thirds (69%) of respondents report that their Committees have some access to "Electronic

Table 6 Literature Distribution		
DATA LABEL	DATA ITEM	NOTES
No. of lit drops before election	2 (median)	Sum of three frequencies
Lit. distribution on behalf of both party & campaigns	48.9%	
Literature distribution volunteers	0.373	# per Committee member
Electronic distribution capacity	78.3% (37.9% for e-mail alone)	e-mail or web-page or list server
Literature distribution — School Committee	19.9%	Committee roles in recent campaigns: School Comm., et.al.
" " — Local Councils	29.1%	
" " - — Mayoral race	14.8%	
" " — County campaign	38.8%	
" " - — State legislature	66.3%	
" " — Governor's race	62.8%	
" " — U.S. Congress	61.7%	
" " — President	52.6%	
Literature distribution area coverage	54.6%	Community-wide
" " door to door	39.9%	
" " both methods	40.4%	Both mail and in-person
Decreasing reliance upon party comm's	39.5%	2nd of major trends affecting... (see next page)
Little or no SC support	32.4%	"SC" = "State Committee"
Increasing difficulty of mobilizing volunteers	67.6%	Only 14 missing responses
Increasing reliance upon...media	31.4%	Non-print media
Small or decreasing supply of materials	19.5%	Lit. & other materials to distribute

distribution capacity" via e-mail, web page or list server. 38% have e-mail alone. These percentages have undoubtedly increased significantly since the survey was completed. Some local Committees [e.g. Burlington (VT) GOP, New Britain (CT) Democrats, Yolo Country (CA) Republicans] have sophisticated web pages with multi-media features. Prizes akin to "Grammies" or other media awards are already being given for the best political web pages. See Chapter 9 for more on the impact of the 'Net and 'Web.

Political Campaign Activity

The responses regarding committee roles in political campaigns largely mirror and reinforce those just noted for "Lit.Distribution." The lowest activity scores are found for both door-to-door activity and local campaigns, the highest, for lit. distribution and state campaigns. It is remarkable, though, how low all scores are for most Committees relative to the maximum achievable. That for "all campaign activity" is 67 out of a maximum possible of 180.

Table 7 LPPC Political Campaign Activity		
DATA LABEL	DATA ITEM	NOTES
Score - all campaign activity	67 (median)	#MV's=46. Max.possible =180
" - door-to-door activity	6 "	" " 3. Max.possible = 45
" - lit.distribution "	26 "	" " 3. Max.possible = 45
" - calling "	23 "	" " 3. Max.possible = 45
" - fund raising "	17 "	" " 3. Max.possible = 45
" - local campaigns "	20.0% (median pct. of maximum score of 60)	" " 3. County campaign roles' activities included.
" - state campaigns "	50.0% (median pct. of maximum score of 52)	" " 3. Gubernatorial campaign roles' activities included.
" - federal campaigns "	39.7% (median pct. of maximum score of 68)	" " 3. Presidential campaign roles' activities included.
" - presidential "		
Door-to-door score pct. of total	11.3% (median)	Maximum is 56.3%
Calling score pct. of total	29.6% "	#MV's = 57.
Fund raising score pct. of total	25.0% "	" " ".
Lit. distribution score pct. of total	29.5% "	" " ".

LPCC's should devote some of all activities to partisan campaigns for their party at all levels. Percentage-wise, they are devoting only 37%. Traditionally, party organizations at all levels urged voters to "vote the ticket."[8] To divide was not to conquer.

To repeat: the prime role of LPPCs is to help their parties win elections; thus, their low campaign activity scores are key indicators of the lesser role of local party committees in electoral politics. So it should hardly be surprising that 39.5% of Committee chairs reported "decreasing reliance upon party committees by candidates or campaigns."

Involvement with Public Issues

Table 8 distills LPPC Chairs' responses on another important area of activity, at least in principle – that of "issues." These are more encouraging in line with the old saying that "If you don't start with high expectations, you won't be disappointed." Only about 37% of respondents indicate that their committees are "NOT involved with issues in any way outside of elections and campaigns." Less than one-third admit that "Public issues (are) not a traditional area of Committee concern…" Only about one quarter believe that there is "Lack of interest in public issues" among either committee members or among voters.

The stat's in Table 8 suggest two major conclusions: (1) Chairs and members of LPPCs are interested in issues, but (2) Committees are not taking advantage of opportunities to facilitate public discussion of issues. Only a minority of survey respondents overall (32.6%) say issues are "of interest

Table 8		
Committee Involvement with Public Issues		
DATA LABEL	DATA ITEM	NOTES
NOT involved with issues	36.8%	Other than elections. #MV's=8.
Forums or mtgs.on issues	41.1%	Sponsorship or participation in
Discussions during Comm.mtgs.	60.5%	
Collaboration with other CBO's	29.5%	On shared concerns over issues
Lack encouragement for att'n to issues	22.7%	One of "factors affecting"; #MVs=17
Of interest only during elections	32.6%	
Lack of interest among voters	23.3%	Interest in public issues
Issues not a traditional concern	32.6%	Concern of Committee
Lack of interest among members	25.4%	
Dominance of TV & media	21.0%	With respect to issues coverage
Frequency of work with CBO's	50.0%	To pursue political &...concerns

only during elections." This is consistent with what we observed earlier – the similar minority that report that their Committees are "NOT involved with issues in any way outside of elections or campaigns." Actually, these results are somewhat surprising in light of the fact that LPPCs are not set up to pursue "issues." The author's own experience with local committees in both parties would imply that, unless the LPPC has a program chairman who likes to invite outside speakers or organize Committee programs around some issues, they are unlikely to be the topics of discussion or deliberation in Committee meetings. Yet, the survey stat's suggest otherwise: about three-fifths (60.7%) of the respondents indicated that there is "discussion of issues during Committee meetings," while over two-fifths sponsor or participate in forums in which issues are discussed or debated.

One-half of responding Committees report that they "work with other CBO's…to pursue political or public-issue-oriented concerns…" either "Frequently" or "Sometimes." "Collaboration" with CBO's over issues is both a stronger form of "work with" and one of several "ways," so the percentage marking this option is much less than half. This represents a largely unexploited opportunity for LPPC's. Joining with other groups to explore issues could help to increase LPPC membership. This represents an opportunity that is also "unexploited" from the CBO side. We noted in Chapter 1 that various programs that attempt to "build civic society" by promoting "deliberation" over issues tend to ignore or overlook LPPCs even while they are searching local political landscapes for "citizens associations and organizations" and the "nodes" of "civic networks."[9]

Two other survey questions attempted to find whether Committees take advantage of opportunities to pursue issues other than forums or discussions; namely:

- preparation or distribution of *white papers* or other issue-oriented materials to inform the public…
- sponsorship of, or participation in, media events or features focused on issues.

We found only a very small minority of respondents reporting the exercise of either option – 15% and 20%, respectively.

Among "factors affecting Committee involvement with public issues," it may be surprising to find that only 1/5 of responding Chairs report "Dominance of TV and other media with respect to issues coverage" to be a factor. Do any make use of public access TV channels? That question was not asked.

State Committee Support

LPPCs are the lowest layer in a three-layer cake of party committees—local, state, and national; thus, it is important to know to what extent the locals get support from the next higher tier, their State Committee. Table 9 shows what can be learned from many survey questions that bear on the LPPC relationship. The overall conclusion from the statistics is that local committees are receiving too little support from their state counterparts. In answer to the question: Is SC support for LPPCs adequate? Sixty-Four and a half percent (64.5%) answered "NO." The highest positive statistic is 77.5% "YES" responses to the question: (Is there) "Occasional attendance at your Committee's meetings by State Committee members?"[10] The median frequency of interaction between LPCC Chairs and the SC is 4 times per year, but the trend of this is increasing for only 31%.

The balance of SC support as between "in kind" and "monetary" is overwhelmingly in favor of the former. Only about 15% receive any "Money support" from their SC and, of these, only 5% report that such support amounts to more than 10% of Committee budgets. Little or none of the so-called "soft money" of ill repute in the campaign finance reform debate (see Chapter 9) has been finding its way down to the local level. This is ironic, for the ostensible purpose of soft money is to finance party building activities. What better use of soft money proceeds than building local party capacity?

A similar 5% report monies going the other way – from LPPCs to SCs. An example of how this reverse flow might come about arose when the Gloucester (MA) Republican City Committee (GRCC) was discussing a new set of bylaws. The SC liason in attendance produced a model set of local Committee bylaws from the the SC. This had provisions that called upon the SC to designate the Chairman of the GRCC Finance Committee and for the GRCC to help raise money for the SC! As a self-governing entity, we at least managed to squelch the designation provision.

Table 9 also reveals the percentages of chairs who report that their Committees receive various kinds of in-kind assistance. There is a clear break between the kinds receiving high marks and low. The highest percentages, ranging from 56% to 36%, are found for Training, Campaign lit. & materials, Computer files and printouts, and Data (polling, demographic). The lowest percentages, ranging 7-17%, are those for Volunteers to supplement your Committees own, Other, Legal assistance, and Political consultants' assistance. Thus, the forms of in-kind help that are less provided or less used are the more labor-intensive or sophisticated services.

The "training" category may be a composite such that the 56% utilization is a somewhat misleading indication of the kind of training that would be directly beneficial to LPPCs. Most SCs sponsor a "campaign school" or equivalent that provides training to candidates, only a minority of whom may be active Committee members.[11] Such could prove to be useful to members but the focus is on winning campaign techniques for candidates, not on the history, roles, responsibilities, functions, and methods of LPPCs. There is very little training for LPCC members or potential members that could be characterized as party "capacity building" training for LPPCs. "Campaign school"-type training sometimes also carries a fee; it's not usually for free usually.[12]

Table 9		
State Committee (SC) Support of Local Committees		
DATA LABEL	DATA ITEM	NOTES
SC support for LPCC's adequate?	64.5% NO	#MV's=16. "SC"=State Comm.
SC member attendance at LPPC meetings?	77.5% YES,	#MV's=78.
Frequency of interaction	4 times per year (median)	#MV's=30. Once a month for 1/4
Trend in frequency of interaction	Increasing for 31.2%.	#MV's=44.
Money support from SC	15.4%	#MV's=3. Among "kinds of support" checked off.
Proportion of budgets from SC	0.0 % (median); only 5%>10%.	Average=2.6%. #MV's=20.
Trend in budget support from SC	6.8% increasing; 20.5% declining	#MV's=126.
Trend in overall support of LPPCs from all sources	27.6% increasing; 29.7% down.	#MV's=14.
Changes in overall support due to SC?	33.1% YES	#MV's=69.
Lack of support from SC as a factor in decline of people's PP	21.1% rank this factor 1-4.	12% rank it #1 or 2. #MV's=5. "PP" = "Political Participation"
More SC support cited as factor "to revitalize" LPPC's.	27.2% rank this factor 1-4.	12% rank it #1 or 2. #MV's=5.
SC in kind support - materials	51.3%	#MV's=4.
" " " " - training	56.4%	" " "
" " " " - computer	42.6%	" " "
" " " " - data	36.4%	" " "
" " " " - legal	16.9%	" " "
" " " " - consultants	17.4%	" " "
" " " " - volunteers	7.7%	" " "
" " " " - other	10.8%	" " "
SC campaign support: LOCAL	42.0%	MV's=10
> Training	23.6%	" " "
> Computer files & P.O.'s	16.7%	" " "
> Literature & Materials	12.8%	" " "
> Monetary	5.3%	" " "

	Table 9 (continued)	
	State Committee Support of Local Committees	
DATA LABEL	DATA ITEM	NOTES
SC campaign support: COUNTY	40.4%	MV's = 10
> Training	25.0%	" " "
> Computer files & P.O.'s	19.1%	" " "
> Literature & Materials	15.4%	" " "
> Monetary	5.9%	" " "
SC campaign support: STATE LEGISLATIVE	60.6%	" " "
> Training	34.7%	" " "
> Computer files & P.O.'s	32.3%	" " "
> Literature & Materials	37.1%	" " "
> Monetary	16.9%	" " "
SC campaign support: STATE GOVERNOR	59.0%	" " "
> Training	23.9%	" " "
> Computer files & P.O.'s	30.7%	" " "
> Literature & Materials	44.0%	" " "
> Monetary	6.4%	" " "
$ contributions from LPPC to SC	5.1%	#MV's=8.

This brings to mind the type of civics training for adults that many did not get in school and that they probably could not find in school today even if they were school-age. This type of training hardly exists at all. Today, where – anywhere and anyhow — are there "lycea" and political education training courses for the general public like those that sprang up over 100 years ago during the last great transformation?

The percentages of responding Committees that have received SC help with campaigns vary in ways like those we observed earlier for Committees' campaign activities. "SC campaign support: STATE" reported is highest at about 60%, followed by COUNTY and LOCAL at 40-42%. The gradations of support received by type of support also fall into place below these overall percentages in the way indicated earlier, as can be seen in Table 9.

The question not yet asked is what to make of the Table 9 stat's? It is a bit of a 'chicken and egg' sort of question. Is LPPC Chairs' felt lack of SC support really a reflection of actual lack of such support or is it a reflection of LPPC's failure to take sufficient advantage of the support made available? And if Chairs are not taking advantage of the support that exists, what incentive do SC's have to expand the quantity or quality of their support? There is ample scope for the latter. It's by no means clear that SCs see their

LPPCs as "customers" or SC assistance as "demand driven." It appears to be more the case that SCs assume that whatever support they can provide is what's wanted or needed. This is a poor assumption for any organization to make.

SC attendance at LPCC meetings, for example: Is the SC member in attendance there to bring SC influence to bear on the LPCC, or to offer support and report LPCC member views back to the SC? And if an SC member is running for office, is he or she there just to blow his or her own horn? How often do SC members report to the SC what they learn from their LPCC attendance? To what extent is any SC a "learning system" that both learns from and assists those "laboring in the vineyards" at the grassroots? Unfortunately, our survey does not help to answer these questions. Some of our interviews, however, reflected upon SC roles in Chapter 4.

The biggest shortfall is on the side of money rather than in-kind assistance. It is both ironic and indicative of the current state of politics in the U.S.of A. that local political committees are typically starved of funds even though the public-at-large views politics as driven by money, especially "big money" or "soft money." Obviously, the concept of general revenue sharing never found its way into the political party arena. SCs could and should provide far more financial assistance. There are challenging ways to do so without undermining or substituting for local fundraising (see Table 10).

Fundraising and Budgets

Table 10 actually highlights just how financially starved LPCCs tend to be even though the survey did not ask for dollar amounts of LPCC budgets. The indications are more indirect, that is, the lack of regular, dependable sources of income. A traditional, tried and true way of Committee fundraising has been an annual dinner. But we noted earlier that only half of responding Chairs report having such events. The median earnings from these, as a percent of Committees' total annual budgets, is only 15%, with only 30% on a rising trend. A median 25% of annual budgets comes from donations, not a stable source, while what might be a stable source – dues – is represented by a median goose-egg, 0% (zero percent). Only one quarter of respondents report dues accounting for more than 20% of their Committees' budgets. The "zero" median is also found for "percent budget from State Committee" (no surprise here), "Sales of goods and services" (remember yard sales, tag sales and garage sales, for example?), and "other sources." The average contribution from SCs is only 2.6% of LPPC budgets and from "Sales…" only 5.3%. The difference between these lies in their trends. The percentage of those who say that the proportion of their Committee's budget from SC is falling exceeds the percentage who say it is "rising" by nearly 14 points. The trend response difference for "proportion of budget from sales" is 12 points toward "rising," as highlighted in Table 11, on Trends).

Only 37% of respondents report using "Membership dues" as a major fundraising (FR) "method." This low percentage may be due partly to some states' legal constraints. Ticket sales for dinners, fundraisers, and other events are the most important method, reported by 59% of survey respondents. "Direct mail" is employed as a FR tool by 46% but this is known to be a low return method. "Sales…" are carried out to raise money by nearly 26% but they take quite a bit of effort to organize. Some of the methods are used to advantage in combination, e.g., selling donated goods and "50/50" tickets at an event for which tickets have already been sold to the attendees. Nevertheless, it is clear from the survey results overall that fundraising is a major challenge for all but the largest, most influential county (not strictly local) committees. A good fundraiser often serves other purposes besides just "FR." The challenge is worthy, but LPPCs could use some help.

Table 10 Committee Fundraising (CF) and Budgets		
DATA LABEL	DATA ITEM	TRENDS / NOTES
% budget from dinner or events	15% (median)	30% rising / #MV's=30
% " " donations	25% "	27% " / " " "
% " " dues	0% " (1/4 > 20%)	26% " / " " "
% " " sales	0% "	17% " / " " "
% " " State Commitee	0% " (average=2.6%)	7% " / " " "
% " " other sources	0% "	/ " " "
FR for contributions to candidates	74.5%	FR=FundRaising / #MVs= 10
" " " " gd. causes	24.5%	For good causes in the community
" " " " SC	5.1%	/ #MVs=8
FR method - Ticket sales	58.9%	/ #MVs=9
" " - Direct mail	46.3%	" " " "
" " - Appeals via media	7.4%	" " " "
" " - Membership dues	37.4%	" " " "
" " - Sales	25.8%	" " " "

Table 11 Committee Trends		
DATA LABEL	DATA ITEM	NOTES
No.of Committee slots authorized	26.5% rising	18.1% declining / #MV's=44
Typical attendance at meetings	27.7% rising	18.6% falling / #MV's=11
Pct.of members actively involved	25.7% rising	19.1% falling / #MV's=26
Committee voter registr'n efforts	16.3% rising	17.9% decreasing / #MV's=15
No.of new voters registered	19.5% rising	7.7% falling / #MV's=30
Proportion of budget from SC	6.8% rising	20.5% falling / #MV's=126
Proportion of budget from events	30.0% rising	7.0% declining / #MV's=99
Proportion of budget: donations	27.4% rising	11.1% " / #MV's=117
" " " from dues	25.7% rising	7.1% " / #MV's=129
" " " " sales	16.7% rising	4.8% " / #MV's=157
Frequency of interaction with SC	31.2% rising	11.0% falling / #MV's=45
Overall support for Committee	27.6% rising	29.7% falling / #MV's=14

Trends

Some topical references have been made to trends along the way, but Table 11 highlights responses to questions on trends in one place. More interesting than the percentages saying "rising" or "falling" are their differences. These differences are significantly positive (significantly more ups than downs) for:

- Number of Committee slots authorized;
- Typical attendance at meetings;
- Number of new voters registered (even if Committees cannot take much credit);
- Proportion of budget from events;
- Proportion of budget from donations;
- Proportion of budget from dues;
- Proportion of budget from sales; and
- Frequency of interaction with SC.

As indicated earlier, the differences are significantly negative for only one indicator: "Proportion of budget from SC." Thus, if we were to balance statistical pluses vs. minus, the prospects for LPPCs would appear to be sanguine. If only the weight of other evidence, plus the views of those "laboring in the vineyards" who were interviewed for this book, would agree;

Table 12
Major Reasons for Declines in People's Political Participation

REASON	TOP FOUR	RANK #1	RANK #2	RANK #3	NOTES
Increasing.domination by political pro's	45.1%	13.5%	8.8%	11.4%	#MV's=5
Women in workforce	30.6%	10.6%	7.8%	4.1%	" " "
Working longer hours	56.5%	19.2%	10.9%	13.5%	" " "
Politics increasingly money & media driven	74.6%	33.2%	16.6%	15.0%	" " "
People increasingly apathetic or cynical	85.5%	48.7%	17.6%	7.8%	" " "
Change in attitude toward parties	48.7%	20.7%	9.3%	8.8%	" " "
TV	32.0%	7.7%	5.7%	5.7%	" " "
Lack of materials or interest from candidates	14.2%	5.1%	3.0%	1.5%	" " "
Other	13.2%	5.1%	2.0%	1.5%	" " "

if only LPPC Chairs were more sanguine on the prospects for "getting people involved."

Reasons for Declines in People's Political Participation

Beginning with the responses shown in Table 12 and the table below, we can see just how un-sanguine they are from the standpoint of political participation. By far the most "winning" responses, ironically, the best indicators of how we all lose through our non-participation, are those of apathy and cynicism. Specifically, over...

- 85% of respondents reported that "People (are) increasingly apathetic or cynical" is a "Major Reason" for "Declines in People's Political Participation" (Table 12) and ...
- 87% marked "Apathy and cynicism" as one of the "Main Barriers and Constraints to People Getting Involved Politically" (Table 13).

Nearly one-half of the respondents ranked these #1, nearly 18%, #2. Thus, a significant majority ranked "apathy and cynicism" first or second as a major reason for declines in people's political participation.

Opinions on "Getting People Involved"

Scores were computed to identify, summarize, and highlight which responses in Tables 12-15 were most important. A score can be computed for each item in each table based on their rankings, simply by multiplying each rank by the number of respondents who assigned that ranking, then adding the products. The top ten results of this scoring are shown below in rank order of their scores.

Questionnaire Rank Item	Rank Score
1. People increasingly apathetic or cynical / apathy and cynicism	1066
2. Exciting political campaigns	519
3. Neighbor-to-neighbor outreach and recruitment	496
4. Charismatic political leaders	480
5. Change in attitudes towards politics overall	455
6. Politics increasingly money and media driven	432
7. Campaigns increasingly dependent upon money rather than people	330
8. People working longer hours	292
9. More and better political leadership	271
10. Changes in attitudes toward parties	270

As is obvious from the last two, the ranked list mixes responses that represent answers to different questions. The interested reader should refer to Tables 12-15 to see which items are drawn from which section of the questionnaire. The common denominator is that the questions all revolved around the theme of "Opinions on Getting People Involved." Statistically, some common denominator is suggested by significant correlations among several of the responses. Many of those, for example, who ranked apathy and cynicism high also believed that politics is driven by money and media (#7) and that campaigns are increasingly dependent upon money (#8). Does this mean that apathy and cynicism are caused by perceptions of politics being a money game? Perhaps, but we cannot say so on the basis of the survey alone. See what those interviewed for this book have to say, too, in Chapter 4. Other significant correlations are noted further on.

Barriers and Constraints to People Getting Involved Politically

The survey results help us to assess the perceived importance of other barriers and constraints to political participation that had been identified earlier through published sources. These include, as shown in Table 13, the time factors attributable to people's increasingly demanding work lives, the fact that "campaigns (are) increasingly run by pro's," and, to some, the greater attractiveness of other civic or communitiy activities. TV, the factor to which Putnam (2000) assigns great importance in his study of the deterioration of public life,[13] appears as a rather minor factor here, with a score of only 101. Not surprisingly, the responses that "campaigns (are) increasingly run by pro's" are correlated with those to the "apathy" and "money" questions. Responses to the "time" and "working life" questions are also correlated. Correlated means that significant portions of respondents assign similar ranks in their answers to both questions.

Table 13					
Main Barriers and Constraints to People Getting Involved Politically					
BARRIERS & CONSTRAINTS	TOP FOUR	RANK #1	RANK #2	RANK #3	NOTES
Working life demands	77.4%	24.6%	25.6%	14.9%	#MV's=3
Two full-time job families	46.2%	10.3%	10.8%	15.4%	" ""
TV	26.7%	2.1%	6.2%	6.7%	" ""
Apathy & Cynicism	87.2%	47.2%	15.4%	13.3%	" ""
Campaigns incr'ly run by pro's	35.9%	6.7%	9.7%	9.7%	" ""
Campaigns incr'ly dependent upon money rather than people	66.7%	15.4%	18.5%	19.5%	" ""
Greater attractiveness of other civic or community activities	35.4%	2.6%	7.2%	10.3%	" ""
Other					

How to Revitalize Local Political Party Committees

The survey also asked "How to" questions – of ways to get people re-involved in the political process. Table 14 shows the answers that emerged. Notice that the way most frequently checked (by nearly 78% of respondents) is one that calls for a change in attitudes towards politics overall. This is also

Table 14					
How to Revitalize Local Political Party Committees					
WAYS TO REVITALIZE	TOP FOUR	RANK #1	RANK #2	RANK #3	NOTES
More active recruitment	40.9%	13.0%	8.3%	6.2%	#MV's=5
Change in attitudes towards politics overall	77.7%	37.3%	16.6%	10.9%	" ""
Change in attitudes towards party	49.7%	8.8%	16.6%	15.0%	" ""
Better candidates	47.7%	13.5%	13.5%	7.8%	" ""
More & better leadership	56.5%	13.5%	13.0%	17.6%	" ""
More attention to issues	32.6%	3.1%	8.8%	11.4%	" ""
Better civic education	35.2%	6.7%	8.3%	7.3%	" ""
Changes in nature of American politics	28.5%	5.7%	5.2%	5.2%	" ""
Other	7.2%				" ""

Table 15					
What Works to Get People Involved					
WHAT WORKS	TOP FOUR	RANK #1	RANK #2	RANK #3	NOTES
Neighbor-to-neighbor outreach	90.2%	29.5%	22.3%	31.6%°	#MV's=5
Exciting political campaigns	88.6%	32.1%	34.7%°	14.5%	" " "
Charismatic political leaders	83.9%	33.2%	21.8%	21.8%	" " "
Non-political leadership	37.3%	5.2%	6.2%	9.3%	" " "
City Hall support	30.3%				" " "
Other	10.8%				" " "

the one that the greatest proportion (37%) ranked first. It points to the possibility of a constructive role for the media — to counteract their leading negative role in aggravating the "spirals of cynicism" and "vicious circles" noted elsewhere in this book (Chapter 8).

The second of the ways most checked (by nearly 57%) was "more and better political leadership by elected officials." This was followed by "Change in attitudes toward party" (50%) and "Better candidates" (48%). Such responses reinforce observations we have seen from other sources, such as the decline in political parties and the feelings of many voters that they are too often faced with the lesser of two evils to choose when they enter their voting booths.

As for leadership, the thirst for this is so apparent in so many ways that it is worrisome, simply because people are so easily seduced by the charms of charismatic types who talk like leaders. One can see this even in the responses of politically sophisticated people, LPPC Chairs, shown below in Table 15. Eighty-four percent (84%) of them marked "Charismatic political leaders" as one of six options of "What Works to Get People Involved." This option, moreover, was more likely to be ranked #1 than the others. Given this book's focus on grassroots politics, however, it is nice to see that "Neighbor-to-neighbor outreach" was the option marked by most (90%), even though respondents were less likely to select it as either their first or second choice. The option most frequently ranked either #1 or #2 as a way to get people involved was "Exciting political campaigns."

How do the opinions on these "Getting People Involved" questions vary among LPPC Chairs, according to differences in their major characteristics, such as political party affiliation, sex, age, and education? Are we likely to find significantly different responses between Democrats and Republicans, men and women, young and old, or well- and less-well educated? Let's look at differences by party to begin to find some answers.

Democrats versus Republicans

First, we can see that there are some significant major party differences in the responses regarding community involvement of Committees and their members. Democratic Chairs were more likely than their Republican counterparts to report that their Committees "work with (other) community-based organizations" (CBOs), 58% v. 46%, respectively. They also tended to report "contributions to good causes" in greater frequency (30% v. 20%). Yet, Republican respondents were about as likely as Democratic to mark "collaboration with CBOs" (31% v. 29%).

Republican respondents are scarcely more likely to be active in a church but significantly greater proportions of them reported that they are active in a civic association or club (75% v. 61%). Which are more likely to be members of local business organizations? No surprise here! – Republicans, with 86%, versus 71% for Democratic Chairs. The incidence of answers to the question of membership in "social service or health-related organizations" may appear to be similarly obvious. And it is, only in reverse. Democratic respondents are far more likely to be members of such organizations – 75% to 55%. The party differences that are statistically significant are denoted by asterisks (**).[14]

Overall, Democratic Chairs are more inclined to work with their non-political counterparts on issues, but the median number of community organizational involvements reported for Committee members is the same (5). In this age of "bowling alone" and documented "civic disengagement," this appears to be a relatively high number.[15] What is remarkable in the stat's of Table 16 is the evidence of considerable engagement in the life of communities among members of both parties, as well as the long term nature of the involvement. The chairs and members of local political party committees are highly involved in the public life of their communities in many ways, not only

Table 16 Community Involvement of Committee Chairs and their Members			
COMMUNITY INVOLVEMENT INDICATOR	OVERALL SAMPLE STATISTICS (FROM TABLE 2)	DEMOCRATS	REPUBLICANS
Extent Committee works with CBO's	50 % "sometimes"	57.6%	46.1%
No. of member CBO involvements	5 (median)	5 (median)	5 (median)
Local business organization memberships	80.5%	71.0% (**)	85.5% (**)
Social service " "	63.1%	75.4% (**)	54.7% (**)
Church/religious " "	89.7%	89.9%	88.9%
Fraternal org'n or sisterhood "	51.3%	46.4% (**)	51.3% (**)

l##

Table 16 (continued)
Community Involvement of Committee Chairs and their Members

COMMUNITY INVOLVEMENT INDICATOR	OVERALL SAMPLE STATISTICS (FROM TABLE 2)	DEMOCRATS	REPUBLICANS
Veterans organizations' memberships	61.0%	58.0%	61.5%
Other politically-related "	42.6%	56.5% (**)	35.0% (**)
Civic associations "	63.6%	65.2%	60.7%
Arts or cultural organization "	50.3%	56.5% (**)	43.6% (**)
Sports "	45.1%	47.8% (**)	40.2% (**)
Attractiveness of non-political community activity	35.2%	31.9% (*)	36.4% (*)
Collaboration with CBO's	29.3%	28.8%	31.0%
Contributions to "good causes"	23.3%	30.3%	20.2%
Years chair resident in community	25.0 years (median)	20.5 (median)	27.0 (median)
Chairs active in churches	66.9%	66.2%	70.3%
" " " frat.or sister society	34.6%	33.9%	34.4%
" " " civic association	69.2%	61.9%	74.6%
" " " sports or coaching	26.7%	24.6%	.27.4%

as participants in politics. In other words, we are not just looking at political junkies; we are seeing community spirits behind the numbers. And one cannot say that "community spirit" is allied with one party any more than the other. Nor is longevity of residence in communities. Relative to the reputed "mobility" of the American population, LPPC Chairs are practically sticks in the mud. Both are deeply rooted in their communities even though Republicans report longer residence in their communities than Democrats.

It is interesting to note a few more of the significant Democratic v. Republican contrasts in some of the community-related stat's. We see that Republican Committee members are slightly more inclined to join fraternal organizations or sisterhoods; the converse is the case with respect to "other politically-related" organizations, "arts or cultural-related" or "sports" organizations, for which the percentages are higher for Democrats. Overall, however, non-political "civic or community activities" are reported as having "greater attractiveness" for Republicans, perhaps thereby amounting to one of the "main barriers and constraints" to their "getting involved politically." Republican Chairs also report a greater tendency to be "active" in a "political club or civic association other than (their) party Committee." These statistics are not contradictory since they represent answers to very different questions.

Table 17

Extent to Which Local Political Party Committees (LPPCs) are Active

EXTENT TO WHICH LPPC IS ACTIVE	OVERALL SAMPLE STAT'S (FROM TABLE 3)	DEMOCRATS	REPUBLICANS
Committee slots filled	89.9% (median)	86.7% (median)	90.3% (median)
Members actively involved	50.0% "	50.0% "	50.0% "
Attendance at meetings	57.1% "	58.2% "	53.5% "
Competition for Committee slots	21.8% (=1)	24.3%	19.5%
Competition for officer positions	30.5% (=1)	33.8%	28.4%
Efforts to recruit new members	79.8% (=1)	76.8%	82.6%
Recruiting candidates - St. & Local - Always or often	87.7.3% 41.5%	88.6% 36.2% (**)	86.9% 43.6% (**)
Annual dinner?	51.3%	52.9%	51.7%
Forums - Issue Forums - Candidate	40.8% 50.0%	48.5% (**) 49.2%	38.8% (**) 51.7%
NON-involvement with public issues outside of elections	36.6%	39.4% (**)	31.9% (**)

Are there any significant contrasts in survey responses by party regarding the vitality of local party Committees – the extent to which they are "active" or "inactive?" By and large, the answer is 'no' but for a few items, marked by asterisks in the table below. A significantly greater proportion of Republican LPPC Chairs indicate that they are involved in candidate recruitment "always or often." Significantly higher percentages of Democratic Chairs report that their Committees both hold issue forums and yet are not involved with public issues. These results seem to contradict each other, and would, but for the tag line attached to the latter question, omitted because of space limitations in the Table. The full text of the response option reads: "NOT involved with issues in any way outside of elections or campaigns." Thus, the responses reported in the last two rows of Table 17 may not be inconsistent if Democratic Committee participation in, or sponsorship of, issue forums takes place only during election seasons, which is likely, perhaps in conjunction with candidate forums. More specific LPPC contrasts on the issues-involvement issue are shown below in Table 18.

Table 17 showed that both parties are more likely to be involved with "candidate" forums than "issue" forums, but we noted that the latter are reported by a higher percentage of Democrats than Republicans. It's likely

| | | Table 18 | |
| | Committee Involvement with Public Issues | | |
COMMITTEE INVOLVEMENT WITH PUBLIC ISSUES	OVERALL SAMPLE STAT'S (FROM TABLE 8)	DEMOCRATS	REPUBLICANS
NOT involved with issues	36.8%	39.4% (°°)	31.9% (°°)
Forums or mtgs.on issues	40.8%	48.5% (°°)	38.8% (°°)
Discussions during Comm.mtgs.	60.7%	57.6% (°)	65.5% (°)
Collaboration with other CBO's	29.3%	28.8%	31.0%
Lack encouragement for att'n to	22.7%	25.0%	21.1%
Of interest only during elections	32.6%	26.6% (°°)	36.7% (°°)
Lack of interest among voters	23.2%	21.9%	24.8%
Issues not a traditional concern	32.6%	28.1% (°°)	35.8% (°°)
Lack of interest among members	25.4%	26.6%	24.8%
Dominance of TV & media	21.0%	31.3% (°)	16.5% (°)
Frequency of work with CBO's (sometimes)	50.0%	57.6% (°°)	46.1% (°°)
Prep. &/or distrib'n of "white papers" or other issue materials	14.7%	16.7%	13.8%
Participation in media events focused on issues	20.4%	25.8% (°°)	18.1% (°°)

that respondent Chairs confused the two to some extent. After all, issues are usually discussed in candidate forums.

Other party contrasts are interesting mostly to the extent that they indicate that, relative to the other major party, one of them is taking better advantage of the "unexploited opportunities" cited earlier. No judgement is made (or possible) here as to which party is doing a better job of treating issues at the local level. The survey results shown in Table 18 suggest that Republican LPPCs could be getting more involved with issues' forums, CBOs and media events to help inform the public on issues. Relative to their Republican counterparts, Democratic LPPCs are less likely to discuss issues during Committee meetings—an obvious opportunity for many of them. To a greater extent, however, Republicans tend to respond that issues are "of interest only during election season(s)" and are "not a traditional area of Committee concern or responsibility." Thus, if may be fair to conclude, on balance, that Republican LPPC's face more "unexploited opportunities" in this area even though these are great for both parties.

More specific LPPC contrasts among other types of activity are shown in tables to follow. Voter registration (VR) has always been one of the traditionally most important activities of LPPCs. From this standpoint, the low majority who report mounting VR campaigns (about 58% in both parties) must be viewed as a negative rather than a positive sign of LPPC activity. The percent should be close to 100%. In my experience, VR was not only the most basic but also a catalytic Committee activity. It was always an important beginning—the way of getting to know one's neighbors, their concerns, their families and who in their families was coming of age. It was also a way to find out who was most interested in the political process, so VR became a seedbed for the identification of possible new Committee members or potential candidates for local offices.

VR by LPPC members who enjoy getting to know their neighbors and take their membership responsibility seriously (now mostly a minority of "old school" members) is very much a personal contact sport. It usually starts by members going door-to-door. It is then supplemented by setting up tables in public places, usually in front of supermarkets or within schools, et.al., and/ or "assisting the efforts of others," often the League of Women Voters. The better, stronger LPPCs conduct VR campaigns involving at least two of the "personal contact" approaches at least twice a year.

Earlier, Table 4 indicated that "personal contact" approaches to VR were reported by distinct minorities of local party Chairs. The stat's in Table 19 reveal that Democrats (Ds) are significantly more likely to use such approaches than Republicans (Rs). The latter are slightly more likely to employ "notices or advertising" to inform people where they should go to register to

Table 19			
LPPC Voter Registration Activity			
LPPC VOTER REGISTRATION ACTIVITY	OVERALL SAMPLE STAT'S (FROM TABLE 4)	DEMOCRATS	REPUBLICANS
Voter Registration campaign?	56.9% yes	58.6%	57.6%
Door-to-door	13.9% "	18.5%	12.1%
Notices or advertising	26.1% "	24.6%	27.1%
Tables in public places	33.3% "	38.5%	30.8%
Assisting efforts of others	21.7% "	26.2%	19.6%
In schools or colleges	24.0% "	30.5% (**)	20.4% (**)
Effect of "motor voter" regist'n	20.4% negative	14.1% (**)	23.1% (**)
No. of new voters registered per LPPC member	1.35 (top quarter) 2.75 (average)	1.40 (top quarter) 1.84 (average)	1.43 (top quarter) 3.37 (average)

vote, although the inter-party difference here is not statistically significant.[16] The average and median numbers of people registered, overall and per member, however, is curiously higher for R's than for D's. Why? It's hard to say from the numbers, especially since many respondents did not answer the question, the numbers are obviously drawn from memory instead of records, and they vary across a wide range. The latter fact, however, is due to a small number of dedicated LPPCs who take their VR responsibility seriously. Their high yield VR activities, moreover, probably owe a lot to the efforts of relatively few dedicated Committee volunteers. Politics, like business and other areas of human activity, seems to follow the "80/20" rule: 80% of the effort or productivity is usually due to 20% of the people involved.[17] High yields by relatively few people lead to high averages.

Recall from Table 4 that the survey sample median numbers of people registered to vote by responding LPPCs is zero (0); otherwise known as a great big "goose egg." Even if there was 100% response on this question, the median would probably not increase, since it is very likely that blanks represent zeros. Most Chairs who had taken the trouble to respond to the survey in the first place and who had non-zero numbers to report on this score would be pleased to mark them down. This is a disturbing statistic for such a basic Committee function. It is also surprising because, as indicated earlier, VR is a good source of recruitment of new Committee members and 80% of Chairs responding reported that "there are active, on-going efforts to recruit new members."

One possible reason why aggressive, regular, periodic and concerted VR efforts are now conducted by a minority or bare majority of LPPCs in both parties is that even they may have become affected to some extent by the "free rider" or "freeloader" disease, noted earlier, that affects politics in the US of A generally. One potentially major infecting agent in the VR arena is the national so-called "Motor Voter" law whereby people are automatically registered to vote when they register their automobiles. Thus, there is at least a temptation for LPPCs and others to say (implicitly or otherwise): "Let the Registry of Motor Vehicles do it." From Table 4, however, we already saw that the "Effect of Motor Voter registration on Committee VR efforts" was registered as "NEGATIVE" by only about 21% of respondents (caps as included in survey question). Now, above in Table 19, we see that R's were significantly more prone than D's to report a negative influence (23% v. 14%, respectively).

This difference may be due as much to inter-party differences in "philosophy" as to considered judgements of the impact of Motor Voter. GOP philosophy is prone to be adverse to the intervention of government into areas that are thought to be amenable to individual or local organizational responsibility. It is also easily possible for quick respondents to confuse any increases in VR overall that may be due to Motor Voter, with any that may have been solely attributable to Committee efforts and thus not think of the impact of the law as "negative." Unfortunately, even though there have been several

	Table 20		
	Inter-Party Differences in GOTV Activities		
GOTV ACTIVITIES	OVERALL SAMPLE STAT'S (FROM TABLE 5)	DEMOCRAT	REPUBLICAN
GOTV campaign?	82.1% yes	88.2% (°°)	77.9% (°°)
Campaign headquarters estab.?	55.1% "	56.7%	53.6%
Calling	76.1 % "	77.9%	74.1%
Driving voters to the polls	58.2% "	72.1% (°)	48.1% (°)
Door to door	26.6% "	35.3% (°)	20.4% (°)
Checking at the polls	50.5% "	54.4%	49.1%
Standouts/signs	64.1% "	69.1%	59.3%
Mailings	57.1% "	58.8%	55.6%
Election day volunteers	0.44 (median, per member)	0.59 (median, per member) (°)	0.38 (median, per member) (°)

studies of the law conducted by political scientists, they have not paid attention to the question of whether Motor Voter has, in effect, had a dampening effect on political participation for the sake of voluntary voter registration efforts.

Earlier, we saw that the "Get Out the Vote" (GOTV) function also involves several activities, as shown in Table 20. Table 5 revealed the overall sample survey stat's. These are repeated in Table 20 for ready reference. What are the differences in these between the major parties? The first one we see is that D's are significantly more likely to mount a GOTV campaign than R's. What about specific GOTV activities?

The survey responses of Democratic LPPC Chairs reveal greater proportions of them undertaking GOTV activities than of Republicans across the board, as shown above in Table 20. Several of the differences are statistically quite significant, as the asterisks in parentheses indicate for specific activities including "driving voters to the polls," "door-to-door" canvassing, and "election day volunteers" mobilized per member. If I were a Republican reader, I would find these contrasts quite troubling, for they mean that the Democrats are doing a better job of getting people out to vote for their candidates. In several Congressional districts, for example, Republicans got snookered in '96 because Democratic Party Committees, aided considerably by union activists using the old brand of people-to-people, shoe leather, "beat the street," "knock on doors" and "pull 'em out" politics, accomplished GOTV with a vengeance and succeeded in considerably narrowing the resurgent GOP's '94 "Contract with America" majority.[18] As shown in Chapter 9, however, the tables were turned during the 2002 election. The GOP did a better job getting voters out for their candidates, at least in key contested districts.

Table 21		
Party Differences in "Literature Distribution" Activities		
LITERATURE DISTRIBUTION ACTIVITIES	STATISTICS FOR BOTH MAJOR PARTIES	DEMOCRATS	REPUBLICANS
No. of lit drops before election	3.66 (average) 5 (top quarter)	3.66 (average) 5 (top quarter)	2.58 (average) 3 (top quarter)
Lit. distribution on behalf of both candidates and party	48.9%	44.8%	51.3%
Lit. distribution volunteers (per LPPC member)	0.437 (median)	0.594 (median) (°)	0.381 (median) (°)
Electronic distribution capacity?	78.6% (38.3% for e-mail alone)	80.3%	77.6%
Lit. distrib'n - School Committee	18.7%	17.1%	19.7%
" " - Local Councils	28.3%	32.9%	25.6%
" " - Mayoral race	13.9%	12.9%	14.5%
" " - County campaign	39.0%	37.1%	40.2%
" " - State legislature	65.8%	70.0%	63.2%
" " - Governor's race	62.6%	65.7%	60.7%
" " - U.S. Congress	62.0%	70.0% (°)	57.3% (°)
" " - President	52.9%	62.9% (°)	47.0% (°)
" " coverage community-wide	54.8%	49.3%	58.1%
" " door-to-door	39.9%	46.3%	38.4%
" " both methods	39.1%	41.8%	37.5%
Decreasing reliance upon LPPCs	39.0%	41.5%	37.5%
Little or no SC support	32.8%	49.2% (°)	23.2% (°)
Increasing difficulty of mobilizing vol's	68.4%	63.1%	71.4%
Increasing reliance upon...media	31.1%	27.7%	33.0%
Small or decreasing supply of materials	19.2%	24.6%	16.1%

Another major LPPC activity introduced earlier is "literature distribution." Here, too, some significant inter-party differences fall out from our survey data, as shown in Table 21, above.

The picture for which Table 21 provides the paints can be described as follows:

- Democratic (D) LPPCs are significantly more likely than their Republican (R) counterparts to distribute their political literature for higher level candidacies, especially those for federal government or national offices. While R's, somewhat more so than D's, tend to focus Committee "lit. distribution" efforts on county or local races, the differences are not statistically significant. The percentages for School Committee and Mayoral campaigns are low because many such races are run on a non-partisan basis, as indicated earlier.

- D's tend to do more "lit drops" before elections than R's and rely more on door-to-door distributions, and each of their Committee members is able to mobilize more volunteers to do so, on average.

- Yet D's, significantly more so than R's, complain of "little or no State Committee support", "small or decreasing supply of literature and (campaign) materials to distribute" and "decreasing reliance upon party committees by candidates (and their) campaigns" while R's, more so than D's, remark on the "increasing difficulty of mobilizing enough volunteers" and the "increasing reliance upon non-print media to deliver political messages" as "major trends affecting the(ir) Committee's ability to serve as a distributor of political literature and campaign materials."

My experience is closer to the Democratic Party local Committee experience. I remember distributing political stuff—"literature" (palm cards, brochures, statements on specific issues) and "materials" (buttons, bumper stickers, lawn signs and other political paraphernalia like combs, pencils and whatchamacallits—your imagination's the limit!) primarily door to door. Stuff was also handed out in front of supermarkets or other public places where people tended to congregate. The old-time Democratic Committee chairs—they were and remain my role models—Mary Perone, for example. See or recall Chapter 4.

In those days, many years ago, Mary and I and others would use only targeted mailings once or twice during an election season. Mailings and non-print media weren't the means of choice for lit. distribution. Besides, the local Committee didn't have enough money to do several city- or town-wide mailings, even at the lower bulk-mail postal rates allowed for political purposes. Many readers may not know, moreover, that it often takes people power to take best advantage of the lowest rates. To get the latter, mail must be sorted by carrier route(s). Or it takes money (capital) to substitute for people power (labor)—either to buy mail printing, stuffing, stamping and sorting equipment or to farm stuff out to a mailing firm. TV was out of the question. The Internet did not exist. We'd sometimes help candidates raise money for relatively cheap local newspaper and radio advertising.

Table 22, below, disaggregates the earlier Table 7 to contrast party Committees' direct involvement in partisan political campaigns. Some significant contrasts here reinforce what we noticed earlier; e.g., the greater emphasis that the Democratic Committees place on federal campaigns and "door-to-door" activity. But there's a lot of additional information to be derived from

TABLE 22			
LPPC CAMPAIGN ACTIVITY: DEMOCRATIC/REPUBLICAN PARTY CONTRASTS			
PARTISAN CAMPAIGN ACTIVITY	OVERALL SAMPLE STATISTICS	DEMOCRATS	REPUBLICANS
Score - all campaign activity	67 (median)	75 (median) (°)	61 (median) (°)
" - door-to-door activity	6 (median)	13 (median) (°)	2 (median) (°)
" - lit.distribution "	26 (median)	30 (median)	23 (median)
" - calling "	23 (median)	27 (median) (°°)	19 (median) (°°)
" - fund raising "	17 (median) 28.3 (top quarter)	14 (median) 30 (top quarter)	17 (median) 26 (top quarter)
" - local campaigns "	20.0% (median pct.of maximum score of 60)	20.0% (median) 33.3% (top quarter)	16.7% (median) 33.3% (top quarter)
" - county " "			
" - state campaigns "	50.0% (median pct.of maximum score of 52)	53.8%(median) 88.5% (top quarter) (°)	50.0% (median) 75.0% (top quarter) (°)
" - gubernatorial "			
" - federal campaigns "	39.7% (median pct.of maximum score of 68)	50.0% (median) (°)	35.3% (median) (°)
" - presidential "			
Door-to-door score pct of total	11.3% (median)	19.8% (median) (°)	7.1% (median) (°)
Calling score pct. of total	29.6% (median)	28.3% (median)	30.6% (median)
Fund raising score pct. of total	25.0% (median)	22.0% (median)	25.0% (median)
Lit.distribution score pct. of total	29.5% (median)	28.6% (median)	30.9% (median)

Table 22 worth noting. First, the Democratic (D) Committees that responded to our survey show a significantly greater overall score for "campaign activity." This owes to higher scores with respect to campaigns at all levels and all activities but for "fund-raising," where the Republican score is slightly but not significantly higher. Even here, the top quarter of the D's do better.

Another remarkable pattern noticeable in Table 22 is the low scores and percentages of maximum attainable scores for both parties' LPPCs with respect to all categories of campaign activity but for "state campaigns." This is a another bad sign from the standpoint of a book focused on grassroots political participation. LPPCs of both parties are playing their political roles at levels far below their potential, more so than even their diminished membership levels would imply suggest. The extremely low door-to-door stat's are especially troubling, but also note the other low activity scores and the far-less-than-50% percentages for all four major activity categories at the end of the Table. LPPCs have been left to languish with politicians' and their campaigns' ever-increasing reliance upon electronic media, political consult-ants, political services firms and other political "pro's;" i.e., upon activities based upon money rather than those that rely upon people.

Earlier, we noted LPPC Chair complaints about the low level of support they receive from their parties' State Committees. The issue of support arises most often during political campaign seasons. Where are the handouts, signs, buttons, bumper stickers and the like? Will the State Committee share the costs of our Committee's phone bank or advertising? Are our political rivals in the other party getting more support than we are? Table 23 builds on the earlier Table 9 to help us see specifically where these party differences lie.

The statistics in Table 23, below, provide the State Committee (SC) support details behind a key observation made earlier: Republican (R) LPPCs do more than their Democratic (D) counterparts to support state and local campaigns. SC support is a two-way street. SC staff do not have time to call around all the LPCCs in their states to ask whether the locals want help or need it. They make known what kinds of assistance the SC is prepared to provide.[19] Then it is up to LPPC Chairs to make their requests. Thus, the major finding of Table 23 can be re-phrased: R-Committees are more likely than their D-counterparts to request SC assistance with local and state-level campaigns. This pertains to all types of assistance other than training for county campaigns, for which the difference is statistically insignificant.

Earlier, we noted the single-digits' level of financial support that LPPCs receive from their State Committees. Such low levels of SC monetary support are also found for LPPCs' involvement in campaigns. Table 24 disaggregates the earlier statistics. Median values of "% budget from the SC" are the same for both parties as for the overall sample: zero (0%); however, the average percent for Democratic (D) Committees (4.6%) is nearly four percentage points greater than that for their Republican (R) counterparts (0.8%). Isn't it curious that we should find such results for what is reputed to be the party of the wealthy?

Table 23

Party Contrasts in State Committee (SC) Support of Local Committees

SC SUPPORT OF LOCAL ACTIVITIES	OVERALL SAMPLE STATISTICS	DEMOCRATS	REPUBLICANS
SC support for LPCC's adequate?	64.8% NO	66.7% NO	63.3% NO
SC member attendance at LPPC meetings?	67.5% YES	66.7% YES	68.3% YES
Frequency of interaction	11 times per year (average) 12 (top quarter)	7 times per yr. (av.) 8 (top quarter)	13 times per yr. (av.) 12 (top quarter)
Trend in frequency of interaction	Increasing for 31.4%.	22.6% increasing °°	36.6% increasing °°
Money support from SC	15.4%	17.1%	11.1%
Proportion of budgets from SC	2.6 % (average) only 5%>10%.	4.6% (average) (°) only 6% > 10%	0.8% (average) (°) only 2.8% > 10%
Trend in budget support from SC	6.8% increasing; 20.5% declining	6.9% increasing	5.0% increasing
Trend in overall support of LPPC's from all sources	27.6% increasing 29.7% down.	19.4% increasing (°) 31.3% down	32.7% increasing (°) 27.3% down
Changes in overall support due to SC?	33.3% YES	33.3% YES	34.1% YES
Lack of support from SC as a factor in decline of people's PP	21.2% rank this factor 1-4.	25.7% rank this factor 1-4 (°°)	16.5% rank this factor 1-4 (°°)
More SC support cited as factor "to revitalize" LPPC's.	27.5% rank this factor 1-4.	30.4% rank this factor 1-4	25.0% rank this factor 1-4
SC in kind support - materials	51.0%	54.3%	50.0%
" " " " - training	56.7%	61.4%	54.3%
" " " " - computer	42.8%	34.3% (°°)	45.7% (°°)
" " " " - data	36.6%	38.6%	36.2%
" " " " - legal	17.0%	14.3%	19.8%
" " " " - consultants	17.5%	5.7% (°)	25.9% (°)
" " " " - volunteers	7.7%	10.0%	6.9%
" " " " - other	10.8%	8.6%	12.1%

Table 23 (continued)			
Party Contrasts in State Committee (SC) Support of Local Committees			
SC SUPPORT OF LOCAL ACTIVITIES	OVERALL SAMPLE STATISTICS	DEMOCRATS	REPUBLICANS
SC campaign support: LOCAL	42.0%	34.3% (**)	44.0% (**)
>> Training	23.6%	54.0%	61.5%
>> Computer files & P.O.'s	16.7%	10.5% (*)	46.5% (*)
>> Literature & Materials	12.8%	13.5%	21.0%
>> Monetary	5.3%	4.5%	6.0%
SC campaign support: COUNTY	40.4%	38.8%	40.5%
>> Training	25.0%	52.5%	45.0%
>> Computer files & P.O.'s	19.1%	15.0% (*)	39.0% (*)
>> Literature & Materials	15.4%	19.5%	25.5%
>> Monetary	5.9%	6.0%	9.0%
SC campaign support: STATE LEGIS.	60.6%	59.7% (*)	40.3% (*)
>> Training	34.7%	33.0% (*)	64.5% (*)
>> Computer files & P.O.'s	32.3%	31.5% (*)	60.0% (*)
>> Literature & Materials	37.1%	45.9% (**)	58.5% (**)
>> Monetary	16.9%	6.0%	13.5%
SC Campaign support: STATE GOV.	59.0%	64.2% (**)	54.3% (**)
>> Training	23.9%	25.5% (**)	43.5% (**)
>> Computer files & P.O.'s	30.7%	40.5%	48.0%
>> Literature & Materials	44.0%	51.0% (*)	72.0% (*)
>> Monetary	6.4%	6.0%	10.5%
$contributions from LPPC to SC (mean)	$273	$234	$253

FUNDRAISING & BUDGET ITEMS	OVERALL SAMPLE STATISTICS	DEMOCRATS	REPUBLICANS
	Table 24		
	LPPC Fundraising and Budgets: Party Contrasts		
% budget from dinner or events	15% (median)	27.5% (median) (°)	12.5% (median) (°)
% " " donations	25% "	20.0% " , (°°)	30.0% " (°°)
% " " dues	0% " (1/4 > 20%)	0% (1/4 > 32.5%)	0% (1/4 > 20%)
% " " sales	0% "	0% (avrge=4.6%)	0% (avrge=5.4%)
% " " State Commitee	0% " (average=2.6%)	0% (avrge.=4.6%)	0% (avrge=0.8%)
% " " other sources	0% " (average = ??)	0% (avrge=6.7%)	0% (avrge=2.0%)
FR for contrib'ns to candidates	74.5%	72.7%	75.4%
" " " " gd.causes	23.4%	30.3%	20.2%
" " " " SC	6.4%	6.1%	6.1%
FR method - Ticket sales	59.3%	64.7%	66.7%
" " - Direct mail	45.5%	32.4% (°°)	54.0% (°°)
" " - Appeals via media	7.4%		
" " - Membership dues	37.6%	38.2%	37.2%
" " - Sales	25.9%	26.5%	24.8%

The other major highlights from Table 24 are that:

- The responding D Chairs reported significantly greater Committee budget dependence on earnings from dinners or other events than the R's, but significantly less dependence on donations;

- The R Chairs reported far more use of fundraising via direct mail than the D's; and:

- D Committees are more likely to raise money for "other good causes."

Trends in these and other features of LPPCs are shown below in Table 25. Consistent with what we observed earlier on the basis of the overall sample (via Table 11), the most remarkable feature of this table is that only a small minority of Chairs report "rising" trends for 11 of 12 aspects of Committee activity for which trends were ascertained through the survey. The

Table 25

Party Contrasts in Committee Trends

TRENDS IN....	OVERALL SAMPLE %	DEMOCRATS		REPUBLICANS	
No. of Committee slots authorized	26.6% rising	26.5% rising		26.9% rising	
Typical attendance at meetings	27.8% rising	32.4% "	(**)	24.3% "	(**)
Pct.of members actively involved	25.8% rising	27.3% "		24.8% "	
Committee voter registr'n efforts	16.3% rising	9.0% "	(**)	21.3% "	(**)
No.of new voters registered	19.5% rising	20.0% "		19.8% "	
Proportion of budget from SC	6.8% rising	6.9% "		5.0% "	
Proportion of budget from events	30.0% rising	42.1% "	(**)	22.0% "	(**)
Proportion of budget: donations	27.4% rising	22.9% "		29.2% "	
" " " from dues	25.7% rising	22.6% "		28.9% "	
" " " " sales	16.7% rising	26.7% "	(**)	8.0% "	(**)
Frequency of interaction with SC	31.4% rising	22.6% "	(**)	33.6% "	(**)
Overall support for Committee	27.7% rising	19.4% "	(*)	32.7% "	(*)

only aspect for which the minority is greater than one-third is the "Proportion of budget from events" reported by D Committees. Thus, for the latter, the proportion is not only higher but more likely to be rising relative to R Committees. A larger proportion of D than R Committees' "Proportion of budget from sales" was also reported to be rising, along with "Typical attendance at meetings." Even so, greater percentages of R Committee Chairs reported the latter rising than falling, along with Committee budget proportions for both "events" and "sales."

Other statistically significant contrasts favouring R Committees trends' rising include:

- "Overall support for Committee" (and, for this, too, the percentage of those rising over those falling is significantly greater for the R's).

- "Committee voter registration efforts" (with the ratios of percentages—of those "rising" to those "falling"—also significantly greater from respondent R's); and

- "Frequency of interaction with SC (but the percentages of those rising are greater than percentages of those falling for both parties).

Table 26

Party Contrasts:
Major Reasons for Declines in People's Political Participation

REASON	TOP FOUR		RANKS # 1 & 2	
	DEMOCRATIC	REPUBLICAN	DEMOCRATIC	REPUBLICAN
Increasing.domination by political pro's	42.0%	45.2%	20.5%	22.6%
Women in workforce	24.6%	32.2%	15.9%	18.2%
Working longer hours	57.1%	55.7%	25.8%	26.9%
Politics increasingly money & media driven	75.4%	73.0%	50.7%	51.3%
People increasingly apathetic or cynical	82.6%	87.0%	63.7%	68.7%
Change in attitude toward parties	58.0% (°°)	42.6% (°°)	34.8% (°°)	26.1% (°°)
TV	31.4%	30.2%	15.8%	10.4%
Lack of materials or interest from candidates	14.3%	11.2%	8.5%	6.0%
Other	11.4%	14.7%	8.6%	6.1%

The most remarkable feature of Table 26 is that, but for one item, it shows no significant differences between the major parties in responses as to the "reasons for declines in people's political participation." The exception is "Changes in attitudes towards parties." Democratic chairs were far more prone than their Republican counterparts to rank this reason 1-4, and a significantly higher percentage of them ranked it higher (#1 or #2). Majorities of respondents from both parties believe that the primary reasons for declines in political participation are that "People (are) increasingly apathetic or cynical" and that "Politics (is) increasingly money & media driven." It is interesting to note, however, that these are not strongly correlated even though strong advocates of campaign finance reform appear to believe that they are.

Earlier in this chapter, we also noted a number of "barriers and constraints" to people getting politically involved. Are there any significant differences between D's and R's opinions regarding these? Table 27 shows there are some. Overall, note that the R Chairs who responded to the survey questions on this topic were significantly more prone to see time factors as major barriers and constraints; D's were much more likely to report money as a constraint. "Time" is reflected in "working life demands" and "two full-time job families;" "money," in "campaigns increasingly dependent upon money..." Does this mean that politically active R's have more money than time, and vice-versa for their D counterparts? Maybe, but the survey does not suffice to answer this question. Given responses to other questions reflecting LPPC's relative reliance upon people or money, a very different inference could be made but it would still not be conclusive—that R-leaders at the local level have a greater preference for an "old style" of politics (per Chapter 4) that relies more upon people's donations of time rather than money.

Table 27

Party Contrasts: Main Barriers and Constraints to People Getting Involved Politically

BARRIERS & CONSTRAINTS	TOP FOUR		RANKS # 1 & 2	
	DEMOCRAT	REPUBLICAN	DEMOCRAT	REPUBLICAN
Working life demands	75.4%	80.5%	34.7% (°)	61.9% (°)
Two full-time job families	40.6% (°°)	50.0% (°°)	14.5% (°°)	26.3% (°°)
TV	18.8% (°°)	28.8% (°°)	4.3%	9.3%
Apathy & Cynicism	86.8%	87.3%	61.7%	64.4%
Campaigns increasingly run by pro's	29.4% (°°)	37.3% (°°)	17.7%	13.5%
Campaigns increasingly dependent upon money rather than people	67.6%	64.4%	45.6% (°)	26.3% (°)
Greater attractiveness of other civic or community activities	32.4%	36.4%	16.2% (°°)	5.9% (°°)
Other				

Perhaps even more surprising are the responses regarding the importance attributed to "attractiveness of other civic or community activities" that might be considered competitive with, or alternatives to, political involvement. Here, the D's have it over the R's, 16.2% to 5.9%, although the percentages are small minorities of either group of respondents. This may seem surprising to the extent that one associates Republicans with greater involvement with charitable activities or other good causes. We found earlier, however, that the D-Chairs were more likely to report LPPC contributions to "good causes."

Earlier in this chapter, we were somewhat surprised to find that there was no correlation between responses regarding "apathy and cynicism" and "politics increasingly money…driven" among the "reasons for declines in people's political participation." Under the heading of the question "What are the main barriers and constraints to people getting involved politically?", we have similar options worded somewhat differently. Are there any significant correlations among the responses to these? Yes, there are, but they are puzzling from the D side, while those from R's conform to our intuition.

R Committee Chairs who thought that "campaigns (are) increasingly run by pro's" was a more important "barrier and constraint" also tended to assign higher ranks to "campaigns (are) increasingly dependent upon money rather than people."[20] But D's who also thought the latter to be important were significantly less likely to rank "apathy and cynicism" as a more important "barrier and constraint."[21] This possible connection is not made by R's, while the connection that R's make, noted above, is not made by D's. These contrasts are puzzling since the more liberal, mostly Democratic, advocates of campaign finance reform (CFR) tend to believe that:

- One reason that "campaigns (are) increasingly dependent upon money rather than people" is that "campaigns (are) increasingly run by pro's;" and that...

- CFR will be an antidote to apathy and cynicism by reducing the importance of "big money" in our political process.[22]

How to explain the puzzle? One can only surmise and hope that academic political science will turn to help. Partly because major unions are such big contributors of both time (people power) and money (direct contributions, "issue advocacy" ads, et.al.) to the Democratic Party, local party chairs may be less prone to make positive connections among "pro's," "money" and "apathy." And since R LPPCs are too often dominated by an "old guard" that tend to take money for granted, they may be less likely to make a connection between "money" and "apathy." Of course, this does not imply that local GOP Committees are more people-oriented. Turning to party contrasts in answers to the "How to" and "What works" questions (reflected in Tables 28 and 29) may shed some further light regarding the questions on "Getting People Involved"" that we have confronted thus far.

Table 28 is interesting as much for the lack of differences it reveals as for its contrasts. We see similar (D,R) responses regarding (in rank order of their statistics, from high to low):

1. "Change in attitudes towards politics"
2. "Change in attitudes towards party"
3. "More and better political leadership"
4. "Better civic education"
5. "More attention to public issues"
6. "Changes in nature of American politics"

Table 28				
How to Revitalize Local Political Party Committees				
	TOP FOUR		RANKS # 1 & 2	
WAYS TO REVITALIZE	DEMOCRAT	REPUBLICAN	DEMOCRAT	REPUBLICAN
More active recruitment	48.5% (°°)	36.2% (°°)	26.5%	17.2%
Change in attitudes towards politics	80.9%	75.0%	51.5%	45.2%
Change in attitudes towards party	48.5%	48.3%	25.0%	24.1%
Better candidates	33.3% (°)	55.2% (°)	14.5% (°°)	22.3% (°°)
More & better political leadership	43.5% (°°)	62.9% (°°)	20.2% (°°)	34.5% (°°)
More attention to public issues	37.7%	29.3%	21.7%	21.5%
Better civic education	39.7%	31.9%	13.3%	15.6%
Changes in nature of Amer. politics	29.4%	27.6%	10.3%	10.3%
Other	4.3%	9.5%	2.9%	9.4%

No.1 was by far the most frequent response, to the extent of 27-32 percentage points over no. 2. This reinforces all that has been written thus far as to the negativity of attitudes towards politics being perhaps the most basic factor inhibiting political participation. While attending a business conference, I had a chance to hear and to question a leading member of the White House press corps on this issue. The question asked, which was reinforced by a follow-on question from another attendee, was (here paraphrased): "What responsibility does the media have for such negativity and what do you suggest the media do to help offset it?" The speaker talked around the question. Two other attendees remarked afterwards that he did not answer it.[23] Yet, we will see in Chapter 8 that mass media are largely responsible for the "negativity," and so they should prepare to play a major role in effecting a "Change in attitudes towards politics" if American grassroots political participation is to make a significant rebound.

Below, significant contrasts are apparent (with ">" denoting "percentage responding greater than") with respect to:

- "More active recruitment efforts" (D's > R's);
- "Better or more attractive candidates for (public) office" (R's > D's); and
- "More and better political leadership by elected officials" (R's > D's).

How to interpret these differences? It's anyone's guess. Perhaps they reflect D's greater emphasis on groups and R's focus on individuals. This interpretation is also consistent with the party contrasts we see below in Table 29.

Table 29				
Party Contrasts in "What works to get people involved"				
	TOP FOUR		RANKS # 1 & 2	
WHAT WORKS	DEMOCRAT	REPUBLICAN	DEMOCRAT	REPUBLICAN
Neighbor-to-neighbor outreach	92.6%	88.9%	44.1%	36.8%
Exciting political campaigns	86.8%	88.9%	16.2%	24.7%
Charismatic political leaders	77.9% (**)	88.0% (**)	25.0%	29.0%
Non-political leadership	41.2%	33.3%	29.4%	23.0%
City Hall support	11.8%	9.4%	1.5%	0.9%
Other	30.9%	30.2%	7.3%	12.9%

The contrasts here are analogous to those we observed via Table 28, but only one is statistically significant—"Charismatic political leaders"—not one that is salutary to Republicans, in this writer's view. A charismatic individual is more likely to be indifferent to, or even an influence quite contrary to, the nurture of the kind of grassroots' political process involving more "ordinary" people that is this book's primary concern. Again, here as in some other respects noted earlier, the latter appears to be a greater concern of D than R LPPC Chairs even though the difference here is not (statistically) significant. There is only a 4-7 percentage points' gap in the response rates for "Neighbor-to-neighbor outreach" as a primary way that "works" to "get people involved." Responses on other options are also similar, although it's interesting to note that a higher proportion of D chairs than R's marked "non-political leadership" as a factor of "what works to get people involved."

Responses to Open-ended Questions

Most (52%) of the Committee Chairs who responded to the survey took additional moments of valuable time to write remarks in response to some of the open-ended questions. These provided many of the most interesting and valuable survey replies, especially to the last two questions:

    # 37: What are the best practices of your Committee?, and

    # 38: Remarks or comments on the questions or content of this survey.

Citations of "best practices" are mostly remarkable for their ordinari-ness—and perhaps for how they remind us of just how much is lost to the extent that the neighborly, community-oriented, people-to-people (P2P) activities of grassroots political activity are let to lapse as they are displaced by a politics dominated by media, political pro's, "robo calls," bulk mail and paid campaign staff. What is best about the practices of LPPC's is best revealed by a number of quotes from the open-ended responses. The usual prefix is "We...

- actively solicit friends and neighbors..."
- conduct a door-to-door (face-to-face) survey...to ask about inter-ests in issues and in working with the Town Committee. We identify the interested and ask them to join."
- have personal contact with people on issues and concerns."
- ask people to get involved."
- Stay in touch locally with all people...(&) be involved."
- do door-to-door (DtD) during each election; it gets great results because they know me and respect my position."

The reason why such practices can be counted among the very best, even from no more than the standpoint of straightforward political effectiveness—

of getting people elected to office—is that, as we saw earlier from one of the more "high tech" political activists:, "people are the killer ap." Or, as a survey respondent simply noted: "People will follow their neighbor whom they trust…"

The overall political effectiveness of the P2P/DtD practices is captured by four C-words that crosscut many of the open-ended responses—Communication, Coordination, Cooperation and Community. Local involvement is most potent when there is:

- **Communication:** Frequent, between and among local leaders, LPPC members, voters, friends, and neighbors with respect to Committee goings-on and public issues;

- **Coordination:** Between Committees and campaigns, especially so that LPPC members are working simultaneously for their entire "ticket" during an election season as facilitated, for example, by a central local campaign headquarters.

- **Cooperation:** Not only between Committees and campaigns but between Committees and other community-based organizations, especially with respect to public issues as, for example, via shared sponsorship of public forums on issues.

- **Community:** When LPPC activities are rooted in a local community as an integral part of its social and public life as, for example, via such activities as reported by survey respondents:

  —"Fund raising for the proposed senior center"

  —"Community-building events"

  —"Community involvement"

  —"One-to-one contacts and community involvement"

  —Community "Pride Day"

  —Contributions to "good causes" in the community

  —Provide "scholarships" to local graduates going on to college

  —"Campaign headquarters in town square"

  —"Soup with your officeholders"

  —"Weekly booth at farmers market"

  —"Talks to classes at the high school"

  —"Make political events social events"

  —"Monthly brown bag meetings"

Thus, as one respondent wrote with regard to the question of "how" to involve people in politics: "Community activists need to take charge." There is great merit to this recommendation.[24] Many more of those who count themselves among "community activists" should be involved with the local clubs or committees affiliated with political parties. But the converse of this is at least as important and desirable. LPPC's need to do far more than they are doing to effect outreach and at least three of the "four 4- C's" with their reputedly "non-political" community-based organization (CBO) counterparts. Survey responses clearly indicate that the needs and opportunities run both ways.

The needs and opportunities exist with regard to public issues, especially. LPPC's attention to these is mostly limited to the ways that they surface during the campaign season. Other CBO's tend to be more issue driven. Thus, there is a natural join to be made between "political" and "non-political" CBO's that, if made, would benefit both types of organizations and help to revive people's interest in politics at the same time.

Those LPPC's that have reported stronger orientations towards issues, other CBO's and the community at large reveal the nature of the opportunity noted above. Even if not a majority, many LPPC's report, among the activities that they regularly or normally undertake:

- Writing "Letters to Editor(s)"—two per month
- Publication of a good newsletter
- Taking strong stands on local issues
- Focus on local issues in town
- Placing a monthly question or issue in the local paper
- Forming committees…to include all interested parties (small "p", per "diversity")
- Providing education, talks, and literature on the (political) process and to connect with their (people's) lives.
- Scheduling interesting (issues-related) meeting topics and speakers
- Attendance at all County activities that promote issue awareness
- Creating ex-officio membership opportunities
- Setting up a booth with a theme and a check-off sheet re: issues at the County Fair
- Conducting issue-based campaigns
- Getting involved with people through church and civic venues

One danger of such positive, pro-active responses to public problems diminishing is that local political participation will increasingly come down to what a number of survey respondents and others indicate that it is already becoming—angry reactions to problems unaddressed and unsolved. The written remarks of several respondents are symptomatic:

> People are reluctant to get involved…until they get mad enough. Unless it (some problem or issue) affects them directly, it's not a big deal.

They only get involved if they are directly affected" (by local issues).

Until people's 'comfort zones' are touched, hence causing them to act, we find it difficult to motivate them.

What works to get people involved?—"outrage over single issues"—"specific community issues"—"gut wrenching issue"—"wedge issue."

As for the first three "C's"—"communication, coordination and cooperation"—the weakening of LPPC's and their major roles that we have observed has weakened these while, vice-versa, the weakening of these has diminished LPPC's and their effectiveness. The reciprocal influences spell yet another "vicious circle" affecting our nation's political life. The basic motivator of people getting involved with LPPCs is that membership enables them to participate in the political process in way that they can "make a difference." If the vicious cycle just identified continues, then LPPC's become increasingly less credible or viable vehicles for such enabling and empowering. People then would be even less likely to join—another negative notch marking another "vicious cycle."

The check-off survey responses reported earlier indicate that negative notches have already been marked in many areas. These are reinforced by a number of open-ended observations:

- "I am a county chair because no one else wanted the job."
- "In the past (note the tense), we had good leadership at the Committee level and active volunteerism."
- "The old practices do not seem to work anymore."
- "We (now) pay someone…people want to be paid"
- We offer "financial rewards for GOTV and changes in voter registration."
- "too much work" (being done by too few)
- "Assumptions with regard to declining interest in political activity are correct."

As we saw in the tabulated results, the "greater attractiveness of other (family and, community) activities" was one of the "barriers and constraints" to people getting involved politically. The trouble is that these other activities cannot substitute for political involvement—they do not effect the distribution of power through which political decisions are made that affect whole communities at various levels.

Ironically, open-ended responses from many of those very much involved in the political process—again, the Chairs of LPPC's—provide an indictment of the current state of our political system that is at least as scathing as much of what we hear from the politically alienated. Note, for example, the following remarks:

- "The pervasive influence of the incumbent/lobbyist complex is hurting the development of new political leadership…"
- "National political reporting and actions have alienated people's attitudes towards government and politics"
- "A politician needs to raise from below…and vote on the basis of what the public needs, not needs of big business or large contributors. People are fed up and the press is a big problem, too."
- "I am afraid Big Money has changed American politics. If you are not rich or cannot raise money, you cannot win political office. He or she who spends the most wins."
- "As campaigns get to be more slick and professional, political committees practically ignore the grass roots except to ask them to raise money."
- "The public views all politicians as being motivated by the self-serving interests."
- "This (politics) is the least desired career choice amongst many good potential candidates (who) have the best intentions, only to be demoralized by the press."
- "Everybody is out to protect themselves! Very few are interested in bettering this country if personal sacrifice is involved."
- "Game playing turns me off!…real life concerns take a back seat…"

Clearly, the survey voices speak with more than statistics. It should be no surprise, therefore, that a significant minority of respondents indicated that they would like to see a "change in the nature of American politics."

Conclusion

Important insights on the status of local political party committees (LPPCs)—the main organizational vehicles for grassroots electoral politics—have been derived from a new primary data source—a national survey of LPPC Chairs. We have found that:

- LPPC Chairs are middle-aged and older; their Committees do not appear to be attracting young people as in the past.
- The Chairs and their Committee members are deeply rooted and involved in their communities. They are long-time residents with many years of involvement in their Committees PLUS participation in many other, non-political community activities.
- Significant proportions of Committee memberships appear to be nominal or inactive because statistics representing Committee activity are significantly lower than percentages of membership "slots" filled. Even though overall LPPC activity scores were not

computed, significant percentages of reporting Committees are inactive in traditionally key areas of LPPC endeavor. LPPCs' voter registration and GOTV activities are weak relative to what they can and should be doing in these major areas. A significantly higher percentage of Democratic Committee Chairs (D's) than their Republican counterparts (R's), however, report undertaking GOTV activities, and more of them.

- Door-to-door activities and others involving person-to-person (P2P) outreach and contact are especially weak, reported by only small minorities of Chairs. They are far more likely to be found among D's, however, than among R's.

- Contrary to one of the myths of American democracy, LPPC campaign activity tends to rise with campaign level from local to non-local campaigns. It also increases with the degree of indirection of campaign methods, from personal to impersonal. The former tendency is much more apparent among D's; i.e., R's place more emphasis on local campaigns. Yet D's are more likely to report use of more "personal" methods of campaigning such as door-to-door. Overall, D's show more campaign activity than R's but both parties' LPPC activity scores are low relative to potentials.

- Committees' involvement with public issues is not bad but there is a lot of room for improvement and opportunities to do more that, if exploited, would increase LPPCs relevance and memberships. There are not significant contrasts between parties in this regard.

- State Committees' (SC) support of local Committees is inadequate, especially financial support. The latter is miniscule even among the very small percentage of LPPCs that receive any at all; the extent of such support, moreover, has been trending downward. R's receive more SC support for state and local campaigns than D's.

- LPPCs lack dependable sources of financial support. R's rely more on direct mail and donations for their fundraising; D's rely more on events.

- Net trends are far from being "bullish" overall, but they are more positive for R's than D's with respect to typical attendance at Committee meetings, voter registration activity and overall Committee support.

The ten most important factors affecting people's political involvement and their Committees were reported by nearly 200 respondent LPPC Chairs to be:

Questionnaire Rank Item	Rank Score
1. People increasingly apathetic or cynical	534
2. Apathy and Cynicism	532

Questionnaire Rank Item	Rank Score
3. Exciting political campaigns	519
4. Neighbor-to-neighbor outreach and recruitment	496
5. Charismatic political leaders	480
6. Change in attitudes towards politics overall	455
7. Politics increasingly money and media driven	432
8. Campaigns increasingly dependent upon money rather than people	330
9. People working longer hours	292
10. More and better political leadership	271
Changes in attitudes towards parties	270

Overall, these summary scores reflect a troubling negativity in attitudes toward politics, political parties, campaigns and political participation. These attitudes are repeatedly regurgitated and reinforced, even generated, by most of the media and entertainment industry in ways that threatens to make them intergenerational.[25] For example, the "Cranium Brigade" show at Disney World ends with a punch line spoken by a chicken: "I don't need a brain; I'm going into politics." Thus, we turn to the media in Chapter 8.

As for party contrasts, there are no significant differences in the responses regarding reasons for people's non-involvement, but there are some with respect to barriers and constraints to involvement and how to get people (re)involved. R's are significantly more likely to attribute non-involvement to time factors; D's, to money factors. D's also tend more to report the "attractiveness" of other, non-political activity options as a "barrier." Respondents from both parties are similarly likely to report, and rank highly, the need for a "change in attitudes towards politics overall" before grassroots political participation can be revived and LPPCs can be "revitalized." D's, however, tend somewhat more to see "neighbor-to-neighbor outreach..." as a method that "works to get people involved," while R's place more emphasis on "exciting political campaigns" and "charismatic political leaders." "Where they should go" is usually the town or city clerk's office in town or city hall.

Notes

1 "Entrepreneur" was not a category included on the survey form. Self-employed and business owners were counted under this heading. Note that, in the tables to follow, the total number of survey responses is 199 and the number of missing values (non-responses to various question items) is indicated by "MV's=".

2 See Putnam, Robert (2000), *Bowling Alone: The Collapse and Revival of American Community*. New York: Simon and Shuster. Highlights of Putnam's findings are presented in Chapter 8.

3 Note that the reporting here of Committee member involvement is indirect. Since Chairs were surveyed, the findings here rest on the Chairs' familiarity with their Committee's members.

4 These low numbers need to be seen in context. Massachusetts is basically a one-party state, given the long domination of the state's politics by the Democratic Party. Some Republicans unkindly refer to their state as "The People's Republic of Massachusetts." Would that it were so.

5 See Chapters 4 and 9. Also see Bearse, Peter (1976), "Report of the City Elections Study Panel on Partisan and Nonpartisan Municipal Elections." Trenton, NJ: Trenton Democratic Committee.

6 As reported in private correspondence by Mike Lynch, Director of Government Affairs, ITW: Mayor Daley's last campaign relied much more on media than precinct workers.

7 As reported by some LPPC Chairs in their responses to some of the survey's open-ended questions, plus late summer, 2000 e-mails to the *MASS GOP Digest* on the scarcity of literature from the Bush campaign in Massachusetts. Federal Election Commission (FEC) Commissioner Bradley Smith attributes this to the centralization of campaigns induced by campaign finance regulation. See Smith's address to the Catholic University Law Review Symposium on "Election Law Reform" in Smith (2000). Obviously, notwithstanding then Gov. Cellucci's strong support of Bush, the Bush campaign was not going to expend resources in a state that Gore was certain to win.

8 Note that McCain Feingold and other campaign finance reforms would threaten this traditional practice. See Chapter 9.

9 The quotes are from references to the Kettering Foundation's program on Community Politics and Leadership in the Foundation's periodical *Connections* (June, 2000, p.20 and 21).

10 SC members frequently attended our LPPC meetings in Gloucester, but it was sometimes hard to tell why they were there – to assist, watch over us or blow their own horn.

11 Note, however, the extent to which LPPC's serve as "incubators" of political talent. Significant percentages of their members have run for office and served in office.

12 In my home state, where Republicans are an endangered species, the RSC candidates' school, too, was in danger of disappearing. The fact that it continues owes more to a dedicated individual than to the SC.

13 See Chapter 8.

14 The double asterisks mark significance at the 5 percent level or less; a single asterisk, at less favorable levels. Most of those marked are significant at levels between five and six percent. This means that the chance that there is no association is 5-6 percent.

15. "bowling alone" and "civic disengagement" again refer to Putnam's landmark book.

16. "Where they should go" is usually the town or city clerk's office in town or city hall.

17. Here, I am again writing from experience.

18. See, for example: "The New Machine Politics" by *Washington Post* Editor Sebastian Mallaby (11/9/99) and "Locals make the…campaigns go," in which Lisa Kocian writes, for the *Cambridge* (MA) *Chronicle* edition of 3/1/00: "These (campaign volunteers) aren't the hired guns, spinmeisters or the professional pollsters. They are individuals who are willing to volunteer some or all of their time to try to fire up an increasingly blasé electorate…" So, as one business columnist wrote: "People are the killer ap."

19. As through SC members attending LPPC meetings, for instance, the frequencies of which have also been reported earlier.

20. The rank correlation coefficient is (+)0.429, significant at the 0.01 level (2-tailed statistical test).

21. The rank correlation coefficient here is (-)0.302, significant at the 0.05 level (2-tailed statistical test).

22. The author believes that these statements are justified in light of his extensive reading and work on the CFR issue as a member of the Business Advisory Council of the Campaign Reform Project. The file of relevant writings is very large, and this is not an academic treatise calling for a long list of citations to back up every statement made. See Chapter 9 for more on CFR.

23. Based on remarks by Tom DeFrank, Washington Bureau Chief, *New York Daily News*, at the Annual Conference of the Community Bank League of New England, Orlando, Florida, September 26, 2000. Please note, however: DeFrank acknowledged the popular, critical view of the press, noted that we had seen a "coarsening of political debate" over the past eight years and remarked that some potential candidates may not run because they don't want to be subjected to media scrutiny. He ended his presentation on a pessimistic note regarding "the nature of the (media) game" – "I don't see it getting any better." See Chapter 8 for more on the media.

24. Recall the remarks of Alissa Batson in Chapter 14.

25. These constitute what Mitroff and Bennis labelled "The Unreality Industry" in 1987, a "4th Estate" that Boorstin had indicted as the generator of "pseudo events" as early as 1961. C-Span is an exception. Perhaps that is why most callers into C-Span's call-in news' review programs say: "Thank you for C-Span."

6.

Political Participation: Barriers and Constraints to Increasing It In the Future

As Sennett, Lasch and others have shown (recall Chapter 2), the social and psychological impediments to political participation run deep. Yet, even those who have overcome these, who have decided that they want to participate in political activities, face a number of barriers and constraints. Earlier chapters have noted or alluded to some of these. Here's a more complete checklist. They include:

- Lack of time given a variety of other life, family and workaday demands;
- Lack of any assurance or confidence or reasonable assurance that any commitment of time would be valued or help to "make a difference;"
- Lack of education or understanding as to how our political system works;
- Lack of appreciation of democratic process(es): Too many people have not seen or experienced the significant differences in the quality of life in political jurisdictions within the U.S. or other countries where political participation is low and/or is discouraged.
- Lack of information: not knowing what's going on, whom to call or where to go;
- The growing sense that one needs to be a "professional" or a "career politician" in order to directly participate in the political process;
- Even if able to locate a campaign or political organization, then, after showing up, facing indifference or even hostility from the political hangers on who are often in charge;
- Lack of transparency or simple guidance: not being informed about who's who or guided as to what to do, even after locating a source or center of political activity;
- Risk aversion: fear and uncertainty of getting involved, compounded by all of the above;
- Lack of psychological and other support for any political involvement among family, relatives or friends; more likely, the contrary—discouragement;
- Negative impressions of politics conveyed by the media and reinforced by others;

- An assumption that one needs money to play in the political game(s);
- A growing sense that most of us "ordinary" people don't have a meaningfully positive political role to play any more in the process of electoral politics, only or primarily a negative role through voting, as indicated by the familiar phrase, for the "lesser of two evils;"[1]
- Few, if any, connections between politics and people's everyday concerns, or between politics and the non-political community-based organizations within which many people get are involved;
- Lack of access to, or facility with, the Internet and World-Wide Web, (but this may be rapidly becoming much less of a problem—see Chapter 8);
- Political parties increasingly devoted to serving as money laundries for media-driven campaigns rather than to their traditional roles of enabling person-to-person/door-to-door contacts, mobilizing people around major issues, and aggregating political positions into meaningful party platforms;
- Lack of leadership that speaks to the need for political reform and inspires people to get involved in the political process (with bows in the direction of Bill Bradley, John McCain and Howard Dean as counterexamples among the rare exceptions).

These represent prevailing barriers and constraints to people's political participation. What about the future? Forecasting is treacherous business. Those taken with the power of the Internet have been waxing eloquent over its promise for democracy, claiming it would empower the individual vs. "the system," and enable more direct, "digital" democracy, etc. (see Chapter 8). Somewhat in the same vein, commentators on "The McCain insurrection" and Dean for America pointed to refreshing signs of political life, respectively during the "Campaign 2000" and 2004 presidential primary seasons (as discussed in Chapter 9). It is also possible, though, that new barriers and constraints may coalesce as structures of money and power arising through the "new economy" get set in place. The new rich may act rather old if they use their resources to protect their own positions rather than to change the system so that the American dream can be realized by a great majority.

Rather than trying to play the forecasting game, let us paint a picture. Imagine the implications if prevailing factors and current trends continue. The real problem is not the number of these but the way they hang together into an overall pattern and reinforce each other. Perceived by the public at large and reinforced by the media, this pattern serves as the single most important barrier to people's political participation. Reactions revealed by poll responses suggest that it discourages their participation in the political process. So where have you seen this picture before?—

- The political process, including campaigns at all levels, dominated by small groups of "pro's"—political junkies or careerists, consultants, P.R.

people, press columnists or media pundits, telemarketing vendors, lobbyists, and other representatives of special interests politically connected lawyers, et. al.

- Pollsters and media commentators calling the results of races before they have been run or polls closed.
- The media "chattering class" or "talking heads" more devoted to shaping than informing public opinion.
- Majorities of the electorate not voting, partly because politicians and the media are talking to each other rather than to voters.
- Most people watching the political game on TV, featuring political celebrities as in spectator sports, as a game played by "them" that is not very relevant to "us."
- Political parties, "issue advocacy" and "special interest" groups effecting outreach to voters through TV ad campaigns, via "attack ads" or other advertising gimmicks designed to get people's attention, rather than through door-to-door or other person-to-person approaches.
- Media coverage focusing on personalities rather than issues.
- Increasing prevalence of increasingly expensive campaigns dominated by money and media, accompanied by a rising perception (whether true or not) that our politics has been corrupted.

The emerging pattern here is not one of democracy, even of a somewhat "representative" variety. It pictures a new political oligarchy powered by incestuous combinations of career politicians, media and money—what McCain called "the iron triangle."[2] Most people would probably not care if "career politicians" included a large proportion of people "like us," but this, too, is becoming increasingly unlikely. We see increasing numbers of wealthy people and members of political "dynasties" on the political "supply side"— the mix of candidates we find on our ballots. "Dynasties," you say?—in a republic that overthrew royalty? Yes. There are Bush, Kennedy, Udall, Gore, Bayh and many other political dynasties.[3]

Thus, the message that most people are getting is that you need substantial capital to play the political game, inherited or earned, either money or a well-known political "name." If this picture, already in view, gets fixed in high relief as a dominant view, the major negative trends exhibited by U.S. politics will continue, such as political parties' decline, decreasing voter turnouts and declining participation in the political process. Elections to the people's Congress may become a rite of inheritance, with candidacies dominated by the children or staffers of former Members.

Note, however, that there is some basis for optimism. Few barriers and constraints yet appear to be cast in stone. As the 2000 and 2004 presidential primary seasons showed, an attractive candidate can win the public's affection in a heartbeat and excite people's interest in politics once again.[4] See Chapter 9. One could also fast forward to "Other seeds of change" (Chapter 7).

One of the political activists interviewed for this book claimed that the only reason Americans are not politically active now is because they don't have to be; when they need to be, they'll step up to the plate and get involved once again. This is another version of the claim that "It's the economy, stupid"—that prosperity has (temporarily?) sold American democracy short, so when the economy turns down, political participation will turn back up.[5] Does this mean that recession or depression sells democracy "long"? Will it take another economic crisis to provoke people to wake up and take part?[6] What will induce a significant, durable return to direct political participation by many more people, one that is not just a blip on the Campaign 2000, 2002, or 2004 radar screens? Do we need a kick in the butt or will it be sufficient to diminish some of the barriers and constraints we have identified? Those involved with development issues in our own and other countries have claimed that all we have to do is lift barriers and constraints to release a new wave of energies. Does this possibility pertain to politics, too?[7]

Others claim that there are no barriers or constraints to people's political involvement; rather, that the electorate is so lazy that it is not taking advantage of existing opportunities for participation. One of our survey respondents, chairman of a County Democratic Committee in California, commented, for example:

"Those who complain about the special interest hold on politicians, and do nothing in terms of getting out the vote, or even voting, must themselves share the blame for the way things are…today."

Besides "lazy," some might add "fat," in keeping with earlier remarks, as in footnote 5, above, about the impact of what had become the longest running period of economic prosperity on record as of February, 2000.[8]

A good rule-of-thumb to keep in mind when there are such polarities in points of view is that the truth (probably) lies somewhere in between. Both viewpoints are partially right. Ironically, their reconciliation may lie more in the domain of economics than politics. Economists have traditionally focused on the factors that induce one choice vs. another. A fundamental economic concept in this regard is "opportunity cost." If the net benefit I would forgo by choosing Option A is less than the lost net benefit of selecting Option B, then I will choose A over B. Another fundamental economic concept is that of scarcity. Well, there is nothing scarcer to most people nowadays than time. Add to this the fact, demonstrated by many economic studies, that the value of people's time increases with economic development and its correlates, rising employment, decreasing unemployment, increasing incomes and higher productivity. Recall from Chapter 4 how one of the interviewees, Mike Lynch, stressed increasing productivity as a factor in people's declining political participation.

Now, let us assume "Option A" is "volunteering for a good cause or community activity" and "Option B" is "political participation." The fact that the scarce, increasingly precious time that people have to devote to volunteer activities is devoted to A over B should be no surprise if the perceived value (resting upon the likelihood that the contribution would benefit one's community) of B is greater than that of A. Unfortunately, given the influence of media, it appears to be more and more the case these days that perception is reality, or that there is little to distinguish the two. In addition, the negative perceptions of politics mean that Option B hardly has a chance to be chosen except by the already politically self-interested. In other words, for most, the "choice" at issue is not even one between a positive and less positive option; it is one between a positive and a negative. So, the option of political participation isn't a genuine option; it doesn't even appear on most people's proverbial "radar screens." Result?: choice pre-determined; the political participation game not even begun.[9]

A lot rides on the media, as discussed in. Chapter 8, including addressing the potential of the Net and the Web. More conventional, established media bear some responsibility for the overhang of negativity that afflicts politics and people's attitudes towards politics today. Contrariwise, it is hard to imagine a shift in attitudes towards politics without active media support. The "public journalism" movement described in Chapter 8 has shown how easily media treatments can be biased by "framing" and selection—by omission as well as commission. Politics is not like the city dump with reporters "objectively" describing how much of a "dump" it really is. When was the last time you saw any reporting on grass roots political activity and how much it means to many of those involved? Or even of non-local actions to restore some grass roots integrity to American democracy? In October, 2000, for example, several hundred protesters gathered on the steps of our nation's capitol to address the issue of campaign finance reform. There was almost no media coverage, even though some of the demonstrators were arrested. Christopher Hitchens was the only reporter to mention this event, in the *Nation*.[10]

The media have a direct conflict of interest in focusing on politics as emphasizing what volunteer political participation is NOT—a money game, and in failing to cover that part of politics which is otherwise—volunteer political participation. For the more it is a money game, the more that media stand to gain by selling ads and airtime. Ironically, efforts to address the issue of money in politics through campaign finance reform (CFR) initiatives at both the federal and state levels have helped to reinforce people's negative perceptions of politics, especially as a corrupt(ing) activity. It remains to be seen whether volunteer political participation will increase in those states where CFR ballot initiatives have succeeded at the polls (e.g., Massachusetts, Vermont, Arizona and Maine). The limited evidence thus far available is not promising and the long-term success of these initiatives is in doubt. See Chapter 9 for more on this.

Featuring "perception" as the major barrier and constraint may seem a bit fuzzy or insubstantial. Its solidity becomes more apparent, however, when we recall two related factors:

1. Most people are shy of getting involved in political activity. Most people haven't been trained to take part in political activity, especially given the atrophied "civics" as curriculum in schools and people's over-dependence upon the media as consumers rather than producers of politics. This is very noticeable to those of us who have served in local government. Even when people have a strong bone to pick with local authorities, they are often nervous or reluctant to stand up like the man in Norman Rockwell's classic painting "Freedom of Speech"—to "speak their piece" and provide testimony before governing bodies.[11]

2. There are a variety of what social scientists call "intervening opportunities" standing in the way of political participation. These include the sorts of volunteer work for community-based organizations and "good causes" noted earlier. Thus, even if political activity were perceived positively, the likelihood of volunteer political participation would be less than that in other activities because the latter are more variously and directly related to most people's concerns. It may also be the case, although a study to document it has not been found, that involvement in intervening opportunities is more "user friendly" than politics; i.e., that it's easier to get involved in non-political activities.

Thus, the negativity surrounding political activity is too easily reinforced for everybody except the politically self-interested; that is, it's just too darn easy for most people to find ready-made excuses *not* to get involved. It's all too easily reinforced, too, on a social basis, because most people are go-along, get along types who imitate others' behavior. Most also don't mind playing the roles of free riders—letting others do "public work," the dirty work (as too many perceive politics to be), or make their political choices for them. Thus, unless there is a strong citizen role model or respected citizen-leader in the ethnic, cultural, social, community or other group to which someone belongs—someone who urges others to get involved and demonstrates what it means—then most people in a group are not likely to extend themselves to volunteer for political activities.

There is a great danger in this behavior pattern, however, as documented by those who have analyzed the complicity of Germans in the Holocaust. One author refers to this as a " 'Contract of Mutual Indifference'."[12] His book provides haunting, unforgettable images—

- The recollection of a child observing her father who "hastily pulled down the window shade" rather than observe (let alone try to do anything to help at any time) a neighboring couple being taken away by the SS.
- A similar image, of a face in a window, watching a group being "assembled...before boarding the death train."

"The face is representative...(of) those who were permanently and merely spectators." Who among you, dear readers, can say for sure that they would behave differently? "The genocide was made possible because 'the vast majority simply did not care.'" The behavior pattern corrupts morality;

some say it is unquestionably amoral. For example, Stanley Hauerwas, a Christian theologian at Duke, writes: "attempts by Christians to avoid political involvement…are rightly condemned as irresponsible, if not unfaithful. Rather, it is the task of Christians to be politically involved…"[13]

Likewise, Baum has written, under a title that unmistakably conveys his condemnation, of the indifference that is "deeply woven into the fabric of modern life."[14] One might add that the transition from "modern" to "postmodern" has only exacerbated this because of the postmodern tendency to "deconstruct" traditional categories and lend support to moral relativism. Deconstruction is simply destructive if reductionist analysis provides nothing constructive to offer in the place of what has been torn apart, undercut and cast asunder. See Chapter 8 for more related to destructive "postmodern" media trends.

So, after all, people's perception of politics is neither insubstantial nor evanescent as a major barrier and constraint (B&C) to their political participation. It should be ranked #1 on any B&C list, for other major B's&C's don't measure up quite as much, and the negative perception dampens efforts to overcome other these. It is compounded of indifference, negativity and fear aggravated by the media. It takes energy to overcome inertia. We assessed the other B's&C's earlier: lack of time; transience or less rootedness in communities; and the narrow self-involvement labeled "narcissism."

Each of the other barriers and constraints to political participation is subject to some qualification. "Lack of time," for example, is more of an excuse than a hard and fast B&C, since political volunteers can make a difference even by devoting, more or less at their convenience, only small increments of time that are much less than the hours they spend watching TV each day. Similarly, the fact that locational impermanence has been greater for the past two generations than for those previous also does not stand up as a "hard and fast," firm, significant B&C except for the small minority of "traveling salesman" types whose locational turnover frequency is greater than once every two years. In most cities and towns, there is an election; that is, some electoral political activity, going on at some level every year; in all places, at least every two years because of federal, state and local election cycles.

The "indifference" factor discussed earlier is due to both narcissism and lack of roots that are far more moral than geographic in nature. We saw earlier, in Chapter 1, how we still suffer from a deeply-rooted historical hangover of narcissism. As for rootedness, a Gloucester fisherman might say: 'We have slipped our mooring or lost our anchor.' Even "lack of time" can be interpreted in the same vein. A major corollary of this lack is fragmentation—of both activities and personal identities. One consequence of fragmentation is reduction, or lack of sufficient cultivation, of a core, firmly rooted, realm of meaningful activity. The apparent lack of this in the public, political arena is one reason why people have retreated more into themselves ("self-development") and/or into their families ("hearth and home" or "nesting") as sources of meaning in their lives, as Sennett and Lasch have shown. Yet, as the interviews help to show in Chapter 4, personal involvement in politics among a community of others can provide a "core…realm of meaningful activity" that helps develop a self of broader scope than can a sole focus on "hearth and home." The home can serve as kernel of a larger community. The latter needs to enter the home; (e.g., through conversations on public issues around the dinner table and other ways reported by our interviewees), else we raise older children, rather than adults from children through our indifference and retreat.

The horrific events of September 11th should be heard as a screaming, two-tone Klaxon wake-up call to Americans that: (1) that their retreat into private enclaves does not serve themselves or their country well; and (2) there is evil in our midst and collective tragedy in post-modern life. Perhaps the World Trade Center should be maintained as what it has become, a mass grave, lest we forget.[15] Now we have to deal with our own version of "never again."

As to the substance of the matter rather than episodic TV coverage: What do we know of the nature of human evil?—not nearly enough, but some profound insights have been put forth by Eric Fromm, Ernest Becker and M. Scott Peck.[16] Peck's book, the most recent and popular of the three, noted something that we may be very reluctant to recognize:

> evil human beings are quite common and appear quite ordinary…They live down the street—on any street. They may be rich or poor, educated or uneducated…They are not designated criminals. More often than not, they will be "solid citizens"—Sunday school teachers, policeman, or bankers, and active in the PTA.[17]

Peck called for "hard science" to study and understand evil. Apparently, Peck's call went unheeded, for we speculated fruitlessly, ad nauseam, about the behavior of Bin Ladin, Mohammed Atta and other terrorists. Among those public figures speaking in response to the Sept. 11th tragedy, President Bush came closest to a meaningful diagnosis when he spoke of terrorists of being the slaves of undemocratic ideologies that honor ideas over lives. He stated flatly: "Osama Bin Ladin is an evil man." Peck came close to providing a checklist of characteristics to look for, including narcissism, looking always for the easy way out, and chronic lying to self and others. Where have we seen these characteristics before?—in ourselves and our politics. It doesn't pay to project evil as something "out there" far beyond ourselves, something whose exorcism is effected by war and professional soldiers. We need to look within and around us for the signs and symptoms of evil. We need to find ways of confronting evil and minimizing its destructive impacts on lives at all levels. Peck provides the basis for a "Neighborhood Watch" far more comprehensive than anything announced by Attorney General John Ashcroft.

The "need," however, means moving beyond a psychotherapeutic approach that tends to focus primarily on individuals.[18] As we saw in the overwhelming worldwide response to the death and devastation in New York

City, the process of confronting evil and human healing is public as well as private. The spontaneous responses of the public at large leads one to ask: What about the responsibility of the formal public sector, government and politics? This question threatens to indict our own government and, by implication, us as citizens, not only the terrorists and obvious evil doers. As noted earlier, we cannot avoid facing the fact that our government failed to fulfill its most basic responsibility—for public safety and security—and that the roots of the failure run to our politics.

The weakening of the CIA goes back to the '70s via a liberal agenda enabled by Watergate. The removal of air marshals from airliners occurred in the early '90s after the airlines complained that they cost too much. In a similar vein, air safety—*A Public Responsibility*—was effectively privatized by the FAA, allowing airlines to contract airport security handling to private firms. For weeks after Sept. 11th, Congress again debated the air safety issue and yet, the public responsibility was again on the verge of being compromised—even in the face of a tragedy of Biblical proportions. Then, when attention was directed to the additional terrorist threat of biological or chemical warfare, we found that we had neglected our public health system. Lobbyists for major airlines and private health providers speak with more powerful voices than ordinary citizens in Congressional committee hearings.[19]

We need to wake up to the fact that our politics and, therefore, our government, has been both too liberal and far too beholden to private interests. September 11th is a wake up in more ways than one. It should be heard nationwide as a nationwide 911 emergency call for us to renew our public life and reform our politics. For too long, we have been living off and cannibalizing the social capital built up by earlier generations. Perhaps 9/11 will come to be seen as a watershed in this respect as well as others. The initial signs were favorable. We saw more people coming together, caring and sharing, giving and helping, and showing a renewed appreciation for the public as well as private values of family and community. We even heard some TV commentators asking: "Will we see a revival of civic awareness?"

Nevertheless, unless we do something about the media, people's negative perception of politics will continue to be the most significant B&C to their political involvement into the indefinite future. Here, "media" should be construed broadly rather than narrowly, to refer to "information" that people receive about politics from nearly all sources. This includes information concerning "civil society" initiatives sponsored by foundations and certain not-for-profit organizations such as Colin Powell's "America's Promise." We noted earlier (in Chapter 2) how these, while extensively promoting volunteerism, have avoided politics like the plague. Media coverage has been highly supportive of these initiatives while, likewise, failing to make the connection with political participation. Improvements in media coverage of all activities that help to build community and improve public life, therefore, need to:

• Recognize and treat positive developments in the political arena, especially grass roots activities;

- Make connections between charitable "issue advocacy" and partisan political developments, and
- Adopt and implement far more of the "public journalism" approach much more widely.

"Connections" are increasingly evident in some media coverage. Unfortunately, this, too, has aggravated negative perceptions of politics because of the way politics has been treated in the context of campaign finance reform (CFR). Ostensibly non-political organizations have been employed or established to put forth political advertisements on "issues" whose thrust is usually negative, with tag lines such as "Call Rep. Smith or Senator Gramm to express your concern(s)". Recall, for example, the ads from "Americans for Tax Reform" attacking Sen. McCain for his stand on campaign finance reform. Such ads are under attack by reformers who are trying to abolish the use of soft money in political campaigns.

The main point here is that revival of grass roots political participation is hardly imaginable without at least the complicity, if not active support, of the media. The media "fourth estate" is simply too powerful and influential. Perhaps one can hope that the most powerful media will, through lack of judgment or self-policing, someday shoot themselves in the foot by running particularly bad stuff, thereby turning people and advertisers away; but it would be quite unrealistic to expect that such turning away would do more than alleviate the most objectionable media behavior. See Chapter 8 for more on this.

Unions' promotion of what one columnist has called the "new machine politics" offers another, albeit also limited, ray of hope that major barriers and constraints can be overcome. The AFL/CIO has (re)discovered the old politics. Surprise!: person-to-person contacts carry a lot more credibility with voters than the usual "30-second sound bites," especially more than the negative "attack ads" that are depressing voter turnouts. The efficacy of reliance upon people rather than TV and telecommunications was apparent in the results of the '98 Congressional elections. Efforts by union canvassers and their Democratic allies, targeted on certain congressional districts, succeeded in the Democrats winning some close races. Having seen this new/old campaign model at work, some of the unions' business counterparts such as Chambers of Commerce were reported to be adapting it for the 2000 and subsequent elections. The question remains, however, especially in light of the discussion of the changing role of political parties in Chapter 4: Have they have seen the light? Will they shift their emphasis from raising money to mobilizing people? Will parties' local political "infrastructure" be rebuilt or revived?

Even if the answers to these questions to all the latter questions were "YES," the major barrier and constraint to people's political participation would still remain—the media altogether—their attitudes towards grassroots politics, how they cover such political activities, their negativity towards politics generally, editorial writing or commentaries that encourage or discourage popular participation, etc. Here, too, there are small but encouraging signs. For the first time since 1992, network news has showed volunteers campaigning door-to-door for candidates in New Hampshire, Virginia and perhaps some other locations.[20]

See chapter 8 for much more on the media as both part of the problem and part of the solution, and Chapter 9 for some more recent signs that it pays to rely more on people and less on media for political campaigns.

Answers to the many questions posed by this chapter also depend partly on the features of campaign finance reform (CFR) initiatives and their likely impacts on political participation. This thread is also picked up and spun out in Chapter 9.

Notes

1. Such a sense has also been conveyed by a popular TV celebrity, that no-one would label as "ordinary"—Andy Rooney, on 60 Minutes (2/27/00, slightly paraphrased): "I usually don't vote for anyone; rather, I vote against most candidates once I settle on the one least unfavorable....The trouble I'm having with this season's presidential primaries is that there's no one to hate."

2. Ben Price, one of the political activists who commented on early drafts of this and other chapters, wrote: "Here you have captured the essence of the perception shared by many people I know! (but) The item not included in your assessment of the new political panorama...is the interloping role of corporations into (a) politics supposedly owned by living humans..." Chapter 8 points to the "interloping (and increasingly interlocking) role of corporations" in the media as part of the problem we face, but this book has not been able to otherwise address the issue that Ben identified.

3. Note, for instance, the September, 2001, *Time* magazine cover article headline: "Camelot lives!"

4. Note, however, Ben Price's counterpoint: "This optimism presumes such a charismatic candidate could be seen crawling out from under the avalanche of vested money that will...be used to create IMAGE in the media for the best-funded, ersatz front-runner" (another comment on an early draft of this chapter).

5. Another variant was put by Lewis Lapham: "Our prosperity finances the habits of indolence" (op.cit., April, 2003, p.38).

6. This "what if," however, quickly suggests a "so what." If the economy tanks, who will have the time to get involved in politics, as people would be working harder just to stay afloat or find a job? And the old leftist assumption that, if the system crashes, the people would rise up, has proven to be BS in the US.

7. Again, Ben Price: "I think if you watch the level of involvement of NGOs (Non-Governmental Organizations) in Seattle as they confront the...power vested in the WTO (World Trade Organization) at the end of November and beginning of December (2000), some hint of an answer to the above questions will become evident. True, it took the slaughter for naught that was Vietnam to arouse a significant citizen participation in the politics...of the 1960s and early '70s. I suspect that it is true that, without burning issues, citizenship is relegated easily to the arena of spectator sport. But I don't believe the...declaration about a "good economy" being a turn-off for democracy. The "good economy"...has...launched a fleet of corporate destroyers and sunk the budget of their shipbuilding employees whose 401k plans...are scant recompense for the loss of democracy through lobbyists' bribery of their so-called representatives. But the citizens don't own the media that keeps repeating the message of "good times." Guess who does?—The same feudal lords of corporate hegemony..."

8. Ben's comment: "No doubt, if you have a good job and a VCR, life is "good." But, really...those who benefit from corrupting the actual democratic nature of the political system...create and fund the lies that depress citizenship and banish hope by active usurpation of the conduits of democratic influence. The real dilemma of the marginalized citizen must be brought into stark contrast with the simplistic and trite statements about a fat and lazy electorate. Let's face it; the average voter doesn't spend millions...of dollars to effect, bend, mold, write and shepherd legislation through the halls of Congress for personal benefit, as do their corporate competition." [editorial remarks to me via e-mail]

9. Ben Price: "If perception IS reality, then whoever owns the conduits of perception (the media) controls and dictates the ersatz "reality" (thus so) The choice between helping "real" people through volunteer work in the community as opposed to getting politically involved...is a "no brainer" for most people (and) ...so the choice seems to be one of serving people you know will benefit by your actions or serving an agenda that is controlled by others who manipulate public sentiment to make it seem otherwise." My rejoinder?: That the latter is a very sophisticated abdication of a citizen's responsibility in a democracy, one that, unfortunately, leaves the battlefield of politics to the powers that be" ("corporate hegemony" in Price's view).

10. Thanks to Ben Price for this example. He was there and he was one of those arrested.

11. Another perspective from Price: "Entering politics has grown as a priority in my life, but for me it seems doomed to be quite a confrontational experience...Expecting the average person to challenge people in positions of authority...is not an expectation grounded in an understanding of the average person's aversion to "difficulties." Conformity is taught vicariously...to be a high virtue." (private communication)

12. See Geras, Norman (1998), *The Contract of Mutual Indifference: Political philosophy after the Holocaust.* London and New York: Verso. The three quotes below are taken from pages 5, 13, 13 and 19, respectively, in order of their quotation.

13. Hauerwas, Stanley (1981), *A Community of Character: Toward a constructive Christian social ethic.* Notre Dame, Indiana: University of Notre Dame Press.

14. Baum, Rainer C. (1988), "Holocaust: Moral Indifference as the Form of Modern Evil," in: Rosenberg, Alan, and Gerald E. Myers (eds.), *Echoes From the Holocaust: Philosophical Reflections on a Dark Time.* Philadelphia: Temple University Press.

15. These reflections on the implications of "Sept. 11th" draw from my article, "Life Against Death," and those of others comprising a post-mortem on the event in *The Ethical Spectacle* (www.spectacle.org, October, 2001)

16. Fromm, Erich (1964), *The Heart of Man: Its Genius for Good & Evil.* NY: Harper & Row. Becker, Ernest (1965), Escape From Evil. NY: Macmillan. Peck, M. Scott (1983), *People of the Lie: The Hope for Healing Human Evil.* NY: Simon & Shuster.

17. Peck, op.cit., pp.47 and 69.

18. There's no such limitation in Peck's psychotherapy. His book also goes into evil behavior by groups and collective responsibility (sometimes misleadingly denoted as "guilt"), with a focus on the massacre of innocents at Mai Lai in Vietnam and our complicity in such acts, analogous to but less overt or widespread than the complicity of Germans in Nazi crimes. See Peck, op.cit., Chapter 6, pp.212-250.

19. This is undeniable; see, e.g., "Bailout for Airlines Showed the Weight of a Mighty Lobby" (*New York Times,* October 10, 2001, p.1), but it doesn't do justice to the ideological cross currents that also influence government policies and decision-making. The call for federalization of airport safety, for example, ran into strong Republican opposition. Republicans tend to neglect the public side of life. They will manage to define and reaffirm the value of the public and public interest in conservative terms or, sooner or later, they will lose.

20. For example, CNN televised a glimpse of workers for McCain going door-to-door for McCain in Virginia on Feb. 29, 2000, Virginia's primary election day, and showed some similar glimpses of canvassing by volunteers during the 2002 congressional and 2004 presidential primary elections.

7.

The Seeds of Change: Agents & Concepts

Introduction

So we need political reform in order to bring people back into the political picture as active agents. But who are the change agents?—"the people"?—not likely unless they are active participants in the political arena. They deny themselves the role of active agents by their absence. Some will say (or hope, of course) that "the people" as in "the will of the people," will come surging forward like a tidal wave, to take back "their" political system with a vengeance once, as in the old movie Network, they're "mad as hell and not going to take it anymore." There's the rub, "with a vengeance." Such a wave of reaction, far from being what some would call "progressive," is more likely to be reactionary. It could even amount to an American brand of facism. So, we must ask again:

Who are the Change Agents?

The major change agent is science, so the leading change agents are scientists. For better or for worse (let us judge as we go), the major sector of our society that has led the way in applying both the techniques and the fruits of science to human behavior and organization is: Guess what!—not politics and government, the sector that one would expect to make such applications. It is not the sector that, presumably, we are most able to control as citizens of a democratic republic—the public sector. It is the one we are least able to control, the business sector. And even though the source of revolution is science, scientists and/or their works increasingly are being turned directly or indirectly to the service of business.

Science-based innovation and entrepreneurship are the prime drivers. The world of The Organization Man is gone. Those among the self-anointed progressives who are looking for businessmen to demonize and capitalist culprits to fight will have to look elsewhere. Anyway, the presumed progressives are not the change agents. They are a very different breed of cat—entrepreneurs and other sources of innovation of two types:

- Private business entrepreneurs, especially founders of science- and technology-based for-profit enterprises;
- Public and Public/private entrepreneurs and innovative organizations, including founders of not-for-profit enterprises that are in the business

REFORM	POLITICS	BUSINESS
Increase participation	N.A.T.O.;2 diminished by the growing influence of money and other influences noted in this book	Increasingly effected via teaming, visioning, flattening hierarchies and other ways
Reinvent relationships	Not at all, or in the wrong direction	More emphasis on relationships that are mutually collaborative & satisfactory
Promote self-organization & self-management	Nil; people & local political committees expected to toe the party line	Encouraged and enabled
Increase responsiveness to "customers," clients or constituents	Only via form letters, if at all	Improved, often inter-actively, in keeping with "the customer is king"3 + "sense and respond"
Empower people to be more effective in their roles	Nil; even dis-empowerment except for check writing & chat rooms	Employees provided with tools, information & authority
Promote entrepreneurship & innovation	Favoring wealthy candidates or the already politically self-interested.	Encouraging & enabling much broader segments of the population
Improve flows and quality of information	Top down	Bottom up and 3-way (up, down & across)
Better leadership	Traditional organizational hierarchy plus media	Enabling, mentoring, facilitating
Better accountability	Lacking but for agency self-evaluation.	Via performance measurement; increasingly transparent, even "open book"
Experimentation	Nil; "Civil society" experi-ments divorced from politics4	Increasingly employed using sophisticated tools
Truthfulness	Not a goal; sacrificed when expedient. "Spin" the way.	Increasingly honored internally; advertising less so. Caveat emptor!
Enhance the power of choice	Power lessened	Power increased
Build community	Divide and conquer; political parties in decline	Recognizing the need to, and increasingly so doing, both internally and externally
Search for excellence	Not widely practiced; good examples scattered & ignored	Greatly increased since Peters' 1982 book.5
Upgrade human resources	Limited political training; decline of "civics" education in schools	Raised to prime concern; tens of billions expended on training and education

of identifying, generating, disseminating and applying new approaches to public policy, and other individual advocates of such initiatives.

Examples of the private type include Ted Turner, Ray Kurzweil, Ray Moore, M.I.T. Media Lab (William Dertouzos, et.al.), Xerox PARC Lab, Kevin Kelly, Herbert Simon, Benoit Mandlebrot, Warren Bennis, Peter Senge, Stuart Kauffman, John Casti and Marvin Minsky.

Examples of the more public cats of the breed include the Santa Fe Institute, Ashoka (Bill Drayton), IIASA (Austria), Brian Lamb (C-SPAN), Jeff Gates, Stewart Brand, Tommy Thompson and Ronald Reagan.

The thrust of the foregoing paragraphs needs another book to develop and justify. The main point from the standpoint of this book, however, is quite straightforward. Anybody looking for the basis of a serious movement for political reform in the U.S.of A. needs to look in places other than the usual political-organizational or reform hangouts. One needs to look for people other than the usual suspects such as self-styled progressives and the media political commentariat. They will be found in places other than the conventional think-tanks and reform-oriented organizations. One place to look is the business community, supposedly the most unlikely locale in which to find seeds of political reform. Within the space of another book, one could also cull such seeds from the entrepreneurial arena more generally, including public or public/private, as suggested earlier.

Revolution in Business as a Basis for Political Reform

Wonder of wonders! Miracle of miracles? Irony of ironies!—business as an incubator of practices and models for political reform! Who'd a'thunk it back in the '60's, or even now?, when there was (is, even now) a strong current of opinion that held (still holds) business to be the source of backwardness in politics—of retrograde conservatism supporting backward powers that resist progressive change. Yet, it is both the gurus and practitioners of the new economy and even some leaders of old big corporations that write and talk of "revolution." When was the last time you heard that incendiary word being used in politics? The subtitle of Tom Peters' summa, *Thriving on Chaos,* is "The Management Revolution." The book's first chapter is entitled "Facing Up to the Need for Revolution." When was the last time a so-called political "leader" even felt "the need," let alone faced or expressed it?

The boxes on the previous page highlight a number of ironic contrasts that might cause Jedediah Purdy to cry in his carrot juice:[1] these are just fifteen differences among the most familiar features of reform. To the extent they are not obvious, the shorthand contrasts will be elaborated as this section continues. Before belaboring the obvious, however, note several contrasts that are not so readily apparent. The reason that some of the most important contrasts are less than obvious is because they appear at what John McPhee (in his remarks on Bill Bradley) called a "higher level of the game" or what philosophers refer to as a "higher level of discourse." That is like moving the level of conversation up a notch from a barroom exchange to a seminar debate. What is interesting to note here is that, unlike politicians, business men and women have addressed their issues at all levels, from the highest to the lowest, from the nitty-gritty to the philosophical.

What is even more remarkable is that business people, unlike their political counterparts, have learned not to segregate issues arbitrarily into categories that presume that some are "higher" and some are "lower." The most detailed features of business practice; e.g., how a low level company representative interacts with customers, may have high level implications (and vice-versa). Thus, unlike political leaders, business leaders have increasingly looked to encourage two-way flows of communications between lower and higher levels. The management revolution which Tom Peters and others have promoted has occurred at all levels to effect changes in attitudes, behaviors and structures. Starting in the '80s, industrial policy in the U.S. began to proceed from the shop floor and the bottom up.[6] The Japanese, once touted as models for U.S. economic policymakers, have continued to view industrial policy as a higher level, primarily governmental, concern.[7]

Thus, the higher levels at which the American business community has addressed issues neglected by those in the political world have to do, not with hierarchy, but with the breadth or comprehensiveness of approaches to change,. These include:

- A systems or systemic approach—business people have really worked to honor what '60s activists only talked about; that is, "changing the system"(s).
- Structural changes that go beyond the '80s fads of "reinvention" and "downsizing" to decentralization via "subsidiarity," flattening hierarchies, self-organization, self-management, broadening ownership, and "disintermediation."[8]
- Reducing or eliminating barriers and constraints to change, so that an on-going process of change is built into business systems.
- Transforming business systems into "learning organizations" so that, not only can people learn from past mistakes, they can proactively learn how to face the future.[9]
- Renewing and refreshing the springs of competition; overcoming some of the faults and failings of market systems;.
- Balancing inquiry and advocacy, little attempt of which one finds in the political arena.[10]
- Recognition of the usefulness and importance of metaphor—largely lost in politics as the quality of political speaking and writing has markedly decreased.
- Recognition of the importance of "environment," not only the natural environment but man-made, organizational environments within which people spend most of their lives; and hence, the need to transform these to make them more enabling of people's goals and "user friendly."

- Institutionalizing science and technology so that the processes through which discoveries are made and applied are integral features of the business system.
- Changing business cultures.
- Identifying and constructively employing patterns, structure and opportunities in the midst of the chaos or turbulence of our times.
- What Tom Peters and other business writers call "Mastering Paradox." This is so generic and fundamental a shift in the very perception of what change is about that we will devote a whole section to it later in this chapter.

Nevertheless, all the changes brought about in U.S. business, even those that can be labeled "radical" or "revolutionary," have not succeeded in improving U.S. politics, democracy or government, nor could they be expected to do so. Business has changed the "system"(s) for which business leaders have direct responsibility—their own. From the standpoint of the larger, overall business-political (etc.) system called the U.S.A., the changes in the business system are a mixed blessing, amounting to what systems analysts would call "sub-optimization." The resultant, growing gap between the business sub-system and the political/governmental subsystem—one progressive (guess which one!); the other backward—is problematic and may be destabilizing for the country's system-as-a-whole unless we can also succeed in improving our political system, too. Many of the changes that business leadership has advocated or effected have been highlighted. By returning to the those identified in the boxes earlier, the nature of the political challenge we face may become clearer if not obvious.

Note that the reference to business "best practices" in the next section does not imply that the practices identified have been adopted by the entire American business community or even a major part of it. The degrees to which they have spread among businesses vary greatly by industry, area, firm-size and other factors. Recent scandals emerging from the "dot.com bubble"—the cases of Enron, WorldCom, et.al.—have given the American public the impression that the American business community is a source of bad-ass scoundrels and problems, not solutions, and certainly not leaders, let alone harbingers of any sort of "reform." The purpose of what follows is to identify business policy and practice models that can help inform a political reform agenda. It is not to discuss the spread of such innovations within the business community but to suggest their adoption and diffusion within political communities. Their promise in this regard is somewhat independent of the extent to which they have spread throughout the business community.

Business Best Practices as Guidelines for Political Reform

One of the innovations in business practice that was first to achieve widespread adoption is a systematic way for businesses to diagnose their own weaknesses and identify ways to improve relative to the "best practices" of their competitors. This is "performance benchmarking" (PBM). PBM has found only limited application within the interlocking worlds of politics and government.[11] By itself, this lies at the core of a basic reform question: How to achieve accountability in those worlds? We touch this issue at points further on in this and later chapters. Isn't it ironic, with all the hue and cry about corporate accountability from those in politics and government, that the latter are hardly models of accountability? Those in glass houses….throwing stones??

Now, let's return to the topics highlighted by the beginning set of boxes at the outset of this chapter.

Increase Participation: The importance of political participation was discussed at length in Chapter 3, as well as the ways it has declined. Thus, the many ways that businesses have increased; indeed, "empowered" employees' participation in workplace decisions may be relevant to a broader politics, not just to the internal politics of corporations.[12] These include flexible teaming arrangements, inclusion of employees in processes by which corporate visions, missions and strategic plans are defined, and encouragement of self-organizing, self-managing work groups.

Business' drive to democratize the workplace began in response to the Japanese threat—the drive to achieve quality assurance. Senge describes the changes that result:

"Levels of supervisory management are removed…Quality inspectors are eliminated permanently. Authority to study and improve work processes is pushed down to front-line workers."[13]

We saw in Chapters 4 and 5 how little of the latter "authority" is enabled or even allowed by the state committees of the major political parties, while grass roots political participation is devalued. The debate on campaign finance reform, moreover,—the only form of "reform" receiving serious consideration— shows how the value of any time that people voluntarily invest in political participation is discounted, denied, or ignored.

Reinvent relationships: In order to spawn the collegial, cooperative, communicative, collaborative and interactive arrangements required by the new economy in all directions, businesses have found that they need to "reinvent" relationships. The implications have been most telling at intermediate supervisory levels. Large numbers of foremen and other supervisors were let go, in spite of aggressive efforts to retrain them, because they were unable to relinquish old attitudes and behaviors in order to develop new relationships based on facilitation and mentoring rather than command and control.

Relative to the business world, the worlds of politics and government exhibit far less awareness of the need to reinvent relationships. It is if the "Third Wave" hasn't yet even curled its lip, when in fact it has long since broken like a tsunami to flood our shores. These worlds still largely rely on hierarchical relationships, one-way information.flows; guarded, self-protective, bureaucratic ("CYA") behavior, and intra- as well as inter-organizational competition.

Promote self-organization & self-management: A prime concept in the new economy is that of self-organizing systems. The concept arose from natural scientists' attempts to understand the dynamics of physical systems.[14] "Self management" arose in a very different context—out of 19th century attempts to bridge the gap between capital and labor by promoting labor owned and managed companies. The two now come together at three levels:

- System-wide: Systems designed for human beings and/or that emerge from their interactions in situations where organizational patterns are perceived, analyzed and deliberately adapted;
- At the company level in the form of profit-sharing or employee stock ownership plans (ESOPs) (even though most ESOPs are not self-organizing); and…
- At the intra-company or micro-micro level in the form of self-organized, self-managed teams.

As we saw in Chapter 4, political parties and their various units are not "self-organizing;" moreover, they are "self-managed" only within constraints that severely limit their ability to provide dynamic, developmental responses to emerging political problems and opportunities. Their hierarchical and bureaucratic forms of organization and management are derived from old economy forces that Toffler called "Second Wave." Relative to developments in the rest of American society, business included, our political parties seem like dinosaurs. Their adoption of the Internet represents a technological overlay, not a revolution or even significant evolution in their organization, management or behavior. When will parties truly graduate from the 19th century to the 21st and "get with the program" of the new economy?

Increase responsiveness to "customers," clients or constituents: The private sector in the U.S. has led the way towards achieving greater responsiveness to customers. "Customer Relations Management" has become a field in itself. The public sector has been playing copy cat by urging its agencies to become "customer sensitive" as part of government "reinvention" initiatives. Some agencies have improved their performance substantially in this regard. Political responsiveness is quite another matter. Neither parties nor politicians are especially responsive to citizens' letters, suggestions or complaints. Nowadays, it is unusual for a citizen who has taken the time to write a letter to an elected official to receive back even a canned, form letter acknowledgement. As for any sort of truly, un-canned, reasonably thoughtful responses, dream on; don't even dare to hope. Write to a national party official and the likelihood of a response is even less. The only letters that the author has received in response to anything sent to a politician are boilerplate thank you's for campaign contributions. Submissions of ideas, comments, complaints or constructive criticism do not seem to count. At best, they earn a proforma reply, not a response.[15] As a South Philadelphia Congressman of ill-repute once said: "Money talks and bullshit walks."

Empower people to be more effective in their roles: Businesses have effectively empowered people in their organizations through:

- Inclusion, in processes of corporate-wide "visioning" to generate and adapt company mission statements and strategies;
- Information flows—requiring and facilitating improved flows of information every which way—vertically, both ways, up and down; horizontally, internally and externally.
- Provision of Tools, such as intranets, extranets, mobile data entry tools, and computer-guided equipment,
- Education and Training—on the job and also that which is not just narrowly job or task-specific—via education benefits as well as classroom and on-the-job training.
- Enabling…
    —Self-organization and/or self-management, as indicated earlier;
    —Employees to get involved as volunteers in activities that benefit their communities.

How much of this does one find in the world of politics?—very little. Many party state committees provide training, but it's primarily for candidates. There is very little training for local committee members to enable them to do their jobs better. There is little "inclusion" in top level strategizing or planning exercises. Information flows are primarily one-way. There is insufficient provision of "tools," "enabling," or other efforts to build the capacity of local political party committees (as revealed earlier, in Chapters 4 and 5).[16]

Improve flows and quality of information: Flows of information from the shop floor have developed way beyond the old model of the employee "suggestion box" model. Pro-actively and systematically listening to people, and engaging them in processes to define how things can be done better, have been keys to improvements in businesses' productivity and competitiveness. In other words, micro-level changes have been keys to the macro-level trends that marked the longest U.S. economic expansion in history. Improvements in the flows of information every which way (up, down and sideways) have already been noted. But the quality of information conveyed through these flows is at least as important as the quantity. The quality lies in concerted efforts to engage everyone in a company, from the bottom up, in processes of "continuous improvement," including changes in business organization and systems, not just incremental changes in the ways things are done.

Meanwhile, on the political side of our society, what have we seen by way of improvements in the flows and quality of information? We have seen the rise of C-SPAN, but this is watched by only a minority of the American electorate. We have seen an explosion in the quantity of information we can access through the Internet and increasing numbers of Cable TV channels. Who among us, however, would claim that there has been any increase in the quality of information on matters political from major media; rather, the contrary.

More specifically, what have political leaders, elected officials and parties been doing to improve the flows and quality of political information? Damn little. The newsletters of elected officials are good examples of self-promotion, one might even say "propaganda." Parties do not engage their members in processes of self-critical self-improvement. Communications run from the top down, not the bottom up. Recall Mike Lynch's remarks in Chapter 4. The ability of parties to provide useful information directly to voters has decreased as parties have let their local "infrastructure" atrophy. Campaign decisions and information provision have been relegated to ""experts" and "spinmeisters."

Better Leadership: The concept of "servant leader" has found its way into the business community but not into the mainstream political arena. Parker Palmer introduced the concept in an inspiring sermon many years ago.[17] The more enlightened segments of the business press and leadership picked it up, gave it currency in the business community and adapted it for application by other business leaders. According to Palmer, a servant leader is one who creates "settings which give you identity, which empower you *to be someone.*" The italicization for emphasis is Palmer's own.[18]

What is it you say?—we elect "public servants," so that our elected officials are "servant leaders"? Look again. The so-called "public servants" of our political system have become its masters. When you hear a candidate say: "Elect me so that I can serve you;" in most cases, you can translate this to mean, "Elect me so that I can advance my political career." When you ask a candidate to sacrifice family, income and peace of mind to be your "public servant," recognize that, if elected, he is likely to act like a devoted servant, even a "Step'n Fetchit" in terms of constituent services. This serves to purchase your continuing support and thus obtain the leeway he wants to exercise power and effect policy at higher levels than the grassroots political hustings. In other words, by playing "servant," most politicians aim to empower themselves, not you.

More Accountability: The American business community has made considerable progress in improving its accountability to the public, notwithstanding some bad examples that seem to suggest otherwise. The most remarkable development in this vein is the adoption of "open book" accounting and management by many businesses, as reported by several articles in INC magazine and some business books.[19] The workings of the political community remain obscure to any except insiders or political junkies and the accountability of the public sector relative to the private would not bear close examination.

Experimentation & Learning from Experience: Even the "old" business community has adopted "new" science. This is evident not only with respect to corporate R&D to exploit advances in the natural sciences but with respect to the application of scientific methods to the many human sides of business. With respect to the latter, the reader familiar with Taylorism and "scientific management" might say, 'So what else is new?' What's new is science. It has evolved far beyond the crude attempts to apply the mechanistic, bastardized paradigm of the old, Newtonian science to business in order to better control the workforce via "time and motion" studies, et. al.

Relative to the old, the new science enables liberation of human beings rather than mis-use to achieve control of people and domination over them.[20] The best examples are provided by businesses that are working to transform themselves into "learning organizations" following Senge, et.al., as referenced earlier. Experiments, both controlled and uncontrolled, are keys to enabling a more systematic approach to business development than simply learning by doing. Many alternative ways to effect a sense of "ownership" of businesses among employees, for example, have arisen in the business world. Many studies have shown that actual ownership by employees in the form of "ESOP's" (Employee Stock Ownership Plans) leads to significant improvements in businesses' performance.

By contrast, what do we observe in the political world?—continued misuse of the old science to increase domination and control by the political class relative to the great majority of citizens. "Scientific human behavioral technology tools" such as focus groups, polling, statistics, controlled experiments and market studies are employed in order to better "sell" political candidates, parties and proposals like business sells soap. This is not science but scientism run amok. Ironically, political consultants have adopted marketing methods from business while ignoring the more progressive scientific directions in which business has been moving. They and their political science colleagues may claim to be "scientific," but they are pedaling an already outdated, ideological, reduced form of science in service to narrow political agendas or campaigns. To them, "power to the people" is just a irrelevant old saying, a leftover from the sixties.

Further on in this chapter, we will see that there are experiments going on to try to demonstrate how people can be empowered. Unfortunately, they are outside of the mainstream of politics and not really empowering, politically, with respect to people's participation in electoral politics where winning power is the aim of the game. Organizations devoted to electoral politics, such as political parties, are not conducting experiments to test how to empower people. They do not even have any systematic ways of learning from their own experience.

Seek the Truth and Try to Effect Truthfulness: The previous section is closely related to this one. For experimentation and learning are major ways to seek the truth about ourselves, how we act and what we can accomplish together. For all the "spin" that businesses may include in their advertising, business has learned that better products and services are based upon truth-seeking procedures, not upon the manufacture of illusions as in "The Unreality Industry."[21] A business that, among other things, does not seek to know the sources of defects in its products or how its customers are using them, is a business that may fail or at least be severely punished for its lack of attention.[22]

As both scientific and religious communities have demonstrated for hundreds of years, truth-seeking is a community activity, not simply an individual undertaking. Thus, Stanley Hauerwas, a theologian at Duke University, shows how it is hard for any of us, individually, to be truthful if we do not live in a "truthful community."[23] More recently, Os Guiness warns us that we are in danger of losing our freedom nationwide as an American community whose:

- Behavior, standards of judgement, language and attitudes have been so corrupted by the moral relativism of a "post-modern" philosophy that truthfulness has little or no currency; and…
- Politicians, exemplified by a Bill Clinton, have so corrupted public discourse and political life through their un-truthfulness that we now live un-free, Guinness would say, in a "world of lies, hype and spin."

Business professors Mitroff and Bennis had issued an earlier warning: "A pervading, powerful sense of unreality infiltrates the land…to avoid coping with a complex world…Unreality is big business." They go on to write that the "end result" is an inability to distinguish between reality and unreality (or between truth and falsehood) and "a society less and less able to face its true problems directly, honestly and intelligently.[24] Pawley had painted a similarly dire picture earlier.[25]

Thus, building a truthful American political community should be a major goal for us all. Find more on this as one of the themes on the media in Chapter 8.

Build Community: Having been a major factor in the destruction of the traditional American community over the past century,[26] American business has nevertheless rediscovered the value of "community" over the past decade or so, both within and without the context of its own organizations.[27] Many businesses are encouraging community spirit, activities and formations as, for example, via:

- Formation of intra-corporate communities such as teams and R&D "skunk works," as well as promoting the corporation as a working community with a shared vision and/or mission overall.;
- Incentives for employees to volunteer to participate in activities that help to build or improve communities, both place-based and issue- or "good cause"-based.;
- Advertising businesses as good corporate citizens of various communities, such as environmental, place-based or American-national.

Meanwhile, our political process seems bent on undermining whatever semblance of political community has been inherited from the past. Our local, community-based political infrastructure has been re-gressively (one dare not say "pro"-) left to atrophy, deteriorate or fall into limbo. Political advertising is often designed to divide the electorate or play upon deeply rooted divisions. The local political "infrastructure," such as it is, is effectively divorced or separated from other community-based organizations (CBO's) whose prime roles are building or maintaining communities. These are among reasons why pointing the way towards rebuilding the American political community from the ground up is one of the prime goals of this book.

Broaden the range of choice: Who would deny that businesses in our consumer-oriented economy have served to broaden the range of purchasers' choices enormously? Development of new products and services plus products' and services' differentiation keep multiplying the variety of offerings available to buyers of all kinds.

By contrast, even though the political class tends to view voters like businesses view consumers, it has been offering a diminishing range of choices to its "customers." Increasingly, we hear citizens say that they have had to vote "for the lesser of two evils." Increasingly, many elected offices are uncontested. Increasingly, people interested in public life are declining to run for office. Increasingly, it seems that politics is becoming a game for the rich and famous. The supply-side of politics is drying up. "Mr. Smith goes to Washington" has become far more of a myth than "Horatio Alger."

Search for Excellence: Ever since the Japanese challenge of the '80's and Peters' and Waterman's 1982 book of the same title, American business has been engaged in a "search for excellence." What about the world of politics and government? No such search process seems to prevail. There may even be a process of adverse selection. Candidates are often elected if they can present an image of being more like us; that is, more like the average Joe rather than someone who has excelled in a demanding field. Politics is demanding but there are also prevailing pressures to "go-along, get-along." Thus, rather than elect someone who has succeeded in a field outside of politics, voters are more likely to go for someone who has shown how he or she can get along in a political environment featuring lowest common denominators—another factor in the "lemons" cycle featured earlier..

Consider education, for example. It's now issue #1. But as of early 2001, only two states were paying teachers on a merit basis by providing bonuses and other stipends to reward exceptional performance. Educational excellence anyone?

Upgrade Human Resources: Many leading large corporations have long provided aggressive education and training programs for their employees. Now, much broader segments of the American business community are engaged in efforts to upgrade their human resources. Some of these efforts are self-defensive or remedial—to make up for shortcomings in public education systems. Obviously, they are driven by the self-interest of companies in having competent workforces in an era of rapid technological change.

What about the interest of a self-interested political system in upgrading human resources? Candidates and volunteers need to be trained. Citizens need to be informed, some would even say educated. The founders of our republic emphasized that the health of democracy rests upon an educated citizenry. Yet, training programs traditionally run by political parties are dwindling. What passes for "civics" education in the schools is sadly deficient, even a disgrace in some areas. Successive reports document increasing ignorance of American history among young people, not to mention practical knowledge of how American democracy works. The human resource base of our democratic system is decreasing in quality at a time when it needs to be increasing.

Master and Manage Paradox: Another Professor of Business Administration, Kim Cameron, has identified mastery and management of "paradox" as keys to "organizational effectiveness" in a time of turbulent change.[28] In the course of so doing, Cameron provides a definition of paradox that is clear and useful. It avoids the confusion that often surrounds use of the term.

"Paradox…involves contradictory, mutually exclusive elements that are present and operate…at the same time. Paradoxes differ in nature from other similar concepts often used as synonyms such as dilemma, irony, inconsistency, dialectic, ambivalence or conflict….Paradox differs from each of these concepts in that no choice need be made between two or more contradictions. Both contradictions in a paradox are accepted and present. Both operate simultaneously."[29]

Cameron borrows from an author whose book on paradox provides an additional slant on "truth seeking:"

"A paradox is an idea involving two opposing thoughts…which…are equally necessary to convey a more imposing, illuminating, life-related or provocative insight into truth than either factor can muster in its own right."[30]

In other words, truth is a two-sided coin.

Paradoxical combinations of qualities in organizations enable them to successfully adapt to changing conditions. Such combinations as observed in the business world are highlighted in the paragraphs to follow.

Ends—Means: Advanced management practice views business as a system of interacting elements, not as a bundle of "means" separable from a bunch of "ends." End products or services are designed so that they also serve as means to other ends. Thus, products are sold in packaging designed to enhance the companies overall image in the mind of the buyer. Means are selected and implemented so that they contribute to desired ends. So a piece of CNC (computer numerically controlled) machinery is not just a tool to produce product; it is a tool that enables quality assurance, higher precision, product development, on-the-job training, et. al. Services and tools developed within companies for internal use (as "means") have been found to be the basis for a new market niche serving external customers ("ends"). The separation and isolation of means and ends helps turn an organization into a non-adaptive creature like a dinosaur.

The latter is one reason why political organizations are quite non-adaptive and why so-called political "leaders" are adaptive only in terms of their ability to change rhetoric in response to polls. Not only do they operate on the basis of artificial, "separation and isolation," the way they do so is often downright unethical, according to the rule: "the end justifies the means." More specifically, any political organization or campaign involves at least two paradoxical ends/means elements: winning elections and building for the future. Even though it is well known to those involved in politics that a truly good campaign brings new blood into politics, the benefit of building for the future has been increasingly less apparent on the radar screens or agenda of the political class. The goals' tension is real; it will never go away, but the possibility of its creative management,—to achieve some balance between goals,—is lost when "winner takes all" and "politics is played in the present tense" philosophies take hold.

Acting—Learning: Real-time business process monitoring and evaluation systems enable producers to systematically learn from experience; for example, to trace the sources of higher product defect rates. More generally, some businesses have been turned into "learning organizations," a la Senge, as indicated earlier. The conventional, long-standing view, that acting and learning are quite separate and conflicting activities, runs contrary to the notion of a dynamic organization trying to adapt to a changing world.

What do we see in the world of political actors that amounts to systematic attempts to learn from experience?—nothing in the political world per se. There are, of course, a variety of external agencies such as institutes, "think tanks" and academic political science programs, but that is not what is at issue here. One can even question to what extent such agencies comprise a "learning system" for those engaged in political-electoral or party activities. Campaign after campaign, as well as in other ways, whatever has been learned on the basis of hard experience is often lost and so has to be relearned another time around. Even though some of the experience gets codified into the practice(s) of political consultants, this means that knowledge obtained in the public arena has been appropriated for private gain. There is no evidence that political consultants, unlike some of their leading business counterparts, are helping clients to transform themselves into political learning organizations. If they did so, perhaps there would be less future demand for their services.

Higher—lower: The growing debate on the issue of growing inequality rests, in part, on an assumption that these are opposite segments of society in conflict. A similar attitude was long prevalent in the American business community but many businesses have moved away from it over the past 10-12 years by recognizing that there are elements of "higher" in "lower" and "lower" in "higher." As indicated earlier, for example, businesses have "flattened hierarchies," involved lower level employees in higher level discussions, enabled two-way flows of information, and "empowered" their employees. Here, too, there will always be tension, but it can be more creatively managed for the benefit of all.

The political world is more strictly hierarchical, as the business community once was. Local committee people defer to state committee people; state to national. Similar pecking orders pertain to candidates, elected officials and appointed officials. Higher is higher and lower is lower, and that's that. Yet, more and more problems come home to roost at the local level as both state and national authorities devolve or impose mandates on localities, etc.

Small—Large: In the past, "small" and "large" were viewed as opposites. A business was one or the other. Successful businesses in the new economy, however, have learned how to be both, simultaneously. Large corporations decentralize, devolve or spin-off operating responsibility to small-scale units so that they can be run in more entrepreneurial ways. Networks, consortia or incubators of small firms can operate as if they were large, by sharing resources and/or engaging in joint marketing, R&D, product design or purchasing.

Corresponding to a stricter hierarchy of "higher" and "lower" roles, the political world also displays greater divides between "small" and "large." For all the talk of decentralization and local initiative, neither national nor state governments have learned enough of how to enable creative localism; that is, how best to pass power and money to "small(er)," "lower" level organizations. Whatever happened to the interest in "neighborhood government" that surfaced during the '60"s?[31]

Public—Private: The larger the company, the more its activities are likely to impact people, areas or factors that fall into the public domain. In fact, however, a strong case can be made that any company, whatever its size, exhibits both public and private features. The larger the size of a corporation, the less it can be viewed as a private "person," notwithstanding the notorious Supreme Court decision of 1889. Perhaps the most obvious example of a public/private mix is the private 501(c)©(3) corporation serving public goals. Like other paradoxical combinations, this one, too, spells tension between the poles. Some businesses manage this tension well; most don't. The ways of mixing and balancing the two continue to evolve. Public/private "partnerships," for example, appear in a variety of mutable forms.

What is most important to note from the business side of society is that businesses have created organizational forms that explicitly recognize, embody and express their public sector side(s). We may not like some of these,; as e.g., in the form of trade associations or lobbying organizations, but they exist for a reason to serve legitimate purposes.

The boundary between "public" and "private" has been blurred, some would say warped.[32] What is private depends a great deal on what rules, customs and/or conventions regarding privacy are honored by the media and others. If the government can require "private" entities to reveal information about themselves, or the media are not constrained in their ability to release their revelations, then the veil separating public and private has been pierced.

Indeed, it has already been pierced; some would say shredded, in the political arena. No instance of private behavior by public officials, however prurient, is beyond public scrutiny. The likelihood that their private "dirty laundry" would be so aired has become a deterrent to many people getting involved in politics.

Quantitative—Qualitative: These terms from social science denote a genuine, paradoxical tension within most organizations. On the one hand, nearly any organization has a need to generate numbers that reflect, at least for management purposes, the financial health and some features of performance of the organization. This is the "quantitative" side of accountability. On the other hand, there's a need to pay some attention, albeit less frequently, to features of organizational structure, incentives, relationships, attitudes and behaviors that cannot be appropriately or completely represented by numbers. This is the "qualitative" side. The latter, in fact, takes priority, Numbers only make sense within a certain context which qualitative indicators can describe.

The tension between the two arises from more than one source. For example, there is the familiar tension between "bean counters" and "decision makers" as to what accounting measures are measuring. This tension is aggravated during a time of increased competition and change, when organizations are challenged to measure their performance at the same time that they may be "reinventing themselves" in ways that undermine or even invalidate existing performance measures.

As some of what was noted earlier indicates, drawn from a renaissance of business literature that says far more, a significant portion of the American business community over the past 12-20 years has succeeded in managing this tension quite well, by…

1. Implementing performance benchmarking, activity-based costing and other sophisticated methods of measuring and diagnosing business performance;

2. Aggressively addressing the "qualitative" side as well, by making significant changes in the attitudes, structures and behaviors that influence business performance; and…

3. Progressively iterating between 1 and 2; that is, using quantitative diagnostics to make qualitative changes and qualitative changes to improve quantitative diagnostics.

Political bean counters prevail. They love numbers—the kinds derived from polls, surveys, Census, political focus groups, market research and other techniques borrowed from business and political science curricula. They use these numbers to do quantitative "analysis" in the form of grade-school statistics that they use to do targeting, profiling and priority-setting for political fund raising and campaigns. As the use of these techniques has spread, people's political participation has dried up and the role of the ordinary citizen has been practically blotted out, as shown in the cartoon below. Now, a political science prof. may call this a "spurious correlation." Who do you think is right, the professor or the cartoonist?

This is quantification, all right, with a vengeance. But it is schlock social science, designed to provide a veneer of analytic scientific authority for an old agenda—political manipulation rather than political empowerment; marketing rather than informing. The "qualitative" side is missing. Like looking at the foreground and ignoring the background. The so-called "quantitative" analysis is anti-structural and a-historical. In order to learn anything of the deeper, longer-run structural factors that might help to explain the snapshots provided by political analysts, we'd have to go back to school and study things other than the political non-science we are being fed. There is no "creative tension" or management of the quantitative/qualitative paradox as in business. It is as if politics had fallen in love with only one industry and one aspect of business success—advertising and marketing.

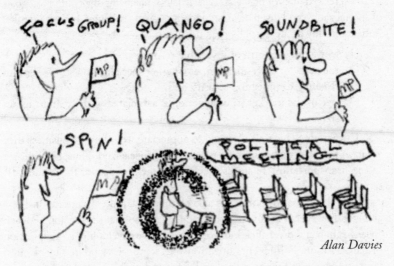

Alan Davies

Loose/flexible organization—Tight/functional organization: Cameron states that: "loose-coupling…encourages wide search, initiation of innovation, and functional autonomy…; tight-coupling…encourages quick execution, implementing…and functional reciprocity…"[33]

As with other paradoxical features, an effective business organization needs to be able to effect both, together, even though they are conflicting qualities. Cameron's studies of business organizations found that "effective" businesses were able to do so.

Political organizations are both too loose and too tight—"too loose" in the sense that lower level committees are left too much to their own devices without knowing what is expected of them; "too tight" in the sense that higher level people both expect too little of them and expect them to follow through on that little without question. They probably would be surprised and concerned if there was a resurgence of lower level initiative. One reason is that the higher levels of political parties have become increasingly focused on fund raising. The fact that some of their power has shifted to campaign committees dominated by existing elected leadership may also be a factor.[34] The hierarchical-bureaucratic nature of political organization has already been highlighted.

Specialization—Diversification: The tension between these poles owes to the fact that any organization needs to build on its strengths at the same time that it needs to diversify in response to new challenges or opportunities. Since the '80's, American business has been managing this tension more sensibly and strategically than during the last wave of mergers and acquisitions (M&A's). That became known as a "conglomerate" fad—the tendency to buy up businesses in unrelated lines of business. During the 90s, conglomerates sold off much of what they had acquired. M&A activity has come to focus on related lines of business. Nevertheless, balancing the conflicting goals of specialization and diversification remains a great challenge. How it is struck both internally and externally depends upon:

(1) leeway in the form of investible resources;
(2) the need for diversification, or whether specialization shows signs of reaching diminishing returns; and
(3) size of the market (specialization is associated with greater market size).

Corporations have also learned to appreciate what lines of business they are in so that they do not become too narrowly specialized. Thus, railroads are in the "transportation" business; steel companies are part of the "materials" sector.

The "business" of politics is also changing. Unlike corporate business changes, however, it is not changing strategically so that the tension between specialization and diversification works to improve development, organization or participation. Political organizations per se, those mandated by election laws, are becoming more specialized—as fund raising vehicles and money laundries. Diversification is occurring by way of politics as a business, as political consultants, political internet firms, political paraphrenalia supply firms and others gradually take over more of the functions of old-fashioned political committees and campaigns, financed by money that the latter have raised. An overriding focus on money may be self-destructive for traditional political organizations. This is no creative management of paradox; it is rather, the mismanagement of.

Continuity—Change: Here is another basic, paradoxical source of tension. As Cameron notes: "Continuity…permits stability, long-term planning and institutional memory." Change… permits increased innovation, adaptability and currency."[35]

Many "old economy" corporations have succeeded in managing this tension very well, maintaining a sense of corporate history, tradition and mission while changing substantially to take advantage of "new economy" opportunities. Some have not; e.g., a major old-line, insurance company that is being sued by its shareholders; one of the "Big 6" accounting firms that failed. Meanwhile, one of the former "Big 6" management consulting firms has been advising clients to honor its "First Paradox Principle"—that "positive change requires significant stability."[36]

This "Principle" is not honored by political organizations. They hardly seem aware of the tension. Thus, they are not consciously managing it at all and, unconsciously, managing it effectively not well. The big change is Internet use—political web-page design(s), "chat rooms," e-mail networks, et. al. This leaves most local political organizations behind and traditional, direct, person-to-person politics unattended. This amounts to placing a premium on discontinuity. As shown in Chapter 5, only a small minority of local political party committees have their own web pages. Chapter 8 will have a lot more to say about the prospects for "digital democracy."

Expansion/Outreach—Consolidation/Integration: Another source of strategic tension is that between expansion into new areas and/or new markets and the consolidation or integration of existing activities. This is obviously related to other paradoxes of the "stand pat" vs. "develop" variety noted earlier. Effective business organizations have recognized this paradox and managed it well. This recognition, reinforced by improved company communications and teamwork, has often pointed to improvements in existing products as opportunities for expansion. This has been the case in the housewares industry, for example, with respect to better design and imaginative use of new materials that have given a whole new lease on market life to many of the most commonplace household items, such as pots and pans.

Political "leaders" and organizations are so fixated on electing their candidates to higher office(s) that they neglect or lose sight of the basis that they came from and the people that voted them into office.[37] These are the foci for consolidation and effective integration of political activities and participants—local political committees.

Entrepreneurial—Bureaucratic: We have touched this polarity earlier, but as a trade-off rather than a paradox. Most organizations need to maintain both types of features even though the degree to which one or the other prevails at any time will depend on several factors, including organizations' stage of development. Organizations of any significant size need to effect both innovation and control. Many "old economy" corporations have transformed themselves from conventional corporate bureaucracies such as those that gave rise to "the organization man" into enterprises that promote "intra-preneurship."[38] Thus, Price Waterhouse also recommends "The Second Paradox Principle: To build an enterprise, focus upon the individual," an anti-bureaucratic advisory.[39] Another major source of advice to business leaders, Peter Senge, advises in a way that is more directly paradoxical. Much of his approach enables a " focus upon the individual" while he also counsels "the primacy of the whole" (organization or enterprise).[40]

Political party organizations haven't followed the lead of their business counterparts to shift emphasis from bureaucracy to entrepreneurship during what President Reagan hailed as the new "age of the entrepreneur." It seems as if fear of political incorrectness has reinforced reliance upon conventional control systems. Meanwhile, political entrepreneurship is alive and well among politically interested individuals who typically invest considerable time and money to build a political base and mount campaigns to get elected to something, usually without any help from their parties. This important brand of entrepreneurship, however, seems more and more to favor those who have either inherited money or invested in building financial assets before they turn to public life. The potentially creative tension between entrepreneurship and bureaucracy is being mis-managed to the detriment of both in public life. Two major reasons may be the following:

1. Higher level political organizations are too often leaving political en- trepreneurs who are promising but not wealthy to "hang out to dry" with their own resources, by providing little support in terms of money or manpower. Ironically, this aggravates political parties' decline because, as more people get elected on the basis of their own individual resources, they owe little or nothing to the parties once elected.

2. Public entrepreneurship is alive and well among many not-for-profit organizations, especially some of those that are issue-oriented, but these have intermittent, weak or opportunistic relationships with political parties.

External—Internal: This is analogous to the paradox of "Expansion— Consolidation" mentioned earlier. Tension is implicit in the underlying ques- tion: Should we "tend to our own washing" as customary or should we diversify our repertory with and/or for a somewhat different set of others? The answer to this question that is evident in the business community is clear: We need to identify and develop relationships with a diverse set of "external" others in a variety of ways—outsourcing, joint ventures, affiliations, partnerships, collaboratives, et. al. Thus, both internal resources and external markets are augmented and enriched.

Higher level political organizations appear to be following the lead of corporations towards one (external) end of this dichotomy like lemmings going over a cliff, somewhat like their fascination for business' marketing techniques. They are outsourcing to political consultants, et.al., with a vengeance while neglecting internal capacity-building. Yet they are far from exploiting the full potential of joint ventures, collaborations and the like with "non-political" public interest groups representing various aspects of civil society.

Symbol—Substance: These are often viewed as opposites, especially by intellectuals who love to carp over fine distinctions that they believe to be substantive. Indeed, advertising and P.R. often seem to favor one over the other (guess which!). Yet, one of the accomplishments of the "top leadership" of effective businesses, according to Cameron, is that they "paid a great deal of attention" to both, as follows.

> On the one hand, structural, personnel and curricular changes were instituted, so that the basic fiber of the institution was altered. On the other hand, substance was ignored in favor of image…to help constituencies interpret events favorably (so that the) core culture…of successful institutions was reinforced…The management of symbols and interpretations was a critical difference between successful managers and others who failed.

Politics has veered towards one end of this paradox, too—"symbol" over "substance." Unless political parties and others can succeed in managing the tension between them better in order to redress the imbalance, they will consign themselves to a state to which many feel they have already fallen—irrelevance and disrepute.

Creation—Destruction: At least since Shumpeter's famous book,[41] business and economic development in a market economy have been recognized as processes of "creative destruction" in which the paradoxical, seemingly polar opposites come together. This has been quite evident in recent years, as business organizations of all types have been reinventing themselves via downsizing, outsourcing, a massive wave of mergers and acquisitions, rapid technological changes, etc. At the same time, we have experienced the longest economic expansion and period of sustained prosperity since series of key economic statistics began. It is also well-known that higher rates of entrepreneurship (new business enterprise formations) go hand in hand with higher rates of business failures.

How the inherent tension between creation and destruction is managed within enterprises in order to exploit their development potential as conjoined processes is, of course, one of the on-going challenges of business management in the new economy, so much so that several books have been written for business readers on how to employ "paradox as a dynamic tool."[42] "The Fifth Paradox Principle" advocated by one of the "Big 6" management consulting firms, Price Waterhouse, for example is: "In order to build, you must tear down."[43]

A question implied by much of the debate over political reform(s) is: How much of conventional politics needs to be torn down or cleared away before we can create a system that works? No one has yet answered this question. Read on and see the final chapter.

Paradox: Revolution in Business a Prelude to Political Reform?

The revolution in American business can and should be considered a prelude to political reform because, if our political system does not adopt or adapt much of what we have seen heralded by the business press, then:

- The political system will fall farther and farther behind the business system and/or…
- The political system may fail…with adverse consequences most of us would not want to contemplate.

The inability of our political system to attract talent, relative to the business community, has also been mentioned. Partly because major segments of the business community have transformed themselves and their ways of operating, business appears to increasing numbers of young people to be more dynamic, interesting, challenging and powerful than politics or government. So, we can see here another vicious cycle at work detrimental to our political system: Talented young people avoiding politics and government; thus, the latters' performance gets worse and more talent stays away, etc.

There are two matters fundamentally at issue here. One is the quality of the political process, a concern which runs through this whole book. The other is power. Business is only a subsystem of the economy and of American society. Polanyi (1957) refers to the market system as "embedded" in society. So it should be, actually as well as desirably. Yet, ironically, the new economy seems to be a replay of the '50's in one key respect. It seems to many as if "the business of American is business" or, to paraphrase former GM Chairman Charlie Miller, as if 'what's good for business is good (best?) for America.'

The organizational development gap(s) that we have observed between business and political sectors of American society—progressive vs. regressive—spells a disparity in power that can only worsen if the political sector continues to lag. This means that Charlie Miller may turn out to be a live prophet, not just a dead executive. His statement may be a self-fulfilling prophecy, but only if you believe that increasing dominance of politics and government by business is good, and not for reasons put forth by those protesting corporate power by demonstrating in Seattle or Washington. The reason lies in the backwardness of the political sector, not with a corporate conspiracy.

We began this chapter with irony; here it is again. Ironically, the great majority of the American people will be increasingly powerless to the extent that they do not take charge of a political reform process that incorporates many of the elements demonstrated within the American business community. The most important of these is people's empowerment. "We, the people…" should be far more than just the opening words of our Constitution. We can begin by recognizing and employing powers already available to us—if we care to take advantage of them—starting, but not ending, with voting.

Paradox or Problem? Big Business Role in Reform Efforts

Another irony is that large corporations have been major players among those pressing for campaign finance reform (CFR). GM helped to lead the way by refusing to play the "soft money" game—a prime target of reformers. Many other large corporations followed. Then the Committee for Economic

Development (CED), an organization representing the views of many blue-chip corporations, published a report that endorsed CFR.[44]

A major critic of corporate, big business support for CFR writes that:

> the type of big businesses represented by the CED don't worry about a loss of influence due to added restrictions on giving...their influence really comes from lobbying ...big business in the United States spends roughly ten times as much on lobbying as it does on all campaign contributions and soft money donations combined.[45]

Meanwhile, polls continue to show that CFR is not a major issue for most voters, notwithstanding the upsurge of energy around the issue during the 2000 Presidential primary campaign season and for some time thereafter. Along with other members of the CFR community, the CED focuses only on money as the root of political evil and fails to recognize the importance of people's time. Thus, a political cynic might claim that large corporations are counting on people not being politically empowered, politically much more involved or even willing to pay attention—and that if the great American majority showed signs of wanting to assert themselves politically, then the public interest and corporate interest(s) would inevitably face off in a great struggle reminiscent of the battle of Progressives vs. corporate Robber Barons of over one hundred years ago.

Given the more entrepreneurial nature of the new economy, however, reformers should not assume that the U.S. business community is either monolithic or adverse to reform. Paradoxically, they will find friends under the business umbrella, as well as some enemies and various shades of opinion in-between. And in terms of the business change models, policies and practices described thusfar in this chapter, they will find much to advance the cause of genuine, overall political reform, far more than is embodied in the various national or state government CFR initiatives.

Notes

1. The author of *On Common Things* has been heralded as an insightful critic of irony and promoter of a refreshingly naïve revival of public life grounded in his West Virginia country upbringing. As this chapter indicates, however, irony has been a constructive tool for political change at least since Jonathan Swift. In spite of the fact that some editions of Roget's Thesaurus treat "irony" and "cynicism" as synonyms, they are not. Even the *New York Times* has made the mistake of practically equating the two, as in "The Age of Irony Isn't Over, After All: Assertions of Cynicism's Demise Belie History" (in The Arts section of October 10, 2001). Cynicism is destructive, while irony accents paradox which, if well-managed, can be quite constructive. See contrasting definitions in Webster's New Collegiate Dictionary, for example.

2. N.A.T.O. = "No Action, Talk Only"

3. For one of the many books on this, see: Bradley, Stephen P. & R.L. Nolan (1998), *Sense & Respond*. Cambridge, MA: Harvard Business School Press.

4. As, for example, those sponsored by the Kettering Foundation through a "community and politics demonstration program". See NACL (1999), "Community Leadership: 1996-1999 Project Report." Dayton, OH: The Kettering Foundation.

5. Peters, Thomas J. and R. H. Waterman (1982), *In Search for Excellence: Lessons From America's Best-Run Companies*. New York: Harper and Row.

6. Bearse, Peter J. (1987), "Industrial Policy From the Shop Floor and the Bottom Up," *The Entrepreneurial Economy*. Washington, D.C., Corporation for Enterprise Development.

7. The author observed this tendency at first hand as an International Consultant for the United Nations Industrial Development Organization in Sri Lanka advising the Minister of Industry. The Japanese continued to pedal their central planning approach to other countries even as evidence of its failure accumulated on the home front.

8. Some of these features have been introduced and elaborated by Charles Handy in *The Age of Uncertainty* and other books.

9. The reference here, again, is to the pathbreaking works of Senge, et. al. (1994).

10. This phrase is also drawn from Senge, et.al.

11. This is not to deny or overlook notable exceptions, such as the Kennedy School of Government's Program of annual awards recognizing "innovations" in state and local government, nor the attempts of some of these to implement PBM. The U.S. Government, Department of the Treasury has also promoted performance measurement and benchmarking by federal agencies.

12. An excellent treatment of these "internal" features can be found in one of the business-focused books that has informed this section: Gareth Morgan's (1997) *Images of Organization*. See especially Chapter 6: "Interests, Conflict and Power: Organizations as Political Systems."

13. Senge, op.cit., pp.38 & 39.

14. For example, in Nicolis, G. and I. Progogine (1977), *Self-Organization in Non-Equilibrium Systems: From Dissipative Structures to Order Through Fluctuations*. New York, John Wiley & Sons, Wiley-Interscience.

15. In fairness to Members of Congress, however, one should recognize the enormous volume of mail they receive, which has been increasing by leaps and bounds, especially via e-mail generated by "grassroots lobbying" (see Chapter 9). It has gotten so that software filters are now used to ascertain what kind of "canned" reply should be sent and to automatically send it, not just to

eliminate "spam." The great volume of mail is just one strong indication that congressional districts are much too large.

16. One ironic twist of the debate on campaign finance reform is that "soft money" was supposed to have been used for such "party building" activities, a purpose whose legitimacy was reaffirmed by decision of the Federal District Court reviewing the latest campaign finance reform legislation. See Chapter 9.

17. Palmer, Parker (1990), "Leading from Within: Reflections on Spirituality and Leadership." Washington, D.C.: The Servant Leadership School.

18. Palmer (1990), op.cit., p.11.

19. See, for example: Case, John (1995), "The Open Book Revolution," *INC Magazine* (June) and Fenn, Donna (1996), "Open Book Management 101," *INC Magazine* (August).

20. See Bearse, Peter J. (1999), for example.

21. The title of an important (1989) book, referenced below in note 24, a book to which we will return.

22. Note, for example, the case of Firestone-Bridgeton tires.

23. Hauerwas, Stanley (1981), *Community of Character: Toward a Constructive Christian Social Ethic*. Notre Dame, Indiana: University of Notre Dame Press.

24. Mitroff, Ian and W.Bennis (1989), *The Unreality Industry: the Deliberate Manufacturing of Falsehood and What It Is Doing to Our Lives*. New York: Birch Lane Press, pp.xi & xii.

25. Pawley, Martin (1974), op.cit.

26. This sweeping claim is generally acknowledged and well-documented by many others too numerous to mention; e.g., with respect to corporate pressures for mobility and post-war patterns of development.

27. See, for example, Gozdz, Kazimierz (1995), *Community Building: Renewing Spirit & Llearning in Business*. San Francisco: Sterling & Stone, New Leaders Press; and Hesselbein, Frances, et.al. (ed.1998), *The Community of the Future*. San Francisco: Jossey-Bass & The Drucker Foundation.

28. See Cameron, Kim (1986), "Effectiveness as Paradox: Consensus and Conflict in Conceptions of Organizational Effectiveness," 32 *Management Science* 5 (May).

29. Cameron, op.cit., p.545.

30. Slaatte, H.A.(1968), *The Pertinence of the Paradox*. New York: Humanities Press, p.4.

31. See Kotler, Milton (1969), *Neighborhood Government*. New York: Bobbs Merrill. The word "enough" suggests that something has been learned, espe-

cially through block grant programs, but the "something" needs to be identified, analyzed, culled, codified and greatly extended. Remember general revenue sharing?

32. See Meyrowitz (1985), and Mitroff and Bennis (1989) on "boundary warping." Also see Chapter 8.

33. Cameron, op.cit., p.545.

34. See Shea, Daniel (1995), *Transforming Democracy: Legislative Campaign Committees and Political Parties.*

35. Cameron, op.cit., p.545.

36. Price Waterhouse (1995), *The Paradox Principles: How High Performance Companies Manage Chaos, Complexity and Contradiction to Achieve Superior Results.* New York: McGraw-Hill, (Pt. 2).

37. Except treating them as "wells" to which they repeatedly return to try to draw out more money.

38. For example, see Lessen, Ronnie (1988), *Intrapreneurship: How to be an Enterprising Individual in a Successful Business.* Ashgate Publishing Company.

39. Price Waterhouse, op.cit.(Pt.3).

40. Senge, Peter, op.cit., p.25.

41. Shumpeter, Joseph A. (1942), *Capitalism, Socialism and Democracy.* New York: Harper and Row.

42. For example: Price Waterhouse (1995), op.cit.

43. Price Waterhouse, op.cit., Pt.6.

44. Committee for Economic Development (1999).

45. Smith, Bradley A. (2000), Presentation to the Catholic University Law Review Symposium on "Election Law Reform." Washington, D.C. (September 23).

8.

DIGITAL DEMOCRACY?
The Media 'Net' and Web of Politics

Introduction

They say that we live in the Information Age—that knowledge is power and that information provides a large part of what counts as knowledge. So the media – prime vendors of "information" – are in the catbird seat of politics. They appear to be the source of power. How so? What influence do the media have on political participation and how do they exercise that influence?

One of the most influential students of the media, Marshall McLuhan, coined the famous phrase, "The medium is the message." Politicians are familiar with this, especially since their ability to win depends upon how their image appears on TV. They don't stand a chance to get elected if they can't get their message out. Here then, we see another dimension of media power: some critics of the media claim, that the "media problem" is deeply rooted and system-wide, not just a topical, current issue. We caught part of the flavor of such a claim earlier, with reference to Sennett, Lasch and Toffler, among others. More recent authors say that the new age we live in is not only an electronic/information age, but a "Systems Age" whose complexity calls for more under-standing, not less, but whose media generate what Mitroff and Bennis have called a "trained incapacity" and a "growing inability" to even face, let alone handle and resolve complex issues.[1]

Obviously, we're not just concerned about campaign messages here. What about the message people are getting about politics overall? We saw in Chapters 4 and 5 how a number of those interviewed or surveyed for this book remarked on how the media were feeding people's negativity and cyni-cism about politics. If they're right, this has influence and it affects candidacies, including people's willingness to run. Many interviewees thought the impact of the media on the latter — what we earlier called the "supply side" of politics — is also negative. So, can we place the brunt of blame on the media for the negatives noted up to this point? The following political cartoon is just one example of very many that provide unflattering portrayals of the political process. Are media responsible for drying up both the grassroots and pools of candidates? Let's take a closer look.

David Horsey, Washington, The Seattle Post-Intelligencer

The way this introduction has proceeded provides a prime illustration of one way the media exert political power and influence. It's called "framing." Politicians, political consultants and media studies claim that the media frame issues, articles, and media treatments to lead the public to certain conclusions. This introduction has framed this chapter to focus your attention on possible adverse impacts of the media on political participation. The focus primarily comes down to identifying WHAT and HOW — <u>What</u> impacts; <u>How</u> generated.

What and How: Reinforcing Vicious Circles

Earlier, we identified several "vicious circles" dragging our politics down. These include the:

- **Political Lemons** cycle: Politics is dirty so good people stay away from politics, making it more dirty.

- **Fear and lack of confidence** cycle: Feeling that one lacks what it takes to become involved with others, politically, a person fails to get involved, and so the feeling is compounded as he or she observes the process being taken over by political pro's or others among "the usual suspects." And so, for lack of being involved, one never gains what it takes and the fear factor prevails or is increased.

- **Voting** cycle: People don't vote, on the basis of feelings that "my vote doesn't count" and/or that "all we have to vote for is the lesser of two evils," but then they truly don't count and potential candidates who might represent a real difference are deterred from stepping forward for fear there is not a sufficient constituency for their views. Then people are even less likely to vote, etc.

- **Political Inequality** cycle: This is the voting cycle with a vengeance adverse to those who can least afford the negative feedback loop: Poor people don't vote because they rightly feel that nobody in elected office is doing anything for them and, indeed, unless they vote, nobody does anything for them. Along with this goes the well-documented fact that the better off someone is economically, the more likely they are, not only to vote but to participate politically in other ways. So to them that has goes the goods and the poor are left with what Rumpy got for Christmas.

- **Public/Private** cycle: The rewards of private life are more personal, direct, less costly and less diffuse; thus, people are less likely to participate in public life. The reduced participation translates into a public life where participation is more costly, less direct (less local, more removed), and thus more likely to be dominated by "the usual suspects" with whom there are no personal, familial or community relationships. Thus, others are even less likely to participate.

- **Party** cycle: Party politics is seen as fractious, contentious, partisan and serving only "them," not "us," so people increasingly stay away from parties as unenrolled or independent; thus, parties become more of what leads to the negative perceptions of them and even less important to people's lives.

- **Independence** cycle: People develop self-images as private, independent people who can think and act for themselves, even in the political realm. This leads to an atrophy of political parties except as money laundries and an increasing dependence upon interest-advocacy groups among whom the citizen consumer can increasingly "shop" to find avenues for representation of particular views. From the standpoint of political participation, however, this leads to growing political independence, the further atrophy of both political parties and of anything that could be called the public interest, and even greater incentives to become independent.

To what extent are the media at the core of these cycles or significant sources of their aggravation? The media as primary producers of images[2] are at the core of the Lemons Cycle because the images that the media present of politics and politicians are predominantly negative. The image of a politician that typically emerges from the media is that of a person who:

- Is ambitious and egotistical;
- Talks out of both sides of his mouth;
- Is beholden to "special interests;" and who...
- Has no special skills or has no career or achievements outside of politics.

The latter point is especially important, as Boulding (1961) indicates that a political system in which the "distribution of images" falls out of line with the "distribution of skills" needed to run it is a system that is or will become unstable.[3] The major skill featured by the media and admired by the public is rhetorical — public speaking ability — the "gift of gab." Ironically, many observers and historians say that even this skill, as exhibited by our current crop of politicians, falls far short of the quality of political oratory heard from past generations of our nation's political leaders. As for other skills, even though we have seen the election of some people to Congress who have built remarkable, prior political careers in fields other than politics, who can name them or their non-political fields? Damn few. There is irony here, too, for the other fields that may be named are most likely centered on the media, like TV acting (e.g., former U.S. Sen. Fred Thompson) or entertainment (e.g., former Rep.'s Sony Bono or Fred Grandy). How many people other than some Democratic activists in Northern New Jersey know that Rep. Rush Holt is a former physicist? Perhaps because of his high visibility as Senate Majority Leader, many Americans know that Sen. Bill Frist is a doctor, but it remains to be seen whether his skills will serve him well in the Majority Leader's position.[4]

The prevailing view of the political process emerging from the media is also unflattering, to say the least. It is a game in which:

- Ethical standards are, at best, grey;
- Truthfulness doesn't count for much;
- One needs a lot of money to play; and...
- Ordinary people have no influence after votes are cast.

Evidence on the other side of the "lemons" coin? — people are shying away from politics. Look at the increasing numbers of uncontested seats, even positions for which there are no candidates at all, incumbent or otherwise, plus some towns where an election was declared but nobody came. "In New Ashford, voters: 202; turnout, Zero."[5]

The media are also at the core of the Party Cycle. This is partly by default, evidenced by decreasing coverage of political party activities. Those of local party committees receive very little or no coverage, so most people do not even know that there are such organizations nearby where they can go to get politically involved. Coverage of higher level political party organizations is also lacking and, when it does occur, negative. Coverage of state and national party conventions has been diminishing. Parties are partisan by definition, but partisanship has been put in an increasingly negative light by the media. Party officials are seen as party hacks who receive their appointments as payoffs for otherwise failed or finished political careers or as favors for party loyalty. Party members are viewed as political "activists" or political "junkies;" i.e., people not like "us."

To feed the other side of the Party Cycle, the media increasingly present declarations of independence from parties as intelligent and principled. One never sees such shifts described as stupid and self-defeating, as Ron Mills indicated in his interview for Chapter 4. Thus, the Independence Cycle and Party Cycle interact. Note, for example, the coverage of U.S. Sen. Jim Jeffords' shift from Republican to Independent. Not surprisingly, numbers and percentages of voters that are independent or un-enrolled continue to rise, political parties continue to weaken and the trend towards independence is reinforced.

The Public/Private Cycle is strongly reinforced by media-generated images even though the roots of this cycle, as noted in Chapter 2, run much deeper than media programming patterns. Questions: (A) When was the last time we saw political involvement or even dinner table political conversations featured in TV programs? (B) By contrast, how often do we see private family life extolled, private recreation activities advertised and self-involved behaviors featured? The answers to this quiz are (A) A long time ago; (B) Innumerable. So, fewer and fewer people even think of participating in politics and there are decreasing numbers of role models that might inspire young people towards such activities. People retreat into private worlds, and the public sector, attracting less talent, is less able to deliver. So, this cycle reinforces the Lemons Cycle and some of the other negative cycles. The most powerful indictment of the media in this respect was provided by *The Private Future* in 1974, a picture that has largely come to pass 30 years later.

As for the political inequality cycle, Barbara Ehrenreich notes the dismissive attitude and sometimes outright erroneous reporting of the media with respect to people who are poor. She also observed: "Forty years ago, the hot journalistic topic was "the discovery of the poor" in their inner city and Appalachian "pockets of poverty." Today you are more likely to find commentary on their "disappearance," either as a supposed demographic reality or a shortcoming of the middle-class imagination."[6]

The possibility that the media can play a different, more positive role, however, one that encourages people to get involved in public life is indicated by claims of a "West Wing flip." Polling of young viewers indicates that they are more favorably inclined towards careers in government than the public at-large.[7]

Manufacturing Unreality and Undermining Truthfulness

The title of this section borrows from the titles of two books, each of which should be far more widely read than they have been:

- *The Unreality Industry: The Deliberate Manufacturing of False-hood and What it is Doing to Our Lives,* and

- *Time for Truth: Living Free in a World of Lies, Hype and Spin.*[8]

As already indicated in Chapter 6, these two books, with support from some others,[9] document dangerous long-term trends away from reality and truthfulness. These trends, moreover, amount to an indictment of electronic media. The fact that some readers may react to the use of the words "reality" and "truthfulness" with skepticism speaks to the danger. Guinness shows how the disease of "postmodern" attitudes — politically correct (PC) relativity without Einstein's devotion to truth-seeking — has many people disbelieving that there is any reality outside of what they can create in their own small, controllable (they think), self-centered worlds. Mitroff and Bennis directly relate to the vicious cycles noted earlier by stating at the outset that the "manufacturing" they point to amounts to a negatively interlocking "combination of mutually reinforcing influences." Just one of the troubling implications of this is that any proposed solution to a public problem usually "consists of intensifying the initial problem." A truly dangerous implication of both books is that we are losing our ability to tell the difference between what is real and what is imagined. "The end consequence is a society less and less able to face its true problems directly, honestly and intelligently."[10]

This is a concern of long standing. Initial symptoms were apparent at least 100 years ago. They were quite visible during the '20's; then they were precisely diagnosed and brought to the attention of wide audiences over 40 years ago. What the two books cited at the outset of this section have served to do is to provide evidence of a long-term trend towards two un's — untruth and unreality. A pretty complete diagnosis of the problem was provided by Daniel Boorstin, former Librarian of the Library of Congress, in a remarkably insightful book that he published in 1961. The more recent books show that the symptoms he identified and analyzed have blossomed into a disease. Mitroff recently reaffirmed the thesis of his 1989 book with Bennis in ways that reinforce the urgency of the far more recent (year 2000) book by Guinness: "The problem (as indicated by the book's title) is every bit as bad and probably worse now... Politics is a media circus. The next step for us as humans is to become unreal, like Cyborgs. What is human? Have we crossed over? We are not just celebrities going for a makeover. The intrusion of media and technology into our lives is now much deeper." (by telephone to this author, August 9, 2000).

One feature of what Mitroff and Bennis called the "manufacture of unreality" by the media, Boorstin had identified much earlier as the creation of "pseudo events."[11] So, if we are looking at trends of long-standing, what's new, and what's so "dangerous?" Mitroff and Bennis say that "what's new" is the new electronic technology, and what's dangerous is its low cost, broad scope, speed of transmission and worldwide applicability. The dangers, however, have long been demonstrated by an electronic technology that is hardly new – television (TV). What is new since the "Unreality Industry" book was released is the introduction and spread of the Internet, whose implications for political participation we will turn to later in this chapter under the heading of "Digital Democracy?".

What is definitely not new is people's tendency to fancy myth, illusion, magic, un-truth and escapism. This tendency is so ancient, so deeply rooted, that it must be recognized as fundamental to human nature. As we shall see in the next section, part of our problem is that the media play upon this tendency, somewhat as they exploit another even more ancient fundamental, sex. The overriding problem, new relative to ancient but already old relative to the 21st century, is that tendencies toward self-delusion became collective, involving millions of people, in the 20th century. These now threaten to become more so as 21st century media technology enables the extension of various forms of collective delusion ever more widely and deeply into the public domain in ways that undermine our democracy.

There is an ancient ordinariness to human behavior in that people in any age feel the need to escape from the ordinariness of their day-to-day existence. This need is paradoxical. It has an undeniably good side insofar as it is a prime root of innovation and creativity. But the bad side, its dangerousness, has been amply exhibited in the 20th century in the banality (ordinariness) of evil and the greater potential of evil over good when the possibilities of escaping the "ordinary" has spread to mass society. Then, via some pretense of democracy, the banality of evil can become the order of the day. [12]

Both the Guinness and Mitroff & Bennis books indicate that the "smoke and mirrors" often attributed to politics now find their true home primarily in the media, to be recycled by the media to give a more professional, highly paid, media consultants' gloss to political imagery. Indeed, it is in the public (political) arena that the trends they alert us to are most perilous, simply (!) because our ability to solve shared problems at any level of community; indeed, the very integrity of "community" itself, is what is threatened and open to question.

One aspect of fantasy is found among several reputable writers urging us to "get a grip" on the real issues of our public life—their reference to the Greeks and their Athenian "polis" or "Agora" as representing a model for democracy via "full engagement with the world at all levels."[13] For a small, 600 B.C century society of slave owners to be so viewed is hardly an effort to come to grips with 21st century reality! So it's no surprise to see a citizen's "op-ed" contribution to a local newspaper titled "Whatever happened to real life?" and commenting: "We have become a nation of voyeurs and exhibitionists. The viewers live out their fantasies…"[14]

From some writers, there is speculation about the applicability in the 21st century here and now of even more ancient, pre-historical models—the "hunter-gatherers" of the Pleistocene age. These were people with no relationship to a place, and a lack of boundaries where everyone was involved with everyone else's business.[15] Such speculations seem harmless except to the degree that they represent a lack of serious effort to grapple with the real problems of real people in real places here in the U.S.of A. As we shall see further on, however, reliance upon old archetypes can become dangerously serious, as when others start to write and talk about a "new Middle Ages." See Eco's chapter on "The Return of the Middle Ages," for example,[16] and recall that medieval motifs figured heavily among Nazi icons.

The books referenced provide few answers but they leave us with questions of the utmost urgency. For example:

- How can we even begin to face, let alone solve "shared problems" if we spend most our discretionary leisure time watching TV?

- How can we come together as a community – as a great American majority – at any level, from neighborhood to nation, if most of us continue to think that quiet time at home is the be-all and end-all of non-working hours?

Answers? We can't provide them. TV is addictive, like a drug, so we need to learn to "JUST SAY NO." It can be done. We did it in our family. We eliminated TV in one house and strictly limited access in the other (summer) house.[17] TV is dangerous to family health. Gee, what do we do if we do away with our TV? We might actually have to do other things, like talk to each other or (God forbid!) read a good book, even one that we can discuss or share! We might learn to communicate with each other (contrary to the following cartoon). We might even talk about politics! Instead, by relying on TV for the sort of political news that some call "pablum" or "sound bites," we gain the sort of "understanding" referred to by the Director of Communications for the White House, below.

"Although humans make sounds with their mouths and occasionally
look at each other, there is no solid evidence that they actually
communicate with each other."

"Americans are leading busy lives…If they can have an instant understanding of what the president is talking about by seeing 60 seconds of television, you accomplish your goals as communicators." [To which a newspaper columnist responded: "Communicators to whom? Children?"][18]

Another impact of TV may be reduced ability to distinguish differences or discriminate among parties or candidates, as suggested by another cartoon, below. So, could time spent watching TV help to explain the oft-expressed feelings of many voters that "there ain't a dimes worth of difference between the major parties"?

David Horsey. Washington, The Seattle Post-Intelligencer

Another question to ask and answer to watch for is whether "September 11th" will turn out to be a "wake-up call for media as well as the rest of America. Initial reactions led one to hope. Some media commentators wondered whether so-called "Reality TV" would still have an audience now that people had found that real life was more dangerous and far more meaningful than the unreality of "Survival" and other such shows. Network news seemed to be somewhat reoriented toward "hard news" and away from news-as-entertainment. Newspapers and TV paid more attention to "the heroes of everyday life" and somewhat less to glitzy stars. There seemed to be more investigative reporting, at least on terrorists and Afghanistan, as a backdrop to "America at War." More Americans were facing the world, not just themselves. Americans were aroused. Unfortunately, it did not take media long to return to reality-as–usual, that is, the unreality noted earlier.

Reinforcing as well as responding to a rising wave of patriotism, the media proceeded to leap from public arousal to support for government, especially for national (central) government initiatives. We saw such headlines as "Bashing Government is Over" and "Terrorism is Making Government Look Good."[19] This shift runs counter to the critical stance toward government failure noted in Chapter 6. It also threatens to reinforce the centralization of government and politics, as every war has done, contrary to the decentralization that would reinforce local democracy and promote greater grassroots political participation.

The family is the first and best foundation for enabling our children to face the world, live in it and make a difference to people other than themselves. They can't do this, however, if their parents are retreating from that world, curling up in their living wombs (sorry; sometimes I lisp) and watching reality (read: fantasy) TV. As shown in the next section, TV is dangerous to community and political health. TV has been with us now for half a century, so there has been plenty of time to recognize the dangers of once new electronic media.

Undermining Public Life and Political Participation in Specific Ways

The danger is that, indeed, the past may prove to be prologue – a predictor of what we may see as the newest of the new media continue their spread across our country and among its people. So, we should really take a look at the effects of TV and other traditional media before turning to prospects for "digital democracy."

Television

The impact of TV on politics and public life has been studied to a fare thee well. What have we learned? – that television:

- Consumes a major portion of people's free time;
- Takes people away from involvement with their communities, partly by substituting viewers' interaction with figures and situations on TV for involvement with real others in real places;
- Privatizes their leisure time activity;
- Blurs the boundary between public and private;
- Drives up the cost of political campaigns;
- Fosters a politics of personality and spectator sports rather than a politics of public issues and participation;

Vic Harville. Little Rock, Arkansas –

- Has turned news into entertainment;

- Still qualifies for that old label "the boob tube;" and

- Distracts people from attention to important issues and shifts their attention to artificial worlds, so that they are "less and less able to face up to true problems."[20]

The preceding cartoon provides a partial illustration of TV's influence. According to Paddy Chayevsky, "TV is democracy at its ugliest."

Based, however, as the lawyers like to say, on the "full body of evidence," the verdict on the impacts of TV is not all negative. We can also see that TV:

- Helps us to see and to understand the "strangeness and otherness of others…to see what other people are interested in or are doing;"

- Broadens our acquaintance with the rest of the world; and…

- Gives the viewer "a sense of connection" with other people in other places.

A more critical view of these positives is that all they amount to is "watching…as a private act…merely observing…dissociating selves from the content" without taking any responsibility."[21] Or: "By making us aware of every social and personal problem imaginable, television also makes us less likely to do anything about it."[22] This view is somewhat unfair, however, since we all know of instances where TV news regarding disasters has prompted outpourings of donations and offers of help from viewers. A more common complaint is that TV news, like much of reporting by other media, thrives on "disasters" (i.e., bad news generally) without covering much, if any, good news on what people are doing to help each other or their communities.

Notwithstanding the occasional "outpourings" noted above, the evidence of negative impacts of TV on our politics and public life far outweighs that of positives. Such indictments have been presented over many years by many

Mike Smith, The Las Vegas Sun, Nevada

analysts, yet the evidence presented most recently by Harvard Prof. Robert Putnam amounts to case closed for the prosecution.[23] He observes, in light of the Nielson ratings for household viewing hours, that: *"the average American now watches roughly four hours a day, very nearly the highest viewership anywhere in the world."*[24]

The cartoon above shows one slant on what this can mean in terms of political participation.

The further observation that "television absorbed almost 40% of the average American's free time in 1995..." significantly underestimates the importance of the time spent watching TV relative to other activities. "Free time" is hardly "free," the use of which is discretionary just because it is defined as time spent not working for pay. As any so-called "soccer mom" (and dad) knows, there are a variety of things to be done during non-working hours, most of which are subject to real scheduling requirements or constraints. These include cooking, cleaning, home repair, child care, shopping and social events, not to mention chauffeuring kids to soccer games (or whatever, wherever). As leading scholars of how and why people spend time as they do, Martha Hill and Tom Juster, wrote:

> The notion of constraints must be a basic characteristic of any analysis that purports to deal with time allocation, simply because total time itself represents a fixed quantity per time period for every individual...[25]

Recall that we earlier referred to time as "the signature of our mortality, definitely "fixed" for each of us, even if we don't know how little is left to us.

Thus, TV watching competes with a variety of other "free time" activities, some of which are higher priority for individuals or families. More time spent watching TV means less time for other things. Is TV watching complementary to any other activities; that is, does more TV watching go hand in hand with more of some other activity? Specifically, what about time devoted to political activities and/or to otherwise taking part in the public life of one's community?

Prof. Putnam's analysis of DDB Needham Life Style Survey data show that there is only one exception to his overriding observation that TV watching is destructive of participation in politics and public life; that is, for the category of "selective viewers"— "the more time spent watching news, the more active one is in the community."[26] Otherwise, outstanding evidence demonstrates unequivocally (with page references to Putnam's book) that:

- "the introduction of television deflated...residents' participation in community activities" (p. 236);

- "Heavy television watching by young people is associated with civic ignorance" (p. 237);

- "TV watching comes at the expense of nearly every social activity outside the home..." (p. 237);

- "those who said they were spending more time watching TV than in the past were significantly less likely to attend public meetings, to serve in local organizations, to sign petitions and the like..." (p. 238);
- "television programs erode social and political capital by concentrating on characters and stories that portray a way of life that weakens group attachments and social/ political commitment..." (p. 242);
- "each additional hour of television viewing per day means roughly a 10 percent reduction in most forms of civic activism – fewer public meetings, fewer local committee members, fewer letters to Congress, and so on." (p. 228)
- "Television...is particularly toxic for activities that we do together." (p. 229).

Even the news-watching aspect needs to be qualified, for many observers of the media agree that there has been a marked trend by the TV networks to turn news into entertainment. This trend poses another serious set of problems, affecting not only political participation but the ability of participants to deal with public issues. Major problems arise from the fact that TV trades in visual images that have nothing to do with literacy, whereas the ability to deal with issues rests substantially on one's ability to read. Visual images may enable each of us, like Bill Clinton, to better "feel your pain," but not help us to understand your underlying problem, let alone how to effectively address it. TV or other electronic media cannot entirely supplant print media. Meanwhile, there are estimates that 23-72 million American adults are "functionally illiterate."[27] The Gallup organization reported that, "on average, 75% of adults have *not* read a book in the previous month."[28] Dear reader, you don't appear to be one of them.

This contrast between reading and watching does not imply that TV is unable to help people understand public issues and deal with them. Actually, if the power of this and other electronic media were exploited for the purpose of providing more and better public information rather than more and better entertainment for profit, the media could add considerable value to the information over and above that which one could get from a book on the same subject. Why? Because the electronic media add information in at least two forms that a book cannot directly provide – audio and visual. This is one reason why "multi-media" applications have such promise. But how much influence did MTV's "Rock the Vote" have on the turnout of young people during 2000 and 2004 elections?

The battle between print and non-print media has been going on for decades. Advocates for the electronic media say that print is a "linear" medium that disables us from taking a "holistic" view appropriate to the "new age." Yet this old printoholic holdover from the Gutenberg era wonders who is the more disabled. It is easier to diagnose "Patterns in the Sand" when the grains are words on a page than when they are pixels on a screen.[29] One wonders how someone can even see, let alone understand, a pattern of visual images if one cannot identify and analyse the underlying elements.[30] It is easy to use the word "holistic" without being able to recognize what the whole represents. Yet, let's not get caught up in word games. From the standpoint of people's role in politics, we may be reflecting two sides of a coin here, not a case of either/or. Combinations of visual images and words can provide a powerful 1-2 punch. They can reinforce each other.

It's possible for TV to be much more effective than print in calling attention to an issue in ways that excites people's interest or concern and sparks their involvement with others to deal with the issue. The dean of public opinion research, Daniel Yankelovitch, calls this "consciousness raising."[31] Once someone is engaged with an issue and trying to do something about it, reliance upon print media may come into play. Print media can be more analytic. Meyrowitz writes: "The logical linking of pieces of information into large, complex and connected treatises and theories is a feature of writing and print."[32] So, if "holistic" is equated or at least connected with the ability to perceive (the) "complexity" (of the "whole" of something), then we can hardly rely on electronic media alone. TV images and multi-media can convey some overall sense of something but sensation is a long way from understanding.

Even the ability of electronic media to "convey more of an overall sense of something" is open to question. Put the power and nuance of the English language into the hands of a great writer and you get both a richer sense and better understanding of the human condition from one book than one can obtain from a month of Sundays of watching TV. This is the gist of the case for print media made by a distinguished author, Mario Vargas Llosa, as he declared "The premature obituary of the book."[33]

> The complex sum of contradictory truths…constitute the very substance of the human condition. In today's world, this totalizing and living knowledge of a human being may be found only in literature…(which) exists only when it is adopted by others and becomes part of social life – when it becomes, thanks to reading, a shared experience.

Which type of medium is more likely to call upon participatory behavior? Print advocates say that good print treatments of an issue are more likely to engage someone's active involvement with an issue because well-written words excite a reader's imagination and thought processes. Both get engaged as a reader tries to grapple with an issue, even while just reading about it. For the sake of this book's purpose, I hope the print advocates are right. My own experience says that they are. Good writing has me thinking about the topic of the writing as I read. As a result, I have developed the bad habit of marking and jotting on the pages of virtually everything that I read unless a quick scan indicates that it is hardly worth reading. Then I just file the item – in the round file.

More specifically, apart from the evidence already highlighted, what do the differing features of print vs. non-print media imply about the likelihood and nature of people's political involvement? Literature is subversive: "This is because all good literature is radical…Literature says that…the world is badly made and that those who pretend to the contrary, the powerful and the lucky, are lying…" (Vargas Llosa, here again and in the next paragraph).

To the contrary, the offerings of non-print media are generally opposite in quality; that is, they are not subversive. They do not promote, as good reading does, "the critical mind" or a "critical and non-conformist attitude towards life."

Remember irony and paradox, whose importance we observed earlier? Well, these can be found in abundance in literature. But what's most ironic in this contrast of media is that both TV and literature rely greatly upon fantasy. Many media critics take TV to task for programming far too much fantasy. But the main point of impact – upon people's willingness to get involved with others in the real (non-fantasy) world – this seems to have been missed by most.[34] Even Vargas seems to have missed it, with a snide, elitist reference to "illiterate people who have been made into idiots by television's soap operas."

Both types of media rely substantially on fantasy, but one type promotes active engagement and the other does not. Why? Because one is an active medium and the other is passive. In order to read a book, one must make a conscious decision to acquire it, open it up and read it. Then, as indicated earlier, if it's a good book, it's more likely to foster an actively open mind and critical attitude towards what's happening in the world. It may be literature that helps you "to understand the impotent feeling of the isolated individual." By contrast, watching TV is a very easy, low-cost, no-brainer.[35] Just press a button or flip a switch to find yourself in transported into other worlds. So fantasy generation is not the main issue.

Unfortunately, for the most part, these "other worlds" on TV are those which value "conformism and the universal submission of humankind to power." Sure, it often seems otherwise; but the brand of individualism most featured is that characterized by differences in personal appearance that can be gotten off the rack or out of a jar or exhibited in terms of personal behavior quirks with no socially redeeming value. Such "seems," such appearances veiling the true nature and distribution of power in society, suggest what is at stake in one's choice of participation or lack of participation in public life. As Bill Kibben, a prominent author and former staff writer for the *New Yorker* said as a 2001 commencement speaker: "We weren't born to live on the couch with the remote control."[36]

Putnam noted that: "If TV steals time, it also seems to encourage lethargy and passivity." In one medium, "fantasy" reminds us of idealism, the tragic nature of human life and "acts of defiance;" in the other, we are entertained and then put gently to sleep. Perhaps this is part of the privilege of being an American. In other cultures, TV may be a technology of liberation. In the old Afghanistan, for example, watching TV was "truly scary," subject to punishment; for the ruling Taliban, a group of Islamic fundamentalists, are (were) watching the watchers.[37]

Yet, the early days of TV were like the early days of the Internet now: Pundits carried on about the wonderful potential of the new medium for reinvigorating American democracy. Then it became "mass media" under the control of major, nationwide networks. Marshall McLuhan, at one time the seminal guru of electronic media, wrote: "Today, the mass audience…can be used as a creative, participating force. It is, instead, merely given packages of passive entertainment. Politics offers yesterday's answers to today's questions."

The potential for TV to do more returned through the development of cable TV on both national and local scales. Nationally, Brian Lamb led the initiation and development of *C-Span*. Local cable channels were required, by law, to enable public access via local channels and training of local activists who wanted to mount their own programs. The primary competition for network TV, however, is turning out to be the Internet rather than cable, especially with respect to people's involvement with public issues via electronic media. That is why, later in this chapter, we turn to "Digital Democracy?" Nevertheless, the *great* importance of the cable options as an antidote to the negative influences of network TV should be noted. *C-Span*, especially, continues to be a dynamic, growing influence with a devoted, participatory set of viewers.

Why do about nine of every ten people who call into *C-Span* with their views, comments and opinions say: "Thank you for *C-Span*"? Because *C-Span* programming is both genuinely and continuously informative as well as somewhat interactive. On *C-Span1*, viewers see live feed of the U.S. House of Representatives in session, unvarnished by interruptions of media commentators trying to put their own "spin" on what is happening. On *C-Span2*, viewers receive a similarly direct view of the U.S. Senate in session. Before the sessions begin, they can tune into *Washington Journal*, a review of the news of the day with a call in feature, often focused on some topical issue. Other programs include: Book TV (a nice integration of TV and print media), "American Presidents,""American Writers," "*C-Span* in the classroom" and many special programs too numerous to mention. The *C-Span* story – the devoted leadership and staff, the many struggles to get it going and its continuing efforts to address emerging challenges – this story has been well told by a Professor at the Naval Academy, Steve Frantzich, whose books make good reading.[38] Some quotes from callers into *C-Span* help to flavor parts of this book. The *C-Span* web page (http://www.c-span.org) is another rich resource that invites people's participation. A third channel, *C-Span3*, was begun early in 2001 to provide additional public service coverage.

C-Span is also a good antidote to print news media that, too often, are prone to provide biased perspectives on the news. Part of the *Washington Journal* program features news stories from a variety of newspapers around the country, and it enables people of all political persuasions nationwide to call in with others. Here again, we have a program that demonstrates how electronic and print media can be mixed and matched with people's participation to take advantage of their potential complementarity. Another good example of this type is *Public Radio International (PRI)*. Besides maximizing information and minimizing editorializing, they mix in reader feedback and music.

Print Media

Why and how do print media often provide biased perspectives? It is important to recognize the ways, especially since most local media markets now lack competitive newspapers. These ways have been set in high relief by a counterpoint movement called Public Journalism which has arisen from the core problem that animates this book – the erosion of citizenship. We already began to confront one source of possible bias at the outset of this chapter – framing. You know what it means to select a frame for a picture. It helps to focus the viewer's attention. Some artists now embellish the frame so that it becomes a part of the picture itself. Starting with the Renaissance introduction of perspective, it became possible to view the individual in context through paintings that presented both foreground and background components. This still provides the best model of framing, because the frame is not leaving out something essential. The individual is not isolated or out of context. Remember: there are two ways for someone to lie: by commission (deliberately) or by omission (leaving out something that may be important).

Cappella and Jamieson, in their landmark study of how the media have served to promote political cynicism, identified two major ways of framing — "strategic" and "issue."[39] "Strategic" refers to a tendency of journalists and others to frame stories to focus the reader's attention primarily upon the machinations, personal characteristics and clashes of politicians and their campaigns that may influence winning or losing a political race. "Issue" framing refers to setting a story or feature so as to maximize its information value on issues to the reader. The studies reported and analysed in the book, properly titled *Spiral of Cynicism,* show how the proportion of journalistic coverage employing the strategic frame has increased relative to issue coverage and how this shift correlates with increases of people reporting increasing alienation towards politics and government. During 2000, we saw predominantly strategic coverage of the presidential race and election aftermath (see chapter 9). 2004?

Another source of bias is a marked tendency of journalists to slant their stories so that they are, implicitly, editorializing in the guise of reporting. There are many ways to do this. One is via selection. A reporter can select certain things to report and not others. Such selection can highlight positives or negative features of a candidate, for example, depending on whether publishers or editors favor the candidate, a certain ideology or other point of view.

A second method is the organization of paragraphs and points. Editors and reporters know that most readers don't get beyond the first page except for gossip, sports, weather or obituaries. So, they will put points they favor up front and relegate the rest to the inside pages. Further selection bias may determine whether the inside story continues on page 2, 5, 15 or 24.

We have been noting the more implicit ways of editorializing. One should pay some attention to explicit methods, too, via editorials labeled as such that usually appear on editorial pages. The history of the media in America began with newspapers that were established by publishers with axes to grind. They made no bones about the fact that they were investing their money to promote their point of view.[40] Most of today's publishers and newspapers are not so intellectually honest. Many (most?) editors have little shame and less humility. They have no compunction whatsoever about using their pages to lecture the rest of us on virtually anything, as if their opinions should somehow count more than ours. Truth or untruth is selective—whatever facts suit their purposes will do; let's not quibble about the rest or even bother to mention them.

Whatever the quality of editorials or reporting may be, serious questions need to be addressed to editors, authors and readers. Here are just a few:

1. Why should we tolerate publishers' policies that allow or require editors to endorse candidates for office on their editorial pages? Is one of the major roles of a newspaper to be an arbiter of power in a community? Should not that role be reserved for the voters, based not on journalists' opinions but on information that the newspaper provides, so that voters can make up their own minds?

2. What are publishers and editors doing to counter the various, more subtle sources of bias in the media cited earlier, not just the obvious "liberal" or "conservative" sources?

3. What are print and other media doing to improve their ability to "police" or govern themselves and improve the transparency and accountability of their ownership and operations?

The Spring, 2003 scandal surrounding a rogue reporter at the *New York Times* served to make an issue of #3.[41] This is an opportunity to enlarge the debate over how the media exercises power and influence. The opportunity may be lost, however, because the issue is too narrowly defined—as a question of how editors can catch deliberate errors like made-up stories and plagiarism. The above cartoon is illustrative. Note some of the categories of concern like "framing" and "reporting-as-editorialising" are missing among the signs. Fortunately, some of the larger issues surfaced as a result of the big stink made by the bad odor of changes in media regulation emerging from the Federal Communications Commission around the same time.[42] We'll turn to these further on.

As someone who has done a lot of statistical work over the years, I am well aware that one case proves nothing. Yet, perhaps some reflection on my own experience with a local newspaper will provide some perspective. As several times a candidate for local office in my hometown, elected at-large, I felt that whenever I ran I faced at least two opponents – whoever happened to be competing with me on the ballot plus the local paper. The only reason that I could figure for this is that I was a declared Republican and the opinions of the newspapers' publisher and editor(s) were those of a liberal rag owned by a non-local conglomerate. I could write a separate book on my experience but a couple of vignettes will have to suffice here and now.

During one of my campaigns for Mayor, a young reporter from another place[43] couldn't resist editorializing in the guise of reporting. While reviewing the report of my campaign committee to the State Office of Campaign Finance, he thought he found a violation – that I had wrongfully accepted a contribution from a corporation! The lawn signs in question were (1) paid for and (2) innovative – the first plastic, indestructible political signs ever seen in Gloucester. They were produced by a small, minority owned business in Chicago that my wife and I had assisted pro bono, so we were able to get the signs at a discount. I found it curious that a liberal paper presumably in favor of helping minorities would try to hang me for buying signs from a minority enterprise on the pretext that the discount provided was equivalent to accepting illegal contributions from a big, bad corporation. Besides the questionable reporting, what we saw in this case was a small local instance of a much larger media problem that has helped to turn people off politics. It's called "gotcha" journalism.

A second type of treatment I experienced locally has come to be observed nationwide as an unfortunate trend towards "personality politics" or, more generally, the confusion of public and private, often leading to the invasion of politicians' personal privacy. More than any other candidate had done in a long time, I put out position papers and press releases on issues, including a handbook showing how I would govern as Mayor. It was very frustrating to me that these were not covered by the local newspaper; rather, the paper tried to focus people's attention on my personality and "style." I would joke that the paper couldn't tell the difference between its (or my) private parts and public parts.

In retrospect, however, this was one feature of journalism that I came to respect. The values I try to honor in both my private and public life are fundamentally public values. A man is either all of a piece in these terms or he is not. If he is, then the word "integrity" means something. So, I have learned this much from my experience with the media – that a candidate should be willing to subject him- or her-self to detailed scrutiny of all aspects of one's life, career and personality. The problem that this raises with the media is more fundamental than one of privacy; it is one of truthfulness. There is no incentive in politics to be truthful; rather the opposite, given the way the media cover politicians and campaigns.[44] Reveal something on which they can put a negative spin and they "gotcha."

There were other instances that I also found more troubling than being attacked as a candidate, because they revealed another basic form of hypocrisy. These were instances where the newspaper would pontificate editorially about the need for people to step forward to run for local office, so that the electorate would face competitive races, only then to undercut a serious candidate who came forward if he or she didn't fit the paper's ideology. This kind of newspaper behavior is troubling because it affects what earlier chapters have referred to as the supply-side of politics, resting on people's willingness to step forward to run for office and expose themselves to media scrutiny. Local editors need to recognize that their tendency to exhume negatives from the more personal sides of candidates lives serves to dry up the pool of potential candidates. Only a very, very small proportion of people are tough, committed and/or masochistic enough to be willing to expose themselves to such treatment.

This brief treatment far from exhausts the identification of media techniques that can bias or color media treatments of public issues, politicians and political campaigns. The point here is not to be exhaustive but simply to heighten your sensitivity to how you, the American citizen, can be led or misled, informed or misinformed. Watch, but watch out. Be skeptical. Question everything from the media and everyone in the media. Rely on those who see their business as informing rather than influencing. Watch C-Span, listen to *PRI*, subscribe to the *Utne Reader*, use most newspapers to line litter boxes and rely more on your own native American common sense than the mouthings of the media "commentariat."

As noted earlier, there is a movement in progress to overcome the journalistic faults noted in this section plus some others. It is called "public journalism." We will turn to it under Options for Change in the concluding section of this chapter.

The Media as a Powerful "4th Estate"

The fundamental issue here is the locus of power, the most basic concern of politics. The media constitute a 4th estate with enormous political power. In a democracy, we are all in trouble when power and responsibility are significantly out of whack. The media has become a dominant sector whose power far exceeds its responsibility.

The basic problems have been documented by others,[45] so let's just highlight here.

- Conglomeration of the media – buy outs, mergers and acquisitions, cross-ownerships of media across media types and locations; growing large corporate domination of media ownership and control.

- Mounting financial conflicts between journalism in the public interest and media owners' pressure for profitability[46]

- Increasing reliance of political campaigns on the media – This was referred to earlier as an "incestuous mix of money and media," amply in evidence during Senate testimony on the McCain-Feingold campaign finance reform bill.

- Increasing media power in the political process – as illustrated by:

  · Increasing reliance upon polls and polling by both elected officials' and the media;

  · The media increasingly seeing their role as primarily that of "opinion management" which "amounts to manipulation of a mass" via polls and other techniques;[47]

  · Politicians' increasingly looking for media exposure and "playing to the (media) galleries"; and…

  · Decreasing factual media news treatments of politics, politicians, campaigns and political parties.

An underlying factor is the need for both media and politicians to capture both people's attention and their money. So, as the media decrease political coverage in order to make more money, politicians need to raise more money to buy media time – yet another vicious cycle. One observer of the media's role in politics wrote:

Journalists interceded more than ever between candidates and voters as they consumed 71 percent of campaign coverage on evening newscasts and left only 12 percent for candidates…The proportion of total election news devoted to issues continued to decline…while the proportion dedicated to "horse race" coverage…rose from 25 percent…to 35 percent…[48]

The media and politics as fabled marketplaces of ideas are both endangered by media conglomeration. It's surprising that anti-trust monitors haven't paid more aggressive attention to what's been going on in the media. The

America on Line/Time Warner merger received a great deal of attention but it was ultimately approved. The erosion of competition in media markets has been going on progressively for a long time. With some justification, reformers on the left regard this trend with apprehension as a threat to progressive politics. Across a broader ideological spectrum, it's hard to imagine how the public journalism movement will succeed in achieving much broader impact in a media world dominated by large corporations whose overriding concern is increasing profitability and company stock prices.

New Dimensions Radio's Michael Toms stated that "The biggest theft in American history has been the theft of the airwaves by corporate interests."[49] He then went on to remark, however, that:

> "the technologies for electronic media are no longer controllable by big money interests. The Internet is an example...We started Webcasting three and a half years ago and it was like having a worldwide radio station without a license."

Nichols and McChesney would agree with Toms' first ("theft") statement but not his second. Their review of the actual and likely impacts of the media on our politics and public life documents "an extraordinary degree of economic and social power located in very few hands" due to a trend of consolidation and increasing domination of media markets by mega-corporate conglomerates that has been aggravated by the 1996 Telecommunications Act.[50] They report that, in 2000:

> "the U.S. media system is dominated by fewer than ten transnational conglomerates: Disney, AOL-Time Warner, News Corporation, Viacom, Seagram [Universal], Sony, Liberty [AT&T], Bertelsman, and General Electric [NBC]...These firms tend to have holdings in numerous media sectors."

An important question that arises here is: With the "4th Estate" dominated by such corporations, to what extent can we rely on the media to police themselves and/or: To what extent is new law and regulation needed, perhaps raising thorny First Amendment issues? During Congressional debates on campaign finance reform, only a few Members advocated provision of free time for candidates for federal offices to "get their message out." The allocation of spectrum to enable the establishment of up to 1000 small, community-oriented FM broadcast outlets is a proposition that brought forth such strong corporate media opposition that licensing of such outlets will be limited to less than 100 stations. Even National Public Radio added its voice in opposition as a large established entity with something to lose.[51] But the American public at-large seemed to be about as complacent as in the direct mail envelope caricature pictured on the next page.[52]

Fortunately, a significant part of the American public began to wake up in response to other FCC proceedings, as indicated further on. The questions at issue are critical to the future of American politics. What is to be the future of public media? Of cable in a new era of telecommunications that will be increasingly wireless? Will changes in federal elections' coverage initiated by the networks in response to the debacle in Florida prove sufficient as a part of overall elections' reform? Wilhelm's major study "on the whole show(s) that (media) technologies as currently used largely unravel the democratic character of the public sphere..." and so calls for "substantial media reform."[53] His call has more recently been trumpeted by others. Nichols and McChesney, for example, say that it's past time for "making media an issue in American politics" – as the linchpin of a broader political reform movement that can "free the political imagination" so that "the supposed apathy of the electorate can be replaced with a level of engagement that suggests that the promise of American democracy might yet be made real."[54] One of those already engaged, a participant in a recent "e-democracy" forum on campaign reform stated:

> The media, having completely abandoned any responsibility to the public or the democracy thanks to..."deregulation," is the worse offender and the biggest roadblock to reform...the airwaves are not a privately owned resource, they are publicly owned...[55]

Relaxation of old rules constraining media ownership approved by three of five FCC commissioners promised to continue the trend towards media deregulation during 2003. Most heartening was the fact that many people finally woke up to the media as a public, political issue. The proposed changes ignited a firestorm of controversy whose consequences still have not been played out. A "key Senate committee voted...to tighten some of the Federal Communication Commission's recently adopted (relaxed) media ownership restrictions, out of concern that the new rules would allow too much media consolidation...The bill also requires the FCC to hold at least five public hearings before voting on future ownership changes...(Senator Byron L.)

Dorgan (D, ND) predicted an "orgy of mergers" if the FCC's ownership rules are not rolled back."[56] As this book was going to publication, it appeared as if the rules would not be cancelled or amended, after all, due to a compromise in Congress to gain support for approval of the 2004 budget.

How the issues raised in this chapter and before the FCC may be resolved is critical. To a great extent, the future of American democracy hinges on the media. The above indictment and other observations up to this halfway point of our "media" chapter indicate that they are a large part of the problem. Moving forward, we will see that they could be the major, underlying contributor to a solution. If only there wasn't a Catch 22 here as elsewhere: People's ability to perceive, and continue to make a stink over, the media as a political issue depends in part on—you guessed it—the media!

Destroyer of Community?

The question mark in this heading needs to be there because it is too easy to place blame for the decline of "community" at the foot of the media while failing to recognize that the media are just another sector of a market economy that has been undermining the community idealized by small town America for at least 150 years. It is too easy to romanticize "community" while failing to acknowledge that small town life can be "cabined, cramped and confined," sustaining a local politics that can be petty, inbred, resistant to change, corrupt, gossipy, hidebound, oligarchic and more focused on personalities than issues. Here, as elsewhere, we need to face facts as they are and not as we may want them to be. This is especially the case as we lead up to a later section in which we will confront the advocates of digital democracy, who believe that there can be such a thing as a "virtual" political community. We need to realistically look at how electronic media may be undermining, even if not substantially destroying, the face-to-face, person-to-person interactions and the "sense of place" which are among the keys to an authentic political community.

Unless our parents are itinerant farmers, employed by the military or corporate nomads, most of us have obtained some sense of place during our childhood. That place is usually the community represented by our hometown. So, our sense of place is colored by childhood memories and dreams. I know. I returned to my hometown after two dozen years away, served on its City Council and hoped to become the City's mayor. A real place, however, is not a projection of childhood memories and dreams. The political community just beneath the surface of the place is something else again. The only way that one obtains a true "sense of place" is by working and living in a community for some years and getting involved with the public life of that community. Again, one should not romanticize "community," even one's hometown.

A real community is a set of real people rooted in a real place – people with struggles, hopes, ambitions, rivalries and the rest, in a community with customs, traditions, power centers, structure, hierarchy, problems and possibilities.[57] The ability to serve a community in a public office depends on much more than willingness. Willingness may depend on ability. Many people are reluctant to get involved because they think they lack ability, but they lack ability because they have not been involved. This is a Catch 22. The way to break it is to act like a swimmer facing the North Atlantic in June – jump in! Start dog paddling with other amateurs. Next season you might be able to swim with the sharks.

We have seen how too much or unselectively watching TV takes significant time and energy away from participation in the political life of a community. Given the connection between "willing" and "able," therefore, TV also detracts from peoples' ability to serve. You can't develop adequate political skills without being involved in politics, even though some political skills can be picked up on the job or as an active member of a church or other community-based organizations.[58] But TV watching is a source of distraction and displacement from being actively enough involved to acquire political skills through any sort of organization. TV watchers are consumers of images of the lives of others. They can indulge their consumption at no direct cost to themselves as they are subjected to advertisements from corporations trying to sell them other ways to indulge their consumption desires. Even selective viewers are consumers. Rather than be even a micro-maker of history, you can be a consumer of history on the History Channel. Rather than making discoveries of your own powers to change things together with others by participating in public life, you can be a consumer of discoveries – on the Discovery Channel.

But it is not consumers but producers who build community. Displacement and distraction from community serve to undermine community. With some notable exceptions, electronic media tend to diminish people's ability to relate to the place where they live as part of a community of shared problems and possibilities.[59] This is also a problem for TV producers as well as viewers. Keith Connors, News Director of *WCNC*, Charlotte, NC, observed: "As much as I've moved in this business, nothing seems like home anymore…It all seems like an assignment."[60]

One might risk generalizing here a bit by also referring to communities of character and truth.[61] The "greatest generation" was raised in place-based communities of character that were not infected by TV. Will the younger generation escape the media's influence enough to try to rebuild such communities? We adults tend to lavish hopes on the younger generation, praying that they will pick up a torch that we have dropped and run with it. And so, Bill McKibben, quoted earlier, also…

> urged students to find pleasure as members of a community, not consumers, adding that no one on their deathbed wishes they had watched more television or made more trips to the mall.[62]

Our sense of place is further diminished by media technologies that have no place reference or significance at all (more on this when we turn to the medium of the Internet). Electronic media news coverage focuses on state and national events. Even local papers are increasingly filled with *AP* (Associated Press) or other distant feeds, relative to the amount of local news. There have been some fine examples of investigative journalism nationally, as seen on *60 Minutes*, for example, but fewer and fewer produced by local or even state-level media. If our sense of place is to mean something more than nostalgia or fond hopes; if, in fact, people living in a place are to learn something of how a community works, then more rather than less local investigative journalism is needed – plus, one might add, more participation in the politics of the place.

There also needs to be greater sensitivity on the part of local boards and commissions as to how developments that they <u>can</u> influence have been undermining community by diminishing the supply of public space that democracy needs to function, as well as in other ways. The most obvious example is the development of a shopping mall that can legitimately be viewed as a "public place" because that is where large numbers of people congregate. Private owners, however, have succeeded in preventing the distribution of leaflets or other political activities on mall premises. Local planning and zoning boards need to attend to such detrimental impacts on public life in their community as well as to their likely negative impact on local shops.[63]

Much more of what is called "public journalism" is needed, too. For a community is more than a set of shared feelings. It is also a matter of public information and, based on this, of shared understandings of how public things (res publica, the latin root of republic) work or don't work in a community. A more public journalism is based upon the truthful, forthright recognition of the fact of media power in any community, and the implications of that power – not the dishonest use of media outlets as expressions of the private political preferences of editors and publishers while pretending to operate in the public interest.

Public journalism media intervene in communities in order to help re-build a civic culture. They not only provide valuable informational reporting on issues of major concern in communities; they sponsor public forums on the issues and urge people to participate in a process of confronting, debating and resolving differences over issues and thereby "coming to public judgement."[64] Public journalism recognizes that the task of rebuilding the American political community is a two-way street, perhaps even a partnership, between citizens and the media. The foundation for this relationship is "a common interest in common affairs." It "depends on the people's willingness to attend to current (and longer-term) issues, (to) take responsibility for public things… Then the media can fortify the public trust that comes with the special privileges granted by the First Amendment…to strengthen…America's civic culture, by which we mean the forces that bind people to their communities, draw them into politics…and cause them to see "the system" as theirs…"[65]

Can these great goals be achieved? Some good local examples show that they can. These examples include newspapers and communities in Wichita, Charlotte, Portland and Minneapolis.

The importance of people's re-engagement at the community level in ways that include direct, face-to-face, person-to-person (P2P) interactions over "res publica" is highlighted by an awareness of how political power, increasingly, is being generated and exercised. Ironically, this is occurring at the community level even while the virtues of the traditional American community are being undermined by the media except through the unreality of nostalgia, fantasy or myth.[66] Political power is increasingly gestated and applied in and through "communities" whose only effective place referent is Washington, D.C. or a state capitol. Consider the House of Representatives, the U.S. Senate or state legislatures. These become effective communities in basically the same ways that other communities are created – through the face-to-face, P2P interactions of people in proximity with some shared concerns. The fact that voters often refer to these groupings as "clubs" is a grudging recognition of their effectiveness as communities. You may hear someone say, for example, something like: 'that Congressman Jones, we elected him to represent us; then he got to Washington and joined the club.'

Now turn to the much maligned "interest group." This is a type of community, too, but one that is even less place-based and more divided into parts than legislatures. Nevertheless, it is an increasingly powerful type of "community." The power of the group is increasingly exercised by a small, close-knit set of activists and professionals (the group's core, who may be co-located in a place) who are supported by members and/or financial contributors who share the groups "interest," whatever that may be. Of one thing you can be sure, no matter how worthy the group's interest (goal, issue, belief, etc.) may be, it is not the public interest but, at best, a part of that broad category referred to as "private interest(s)."

You may question the use of "community" to denote "interest group," but few would question the observation that interest groups wield increasing power along with the legislative "clubs" that the groups lobby. Their power derives from their organization as a community of individuals determined to make a difference in a certain direction. By themselves, the individuals involved would be powerless except in very rare ("Erin Brockovich") instances.[67] Yet, the exercise of the groups' power in Congressional committee hearings, et.al., occurs on a small group basis. Congressional power itself is exercised substantially on a small group basis in committees.

The antidote to the growing influence of interest groups is not more interest groups but groups of citizens actively involved in the politics of place-based communities where citizen participation in public affairs provides some real sense, not only of the value of community and place but of what public interest can really mean — because people have worked to recognize what "it" is or can be by "coming to public judgement." Following the great political philosopher Hannah Arendt, Dan Kemmis directly connects place and public via the metaphor of a table at which people are sitting:

> To live together in the world means essentially that a world of things
> is between those who have it in common, as a table is located
> between those who sit around it…[68]

The root of our political problem, Kemmis writes, is the "vanishing table,"
the "res" in "res publica."[69] The sense of place is the thing (res) that has been
diminishing to the point that the public (publica: public interest, public things,
&c) has been diminishing, too. To be a public, we need a place for which we
care and to which we can repair, to talk, debate, deliberate and reach public
judgement. Instead, as Kemmis remarks as if commenting on fast food indi-
gestion:

> Public life as we all too often experience it now is very much like
> a Big Mac—it can be replicated in exactly the same form,
> anywhere…placeless "food" consumed under placeless yellow "land-
> marks," weakens both our sense of food and of place, so too does
> the general placelessness of our political thought…[70]

Kemmis' aim resonates with that of this book. He writes of rebuilding a
"political culture" that is unmistakably grassroots – grounded in locality and
community. He refers to the preamble to Montana's state constitution as
indicating "that the political culture of a place is not something apart from the
place itself." What is a place that counts as a community? Here, he justifiably
turns to the eloquence of another author, Wendell Berry. It is where "all who
are living as neighbors…are part of one another, and so cannot possibly
flourish alone…"[71]

There is a paradox here that should be confronted along with others. It
is a paradox along several overlapping dimensions, such as:

1. Place…non-place
2. Close…distant
3. Organization…non-organization
4. Voters…citizens
5. Consumer…producer
6. Affective…effective

An effective political community has features that:

1. place it, strategically, somewhere along the line of each of these
   paradoxical dimensions, so that…
2. its defining strategy is designed to "make a difference" to and for
   the community by acquiring and applying power through a political process.

The first placement is that of "place." Any community needs a place
where political activity, power and influence can be exercised and where
participants can see, close up and meaningfully, how they can make a difference. This is why we pointed to the "diminishing…supply of public space,"

earlier. BUT, paradoxically, there also need to be non-place features, even in places where several generations have grown up. A small town with a tight network of community relationships can generate conflict as well as consensus. The late, great city planner Lewis Mumford once wrote: "When people share the same environment, they often see more differences among themselves." Meyrowitz notes that the introduction of print media 500 years ago served to "distance people from sound, touch and direct response (and give them a) break from total reliance on oral communication."[72]

These days, people say they need "space." Sometimes, they have to ask others to "get out of my face." Indeed, everyone needs some effective distance as well as closeness to others. This is the second placement. How close or distant we choose to be from others will vary, person by person. Among these will be people who we will want to count among our strategic allies, not necessarily among friends or relations. Some of these will be "non-place," living or working in locations other than "our place," or otherwise located some effective distance from us (social, financial, political, et.al.).

To be effective, politically, we need both organization and non-organization in our community. The lack of organization on behalf of "community" is one reason why this feature of our national life is disappearing except for its honorable mention in commencement speeches. What voice does the community of Merrimac, Massachusetts, have in the state legislature, for example? None qua community, even though the Chairman of the Board of Selectman may be able to get the State Representative representing Merrimac (among others) to introduce a "home rule" petition regarding some specific issue. Merrimac is better organized administratively to manage its self-governing polity internally.

Even in this respect, however, it's not well organized politically. Local political party committees in the town are in limbo. The Town has trouble getting quorums for Town Meeting(s) because there's hardly anyone out "beating the bushes" for people to come, and most voters don't recognize that attendance at Town Meeting is their responsibility as citizens.[73] By contrast, some municipalities are over-organized. Town or city politics may be dominated by one party, one interest group, one industry or one local newspaper. Any community needs some degree of dis-organization to make room for effective dissent, innovation, "new blood" and the like.

So we've already reached dimension #4: "Voters…Citizens." Citizens of a federal republic have a responsibility to do more than just vote. That doesn't mean that we all have to be activists or political junkies" heavily involved or "participating" most of the time or even frequently—just that we all recognize that we have some (shared) responsibility that we fulfill when, if and as we can. Voting and other activities of citizenship go together. It's hard to make your vote count if you don't have good choices and it's even harder to get good choices to vote for if there aren't more than the usual suspects involved in the process that determines what those choices might be. Every adult American needs to ask where he or she stands along the "Voter…Citizen" dimension and then, like a politician, ask not only "where" but "when", "how" and "with who(m)"? Unfortunately, the local media as they typically operate will not help you in this.

In terms of the fifth dimension, most of us may have to say "beam me up, Scotty," because, politically, we are consumers, not producers. But, as the public journalists say, if we want to "take our (political) system back" or "make it ours," we will have to start acting as producers, not just as consumers of whatever the media and the political class throw out at us. We will also have to be more selective as consumers of media offerings and political fare. Unless you are in one of the cities already tuned into public journalism, your local media will not help you here, either. You will not be informed as to where to go or whom to call to get involved, politically.

Now we can be more specific as to what the question mark denotes in the title of this section. Whether or not the media are partly responsible for "destroying community" as some have claimed, we can recognize the ways that they are undermining community directly or indirectly, by design or default. More specifically, we have seen how the media undermine politics at all levels, but especially at the local or community level, while doing nothing to promote or assist the building of a political community at any level. Those media that have adopted the philosophy of public journalism provide some exceptions, but they are few and their numbers are unlikely to increase without considerable public pressure.

Digital Democracy

"The Internet will save democracy. Or so the early 1990's technohype led many to believe. With each new communications medium comes a wide-eyed view of its potential. I'd like to suggest that, just as television saved democracy, so will the Internet."[74]

Introduction

I first got acquainted with the wonderful potential of the new electronic media based upon fast, broad bandwidth technology through my subscription to *Wired* magazine and a round of correspondence with one of its writers, Jon Katz. Jon thought he had seen the emergence of a "new political sensibility" in "Cyberspace." The magazine referred to the bearers of this sensibility as "netizens." Then *Wired* teamed up with the Merrill Lynch Forum to sponsor a survey in 1997. The December, 1997, issue featuring the survey results showed Norman Rockwell's painting "Freedom of Speech" on the cover. The central figure in the painting is that of an American workman standing up to speak his piece at a town meeting.[75] If there is a single motif for American democracy this is it. But does the figure of then — one of the "greatest generation" participating in a public meeting – bear any resemblance to the figure of now, a "netizen"?

The *Wired* survey data, viewed in light of the more complete and trend-wise data compiled and analyzed by Putnam, suggest that the answer to the above question is NO. The American workingman is highly unlikely to be seen in the foreground of such a scene today. The typical "netizen" is not a workingman but a "super-connected" or well-"connected" upper middle class professional. Here, "connected" is akin to "wired."[76] Less than half of those connected through the "Net thought that "who you know" is more important to getting ahead than "what you know." Perhaps they took their better connections for granted. The connected set closely overlaps those who are better educated, with better jobs and higher incomes than the "unconnected." These are the ones more likely to vote, to be "participatory" (though neither the survey nor Katz specify what this involves), to know the name of their Congressman, etc. It is not surprising they are more likely to own a PC and otherwise be tuned in, technologically.

The *Wired* crowd reacted as if this group of wired clientele had just been discovered and, moreover, as if the same crowd was thought to be "alienated" from the political system. Of course, as the Verba, et.al.(1995) study, could have told them if they had crawled out of their techno-bubble long enough to look before commissioning their own survey:

· "Digital Citizens are not alienated…"

· "the online world encompasses many of the most informed and participatory (?!) citizens…"

Unfortunately, the *Wired* survey did nothing to negate the gnawing anxiety that Putnam's *Bowling Alone* thesis might be right – that both the connected and the unconnected might be equally alienated from direct political involvement with others.[77] The question of whether the new digital media enabled such participation or rather presaged a participatory oxymoron — being involved by "surfing" alone at one's PC – this question was not addressed. Being involved as a political volunteer with others was not included among the participatory options in the survey questionnaire.

Swept along by the wave of an "electronic outpouring" over the *Wired* survey results, Katz asked: "Can we build a new kind of politics?…Or are we nothing more than a great, wired babble pissing into the digital wind."[78] Six years later, it appears that the answers to these key questions are, respectively, NO (at least not thusfar) and MAYBE (there's still a lot of babble and some pissing). The high tech political enthusiasm that Jon and many others felt at the dawn of the digital age now seems naïve and exaggerated. Not much of the promise of "a new kind of politics" has yet been realized. The jury is still out in 2004, notwithstanding the huge media hype over the waves Howard Dean made in the early part of the 2004 presidential primary season. We still don't know what became of the waves of volunteers that were aroused by the real pioneers in use of the Internet for major political campaigns (McCain, Bradley and Ventura). We know even less of whether the latest up-blip of political participation aroused by Dean will endure. Look for more on the latest efforescence of digital democracy (Dean, Moveon, et.al.) in the next chapter.

The *Wired* hype over "netizens" might appear to be little more than a curious footnote in cyber-political history but for the fact that the history is repeating itself. A 2004 report from the Graduate School of Political Management at The George Washington University [a school to paper over the pseudo-science of political pro's with the veneer of an academic degree] reveals a new class of "Online Political Citizens, over two-thirds of whom "qualify as Influentials" – another great survey discovery akin to that of Katz. The new 2004 Influentials seem curiously like the 1997 Netizens. They are:

- twice as likely as members of the general public to have a college degree; they

- have higher incomes, are slightly younger, and are more likely to be white, single

- and male…the Americans who "tell their neighbors what to buy, which politicians to support, and where to vacation…[79]

Thus, the pollsters (Roper ASW and Nielson/ /NetRatings, who conducted the "innovative study") discovered another group that is a prime target for the pro's that love to apply their marketing techniques to sell candidates like soap. But are Influentials political leaders or just opinion leaders? Are they directly involved in political organizations? Are they reaching out to less elite others, helping to increase political participation and build political organization across class and group lines, so diverse cross sections of people in their political subdivisions can be politically more active and effective, not just the Influentials themselves? The answers to these questions appear to be NO. Even though they are described as "politically energized," their political energies primarily appear to be focused as Cyber couch potatoes:

They support their candidates by visiting their Web sites, joining Internet Discussion groups, reading political Web logs and making political (money) contributions over the Internet." [80]

Is there more democratic promise to be fulfilled in our wired society? Let's hope so. The TV news media seem to think so, as they solicit viewer e-mails in response to questions they broadcast in response to the news of the day. This is a variation on "instant polling." Those few whose e-mails are broadcast may feel empowered. What about the rest of us?, or even the chosen few. Does their brief moment in the TV sun amount to citizens' influence on decisions being made by few others far away? Or is it more like a lesser version of the brief moment of glory felt by those exposing themselves on "reality TV," that has little to do with reality?

Another term in the new digital technology dictionary that is a contradiction in terms when used in conjunction with "citizen" is "dis-intermediation." This term connotes one of the most profound impacts of the Internet – the ability of people to use the World Wide Web (WWW) to go right to the source – of products, services, information…you name it – and bypass the usual intermediaries, such as travel agents, banks, retail stores or, in the case of public life – political parties. But in political terms, dis-intermediation means dis-organize and thereby, dis-empower — unless, of course, as an article of faith, one believes, as many digital-democracy advocates apparently do, that the new technologies will enable a libertarian electronic fulfillment of Jeffersonian democracy (more on this further on).

We have nothing to lose but our high tech toys! The individual American, "superconnected" via his keyboard, cell phone or Palm pilot, will have as much power to shape our collective future as the K Street lobbyist backed by an industry trade association! During the late '90's, this viewpoint, not unlike some of the other hype endemic to the "dot.com bubble," was advertised as shown below.

The sentiment is admirable but the means of its fulfilment are not – as if all we have to do is look to "high tech" to revive political participation. So some of the pundits inclined to make a fetish of technology would have us believe. The ad text accompanying the above picture is indicative: "In-House Lobbyist (software) can transform a computer novice into a lobbying…powerhouse…we just made it (politics) a lot more fun and easy."[81] As if satisfaction of our civic responsibility is only a click away!

A cartoon spoof of this technological euphoria is shown below. The cartoonist may be closer to the likely truth of how the new electronic technology could affect "American Civic Life."

A FIVE-STEP PROGRAM by Steve Brodner

Technology

Technology

After all, technology is a tool; indeed, it helps to think about digital technology as providing a set of power tools like those some of us have in our basement workshops, kitchens and garages. We use our tools to do things that we want to do or that need doing – to develop, make or create; communicate, inform, influence, repair or renovate, sell or trade, travel, improve our health, etc. Digital technology is like a small power tool, only with potential far greater than "small." Our purchase of it is the result of an individual choice but our ability to use it depends on affordable access to a network whose existence, affordability and capacity is far from being the result of individual choice. We overlook the latter because we now take access to electrical power for granted. People in the U.S. did not always do so.[82] The Rural Electrification Administration (REA) during the New Deal was a big deal. So was Lyndon Johnson's stint as REA Director, long before he became a U.S. Senator and President. Ask old Texans and others who grew up in rural counties what difference electrification made to them.

The power tool analogy is a good one because it helps us to make some basic distinctions as well as to focus on "power." Digital technology is not the same as TV. A power tool is an active technology; i.e., it requires at least some amount of continuous, active concentration and skill by its user. As we noted earlier, TV is a relatively passive medium. Until interactive television becomes a widespread reality, TV cannot be properly viewed as a tool even though, for some how-to programs, there may be some tool-like acquisition features in the viewing. Other tool-like features to consider? – speed, selection (choice of technology) and individuality in use as well as choice. You may have a ¼" or 1/3" power drill but there is no question that you can get the drilling job done at a higher speed than with a hand drill. Analogous digital technology speed has already led to similarly obvious contrasts; e.g., e-mail relative to "snail mail."

Perhaps the single most important feature from both business and political standpoints, however, is that of individualism or individuality in the selection and use of the new digital technology. The use we make of the new tools is up to us. There are no prescribed adoptions, roles or functions to follow. Keep this point in mind, for the prophesiers, pundits, futurists and other salesmen among us are putting out all kinds of nostrums that may suggest otherwise. Some seem positively Lincolnesque – that the new technologies may provide "a new birth of freedom." Perhaps, but not necessarily if used as AOL/Time Warner, NBC or CBS would have you use them. The choice is yours but, for many, any saving grace may appear only if there are bugs in the programs, as suggested by the cartoon below.

"The beauty of this system is that there are a few small errors programmed into it, which helps to avoid total depersonalizations."

The choice and use of technology always involves pros and cons. The main "pro" is that some important tasks can be done much faster,[83] although this is a mixed blessing. Some chalk it up as a "con," especially with regard to the political impact of the media. Intense media competition during the 2000 election – the need to "call it" first, for example, contributed to the Florida election mess, which has been examined exhaustively elsewhere. The most important adverse impact, however, arises from the other side of the new technologies individualistic coin. Narrowly private decisions about the use of a new technology that has wider, public impacts may carry consequences adverse to a democratic republic. Some even label this, following colleagues in the environmental movement, "the tragedy of the (digital) commons." This is such a serious concern, let's return to it later in this chapter when we can pay it more attention.

Uses, Users and Utilization

We are all more or less familiar with the uses of digital technology but it may help to classify and lay them all together for easier review. From the standpoint of prospects for a digital democracy, it's also important to see how the technology is being used by various types of users. Will the uses enhance the already dominant political powers of the "powers that be" or give the rest of us chances to play more effective roles in public life?

There are two major uses of the Internet—to:

1. Get information, and to

2. Send and receive e-mail.

They overlap, as anyone who has received files attached to an e-mail can attest. The files add to the information value of what's in the e-mail itself. Why is information important?—mainly to find out what's happening in some larger world. This is one reason why web pages set up by major news channels have become increasingly popular sites on the Internet. But what's the point of knowing more than we did before we opened a web page, e-mail, newspaper, book or magazine? Does the information have a use? Is information power, or is it a stretch to go from information to knowledge to action?

Questions of "why" and "what for" may seem obvious, even trite, but they become increasingly important as we move to assess the real potential of digital democracy. Moving from information to knowledge is indeed "a stretch." The challenge starts with a choice of a search engine. You enter a word or phrase, click on "go" and the typical general purpose, pre-packaged search engine like that built into systems by Microsoft or AOL will spit out a minimum of dozens of references, sometimes hundreds or thousands. You thought finding needles in haystacks was an old problem?

Let's say you narrow down the list to a dozen items. So you print them out. Anyone got time to read? What about analyze? Digest? Notate? Synthesize? Draw conclusions? Then to do what? Write a letter to the editor of your local paper? Good idea, as long as your thinking doesn't run against the grain of the paper's bias. Write to your Congressman. Try it, but don't hold your breath for any but a form response, maybe not even that. So let's ask again: What's the point? Just to sound well-informed in a group of others indulging in cocktail party chatter? The two problems we've identified thusfar seem curiously similar to those that afflict political participation: time and efficacy. Who has the time to run a gauntlet with an uncertain result at the end of the line? How effective might any investment of time prove to be? Remember Mike Lynch's remarks in Chapter 4?

Those promoting a more "deliberative" democracy need to ask: If democracy can't be deliberative without more knowledge of public issues among more people, and the Internet doesn't make it any easier for people to be knowledgeable, what are the consequences? One dire forecast makes the digital divide look like a dividend – that our society could break up into two cultures, one a group of wired "netizens" like those touted by Katz; another, a group of couch potatoes that will be satisfied with political pablum fed by major networks that dominate both TV and 'Net channels under conglomerate ownerships. Guess who's left out of the political picture in this scenario? Most likely; you are and, as a cyber-citizen, perhaps even more so. Note that using the 'Net as a consumer to buy things wasn't highlighted earlier as a major use, because it hadn't yet become so. But now it's become so, and the private commercial/advertising/ purchasing functions of the medium may come to crowd out its still undeveloped public potential as a people's political tool.

The late, great Christopher Lasch had it right here as well as on narcissism and elites: Information and deliberation have little practical value in the absence of political debate. "What democracy requires is public debate, not information," he wrote, just before he died in 1994. Why? Because of the old maxim: "If you don't ask the right questions, you'll never find the right answers." Lasch continued: "we can identify the right questions only by subjecting our ideas…to the test of public controversy." In other words, information of real value to real people dealing with real issues in the real world is partly the result of debate, not some abstraction of academic value prior to or apart from debate. And what kind of debate? – P2P or face-to-face, where people face each other across aisles, tables or rooms. Not faceless, often anonymous interchanges over the Internet. Lasch lamented the loss of political debate starting about 100 years ago—healthy, vigorous debate aided and abetted by journalists. He noted:

> It's no accident that journalism of this kind flourished during the period from 1830 to 1900, when popular participation in politics was at its height. Eighty percent (80%!) of the eligible voters typically went to the polls in presidential elections. After 1900, the percentage declined sharply…[84]

What about e-mail? Here's something we can all do in small doses. As a way of communicating with friends, relatives, colleagues, anyone, it's a lot more quick and convenient than "snail mail." It's tit for tat, send and receive. No response? Not to worry; there's always Aunt Helen. And if you get additional information, attached, it's probably something you requested or something that somebody has some reason to believe you might want.[85] The beauty of e-mail is that it's something that each of us can do to be in contact with others, quickly, in the limited time that we have at odd hours, to sign on, send and receive. It's also a much more effective political tool than receiving more information, as we'll see; but e-mail is no substitute for face-to-face interactions. According to Janet Bruno, CEO of Marlboro Cooperative Bank and Chairman of the Board of Selectmen in the Town of Merrimac, MA, it is neither a genuine nor an adequate means of communicating with others over either business or political matters. She would never provide a loan nor hire someone simply on the basis of e-mail or other electronic submissions. People who send in job applications via e-mail without coming into the bank receive automatic form-letter rejections. She thinks that Di-Tech.com, the online mortgage lender, will eventually get into trouble.[86]

The Internet and Political Organization

After all, organization is key to politics in a variety of forms – political party committees, campaign organizations, governmental boards and commissions, et.al. Information is a product of organization rather than vice-versa. E-mail is more likely to be a tool of organization than a conveyor of substantial information. The Internet, therefore, is potentially more important as a facilitator of political organization than as a provider of information. This potential is already apparent. Recall Ingrid Reed's remark (in Chapter 4) on how the 'Net served as an organizing tool to those in the Princeton (NJ) area who were concerned about the imposition of state highway plans. Scan the Appendix on political 'net resources and notice how the organization of many political groups around all kinds of causes and concerns has coalesced through the Internet. Much of this organization has begun by way of an e-mail two-step:

1. <u>identification</u> of a core group of people with shared concerns through searches of political web sites and early e-mail exchanges; and...

2. <u>construction</u> of a group e-mail list, perhaps followed by use of a list-server, to enable intra-group communications and continued organizing around issues, events, ideas and political positions.

Steve Clift, founder of what is, in this author's opinion, the single best digital e-democracy website on the Internet, confirms the effectiveness of e-mail: "Almost by accident, we discovered that the most valuable thing Minnesota E-Democracy created in 1994 was the *MN-POLITICS*....e-mail discussion forum – our online public commons (which) quickly became a part of real politics in Minnesota."[87]

In 2001, Clift noted: "This is pretty amazing. The new Prime Minister of Japan, <http://www.kantei.go.jp/>, recently launched an e-mail newsletter and it already has 1,000,000 members."[88] About two years later, he wrote: "In my opinion, any member of Congress that does not provide a simple e-mail address for their constituents are acting in a fundamentally undemocratic manner. E-mail is the clear choice for citizen communication in social and business life."[89] Here, as Janet Bruno did earlier, we might ask what is the quality or adequacy of e-mail communications, especially when members of Congress rely on "auto-reply…processes." Clift's promotion of e-mail above has to do with e-government rather than e-democracy. Among the many ways he has promoted e-democracy, however, he has urged that any political campaign website is neither complete nor effective without an e-mail newsletter that enables those interested in getting involved to see what's going on, how to participate and how to get together with similarly motivated others.[90]

The downside of the Internet as a tool of organization is also apparent, perhaps even above. It has been the subject of increasing attention, especially since the publication of Cass Sunstein's book *Republic.com*. It is interesting to note how the attempts of "ordinary" individual Americans to empower themselves even a little bit through the Internet often earn critical comments in major media outlets. The danger of the downside was apparent long before Sunstein's book was released in the early Spring of 2001. The danger is that of fragmentation—a citizenry increasingly divided into a multiplicity of non-interacting, uncompromising groups as individuals identify like-minded others via the 'Net. Anyone using the 'Net for political purposes has seen this happening. Whether via "UseNet," Yahoo "e-groups," AoL groups or whomever, group-wise citizen "organization" has multiplied over the Internet, but there's very little interaction among the various groups. It's become like a paraphrase of an old Kingston Trio song: 'The English hate the Irish and the Irish hate the Dutch, and I only like those who share my crutch.' (originally: "I don't like anybody very much," which is largely still true if we insert "politicians" for "body").

The word "hate" here may be too strong, but it does suggest the kind of coverage that the media have given to people's attempts to come together over shared concerns via the 'Net outside of established channels. These attempts are viewed as catalysts for extremism. A recent headline is illustrative: "Adding Up the Costs of Cyberdemocracy: Experts Worry That the Web Encourages Extremism."[91] There is no question that many hate groups have found the Internet provides convenient, low-cost ways to identify similarly angry others. But to play on this feature? One wonders what the so-called "experts" have to lose.

The real danger is the continuing loss, aggravated by the Internet, of the sort of genuine public that is so crucial to the health of American democracy —citizens who pay attention to public issues, debate them in order to arrive at informed compromises or common ground and then find ways to act together on the issues that most concern them. Media leaders would do well to consider how they can counter this danger rather than contributing to it—by promoting cross-group Internet interaction rather than casting a negative pall over citizens' self-organizing efforts to come together over shared concerns. As one commentator noted: "The point is not which party is more extreme, but how the media characterizes the parties' respective positions."[92]

Recently, websites have popped up that are designed to bring people together face-to-face, to overcome the impersonality, inadequacies (and sometimes, the dangers) of e-mail "communication" at a distance. These include meetup.com, twofortheshow.com, friendster.com and craigslist.org. One headliner wrote: "Web sites that create new acquaintances are making local connections…" while the article itself quoted a website-inspired get-together participant as saying: "This mobilizes people." All to the good. Right? Yet the websites ask potential participants to "pick a topic," or "create a profile" and "meet with people with similar interests" – not exactly venues for generating debates that could generate understandings or hammer out compromises over controversial issues. [93]

So, as Sunstein lamented at length, there's damn little "cross-group Internet interaction."[94] As David Brooks continued more generally in "People Like Us": "what I have seen all around the country is people making strenuous efforts to group themselves with people who are basically like themselves."[95]

The preceeding remarks amount to one big reason that Steven Clift has been fostering "a simple concept" that he calls the "Public Internet." In his own words: the private sector, government, non-profits, educational institutions, and others need to work together to develop and apply the Internet in public interest ways that none of them can do on their own. Unfortunately, we are constrained by our notion of public broadcasting as an alternative channel or that government alone is responsible to solve public problems. We have a hard time seeing that a new model—only possible because of the Internet—is emerging.[96]

The organizational arrangement implied here is hardly "simple." Thus, it is no surprise that it has not yet emerged front and center through the unadulterated dynamics of the Internet. If the 'Net is to facilitate political participation, especially at the local level, a good deal of public-spirited leadership, including political and governmental, will be required to effect new, creative public/private collaborations. Instead of citizens' leadership to foster e-democracy, however, we see "e-government" being promoted by private, for-profit Internet software and systems' vendors. This enables you to "participate" in public hearings without showing up at city hall or a legislative chamber. It doesn't help you to organize others so that, altogether, you can make a far more significant difference.

A simpler "e-"model, albeit one that requires substantial volunteer effort to get underway and work well, has been demonstrated by another fellow from

Minnesota, Tim Erickson, via e-mail *Politalk* issue forums that facilitate one essential element of a democratic process – deliberation.[97] These have taken place on a variety of issues, both state and national, via e-groups that are now accessible through Yahoo. The issues thereby debated have all been important, including campaign finance reform, globalization, transportation and war with Iraq. What's most important to note here, however, in light of Sunstein's criticisms, is that the forums have enabled a diverse set of opinions to be represented. They have avoided the "flaming," "spam," ideological fixations and personality colorings that have afflicted other e-mail interchanges.

What have been key features of *Politalk* that have enabled the forums to work well?—

- Recruitment of a cross section of resource people who initially post background information on the issue at hand, including government officials, experts and legislators. These "resource people" also participate in e-mail exchanges as the forum proceeds.[98]

- The care and attention of a good moderator who sets ground rules, distills debate interactions daily and archives the proceedings for retrieval later by a wide variety of others, including elected officials.

Two questions remain, however, that need to be addressed by any evaluation of this model:

1. Among those participating, how many minds have been changed to any degree as a result of interactions with others with different points of view on the issue(s)?

2. Have the forums influenced anyone in a position to act on the issue(s); i.e., have any influences on government policy, program or legislation been apparent as a result?

As we have seen, expectations of the latter influence the likelihood of people participating in political forums of any sort.

The possibility that the Internet could empower us has inspired e-democracy guide- books to help citizens realize the possibility. These include:

- *Cybercitizen: How to use your computer to fight for all the issues you care about;* and

- *Modem Nation*: *The handbook of grassroots activism online.*[99]

Both of these are marked by their orientation to issues activism and to enabling readers to use the Internet to communicate with the powers that be, including established media (e-government), rather than to enabling Internet users to politically self-organize, to empower each other and or participate in partisan, electoral politics in order to help make a difference across a set of issues (e-democracy).

Political Campaigns

Candidates' campaigns are another form of political organization that, increasingly, is finding form and expression over the Internet. Website designers have entered the stable of political consultants as other consultants have told candidates that having their own campaign website is a sine qua non of a political campaign in this high tech day and age. There is even now, as in other areas of media accomplishment, a set of annual awards for the best political websites. What are they called?—"Webby" awards, of course.

The McCain and Bradley 2000 campaigns for President, building on Ventura's 1998 campaign for Governor, did a lot to establish campaign website development as a trend. McCain raised over two million dollars via the Internet during the salad days of his primary campaign in New Hampshire (NH). Bradley raised thousands of volunteers through the 'Net from all over the country. I can speak to this from experience since I was a volunteer working for Bradley in NH. In one city, I was teamed with a volunteer from Virginia to go door-to-door during a cold February weekend. He had found the Bradley campaign through the Internet, and he questioned whether he and other volunteers from out of state would have been located and induced to volunteer in NH without 'Internet interactions via campaign websites.[100] A good feature of both the McCain and Bradley campaign websites was also their self-organizing features – encouraging people who signed on and decided they liked the candidate to help identify and organize others, friends and neighbors via e-mail. Ventura's "cyber volunteers… were able…to follow Jesse…around the state and post messages on the bulletin board… the Web…allowed his supporters to keep in touch and spread his message."[101] Thus, McCain, Bradley and Ventura were the early leaders and role models of the "virtual activism" and Internet fundraising that, much later in 2003, gave former Vermont Governor Howard Dean such an early jump to the head of the pack of 2004 Democratic presidential candidates.

For the sake of a perspective that can only be provided by a real person, a non-digital, non-virtual sidelight on my volunteer partner in New Hampshire, 2000, should be inserted here. He was Bob Smith, from Alexandria, Virginia. He had been involved in local politics. He had led a fight to keep his kids' high school open. So he ran for School Board. Neighbors didn't talk to him for months afterwards. He agrees with what we found in Chapter 4 – that local political party committees have atrophied — so it's unlikely that he would have gotten involved in the Bradley campaign via that route. He also observed that people don't understand or appreciate what it takes to be a "public servant."

Political Parties

Political parties have found homes in the Internet, too, at all levels from ward to national. It's interesting to note that, as between the two major parties, the Republicans have most aggressively exploited the 'Web and 'Net at all levels, recruiting over 300,000 "e-Team Leaders" nationwide. We saw this earlier at the local level in the survey results reviewed in Chapter 5. The power of the Internet in helping to communicate, inform and mobilize citizens with shared concerns has been amply demonstrated by all parties, including the Green and Libertarian parties among the non-majors. From the standpoint of place and community, it's important to recognize that the power of the tool can be as great at the local level as at higher levels. Some good model local websites are cited in the political website resources' Appendix.

Dependence on other media needs to be noted. Websites cannot be viewed as stand-alone entities. Their viability depends on two factors – their linkages and how many people know to go there. The last is first. Websites need to be advertised widely in other, "old economy" media for people to know that they even exist. McCain knew that. Every one of his campaign posters, signs, palm cards, brochures and letters; that is, all the traditional campaign items, included his campaign's web address.[102] Why did commercial websites spend millions of dollars on advertising during Super Bowl 2000? The dot.com post-mortem cynics would say: so that they could use up their financing and go out of business. The fact of the matter is that if you don't advertise or otherwise get the word out that your site exists, very few will know to visit it.

The main "otherwise" is linkages. Other, related political sites need to include references to yours to bring people to your site who are likely to share your concerns. So, for example, state political party committee websites like those referenced in the Appendix Directory of Internet Political Sites usually contain references to local political committee websites, other politically relevant sites, or relevant e-mail addresses. Linkages are so important that internet services' providers (ISP's), website designers and search engine managers are charging extra in order to place customers' websites near the top of lists that search engines would generate for those searching for sites with certain qualities.

Having recognized the centrality of websites to their activities, what are parties doing with them? – still primarily using them to raise money rather than revive grassroots' political participation. An August 27, 2003 letter to the Republican Party's "Sustaining Members" from the new Republican National Committee Chairman, Ed Gillespie, is indicative. After he appeals to me in the body of an e-mail to "renew your membership in the RNC with a contribution" (of $$), he continues with a "P.S. The RNC is currently laying the groundwork for winning campaigns in '03-'04 (with) the support of grassroots activists like you…" Trouble is, this appeal seems remarkably similar to disingenuous fundraising appeals that I have often received in the past that claim to be raising money for local or regional campaigns and party organizations. As an active member of a political party, however, I have never seen any such contributions filter down to the local level – rather the opposite, in fact, as reported earlier in Chapter 5. As for the real, substantial contributions of time invested by party members and other interviewees observed in that earlier chapter—what of these? We can see signs, noted in a later section of this chapter, that parties may be waking up to the value of people's grassroots political participation.

Electronic Government

A third major organizational form implicated by the notion of digital democracy is "e-Gov" – electronic government. This is the topic of frequent articles in the business press as digital systems' integrators and a flock of e-business others seek to sell their products and services to governments at all levels.[103] What does this have to do with political participation? Perhaps something. The negativity of people's attitudes towards politics – a factor in their non-participation – is partly attributed to the shortcomings of government as well as those of politics and politicians. These include lack of government responsiveness, inadequacies of various government services, poor channels for citizens' input into governmental decisions and other factors that advocates of e-Gov say that their systems would remedy.

So, for example, some local governments have set up public information kiosks with keyboards and screens to enable citizens readily to find information and services from government agencies without having to go to City Hall to get them. Others are taking steps to electronically enhance local government by enabling e-mail interactions among and between citizens and government officials, including on-line, real-time debates over issues. As e-Gov initiatives take root and systems are improved, however, researchers would need to address two key questions:

1. Will improved government access, enhanced citizen input and better services help to offset people's political apathy and cynicism?, or…

2. Might e-Gov further reduce political participation to the extent that it enhances government's ability to "do its job" without increased citizens' participation, as if government had been put on automatic pilot via new technology?

One student of e-gov titled an article "E-Government vs. E-Democracy" (emphasis mine), observing that: "Encouraging e-democracy is less desirable to elected officials (because) E-democracy uses information technology to make (them) more accountable to the public."[104] So, which one is going to be encouraged and the other, discouraged?

Direct Democracy / Digital?

The major use that the advocates of digital democracy see for the new technology is realization of the Jeffersonian dream of direct democracy. Ironically, this dream is closely related to the use of polling, which has been the target of complaints from many of those most concerned with the health of

American democracy. Superficially, the dream of an electronic direct democracy seems attractive, including:

- Issues to be decided by citizens directly through electronic voting and instant tallies (polling), and so there would be...

- Internet "disintermediation" – no need for political parties, pundits, editorialists, representative or other intermediaries standing between citizens and the making of decisions that affect their lives.

Instant polls seem to provide a starting model. We now see them frequently on the Internet, via AoL, CNN, Yahoo, interest groups and others. Some of these provide input so interest groups can deluge legislators with messages such as "Two-thirds of people polled say they favor 'x' or oppose 'y'." For example, on May 8, 2000, CNN put forth two questions to poll those tapping into its media:[105]

1. "Do you think that India can succeed in reducing its population growth?"

2. "Can a computer virus spread accidentally?"

Are such questions the prelude to making government policy on the basis of direct/digital democracy? Is this really imaginable, even in a dream? The factors inducing population growth in any country are many and their interrelations are complex. Would my uninformed YES or NO answer to question #1 mean anything at all? Or even to #2? The questions quoted above are only two examples but they are not untypical of many others. What's the sense of asking such questions to get only yes or no answers?[106]

A company named "21st Century Faxes" also conducts such polls via fax, the results of which are posted at http://www.poll-results.com. These polls also ask questions requiring only a "YES" or "NO" answer. This is OK for questions like: "Do you still want to receive your mail on Saturdays?," the answers to which will be forwarded to the Postal Workers Union, General Accounting Office and Congress; but other questions, such as those mentioned above?[107]

So we again face a question that we confronted earlier, only now with a high tech twist: Except for decisions that can be made on the basis of simple yes or no answers, can electronically mediated direct democracy replace representative government? The answer, again, is NO. The digital direct democracy dream is an illusion. We can't get most voters to come out for Town Meeting or to cast an unspoiled ballot for President, and yet we expect them to take the time and effort to think about the U.S. stance towards population policy in India?[108] Some matters are properly left to representatives for final decision.[109]

So, the punster asks: What do you get when you combine the new technology with direct democracy in California?—a bad joke—an election with 135 candidates that quickly became one the most multi-ring of the political media circuses of 2003.[110] This media event not only brought out a lot of strange political characters, it led to some very curious turns and contradictions; like, liberals who are self-described "progressives" turning against the Progressive initiative and referendum provision in the state's constitution that enables people to recall a Governor. Liberals opposing direct democracy—is this an example of "the politics of paradox" described in Chapter 7, or just another instance of the kind of political hypocrisy that turns most people off politics?

Long after the California recall election is history, the most important digital democracy question will remain: whether our representatives will use the new media technologies to enhance their ability to provide both representation and leadership for "constituents"—a.k.a. concerned public citizens with an ability to play a greater role than that of just "customers" of whatever their "representatives" care to provide? Will they use digital technologies to better effect more and better outreach to people, to engage them in the political process?—Or to tap into both individual and collective intelligence residing in the public at-large in a process of co-deliberation and co-determination on issues?[111] In other words, will elected representatives work to make our democracy more direct by reducing the effective distance that people feel from both the political process and the people elected to advance it? Who would lay odds on a 'yes' answer to any of these questions?

So the key factor affecting the political process that the new technologies can alter is "distance," a factor that we touched in the section on community. And the key corollary question is: Alter for the better? Our earlier focus on place was not misguided, for it is at the community level in a real (i.e., not a digital-virtual) place that people can make a difference, see the fruits and realize appreciations for their efforts. So, in addressing the "key corollary question," above, we need to confront the fact that the digital tools provided to us by the new technologies are double-edged swords. On the one hand, they can help us to be more politically effective wherever we are, in any real place. On the other hand, they know not "place;" they are place-less. In fact, as many students of the media have pointed out, they blur, undermine or erase boundaries; they consummate people's leaning towards the "non-place urban realm."[112]

The dangers of this trend are suggested by the following quotes:

- "Nothing can be further from the new technology than "a place for everything and everything in its place."" (Marshall McLuhan)

- "Our world may seem suddenly senseless to many people because…it is relatively placeless."[113]

- "As place and information access become disconnected (via the new information technologies), place-specific behaviors and activities begin to fade…so now do many live relationships take on an ephemeral and sporadic quality." (Meyrowitz, op.cit., p.148)

- "direct physical presence and mutual monitoring are still primary experiential modes." (Meyrowitz, op.cit., p.312)

It's important here to recognize that distance means more than mileage; i.e., distance has more dimensions than just geographic ones. So we need a broader notion of distance; call it "effective distance." There's social distance – if someone's not part of your social, cultural, ethnic or other group, they may as well be on the dark side of the moon. There's psychological distance. If you've had a falling out with a former friend, then the effective distance between you and that person is infinite, even he or she lives next door. There's intra-family closeness (the inverse of distance), as in the old saying "blood is thicker than water." So, from now on, when you see the word "distance," realize that we're looking at something with more than one dimension.

Digital media are a plus from the standpoint of effective distance because they reduce it – between people, places, groups and otherwise. The non-place aspect of digital democracy is hardly all bad. Even TV. We see, or we can interact with, all kinds of people reflecting situations, interests or concerns that we would not otherwise encounter. We are brought into visual, informational or e-mail contact with people in vastly different places all over the world, so our horizons are broadened, virtually on a daily basis. TV, for example, has told us the story of the "Lost Boys of the Sudan" and how they have adapted to life in communities very foreign to them (as they are to us), like some in North Dakota. *60 Minutes* has brought to our attention the plight of abandoned children in Romania. We can then follow up at websites to see whether there's anything we can do in response to such situations.

There are countless other examples of how digital media break down boundaries between here and there, public and private, leaders and led, and our place in the world and that of others. This digital process of "breakdown" is not an unmixed blessing, but it is necessary and OK. There are still many more artificial walls to be taken down between people, groups and places.[114] Meyrowitz has pointed out that "to merge information worlds" (via digital media) is to "encourage egalitarian forms of interaction," [115]a definite plus for digital democracy.

Guinness remarks how difficult it is to have a more truthful politics in the face of the fragmentation brought about by the "partitioning" and "compartmentalizing" of people and information. Ironically (since much of his book is critical of the media), he credits media coverage of the Clinton/Lewinsky scandal. The media role in blurring the boundary between public and private in this case may have the salutary effect of raising the moral standard of public life. His remark that "there can be no liberty for a community that lacks the means to detect lies" implies a challenge to the media to play a greater, more positive, investigative, informational role in the future.

Like so much in this book, the role of the media is paradoxical. The digital media are simultaneously serving two opposing tendencies: to break down walls and link people up while creating new nodes of fragmentation. Again, the new technologies can serve to build community, including a larger, more inclusive sense of what "community" can mean, or it can help to destroy it as groups and individuals in cyberspace "do their own thing," virtually and sometimes with virtuosity, but with little public virtue. The response to the negative tendencies is partly one of attitude: Treat the new technologies as tools that you can (or should) control and use (or be able to use) in ways that can improve your private, public and public/private lives. The only new walls that should be built are "fire walls" to ensure privacy under the Constitution. All others should be warped, blurred, broken down or eliminated. "The opening of closed situations is the reversal of a trend several hundred years old." Thus the media's influence could prove to be quite revolutionary.[116] But, for now, you have reached digital democracies'…

Last Page

You have reached The End of the Internet

Thank you for visiting the Last Page.

There are no more links. You must now turn off your computer and go do something productive.

And So…

An old saying left over from the '60s is that "You're either part of the problem or part of the solution." As someone who is, in part, a child of the '60s, I have continued to swear by this saying even as others of my vintage would just as soon forget it. Anyway, a reference from that period is not out of place in a chapter on the media for, at one and the same time, the media are both a prime source of the problem of declining political participation our country and a prime source of any solution. Another reason reference to the period is not out of place is that the '60's generation, as the first whose politics were largely shaped by and played to the media, is another source of our problem; i.e., a generation that we have to move beyond. Media/consumer politics needs to be supplanted by grassroots/producer politics.

Changing attitudes and behaviors is the key. Those derived from the '60's are destructive of American democracy. Those demonstrated by "the greatest generation" are otherwise, and it is from these that we can derive and adapt attitudes and behaviors sufficient to the challenges of our own. Influencing attitudes and behaviors is something the media are good at. Observations of what was called the "West Wing flip," noted earlier, reveal the media's potential as an instrument of change with respect to attitudes towards government and politics. As media leaders become more aware of the adverse political consequences of their programming decisions, along with their public power and corollary responsibility, they can modify their decisions accordingly. Whether they will do so depends, in part, upon concerned Americans and their representatives in Congress – whether we and they have the balls to make media power a political issue.

The first test of this will be how the Congress deals with outrage over the recent FCC rulings that would enable big corporate media interests to increase media cross-ownerships and to dominate more of media markets. The fact that, according to Common Cause, "nearly two million Americans have contacted the FCC and asked the agency not to make it easier for media giants to acquire even more media properties," is encouraging but who would like to bet on the ultimate outcome, especially since the President has said he would veto any attempt by Congress to overturn the FCC rulings? [117] The House Appropriations Committee, against the "weight of corporate pressure…approved an amendment that would deny the FCC the money to implement the new FCC rules…" [118] As of this writing, however, it does not appear that this amendment or other bills in Congress that would "overturn the FCC rulings," survived compromises to pass the 2005 budget. In the ongoing battle between corporate lobbyists and popular pressure, chalk up another big win for the former and a loss to the latter.

The second big test depends on the extent to which we are willing and able to make use of the new, digital media technologies in ways that assert and effect some significant degree of independence from established media. During 2000, a survey conducted by the University of Connecticut found that "51 percent of Americans believe the press has too much freedom." [119] This should have been a wake-up call for all the media. The issue is not one of freedom but of political power.

The sometimes paradoxical combination of problems and opportunities created by the media in the political arena can best be addressed by keeping some basic guidelines in mind:

- **Openness**: A more open system is better than one that is relatively closed.

- **Truth-seeking**: Providing information based on in-depth investigation and fact-gathering is better than attempts at "spin," opinion-shaping and punditry.

- **Competition**: Opening up opportunities for increasing media competition and new, more localized media outlets is better than allowing continued media conglomeration.

- **Linkages**: Promoting cross-fertilization among websites on the Internet is better than smirking at their fragmentation, or behaving as if the Internet is naturally an archipelago; i.e., assuming that, as long as we have discovered our island of co-believers in cyberspace, we don't have to bother with others who may disagree with us.

- **Public space**: Creating more public and public/private media channels would give American citizens much more "space" to discover common ground (i.e., to become a public with an interest broader than the narrowly private) than if we allow media to be pre-empted or dominated by the private-market and its advertising. If the latter trend continues, then "I believe we're going to see something like the Microsoft Grand Canyon National Park..."[120]

- **Coverage**: Competitive media will cover more of what Americans want if both they and the officials they have elected indicate what they want and find ways to exert pressure on media outlets to supply more of it. The "it" needed to help revive American grassroots political activity is a two-sided coin: (1) more coverage of politics that treats more of issues and less of personalities; (2) coverage of the political involvement of ordinary Americans, especially at the local level.

- **Public journalism**: The guidelines represented by this approach.

Let's reflect on these before we try to draw up an agenda for action that we think would remedy media failings identified in this chapter. Per the paradoxical nature of these, note that nearly every weakness of current media could be turned into a strength. "Coverage of the political involvement of ordinary Americans," for example, could employ media techniques now used to turn news into entertainment or sell issues of *People* magazine to tell some really engaging stories of "ordinary" Americans who are political "heroes of everyday life."[121] The popularity of *Erin Brockovich* suggests the media potential of such stories without the media having to embellish the tales or focus on some latter-day Joan of Arc.

NOTES

1. The quotes here are drawn from Mitroff and Bennis (1989) but their views as to the systemic nature of the problems we face are shared by many others who will be referenced elsewhere in this chapter.

2. The view put forth by Nobel Laureate Kenneth Boulding in his book *The Image*.

3. Ibid., p.106 of Chapter VII: "The Image in the Political Process."

4. Early indications are that they may in terms of his image but may not in terms of the insider dealings of the political world of the U.S. Senate. See Gram, David (2003), "The Price of Power," *New York Times Magazine* (May 11).

5. *Daily News,* Newburyport, MA (October 2, 2000), originating as an Associated Press story out of Boston.

6. Ehrenreich, Barbara (2002), *Nickeled and Dimed: on (not) getting by in America.* New York: Henry Holt & Co., LLC, Owl Books, p.216.

7. As reported by Public Radio International's "Marketplace" program of June 13, 2001.

8. Respectively, see Mitroff and Bennis (1989) and Guinness (2000) among the References for full citations.

9. Others include Cappella and Jamieson (1997), Putnam (2000), Wilhelm (2000) and Guinness (2001).

10. Mitroff and Bennis, op.cit., p.6.

11. Boorstin, Daniel (1961), *The Image: A Guide to Pseudo Events in America*. Reprinted in 1987 with an "Afterword" by George Will. It is remarkable that Boulding's book was published in the same year with the same main title and some overlapping, supporting observations. They were written independently. There is no reference to Boulding in Boorstin's extensive bibliography or index, even in the later edition.

12. The potential pointed to here did not end with 2000's millennial celebrations. Recent coverage of the crime of Timothy McVeigh has recognized the "banality of (his) evil." We also need to recall that Hitler was brought into power through the abortive democracy of the Weimar Republic.

13. Ironically, the quote is from Mitroff and Bennis' book, page 161. Another, more recent example is provided by Jonathan Wallace (jw@bway.net) in his article "Minority Rule," in *The Ethical Spectacle* (http://www.spectacle.org), February 2001.

14. Lee Heffner writing in *The Daily News*, Newburyport, MA (May 1, 2002, p. A8).

15. The sentence paraphrases Meyrowitz (1985, p.316).

16. Eco, Umberto (1986), *Faith in Fakes: Essays*.

17. As further noted by "Throw those TV's out with the trash", a letter to the editor of the *Gloucester Daily Times* published February 7, 1997, which seconded an earlier, similar letter from Peg Sibley, a member of the City's School Board.

18. Quoted by Seaquist, Carla (2002) in "America, we need to talk—*seriously*," *The Christian Science Monitor* (June 24).

19. The latter was seen in "The Arts" section of the *New York Times*, covering many media, on October 10, 2001, p.F1.

20. Mitroff and Bennis, op.cit., p.xi.

21. The quotes here are from Meyrowitz (1985), pp. 85 and 89.

22. Putnam (2000), p. 242.

23. The highlights presented here are drawn from Chapter 13 of Putnam's book *Bowling Alone*, cited earlier.

24. Although Putnam qualifies this to say that the average could be as low as three, other studies indicate that it could be as high as 6 and 2/3 hours per day across virtually all income groups in our society. See Meyrowitz' (2000), footnote on page 79, for example. The higher estimates are per household. Families are watching instead of talking, least of all talking about politics or public issues.

25. Hill, Martha S. and F. Thomas Juster (1979), "Constraints and Complementarities in Time Use." Ann Arbor, Michigan: Survey Research Center, Institute for Social Research, University of Michigan.

26. Putnam (2000), p.243. As documented by the research of Verba, cited earlier, and others, "selective viewers" are primarily those of higher socio-economic status. Thus, again, those most in need of political influence are swayed away from political participation even if they could afford the time.

27. Reported in Meyrowitz (1985), footnote on p.75.

28. Reported in Meyrowitz (1985), footnote on p.80. This is not to imply that one must read in order to participate in public life. Forums on public issues sponsored by the Kettering Foundation and Public Agenda have demonstrated that diverse cross sections of citizens participate enthusiastically and effectively once they are convinced that their involvement is meaningful—that their views will be taken seriously.

29. The quoted phrase is the title of a neat little book by Terry Bossomaier and David Green (1998), the subtitle of which is "Computers, Complexity and Everyday Life."

30. People are easily fooled by optical illusions such as the the Ouchi pattern [as found on http://www. expert.booksonline.com], and the ability of TV to convey other illusions is even more sophisticated.

31. See his insightful book: *Coming to Public Judgement: Making Democracy Work in a Complex World.* "Consciousness raising," however, is only the first step in moving from public opinion to the kind of public judgement needed in a healthy democracy.

32. Meyrowitz, op.cit., p.79.

33 Vargas Llosa, Mario (2001), "Why Literature"? *The New Republic* (May 14). It's interesting to note that he doesn't treat the distractions of electronic media as the reason for why people are reading less; rather, he opens by attacking people's excuses for lack of time to read—that "literature…can be sacrificed without scruple when one "prioritizes" the tasks and the duties that are indispensible in the struggle of life." There is a curious parallel here with political participation. The same excuses for non-involvement are trotted out for an activity that is similarly "indispensable." Several quotes following are also from Vargas' article unless otherwise indicated. Vargas is Professor of Ibero-American Literature and Culture at Georgetown University.

34. It was not missed by Putnam. His evidence showed that people who read are more likely to be involved, but he did not go into the contrast of TV with literature.

35. The low-cost feature has been highlighted by Meyrowitz; however, this is only the direct, private cost. The indirect cost of being such a "free rider" is immeasurable —the social cost of the erosion of our democracy.

36. Ingraham, Jeson (2001), "GDA grads told to strive for community, not con-sumption." Newburyport, MA: *Daily News* (June 3).

37. See Bearak, Barry (2001), "This Job Is Truly Scary: The Taliban are Watching." *New York Times* (June 1). The 'job' referred to is that of TV repairman.

38. See Frantzich, Stephen, and J. Sullivan (1996), *The C-Span Revolution.* Norman, OK: The University of Oklahoma Press; and Frantzich, Stephen (1999), *Citizen Democracy: Political Activists in a Cynical Age.* New York: Rowman and Littlefield Publishers.

39. Cappella, Joseph N., and K.H. Jamieson (1997), S*piral of Cynicism: The Press and the Public Good.* New York: Oxford University Press.

40. Tebbell, John (1974), *The Media In America.* New York: New American Library.

41. And served to impel or induce a response – appointment of an "ombudsman" by that newspaper and many others.

42. See, for example, the editorial in *U.S. News & World report* by Mortimer B. Zuckerman: "A sure-fire recipe for trouble," which remarked that "The FCC's recent decision to ease ownership rules on big media companies, if not reversed, will deliver a body blow to our democracy" (June 23, 2003).

43. Two features here are apparently characteristic of many local papers along with a third mentioned earlier, lack of an alternative or competitive paper. One is a tendency to recruit and employ reporters that arrive from someplace else, work a couple of years locally and then leave by the time they undergo enough on-the-job training to get acquainted with the community they are covering. Julie Salamon, a reporter for the *New York Times,* wrote: "Increasingly, local news isn't reported by home-grown reporters with an indigenous passion for the place they live" (October 10, 2001, p. E8). Another feature is non-local ownership, increasingly conglomerate in form. Neither of these is conducive to community-building, let alone a community-based politics. My hometown newspaper, for example, was owned by Essex County Newspapers which, in turn, was owned by Dow Jones, which sold it to the *Eagle-Tribune.*

44. This point was elaborated in an "op ed" piece entitled "Truth Isn't a Political Priority," published by the *Gloucester Daily Times* (April 24, 1987).

45. For example: Nichols, John, and Robert W. McChesney (2000), *It's The Media, Stupid'.*

46. See Barringer, Felicity (2001), "Unresolved Clash of Cultures: At Knight Ridder, Good Journalism vs. the Bottom Line." *New York Times* (June 1). Note also the PBS series on "Local News: One Station Fights the Odds." Julie Salmon's review of this five-part profile of *WCNC* (Charlotte, NC) included this sketch of Keith Connors, the new director: "a decent and compelling soul, trying to cheer his staff and encourage good reporting while answering to the corporate bosses. It's a tough job" (*New York Times,* October 9, 2001, p. E8).

47. Thelen, David (1996), *Becoming Citizens in the Age of Television* (p. 195).

48. Thelen, op.cit. His statistics are from 1988-92 but the trends he reports have continued. "Horse race" coverage was amply apparent during 2000.

49. As stated during an interview with Karen Olson, Assistant Editor of the *Utne Reader* (March-April, 2001, pp. 84-86). New Dimensions is "the longest running independently produced program on National Public Radio" (NPR).

50. Nichols and McChesney (2000), op.cit., p. 29.

51. Michael Toms also claimed that "Low-power FM would recreate democracy, which we have never really tried successfully." *Utne Reader* (March-April, 2001), p. 85. Unfortunately, Republicans in Congress backed "big broadcasters" and "sought to block a Federal Communications Commission program to license hundreds of new, low-power radio stations." (New York Times, May 27, 2001, p. 1).

52. From a solicitation for subscriptions received from *In These Times,* a periodical published in Mt. Morris, IL (P.O. Box 1912, 61054-9885) oriented to liberal political activists.

53. Wilhelm, Anthony (2000), *Democracy in the Digital Age.* New York: Routledge (p. 10).

54. Nichols and McChesney, op.cit., p. 92.

55. Remark of Vivian Tenney via e-mail to the *Politalk-US1* forum on campaign finance reform (3/4/2001).

56. Ahrens, Frank (2003), "Senate Panel Approves Tougher Media Rules," *Washington Post* (June 20, p. E01).

57. What is "real"? – not a creature of the media.

58. See Verba, et.al. (1995), whose study reveals to what degree "willing" is dependent on "able," and vice-versa.

59. The notable exceptions are community-based sites.

60. Quoted by Julie Salamon in "A Station Pursues Both the News and the Audience," *New York Times* (October 9, 2001, p.E8).

61. As with the reference to "character" in President George W. Bush's Inaugural Address and Stanley Hauerwas' reference to "truthful communities" in his book *A Community of Character.*

62. McKibben, op.cit. (see footnote 36).

63. For more on this, see Kohn, Margaret (2001), "The Mauling of Public Space," *Dissent* (Spring).

64. The quoted phrase is the main title of the book by Daniel Yankelovitch (1991), cited earlier, on how the media should do more than use polls to reflect the opinions of the moment or as fodder for the evening news. See also Kay, Alan (1998), *Locating Consensus for Democracy.* St.Augustine, FL: Americans Talk Issues, on "public interest polling."

65. Quotations here and preceeding, as well as the following examples, are drawn from Rosen, Jay, and D. Merritt, Jr. (1994), "Public Journalism: Theory and Practice." Dayton, OH: the Kettering Foundation.

66. As in TV renderings of "Little House on the Prairie" or Garrison Keillor's "Lake Wobegon" monologues on "Prairie Home Companion." A much longer list of examples could be compiled.

67. The movie is an inspiration and the reception that it received was heartening, but the word "rare" is important. The movie also misleads. You don't have to be like the heroine – you don't have to sacrifice your all on the altar of political activism to be able to make a positive difference to the quality of life in your community.

68. Kemmis, Daniel (1990), *Community and the Politics of Place.* Norman, OK: University of Oklahoma Press. Dan is a former state legislator, Speaker of the House in the Montana Legislature and Mayor of Missoula. He is quoting from Arendt's book *The Human Condition.*

69. "vanishing table" also refers to the lack of conversations on politics and the issues of the day around family dinner tables which have nurtured both public and private leaders. Anne M. Mulcahey, Chief Executive, the Xerox Corporation, for example, recalled from her childhood that "dinner was a time to be provocative, to discuss politics, religion, current events, anything that was contentious. You had to participate…" See "Shaped by Family Debates," New York Times (October 10, 2001). Many more such recollections have been seen or heard from political leaders as well. Thus, both public and private-sector leadership may spring from the same (diminishing) family "table" source.

70. Kemmis, op.cit., p. 7.

71. Kemmis, op.cit., p. 7. The quote is from Berry's book *The Unsettling of America*.

72. Meyrowitz, op.cit., p. 17. He continues, wondering whether "electronic sensors will return us to village-like encounters but on a global scale." (p. 18) Others wonder whether they will "return" us to "1984."

73. For instance, during the winter of 2002-03, Town Meeting had to be convened three times before a quorum was present, even though tax bills and other town business had been held up.

74. Clift, Steven (2000), "Democracy is Online," *OnTheInternet magazine*. Internet Society (March/April 1998, p. 1). Did you sense the sarcasm in the final line of this quote? If you did, good for you. I didn't. Via e-mail, I questioned Clift about his reference to TV and, of course, he set me straight. Boy, did I feel dumb when I received his response!

75. You can tell that the central figure is a "workman" by looking at his hands even though there is also a contrast of dress. The figures on either side of him are wearing suits.

76. A "superconnected" person exchanges e-mail at least three times a week and uses four technologies: cell-phone, beeper, PC and laptop. A connected" person uses three of the four technologies. A"semi-connected" person uses some of the technologies but not e-mail; "unconnected," none of the technologies.

77. Long before either his book came out or the survey was done, Putnam had put forth his thesis in an article with the same title that, like the book, received a good deal of attention and generated a great deal of controversy.

78. Katz, Jon (1997), "The Digital Citizen." *Wired* magazine, no. 5.12 (December).

79. Keller, Ed, and Jon Berry (2004), *The Influentials*, Washington, D.C.: Institute for Politics, Democracy & the Internet, Graduate School of Political Management, The George Washington University (quote from the Executive Summary accessed via http://www.ipdi.org/Influentials/Report.pdf).

80. Ibid., op.cit.

81. Advertisement of Starboard Response, San Luis Obispo, CA 93406, in T*he Washington Times National Weekly Edition*, Family and Culture section (July 6-12, 1998).

82. Nor perhaps even now. In 2002, largely because of screw-ups by their Governor and elected representatives, people in California found that they couldn't take electric

power for granted. In 2003, people in New York and a broad swath of states through Ohio and into the Midwest found out the same thing during "The Great Blackout." Thus, *The Economist* could refer to "the powerless masses" in the August 25, 2003 issue. The double meaning here was apparently deliberate. Faith in technology was undermined by "a system in chaos," yet people's response to the crisis, especially in New York City, seemed to boost their faith in each other and their local communities, at least for awhile. See *U.S. News & World Report* article by Marianne Lavelle titled "Gridlock," September 1, 2003, p. 30.

83. Two books highlight this aspect: Gleick (2000), *Faster,* and Davis (2001), *Speed is Life.*

84. Quotes from Lasch here and just prior are drawn from his article "Journalism, Publicity, and the Lost Art of Argument," *Kettering Review* (Spring, 1995, pp. 44-50).

85. A problem we're running into here, however, is a possible "privacy" issue. Advertisers are trying to reach you with customized ads but they can't customize without knowing a lot more about you. So they are building massive data bases on business customers so that they can do targeted marketing focused on a target of a single individual—you. Political candidate marketing is going the same way.

86. Views conveyed to the author in private conversation, August 26, 2003.

87. Quoted from Chapter 7, "Building Civic Life Online", of Clift's (2000) opus: *Democracy is Online 2.0,* the closest thing to a "bible" for e-democracy that I have yet found. As of this writing, it is still available only online via www.e-democracy.org/do; that is, via Clift's excellent *Do-Wire—Democracies Online Newswire.* The *MN-POLITICS* site is at www.e-democracy.org/mn-politics.

88. *Do-Wire* of 6/14/2001 (from clift@publicus.net - click here to send an e-mail to Steve).

89. *Do-Wire* of 8/18/2003, p. 1.

90. As emphasized, for example, in Clift's *[DW] Report* of 2/5/2004: "a single, well-edited, concise, weekly e-newsletter…is essential."

91. *New York Times,* "Arts and Ideas" section front page article by Alexander Stille (June 2, 2001).

92. Limbaugh, David (2001), "Moderation in all things? Not quite." *Jewish World Review* (June 6).

93. Quotes from "Want 2b Friends," by Kristi Palma in the *Sunday Eagle-Tribune* (August 17, 2003, p. E1).

94. Sunstein, Cass (2001), op.cit. Note, moreover, that a study on "The Consequences of Cross-Cutting Networks for Political Participation" observed that "social accountability (peer) pressures in cross-cutting networks discourage political participation." See the article by Diana C. Mutz in the *American Journal of Political Science* (Vol. 46, No. 4, October, 2002, p. 838).

95. Quote from *The Atlantic Monthly* (September 2003, p.29).

96. Clift, Steven (2000), op.cit., p. 2 of Chapter 7, Draft 3.1.

97. Is there something in the water of the state of Minnesota that has given rise to models of democratic process that can inspire those of us in other states?—not only e-democracy and *Politalk* but the three- way gubernatorial debates that led to Jesse Ventura being elected?

98. I was both a resource person and a participant in the forum on campaign finance reform, for example.

99. Cited in the Bibliography, respectively, as Kush, Christopher (2000) and Bowen, Charles(1996).

100. McCain also elicited a great number of volunteers for his campaign, too, but I can't relate to that from my own experience. One of the big questions left over from the 2000 political season is what became of the McCain and Bradley volunteers after their candidates dropped out. Are they still involved or did they drop out, too?

101. "Politics Online: Internet Tools for Politics" (www.politicsonline.com), 1/31/2002, p. 1.

102. This is truly a "footnote" to McCain's 2000 campaign. One of his Internet addresses was for sale on the Internet. Anyone want to spend several thousands of dollars so that Americans can continue to channel on "straight talk" via the 'Net without having to read the usual promotional newsletter(s) from an elected official?

103. See, for example, the publication *Washington Technology*.

104. Snider, J.H. (2001), in *Government Technology* (August 1).

105. CNN has a website as well as a TV channel, as watchers are frequently reminded.

106. The answer, according to Alan Kay, is 'not much,' which is why he has devoted so much of his valuable time and creative talent to designing and advocating an approach to what he calls "public interest polling." See Kay (1998), op.cit.

107. 21st Century Faxes, Ltd., 331 W. 57th St., PMB 504, New York, NY 10019. A response fax to 1-900-370-3200 (YES) or 1-900-370-9400 (NO) costs $2.95 per minute.

108. This is hardly an academic concern since President Bush cancelled Clinton's rule allowing the use of federal funds to support population planning initiatives that include counseling on abortion in such countries as India.

109. A key question that seems unavoidable here, however, is: What does it mean to be an elected representative? If a poll showed that most constituents were against a certain measure, can the representative vote against it and still be (a) "representative"?

110. Cartoonists had a field day along with late-night comedians. One cartoon pictured a joking face on a map of the U.S. highlighting Florida and California, with the face in Florida saying to that in California: "We're not laughing with you." See cartoon by Bill Mitchell in the *National Journal* of August 13, 2003.

111. The key potential, the greatest enabling potential of the new technology, in my opinion, is "distributed intelligence." See "Mining the Minds of the Masses: Researchers Muster Online Volunteers for Collective Brainpower." *New York Times* (March 3, 2001).

112. This designation was coined by urban planner Melvin Webber (1964), in *Explorations in Urban Structure,* and employed more recently by Sharpe and Wallach (1987), "From the Great Town to the Non-Place Urban Realm," in *Visions of the Modern City.*

113. Meyrowitz, op.cit., p. 308.

114. At this point, if this were an electronic, multi-media book, you would hear a passage from Pink Floyd's *The Wall:* "Take down the wall! Take down the wall!" (EMI Records, Ltd., United Kingdom, 1994). Recall that one of the greatest boundary-busting events in history was the destruction of the Berlin Wall not long after Ronald Reagan, with an only slightly different combination of words, said "Take down the wall" to Mikhail Gorbachev.

115. Meyrowitz (1985), op.cit., p. 64.

116. The quote is from Meyrowitz, p.310, but it is based upon work by the French sociologist Foucault which documented the "trend." More recent work by James C. Scott (1998), *Seeing Like a State,* is also illuminating in this regard.

117. Quoted from a July 31, 2003 press release of Common Cause titled: "In the FCC Rules Debate, Will Two Million Voices Trump $124 Million." See www.commoncause.org.

118. The Senate bill is titled "The Preservation of Localism, Program Diversity and Competition in Television Broadcast Act of 2003." The quote here is from another Common Cause press release, dated July 18, 2003, titled: "July 18 Report from the House of Representatives: House appropriations committee stands up to big media."

119. Quoted in an editorial in the *The Eagle-Tribune* (Lawrence, MA, Tuesday, July 4, 2000, p. 6).

120. Bill Carter's remark in "Survival of the Pushiest," *The New York Times Magazine* (January 28, 2001).

121. Similar to stories our fathers and grandfathers read in school nearly 100 years ago, as in: Coe, Fanny E. (1911), *Heroes of Everyday Life: A reader for the upper grades.* Boston: Ginn and Company. The preface to this delightful old book observes that: "A rarer quality than military valor in the citizens of our own land or of any land is that form of moral bravery known as civic courage." (page v). We saw such courage exhibited most recently on September 11th, 2001.

9.

Year 2000 and the Agenda for Reform

- 2000: What a Year! Threshold of Change? Reform as a Subtext of the Year 2000 (and 2004?) Presidential Campaign
- Populism and Participation in the Politics of a Presidential Election Year

    —The 2000 Primary Season & Reform
    —Presidential campaigns
    —Campaign Finance Reform: Debates
    —Campaign Finance Reform: Legislation

- Other Reform Initiatives Stemming from 2000

    —Florida, the Count and Election Reform
    —Other Propositions for Election Reforms

- Postscript to the 2000 Election
- Goodbye to Bill Clinton
- Prognosis, Postlude, New Beginnings and Reform Redux

Executive Summary

From the standpoint of real political reform, election year 2000 started with a bang and ended with a whimper. Ironically, campaign finance reform (CFR), though supposed to reduce the role of money in politics, focused only on money. No value was assigned to the people's time as political volunteers. Both CFR and election reform initiatives took steps to federalize campaign finance and elections that bordered on being unconstitutional. Bill Clinton's exit served to remind us how he depreciated the coin of political life even while focusing attention on an imperial Presidency and national politics. Both our attention and the reform agenda need to be refocused on state and local initiatives and political parties that recognize the value of people's participation in the whole process of electoral politics, not just voting. In these terms, 2000 revealed some signs of hope, that the "old politics"— bringing people back into the process—could make a significant difference to the outcome of new political races, as witnessed by the impact of Democratic labor unions putting more workers on the streets, and by Republicans mobilizing people to get out the vote in key Congressional districts.

Introduction:

2000: What a Year! Threshold of Change? Reform as a Subtext of the Year 2000 (and 2004?) Presidential Campaigns

This book was being written during one of the most remarkable political years in our country's history. The Presidential campaign playbook came to a final episode far more remarkable than the political game preceding. As a result, all of a sudden, there was talk of "reform" once again at the end of a year that opened with talk of reform by challengers during the Presidential primary season. The scope of the year-end talk, however, was limited largely to "electoral reform"—changes in voting arrangements to ensure that every vote would count. This was followed by another round of talk on campaign finance reform that seemed like déjà vu, harkening back to the year's beginning. Those who talked the talk, however, were not able to walk the walk in ways that would help the great American majority to become more active and effective political actors. In other words, another great Presidential election year opportunity to grapple with the true challenge of political reform was lost. Perhaps the most hopeful sign was seen at the White House exit. The entry of another occupant seemed sanguine, at least in terms of inaugural rhetoric. But, harbingers? Preludes? Some real hope for reform by 2004 or for opportunity to be realized during the 2004 Presidential election year?

Who will turn out to be the "Reformer with Results" after all is said and done on the issue of reform? A common slice of political advice tendered to those running for office is that the candidate should always try to set the agenda so that the campaign debate is carried out on his terms, not those of the opponent. Bush's political advertising slogan was a backhanded compliment to his opponent at the time, testimony to the fact that McCain had succeeded in setting the Presidential Campaign agenda for awhile, even taking it away from Bill Bradley so that reform became the subtext of the 2000 Presidential campaign. This is how things looked in naked (calculating, short-term) political terms for awhile during the Spring of the year 2000.

Given the passage of time since and the perspectives found in Chapter VII, we can now get a better, broader slant on the political workout on reform during the year and its immediate aftermath. Who actually set the agenda? How was the reform issue defined? What kind of reform did the issue definition represent? And what are actual or likely repercussions to deal with now and into the future?

Populism and Participation in the Politics of a Presidential Election Year

The 2000 Primary Season & Reform.

Hopes rise at the New Year and sap rises with the onset of Spring. So, too, with the primary season of the 2000 Presidential race. For awhile, it seemed as if "reform" might be the prime driver of the year's political season. Words resonant of the Progressive Era of 100 years ago brought out thousands of new, young and independent voters, putting new energy and life into a race in ways and to an extent that had not been seen during the previous Presidential election campaign of 1996. The challengers attracting media and primary voters' attention, John McCain and Bill Bradley, were on message re: reform like Frik and Frak. Thus, primary questions at two levels came to the fore:

1. Would a reform message move to the top of the public agenda, notwithstanding polls that repeatedly said "no;"

2. Who would win out as the message bearer?

Remember the joint press conference in New Hampshire at which Bill and John shook hands and pledged mutual devotion to a reform agenda? That reminded me of the handshake between another Bill and his buddy Newt that accompanied a similar declaration – like that emerging from a NATO meeting: No Action; Talk Only. Nothing happened as a result.[1] The encounter between "Dollar Bill" and "Straight Talk McCain," however, was like a coin toss that Bill lost. Afterwards, it was downhill for the Bradley campaign. This Bill had some good things to say, but he never did overcome his (public) speech handicap and John had it all over him for charisma. It's tough running against a real war hero who preempts your main message. Though Bill's lackluster campaign may be blessedly forgotten, we should recall the reform part of his platform.

Looking back, who among the political pundits noticed a disconnect between early and late 2000 in terms other than number of months passed? The early Presidential primary season was marked by political participation in New Hampshire that could nearly darn well be called populist. People from all over and many walks of life converged on the Granite state to walk, talk, mail, call and otherwise work for various Presidential candidates, not only McCain but Bradley, Forbes, Keyes and others. Old fashioned people politics seemed to be back with new faces and flavors. Now recall the late Y2K political channel. What did we see?—The people appeared to have left the scene. The reform issue was reduced to S.27, "McCain-Feingold," a Senate Bill that mentioned only money. What happened to all the political volunteers that we saw in New Hampshire, those who thought the political process might still have some life left in it after all? Were some of them the same people we saw standing outside courthouses in Florida? Were they the ones attracted by Al Gore's pretend populism? How many even bothered to vote once the McCain flame had died out? How many moved over to Nader or voted Green, Libertarian or other 3rd party? According to the leading scholar on political participation, Sidney Verba, we still don't know the answers to these questions.[2]

Presidential Campaigns

While he was running, President G.W. Bush never had a Republican reform proposition that had much more to offer than that of Sen. Mitch McConnell, the prime opponent of McCain-Feingold and other campaign finance reform (CFR) legislation. To his credit, however, Bush's actions demonstrated the value of McConnell's main proposition in ways that words could not. His campaign provided quick and "full disclosure" of campaign contributions via the Internet.

Meanwhile, his opponent was playing the populist card. Not only did Mr. Gore repeatedly say that he would "sign" McCain-Feingold once it reached his desk as President, he railed against "big money" and "special interests," as if he were running his campaign according to a Progressive Era reformers' playbook. Then, in its desperate last days, the Gore campaign appealed to "the will of the people" and "the voters' intent" to justify repeated efforts to find enough voters in Florida to validate Mr. Gore's presumption of the Presidency based on a national popular majority, as if the U.S. was a foreign, unitary state with a different constitution. His appeals were those of a demagogue, not those of a man who would be President of an American federal republic.

For the tradition that Al upheld was otherwise. He was the latest in a long line of American demagogues—pretend populists who play on people's passions without informing them as to what they can or should do other than vote for the "man of the people" if they really want to "count." The appeals of such pretenders also rest upon what they do not say. They rely too much on people's ignorance or inexperience of what it takes to make a democratic system work. One was hard put to hear, however, even if one had a political hearing aid to turn up, how Mr. Gore's election would bring people back into the political picture and enable a government of and by as well as for, the people.

The Supreme Court properly focused on HOW votes need to be counted to ensure equal protection under the law. No totalitarian allusions to "will of the people" here. Voter is as voter does. Whether or not the vote can be counted is unambiguous according to a uniform standard, or the vote is rejected or not recounted. No impressionistic reliance upon various interpretations of "voter's intent" here. We do not live in the Republic of Chad. Our ox was not Gored, Babe.

Yet the Supreme Court was wrong to put itself in the position of effectively deciding the outcome of the 2000 presidential election. Yes, there was a Constitutional "equal protection" issue, so the Supremes were right to take the case on even though (or because?) it sang to the country with dissonant chords. There were also voting inequities, although reliable, convincing evidence of these did not arise until later. Yes, an election result needed to be certified within no more than a few weeks. The Court's decision would have been wiser, however, if it had enabled the federal nature of our election process to work itself out, with clearer standards, to be sure, but at the state level first and foremost, then passing to the Congress as specified by our Constitution, if necessary. The process would have been a bit further prolonged and even more contentious, partisan and noisy. The outcome would have been no different but it would have been more satisfactorily consistent with the de-centralized, federal nature of our Republic.

We can now look back at the 36-day episode as a much needed civics lesson on what we as citizens need to do if we really want to count in the future. We don't have to buy into continued, misleading, negative interpretations generated by the media "commentariat." The brunt of the lesson is positive, promising and constructive if the majority of the American people see that they need to be active participants in the political process if they want the political system to be authentically as well as legitimately theirs. The impor-tance of voting is now obvious to all. But democratic political participation means more than just voting. People need to participate actively in the political process through which candidates are selected and elected. At the local level, this process includes ballot design, designation of poll workers, and selection of people to serve on election boards.

The example of Florida is hardly negative. We saw dozens of volunteers helping to count thousands of ballots over hundreds of hours. We observed the critical importance of many more people than those in the political class paying attention to basic features of how "our" political system works (or sometimes falls short)—as in ballot design, voting machines and procedures, whether voters pay attention, protest demonstrations, influence of the media, poll closing times, and so on.

If these lessons are taken to heart and acted upon, then the experience we have been through as a nation will turn out to be a big plus. Our federal democratic republic will be the better for it. We will continue to light the way for other nations whose people were as fascinated with the counting contro-versy as ourselves. If the episode rings like a wake up call for American democracy, then our children will benefit most of all, in more ways than even the Count of Sesame Street can "count." They will benefit by example—seeing more parent-citizen role models as actors, not just spectators, of the drama of American democracy. They may even get involved enough to "Take Back" their government, as the non-science fiction book by science fiction writer Robert Heinlein would help them to do if they were to read it and take it to heart along with this one.[3]

As for Presidential campaigns, it remains to be seen whether a genuine populist will emerge as a strong contender during 2004, whether real reform will be more than a "subtext," or whether "digital democracy" will emerge as a real force. The folks at the website moveon.org—"Carrie, Eli, Joan, Peter, Wes, and Zack"—seemed determined to realize all three. They called for a much earlier than even New Hampshire primary via Internet voting on June 24, 2003, while featuring e-mail statements from Howard Dean and two other Democrats—would-be populists that hoped to be anointed via e-voting. Moveon's Internet newsletter of 6/18/03 reminded me of the 1998 notice featured in the last chapter suggesting that democratic political participation is "just a click away."

Former Vermont Gov. Dean's e-mail in that newsletter, if it had been designed for audio streaming, would have rung aloud with populist noises, such as:

> Defeating George Bush will take nothing short of a grassroots movement. That's why we've... provided tools on our website to help you build the movement in your community. Click below...I want everyone to know that there is a way to get involved...no matter how much time they have...

Dean's campaign manager Joe Trippi claimed, presumably without blushing, that: "This is the first great grassroots campaign of the modern era."[4] Dean appeared to be already anointed by Moveon as his letter appeared as the first of "three candidates who polled highest with our members." Rep. Dennis Kucinich and Sen. John Kerry were the other two. One had to click on "Read letters from all the candidates here" to find the other six of nine Democratic candidates for Moveon's presidential primary.[5] Thus, it was no surprise to see the results of "the first Internet primary in recorded history"—Dean, Kucinich and Kerry placed 1,2,3, with Dean far ahead at over 43%. Democracy in action?

What was surprising was the demonstration of how quickly a national primary could be organized and executed via the 'net and the size of the "turnout." Certified at 317,647 Moveon members, it was larger than the combined turnouts of voters in the New Hampshire and South Carolina primaries and Iowa caucuses during the 2000 presidential election season. Thus, the power of the Internet as a political organizing tool, to which the previous chapter pointed, was demonstrated nationwide. It still remains to be seen whether this power will be translated into a durable revival of people's direct political involvement—"We, the People" empowerment—or into another transient increase in political participation plus another demonstration of the power of Internet political fund-raising to finance political business-as-usual.

Ironically for many Moveon members who see the need to revive the Democratic Party as a progressive force vs. a resurgent GOP, reliance upon such an Internet procedure would serve to weaken the Party. I was allowed to participate in the primary, and my vote was counted even though I am a registered Republican. Many who voted may not have been registered to vote in a regular election. The only requirement was that one be a Moveon "member." Moveon did not use the occasion to urge members to go down to their city or town halls to register to vote. Nor to enable "Instant Voter Registration," as urged by many liberal activists, for participation in their

Internet primary. One had to be "registered" as a Moveon member by the evening of the day before voting began. According to the avowedly liberal magazine, *The American Prospect*, the main winner of the primary was Moveon: "the group has managed to induce some of the highest profile Democrats in the country…many of whom are part of the party establishment and had not felt a need to join up with Moveon…into conducting a massive, no cost membership drive for them…"[6]

Campaign Finance Reform: Congressional Debates

Unfortunately, as 2000 wore on and slopped over into 2001, the reform issue became only a matter of money with respect to either side of the 2000 reform coin—election reform or campaign finance reform (CFR). "Thank God for C-SPAN." C-SPAN2 carried the U.S. Senate debates on CFR in their entirety. Political commentators fell all over themselves to compliment the Senate and many of its members for the quality of their deliberations—as if political speechmaking had been sadly missed and posturing for the cameras was something new. No one seemed to notice how even the most populist members among the Senators failed to define the issue so that people could come back into the picture. There were two exceptions that prove the rule— Barbara Mikulski and the late Paul Wellstone. Especially Barbara. Her nostalgia was eloquent. She recalled how, with the help of political volunteers in Baltimore at the outset of her political career, she knocked on 10,000 doors to "beat the machine" and win a seat on City Council. But did she move from this recollection to observe how there seemed to be no room for volunteers in the "reform"(ed) political future envisaged by McCain-Feingold? No.

Sen. Wellstone's performance during the debates was marked by two proposed amendments:

1. One to extend the ban on "issue advocacy" by corporations and unions to non-profit organizations, an amendment that many political commentators and opponents of Wellstone (like Sen. McConnell, who voted for it) thought would ultimately sink the McCain-Feingold ship because of its likely unconstitutionality. This amendment passed in spite of McCain's opposition.

2. Another amendment to give states the option of extending public financing (a.k.a. "Clean Money") to federal office candidacies. This amendment failed even though supporters pointed admiringly to the "Maine model" and tried to force federal reform into a "states rights" wrapper rhetorically embellished by some Senatorial rappers.

The only concern expressed for time as a resource in politics was a concern for Senators' time—the time they need to spend (too much) raising too much money in order to finance multimillion dollar campaigns. The value of time contributed by political volunteers had disappeared from their radar screens as a result of "the money chase." In the old days, candidates would spend more time calling for volunteers than dialing for dollars. The Senators felt free to blame TV for most of the time they had to spend fund raising to feed the maw of the media. None of them, however, felt strongly enough to introduce an amendment calling for even minimal allocations of free TV time to enable them to "get their message out."[7]

The fact that they had to raise money to pay big bucks to political consultants who also stood to make more big bucks from media "buys"—this fact earned (dis)honorable mention by some. But the connection with people's absence from politics was lost. No one observed that political consultants are increasingly taking over grassroots political functions that used to be performed by volunteers—one of the basic reasons why the cost of political campaigns continues to rise at three times the rate of inflation! Also, no one in the Senate thought to suggest that the increasing costs of campaign finance regulation might itself be a factor aggravating this incredible rate of inflation. Even though there was some high flown rhetoric about a political system in danger of sinking, no one used the Titanic as a metaphor. Perhaps they didn't want to be seen to be rearranging deck chairs.

Opponents of McCain-Feingold pointed to another danger—federalization of elections. The danger was already apparent in a memo to the Federal Election Commission (FEC) from the Commission's General Counsel that was discussed at the FEC's September, 2000 meeting. This memo also reveals that the urge to control the political process to remove any possible perception of "corruption" knows no bounds. As Bradley Smith, FEC Commissioner, indicated: "McCain-Feingold threatens to limit the voter registration and GOTV activities of state and local committees."[8] The reason why a lawyer can make a case for state and local controls under federal law ("federalization") is that political party activities, traditionally, have involved "working for the ticket" at all levels, from local to federal. The mix is called "bundling."

Thus, the FEC General Counsel proposed regulations in the form of financial allocation rules and federal oversight that amount to a crude, perverse form of unbundling of political activities that belong together. Look at this from the standpoint of a party precinct worker (political volunteer). Rather than going making two sets of door-to-door visits, one time for non-federal candidates with one set of handouts and another time for federal candidates with another set of handouts, wouldn't you want to go once around for all your party's candidates (the entire "ticket")? If you were the Chair of an LPPC, like one of those surveyed for Chapter 5, would you want to keep time accounts for each canvasser, in order to report to the FEC how much time your Committee people spend working for candidates to federal office? After McCain-Feingold was handed over to FEC staffers to set the rules for the law's administration, the issue of federalization arose with a vengeance once party committees were faced with implementation and enforcement of the new regulations. It has also arisen in the context of pressure for other reforms, as we shall see further on.

Yet the *Christian Science Monitor* concluded, immediately after U.S. Senate passage of McCain-Feingold as amended:

> Perhaps the biggest benefit of this legislation: Citizens might feel they can return to civic participation in this new political space created by the lessening of money influence in Washington...the American people can...lose some cynicism, and more actively participate in national politics.[9]

This statement is exceptional. It's also quite a reach or stretch. There is little basis for it. One can only hope that it turns out to be more than an article of Christian Science faith.

CFR: Legislation

Lest McCain-Feingold be seen as the be-all and end-all of reform in legislative terms, let us note that the most energetic and extensive efforts at reform have been occurring at the state and local level. Sub-national units of government are "laboratories of innovation" in a federal system.[10] As already noted, the "Maine model" earned a good deal of attention during debates on one of the Wellstone amendments to McCain-Feingold. State efforts have come to focus primarily on the so-called "Clean Money" ballot initiatives which pretend to try to take big money out of politics by substituting one form of money for another—public money for private. Such initiatives have been passed, not only in Maine, but in Arizona, Massachusetts and Vermont. In the past, similar initiatives have been passed in New York City, New Jersey, Minnesota and a few other places without relying on the apocryphal "Clean Money" billing. The latter label is used as if it were a political counterpart of the "Good Housekeeping" seal of approval.

It helps to have an ironic sense of humor in this business, for ironies abound. Another is that the Clean Money ballot initiatives that have succeeded owe their success to political volunteers doing old-fashioned people-to-people, door-to-door, street-wise politics—canvassing, getting signatures, writing letters to editors and getting out the vote. It's interesting to observe that many of these volunteers arrive in buses from locations outside the state where the initiative would be voted on by in-state voters, but that's another issue which we can table for now. What's even more interesting is that the interest in political volunteerism seems to wane once initiatives are passed. Politics is still a money game; just that it's played with someone else's money.

Consider the highly touted "Maine model," for example. How do its admirers measure its reputed success? Let us count the ways. Quoting statistics on people's political participation—to see whether the "reform" may have led it to increase in terms of voluntary commitments of time—this is not among them. The primary indicators are otherwise—increases in numbers of candidates and seats contested. So let us sing hosannas for reform—the fact that we have increased political opportunities for the usual suspects—the already politically self-interested—to run for office and build their political careers at lower cost to themselves, their families and their friends because we, the taxpayers, are financing their campaigns with public money.

We probably should not sneer at the Maine performance benchmark in a state like Massachusetts where there are so few competitive races for state offices and the disease has been spreading to the local level. As one columnist noted: "In both 1998 and 2000, Massachusetts was tied for last among the 50 states in the percentage of contested primary races. Last. Virtually the entire Legislature and congressional delegation returned to office on a pass."[11]

This columnist also remarked on frequent references to "the will of the people" by proponents of the Massachusetts' Clean Election Law – "a well-intentioned if deeply flawed effort to reduce the decisive role money plays in state politics." Many would challenge use of the word "decisive" here but not the phrase "deeply flawed." One flaw is that the "Law" recognizes candidates but not parties as actors in electoral politics. It would provide no public funding to or through political parties even though the ballot question as worded would not preclude a law enacted by the Legislature from doing so.[12] "Clean Money" would go only to candidates, thus further diminishing the role of parties in the political process. Reliance upon initiative and referendum (I&R) as the primary tool of reform undermines the role of parties in the first instance, even before an initiative would take effect if passed. In Massachusetts, ex-Governor Cellucci is recognized as someone who successfully promoted the use of I&R but who whose leadership of the state GOP served to further undermine his already weakened Party.

Recall remarks in earlier chapters [with reference to Lipow (1994)] that point to the undemocratic nature of "plebiscitary" democracy via I&R—another irony that should earn a frown rather than a smirk. So, here is yet "another nail in the coffins of parties" brought about through well-intentioned efforts of those characterized as "reformers" by media writers who understand no more of the political process than the reformers do. Ironically, I&R advocates may provide a nail in their own coffin as the hilarious example of the 2003 California recall rebounds. The undemocratic paradox of direct democracy being bankrolled by a rich pol, yielding a crop of 135 candidates, a media circus and an election in which a governor could have taken office by winning as little as 10% of the vote, is almost too rich or too funny for words.

More generally, the debate over Clean Elections initiatives features those who favor "direct democracy" vs. those who respect the fact that our governments at all levels, constitutionally, are representative democracies. Another basic controversy implicit in the debate is that between "public" and run-of-the-mill journalism. Journalists like the one last quoted did nothing to probe the issue sufficiently to inform the public before they voted on it. When the voting is over, they hide behind the "popular will" as sufficient justification for ex-post rationalization of an initiative that some recognize as "deeply flawed."

Yet another irony seems to have escaped observers of reformers' efforts even though it is well known to public finance economists. This is that the introduction of significant amounts of public money into some segment of the political economy almost invariably has an inflationary effect. Goods and services purchased with public money tend to increase in price faster than the CPI. U.S. Senators participating in the CFR debate called attention to political inflationary factors in a situation where the only public money has been that committed to Presidential campaigns. Clean Money reformers, like others who have had to face the lessons of past reform history, can anticipate seeing their initiatives fulfill the "law of unintended consequences." By centering their reforms on money, they will increase the cost of campaigns and make them more, not less, dependent upon money over time.

The latter irony does not begin to speak to yet another. Reformers, most of whom are fundamentally apolitical, perhaps because they view politics and politicians as representing lower life forms than themselves, are putting "Clean" campaign financing increasingly at the mercy of politicians. At some point, once all the reformers' hype and media attention to it blows over, state legislatures will be increasingly reluctant to budget public money for private campaigns. This was the case in Massachusetts even at the beginning of Clean Money initiative implementation. The state legislature's reluctance to appropriate money led the Supreme Judicial Court to intervene. They ordered the auction of public property to raise money to implement the Clean Elections Act.[13] Enough was raised to enable Warren Tolman to undertake a multimillion dollar campaign for Governor whose reliance upon negative advertising helped to discredit the Act. Thus, when legislators hostile to the Act, headed by the Speaker of the House, put up a ballot question that asked whether voters wanted to use public money to finance political campaigns, the initiative passed. Thus, Clean Elections became a dead letter in Massachusetts. These initiatives haven't fared much better in other states. As indicated earlier, Maine reports some limited positive impacts, but a recent study may serve to further undermine the credibility of Clean Elections, even in Maine.

The field of public finance helps to provide some additional perspective on the issue of taxpayer subsidies for political campaigns. This is the so-called "dead weight" issue. Subsidies are a wasteful dead weight to the extent that they subsidize activity that would have been undertaken anyway. There's a lot of this in Clean Elections. Nearly all of incumbents would be running for re-election. They're subsidized, along with a significant portion of the politically interested who would run for office even if public funding weren't provided. Especially from an economist's standpoint, it's pretty amazing that this issue was not raised in the Clean Elections debate in Massachusetts. Already, in a state where the Legislature was challenged to appropriate $10 million to implement the Act, there were complaints from proponents that Clean Elections would be under-funded at a level of $22 million. Given the inflationary issue already noted, the amount of subsidy is likely to be a bone of contention year after year in state Legislatures faced with the challenge of implementing such initiatives. The state fiscal crisis provided the final death knell, providing a ready-made excuse for the state legislature to kill the Clean Elections Act in Massachusetts in 2003.

Given the high degree to which the overall elections' subsidy is "dead weight," an economist would have to conclude that Clean Elections is a pretty inefficient solution to the campaign financing problem. In a way, that's not surprising, since the costs and benefits of people's time hasn't been figured into any overall cost/benefit analysis (there hasn't been one). What's ironic here (again!) is that reformers tend to want efficiency in politics.[14] As if anyone with any political experience had any reason to believe that politics could be efficient. Or shall we count inefficiency as another feature of "the law of unintended consequences" that has plagued CFR initiatives all along?

Overall, the most important legislative common denominator between the federal-level McCain-Feingold and state-level Clean Money reform initiatives is clear: They both certify the dominance of money in politics and further diminish the importance of people. The latter irony is not funny at all. It is rather threatening to the future of our democratic republic.

Recall the remarks of Ben Franklin to those waiting to hear the results of the 1787 Constitutional Convention in Philadelphia. When asked what the Convention had accomplished, he responded: "A Republic, if you can keep it." The danger of losing it is further aggravated by the fact that so-called reforms at both levels will weaken parties that, as the national survey revealed in Chapter 5, are already weak at the grass roots—with respect to their local party committee foundations. Traditionally, these committees have relied heavily upon volunteers. It is also ironic that McCain-Feingold would ban "soft money" intended for "party building" and that could and should have been devoted to such activities by re-directing such money rather than banning it.

During the Senate debate on the Hagel amendment to S.27, Senators Hagel and McConnell pointed to the negative consequences of the bill for political parties—another common denominator of state and federal reform initiatives. Unfortunately, as indicated earlier, the negative consequences of state-level reforms for parties has not figured in debates over Clean Money initiatives even though they are potentially more adverse. Without strong parties, how is the great American majority of unorganized, unaffiliated, "independent" individuals to make a difference in the political process? The answer is: They won't. They will be effectively dis-empowered—"spectators" of the political game and consumers of pundits' political pablum, their role simply that of voters for the "usual suspects," not that of citizen producers or political players. Some years hence, when it becomes amply clear that the political class can't do it all for us, there will be hell to pay as the class minority faces an angry majority.

As this book initially went to press, the Bipartisan Campaign Reform Act (BCRA) had just passed Supreme Court review. A federal district court had ruled some of the Act's soft money and issue-advocacy advertising prohibitions unconstitutional. Then the Supreme Court, ruling on another case, found in a 7-2 decision that a North Carolina anti-abortion group should not be allowed to make direct contributions to candidates and campaigns from its general fund instead of its PAC. A decision in favor of the group would have resurrected soft money with a vengeance, since corporations and/or unions could make unlimited contributions to such general funds. Thus, one editor was led to comment that this "ruling is an encouraging indicator that the court may not be too hostile to the….Act. This proved to be prescient, as the Supreme Court upheld most provisions of the BCRA in time for it to govern financing and expenditures for the 2004 campaigns. Whether this decision, however, will serve to resurrect people's political participation is another matter, one on which one is hard put to be optimistic.

It's easy to criticize and forecast dire consequences due to various reform initiatives. But can one come up with a better way? We can, one that recognizes the value of peoples' contributions of time, and provides incentives for them to be involved as actors, not just observers and voters. Now that you've seen this bold claim, you'll have to wait or skip to Chapter 10 to see how it can be fulfilled. Remember, short-term-itis, our hankering for instant gratification, is part of our problem!, so don't be tooo impatient. Read on!

Other Reform Initiatives Stemming from 2000

Florida & the Count

In addition to and advance of final passage of McCain-Feingold, the last hurrah of the 2000 wavelet of reform was the reaction to the Florida recounts. The hue and cry over the extended count led to a flurry of electoral reform proposals, some of which are still floating around the halls of Congress and various state legislatures. These focused on changes in voting machines and procedures, rosters of registrants, ballot designs and election board workers. It would be very easy to get tangled among the trees of various proposals and quite lose sight of the forest of reform. It is remarkable, in fact, how this "electoral" category of reforms was disconnected from any larger reform agenda, including even the money-only agenda of McCain-Feingold. Is this another example of the right hand of government not knowing what the left hand is doing, or of legislators being unable to balance or connect two thoughts in their minds at the same time?

"Ironically, the state of Florida, where the bomb went off, is one of the first states to rebuild," remarked Kay Albowicz, Communications Director for the National Association of Secretaries of State.[15] Early in May, 2001, the Florida legislature approved and the Governor, Jeb Bush, signed, a bill to overhaul the state's election system by:

- requiring manual recounts of ballots in close elections.
- banning punch-card ballot machines.
- streamlining absentee balloting.

- lengthening from 4 days to 11 the amount of time allowed to certify general election results.

- appropriating $24 million to help finance the acquisition of new voting equipment—by providing $3500-7500 per precinct to pay for optical scanners. Counties that want to use touch-screen technology could opt for this if they could afford it.

- providing $6 million for better education and training of poll workers and voters.

- setting uniform guidelines for manual ballot recounts.

The only link to CFR was a provision that would eliminate state matching funds for out-of-state campaign contributions. This is a feature that should be picked up by other states. It's the state analogue to federal law designed to cut the influence of "foreign" money. Out-of-state money could talk with a louder "voice" than the views of down-home voters. This provision was "denounced by the Democrats," who were looking to out-of-state contributors to help unseat Gov. Jeb Bush in 2002. As for the "education and training" feature, this promises to circumvent the traditional role of political parties in this regard. To the extent that it does so, it would serve to further weaken parties.

Florida put money on the table to fund its reforms. The failure of other states to do likewise truncated reform efforts or put their implementation on hold. Such was the case in Georgia even though Georgia's effort was ahead of Florida's both technologically and in time. Gov. Roy Barnes signed legislation in April, 2001, to place touch-screen voting systems in all precincts, but Georgia was "waiting for the money."[16] So were election officials in many other states, even though more than 130 bills related to election reform had been signed into law and more than 1,000 were pending in 35 states as of summer, 2001.

Another remarkable feature of these reform debates is how the political role of the great American majority was, once again, excised or diminished in the reform picture. Most attention focused on "technology" as the source of solutions. So manufacturers of high tech voting machines had a chance to peddle their wares, and advocates of electronic voting via the Internet could tout "digital democracy." We've already encountered the latter in the last chapter. It's so typically American to look at technology for a fix. Reform was very narrowly construed even though the claims of "disenfranchisement," etc. could have been heard to raise broader issues.[17]

So what people were talked about?—election board workers, among the pillars of local democracy—those who work long hours at low pay on election day. They are among your neighbors. They check you in, check you out and help you out, if you need help, at the polls on election day. They include many grandmas, some disabled and some un-or underemployed locals who could use the beer and pretzel money ($25-75 per day in Massachusetts) supplied by city or town clerks.[18]

And how were they talked about?—as among the sources of electoral malfeasance or incompetence thought to have denied some people their vote, rather than as essential sources of help in the elections' process. Thus, among proposals for so-called "reform" are those that would remove the role of political parties in nominating board workers by selecting election helpers on an "independent" (non-partisan) basis, with training and oversight to be provided by state agencies rather than political parties or local government. One of the last little "perks" that parties can provide to local activists would be gone. Rather than recognizing the role of local political party committees and building on their ability to mobilize volunteers, reformers are trying to put more nails in the coffins of parties and to take another step towards federalization of elections.

The role of local government in elections is being scrutinized with a very critical eye by national observers who appear to have little or no political experience, for they have finally woken up to the fact that the conduct of elections is a localized responsibility. The *New York Times* editorialized: "For too long, local governments have been left to conduct elections with insufficient resources and guidance" (Feb.5, 2001). The *Times* was shocked, "shocked to learn that the margin of error could vary so widely across jurisdictions" (December 17, 2000). So some are now calling for national election standards, at least for Presidential balloting at the federal level, or at least to ensure uniformity within states. The *Economist* pronounced, for example:

> America needs a root-and-branch reform of its voting system…It needs a national system of voting…and it needs to embrace the wonders of modern technology. [December 9, 2000]

In keeping with the above thinking, Democrats on the U.S. Senate Rules Committee deliberating on what the Congress should do in the wake of Florida 2000 were pushing for federal mandates "that the states take certain actions."[19]

If some people are losing their votes at local polling places, is the state or national elections system to blame? Hardly. Where were the voters of Palm Beach County when the fabled "butterfly ballot" design was up for review? Who among them was present at a County or City Council meeting or election forum to ask questions when a candidate for City or Country Clerk was up for the job? Here, as in other areas of concern, local voters' lack of attention is the root problem. What's the most appropriate solution in a decentralized system?—not federalization of elections or even greater state control, but local initiative. As Chris Matthews, host of "Hardball" put it on C-Span: "People must put the pressure on locally" [*Washington Journal,* with Brian Lamb, on Friday, the 13th of April, 2001]. Of what value is a "Voters Bill of Rights" if there is no voters' responsibility?[20]

The latter issue was nicely highlighted in a letter to the editor of *USA Today* in response to the Florida reform package described earlier:

"…in all of this, no mention is made of the voter's responsibility to vote correctly… there are several safeguards to be sure that the process is carried out correctly.

- First, be familiar with the ballot. It's usually sent out 1 to 2 weeks prior to voting and is published in the local newspaper. If you don't understand your ballot, consult a friend, relative, attorney or your (local) supervisor of elections.(or town or city clerk, et.al.)

- Second, be sure you have the required proper identification with you at your voting precinct…

- Third, know your precinct and polling place to avoid going to the wrong place…

- Last, and by far not least, do your homework with regard to the candidates…"[21]

To the latter, one might add "with regard to" ballot questions. I am especially sensitive with regard to these, not only because such questions reflect the closest thing that we have to direct democracy, but because my own failure to vote on several of them during the 2001 Town of Merrimac election provides a good example of how easy it is to fail to exercise a voter's responsibility. What did I fail to do?—to simply turn the ballot over after voting for candidates. Boy, was I pissed when I realized that I had not voted on the questions after casting my ballot! There were four. They were all important. Most were controversial, including funding for the school budget, a new library and the Town's share to enable participation in the state's new "Community Preservation Act." All had been discussed in a prior Town Meeting which I had attended. I prayed that the vote tallies on these wouldn't be as close as the election in Florida, so that my failure would spell results one way or the other. Luckily, this was not the case.[22]

Who did I blame for my "undervote"—the Secretary of State? The Town Clerk? The Election Board workers? The Supervisor of Elections? None of the above. Like those who railed against the "butterfly ballot" in Florida, I suppose I could have complained that the ballot was poorly designed. After all, the "Instructions to Voter" box at the top of the ballot did not advise the voter to look for "Ballot Questions" on the other side. But there was a reminder to 'turn ballot over and continue voting' at the bottom of the ballot. Should I blame the Town Clerk for the fact that this was tucked without super highlighting just below "Sewer Commissioner," an office for which there was no contest? I blame only myself. I wanted to vote on the questions, and there had been a sample ballot posted inside the polling place with both sides showing, just before the table where voters check in with the election board workers and registrars.

This personal aside reinforces the point made by the letter writer to *USA Today* It's rather curious, in fact, that politicians running about and speaking out to show that they were doing something about the problems in Florida

were loathe to ask what proportion of the problems might be due to individuals' mistakes or shortfalls in voter's responsibility—those things that we are
capable of doing ourselves if we simply pay attention and follow the basic
steps noted in the letter to the editor.[23] These days, with people and media
being the way they are, one sometimes has to sound outrageous to make a
point. So, here it is from George Carlin:

> I think that if you are too stupid to know how a ballot works, I don't
> want you deciding who should be running the most powerful
> nation in the world for the next four years.[24]

Thanks for the slap, George; I needed that! (and did you, too?) Isn't it
ironic that we're trying to export American electoral democracy to Iraq while
voting turnouts continue to be embarrassingly low at home? How many voters
would react to more aggressive GOTV efforts as in the following cartoon?

Signe Wilkinson, Pennsylvania,
The Philadelphia Daily News.

It's important to note that the problems uncovered in Florida were not
new; they were simply thrown suddenly into high relief, given the lack of
attention previously paid to them and the closeness of the Presidential vote.
Various improvements that might have avoided the Florida debacle had been
on the table for over many years. According to Sharon Priest, Arkansas
Secretary of State and Chairwoman of the National Association of Secretary
of State's Task Force on Election Standards:

> we've got resolutions from meetings going back twenty
> years…There is nothing, at least to people in the elections busi-
> ness, new or earthshaking…Part of it is the simple task of following
> the laws that are already on the books…and part of it is looking

at what the best practices are…There is no need to reinvent the wheel.[25]

A former prosecutor in northern Florida, David McGee, said "voting fraud was also a "great tradition" in the state, although malfeasance is most likely in races for local offices…"[26]

There are best practices as well as bad examples to be seen at the local level as well as across states. They range all the way from Princeton, NJ (among the best) to St.Louis, MO (among the worse). Local variations are due primarily to local factors, including citizens' political participation. Those of us who vote get to know their local election board workers. They are often sweet little old men and ladies who have lived in the area since Hector was a pup, who may have been recommended by local party leaders and who need a few extra bucks in their pockets. The City, Town or County Clerk need not be a stranger, either, and if you don't like him or her, you can show up and speak out at the annual public hearing where the Clerk's performance is up for review. You can also show up at the Clerk's office when there is a drawing for ballot positions, to check whether there are any "sticky fingers" at work. You yourself can volunteer to be a Board Worker or poll checker. You can check on the local ballot design. You can gather at City or Town Hall to observe the counting of ballots, cheer the winners and console the losers, some of whom are likely to be friends or neighbors. Etc.

Thus, even though the U.S. Civil Rights Commission Report on Y2K voting in Florida disagrees, the roots of election reform also lie in local action.[27] If state or federal authorities can provide incentives or matching grants to local authorities to help the less-than-best finance local improvements, including improved equipment and higher pay for election board workers, so much the better.

After all the hue and cry generated by Florida had died down, the elections reform issue, like McCain-Feingold, also came down to a matter of money. Good intentions and high rhetoric ran into low budgets as state finances hit the wall of the recent recession, growing deficits and Republican federalism. Hundreds of bills were introduced into state legislatures all over the country. Then they waited upon federal assistance to buy new voting technologies, etc., and they waited, and waited…. As of this writing, only two states had passed major election reform initiatives—Florida and Georgia. To avoid a repeat of the Florida 2000 controversy, the Florida legislature enacted clear standards for ballot recounts and provided funds for new voting machines. There were some good results to be seen during the 2002 elections.

Other Propositions for Election Reforms

Even while all this was going on, some election reform nostrums left over from past waves of concern were getting some attention, too. Term limits, for example. These had been passed in many states and cities during the 90's.

Now politicians and some voters were facing the consequences of their past I&R success.

The New York City Council, for example, woke up to the fact that a few dozen of them would be required to give up their well-paid, perk-laden positions. A motion to overturn voters' intent was narrowly defeated. Term limits there and in many other locations caused the music to start earlier in the political game of musical chairs. Many incumbents hustled to find other positions to run for so that they could continue in "public service" (not necessarily the same as service to the public). More recently, San Antonio voters were scheduled to vote on May 15, 2004, "to decide if the nation's strictest term limits should be relaxed..." An elected official who views himself as a "living example" of term limits was Gov. Mark Johnson of New Mexico. He viewed his public service stint as a great opportunity, something he "always wanted to do," but not as a career. He had a successful career as an entrepreneur before entering politics and perhaps looks forward to a successful second (or 3rd) career outside of politics.

Long-standing but relatively dormant recommendations for other election reforms resurfaced in light of alleged civil rights violations in the Florida voting and of Reform and/or Green Party candidates not being allowed to participate in Presidential or Congressional debates during the 2000 election season. These other reforms include:

- Proportional representation
- Instant runoff voting
- Changes in redistricting and/or the sizes of legislative bodies
- Abolition or reformation of the Electoral College
- Voting "outside the box"—via mail, on-demand absentee voting, or in-person early voting.
- Cumulative voting

The first five have been getting some serious attention. Let's focus on them. Remember Lani Guinier, Clinton's erstwhile appointment to the Justice Department, withdrawn because of her supposedly extreme-liberal views on affirmative action and voting rights? Well, she has been one of the leading proponents of proportional representation(hereinafter referred to as "PR"). This is an election system much used in Europe and many other countries worldwide whereby the number of seats in a legislative body are allocated in proportion to the votes gotten by various parties who qualify to participate in an election. It is very different from our "winner take all" system. As things now stand, the Reform Party would have to win a majority of voters in each of 44 Congressional Districts in order to hold at least 10% of seats in our House of Representatives (10% of 435, rounded off, is 44). Under a PR system, the Reform Party would get 10% of seats if it earned 10% of votes nationwide.

328   Peter Bearse

Advocates of PR claim, with some credibility, that such an elections arrangement would overcome obvious shortcomings of "winner-take-all;" specifically:

- Low voter turnouts: Turnouts in countries with PR are much higher than in the U.S.

- Inadequate representation of minority groups, interests or parties: As indicated above, these can be represented and have some influence even without winning majorities.

- Gerrymandering = the manipulation of legislative district lines by state legislatures to create districts with boundaries tortured to suit powerful incumbents or minority groups. PR makes this "far more difficult."[28]

Two of the primary objections to PR focus upon:

1. Loss of representation based on geography: "With PR, voters find an ideological "home" rather than a geographic one."[29]

2. Possibly insufficient transparency, accountability and/or governability due to shifting inter-party coalitions and a weaker connection between public opinion and public policy, among other factors.

PR is not a new idea. It's left over from the Progressive Era of about a century ago. Several cities adopted and later repealed it. The approach is still used by only one, Cambridge, Massachusetts to this day.[30] As a result of both domestic and foreign experience, a great deal has been learned of how to adapt PR to various goals and circumstances. It is adaptable. It could be mixed and merged with our current system, for example. The advantages of PR relative to its disadvantages are sufficiently strong to justify its adoption by some states, which could then be viewed as "laboratories" for testing the approach on a broader scale. It's a big country, with lots of room for creative variations in election systems to better align them with regional, state and/or ideological preferences. There's not a Constitutional issue here. Changes in state and federal law would suffice.

A bill was introduced in the House to enable states to adopt PR. During the 108th Congress, this was referred to as HR 1189, the Voters' Choice Act.[31] It would have repealed a 1967 statute mandating single-member districts. The billing given this initiative by the Center for Constitutional Rights, however, seems quite exaggerated:

> The goal of the Voters' Bill of Rights is to correct the flaws in the administration and machinery of elections and to press for far-reaching reforms aimed at creating a more participatory democracy in our country.[32]

Adoption of PR by some states would help to loosen up the system as it currently stands, reduce the sense of disenfranchisement felt by many voters and encourage the formation and growth of new parties.

Another reason for giving serious consideration to PR is that it would or could dovetail nicely with two of the other election reforms mentioned earlier—"instant runoff voting" (IRV) and changes in the sizes of legislative districts. Look at the latter first. The number of Congressional Districts has remained unchanged as the country's population has grown, so that the ratio of U.S. Representatives to population (now about 1:500,000) is much, much larger than the founders ever envisaged. Thus, a strong case can be made for increasing the number of Districts and/or increasing the number of representatives per existing District. The latter would jibe with PR, which requires multiple rather than single-member district representation.

PR also goes hand-in-glove with IRV, via which voters rank their choices. If one fails to get a clear majority, then the candidate with the fewest first-place votes is eliminated, and ballots cast for that candidate are transferred to the second choices on voters' ballots. This process of transferring votes "simulates a series of runoff elections… until one of the candidates has a majority."[33] Thus, IRV can serve two purposes:

1. "save money for taxpayers and campaign cash for candidates by combining two elections into one;"[34] i.e., by eliminating another leftover from the Progressive Era—primary elections, which have become increasingly wasteful and dysfunctional as primaries attract very low turnouts that are dominated by highly motivated political factions rather than by voters representative of the public at-large.[35]

2. Elect the top two or three candidates from a longer list.

Surprisingly, IRV appeared to receive no mention in media coverage of election reforms that were reactive or responsive to the Florida controversy. This is surprising because, otherwise, IRV seems to have been the topic of increasing coverage in the news. This is evident from "Electoral System Reform in the News," a tracking service of the Center for Voting and Democracy accessible through the Center's website. Over the period Nov., 2000 to June, 2001, two-thirds of 118 "in the News" citations provided some focus on IRV.

The journalistic interest in IRV has been reflected in a number of legislative initiatives. Of four bills dealing with various aspects of electoral reform introduced into the 107th Congress, one would study IRV as well as PR and other pro-democracy reforms.[36] At the state level, 9 of 12 states where electoral reform legislation has been introduced report initiatives that would provide for IRV use for various elections. A bill introduced in Massachusetts would have that state study the feasibility of introducing IRV.[37] A former Member of Congress, Mickey Edwards, formerly at the Kennedy School of Government and Harvard and now at Priceton, has been advocating IRV adoption as a way to make elections "more democratic" (as in the op-ed piece cited in footnote 35). A more recent newspaper article announced that Roseville, Minnesota, "may put instant runoff voting to the test in an April

20 (2004) special election...in an experiment that could change the way Minnesota elections are won... The Minnesota Senate approved the Roseville experiment..."[38]

As for the Electoral College, it's interesting to note that some of those advocating its reform rather than its abolition are, in effect, advocating a form of PR for the College whereby the number of electors designated to vote for each Presidential candidate would be proportional to the popular vote received by each candidate by state and, thereby, overall, so that the vote in the College would reflect the popular vote. As suggested earlier, the danger here is that some advocates, contrary to the very nature of our Constitution, would rather see the U.S.A. be a unitary state than a federal Republic. Thus, they would federalize elections, preferring to perfect our elections system from the top rather than have to deal with a messy, error-prone patchwork of arrangements from the bottom. Rather than this unconstitutional approach, several states have introduced, and some have passed, legislation that aligns the number of the states' electors more closely with their popular votes for President. This is the way to go.

With respect to "voting outside the booth," the jury is still out as to whether changes in election laws to enable this are a step forwards or in the wrong direction. Opinions differ. Many view changes that in any way make voting easier or more convenient to be desirable changes.[39] The National Commission on Federal Election Reform, however, endorsed the proposition that:

> voting at the polls serves basic and historically rooted objectives," adding that "The gathering of citizens to vote is a fundamental act of community and citizenship...Though this (voting outside the booth) trend is justified as promoting voter turnout, the evidence for this effect is thin...voter turnout may even decline, as the civic significance of Election Day loses its meaning.[40]

In a letter to the editor commenting on the article in which the above quote appeared, Mr. Jim Triggs of Edina, Minnesota wrote: "voting is not meant to be convenient. It's a responsibility that we should all cherish." Another letter writer, William C. Brown, of Urbana, Illinois, chimed in to admonish: "'The Dangers of Voting Outside the Booth'...does not go far enough. Not only should citizens vote in person, but those votes should be counted by people."[41]

Postscript to the 2000 Election

So much for voting. Notwithstanding "the count," was there any sign of people's participation in the 2000 election after the presidential primaries? Yes, there was, followed by more in 2002 and more yet again as this book goes to press during the 2004 Presidential primaries. While not enough to mark a remarkable change in American politics, there are clues from the past 3-4 national elections to suggest that political parties and campaign managers can win by bringing people back into the political game.

The last several days of campaign 2000 were characterized by "Ringing Phones, Chiming Doorbells, Stuffed E-mailboxes: The Great Voter Roundup." But "last minute exhortations were...just the warm-up for Tuesday's main event: a military-style mobilization of hundreds of thousands of campaign workers...to drive people to the polls, hand out literature outside polling stations...knocking on doors and making phone calls..."[42] This is a latter day sidelight of politics as it used to be. Does it show signs of what could become a significant upward trend, or just a transient blip on the radar screen of the potential renewal of an new/old politics. Are we seeing a temporary renascence or a more durable renaissance?[43]

The pre-election day report from which the above quotes are taken noted that the Republican Party expected to field 100,000 volunteers; the Democratic Party, surprisingly, only 50,000. The AFL-CIO, however, expected to put "100,000 campaign workers on the streets," while the UAW hoped to swell these ranks with 800,000 "members who, for the first time, have been given Election Day off as a paid vacation day." Meanwhile, the National Abortion and Reproductive Rights Action League was pulling to call another 800,000 and the Sierra Club, 75,000. Can these impressive numbers be registered as representing a resurgence of grassroots political participation, when most seemed to be involved because they already had a political ax to grind?

Also: "For all that effort, political analysts still predict(ed) that Tuesday's (November __, 2000) election will continue the historic slide in voter turnout, which dipped below 50 percent in 1996."[44] Yet, here, and later in 2002, the pundits were wrong. "There was a modest turnout increase in both...caused by something that had almost been seen as extinct—grassroots mobilizing and get-out-the-vote activity in key states."[45] Earlier, we noticed earlier that similar activity had made a difference in key congressional districts in the '98 mid-term elections. In 2002, "The largest turnout increases were largely concentrated in states with high-profile close contests and where the candidates, parties and interest groups put...greater resources than in recent elections into grassroots get-out-the-vote efforts. If there is any doubt that such efforts "made a difference," look at the close races where the swing votes served to change the power equation in the Congress; again, contrary to the prognostications of most so-called political "analysts." Also contrary to the usual political expectations (or stereotypes): "The Republicans clearly out-organized the Democrats."[46] So, are we seeing signs of a "conservative populism?"[47] Whatever. If "ordinary" people can have such an impact as little tails wagging on the big money dogs of national election campaigns, imagine what they can do as citizens taking responsibility for their own politics! Put the recent experience in context and then extrapolate. As the CfSAE observed in its release cited earlier:

while the budgets for such (grassroots) activity in both (2000 and 2002) elections did not come close to rivaling the moneys poured into political advertising, any commitment to personal (political) contact activity is a welcome change.

Indeed, and recent election results provide some hope and point the way, that such activity may increase.

Indeed, some observers have seen the formation of "trends" towards an increasing reliance upon the "grassroots" by political parties, major non-party organizations and some political consultants. "Grassroots lobbying" was even referred to as an "industry" in *Campaigns & Elections*, the magazine of the political pro's, in early 1999.[48] The success of targeted people-to-people GOTV efforts in past congressional elections, noted earlier, has led to increased attention upon such efforts in planning for the 2004 elections. Rep. Buck McKeon (R, CA) is "leading the GOP program called STOMP…(Strategic Taskforce for Organizing and Mobilizing People)…and "Grassroots (are) replacing soft cash in campaigns."[49] Does all this mean that we are seeing the beginning of a renaissance of people politics or a conservative populism to supplant '60's-brand politics? The language seems promising. In August, 2003, the GOP released an "Ask America National Policy Survey and announced: "The Republican Party is conducting this nationwide grassroots project as a critical part of our efforts to strengthen our Party by getting more Americans involved." Unfortunately, there is nothing else in the announcement, the survey or other GOP materials to indicate that the party knows how to walk the talk. The GOP has either forgotten what the Reagan legacy means or not yet found a strategy to translate the legacy into action. Ironically, the legacy was perhaps best stated by a progressive Democrat, Will Marshall when he wrote: "a more fundamental task beckons: returning power and responsibility to local institutions and individuals…In their haste to shrink government, the Republicans have missed this essential aim of devolution" (and I would add, as earlier, *decentralization*).[50]

As for the other major party, they apparently see Al Gore, Howard Dean and Moveon.com as representing "populism." For all parties, money rather than people is still the key resource of political campaigns. The "pro's" are in charge. What the grassroots "industry" represents is using the Internet to get people "bombarding House and Senate offices" with e-mails on interest-group issues. "STOMP…calls on lawmakers (rather than local political committee leaders) to recruit volunteers for battleground races."[51] Both major parties' web pages are trying to recruit volunteers for congressional races that are now treated as national campaigns as the parties vie for control of the Congress. Tip O'Neill must be rolling over in his grave.

What the major parties call "grassroots" recruitment efforts, unfortunately, make no reference to local political party committees or to other than the select "national" battles. Thus, if emergent "trends" are any indication, the major parties' local infrastructure will continue to atrophy while the "obvious suspects"—the already politically interested—will continue to be recruited as shock troops to help win the GOTV end-games of congressional campaigns in races that are important to the national party committees. Indeed, "political operatives (a.k.a. "pro's") are discovering that direct voter contact is often more effective than media advertising."[52] What side of the political hay wagon did the "operatives" have to fall off of in order to make this momentous discovery"?—the T.V. media side. It finally hit them that negative and saturation TV ads for political campaigns have hit diminishing returns and that decreasing proportions of people in TV "markets" are paying attention.

So, while the new attention to the grassroots is welcome, it does not yet represent by a long shot the rise of a more people-based politics nor a systematic effort, if any, by political parties to recruit the politically turned-off or to revitalize grassroots politics via their own local committees. National party leaders take note: Your congressional and national power may be built on a bed of sand. Will you be inspired or impelled by the Supreme Court decision on campaign finance to truly return to your party's local organizational roots? Will you agressively seek to recruit a new, broader and more diverse party membership,working with and through local leaders to build the party at the grassroots? Or will you just dip into the same old well by continuing to call upon the already committed, and see the use of money at the local level as a way to continue to support the campaigning, lobbying and political consultants' industry?

Goodbye to Bill Clinton

Clinton's departure from the White House: Was it a climax to the "Politics of Narcissism?," or a prelude of more to come? What legacy has been left to us by a man who often seemed preoccupied with the question of what his "legacy" would be?

Clinton served to bring democratic politics to a new low. This is a point now from which, hopefully, it has nowhere to go but up. Let us hope that he was the last great star of a political star system promoted by Hollywood, the media and the high proportion of people who look to charismatic leaders and political careerists for solutions to our political problems. "Bubba" advanced the politics of spectator sports, of personality, of political careerism, of "pseudo events" and of money and media—all the features of politics that have turned it into a pol's game rather than a citizens' exercise. Notwithstanding his talent as an eloquent public speaker, he lowered the tone and depreciated the coin of our public life.

Unfortunately for a man of great ability who modeled himself after JFK, the main postcript centers on his sex life, "or, as he would have it, 'nonsex' " activity.

> To the insecure male, power without access to and dominance over women is not worth having…A significant portion of a generation

of aspiring Democratic politicians patterned themselves after John F. Kennedy. This emulation…sometimes included the pattern of "scoring" with as many women as possible…It may be that he (Clinton) was willing to risk his power for this because being in such a position relative to women has been the subconscious objective of his quest for power all along.[53]

When the quest for power comes to focus on empowerment of self over (an)other, then the ideal of democracy as expressed by Lincoln has been lost, by definition as well as in actuality. This is why Clinton's legacy represents an abridgement of the American dream found in Rockwell's painting(s) as well as in Lincoln's language. It's ironic that such a big-D Democrat turned out to be such a small-d politician and that a man who was so inspiring a leader in words should be so lacking true political leadership in terms of action. The upside, as others have remarked, is that Clinton's final term may have marked the end of the "imperial Presidency."[54]

Prognosis, Postlude, New Beginnings and Reform Redux

Where will the so-called reforms of the Year 2000 take us?—Toward "1984" as pictured by Orson Welles, or towards "2001" as envisaged by Stanley Kubrick?—our lives directed by a controlling authority, whether computerized like the movie's "Hal" or not, everything OK as long as we stay asleep and don't question the system? Or, in the words of Abraham Lincoln, towards a "new birth of freedom…so that the government of the people, by the people and for the people shall not perish from the earth."

We have seen that the year which, in terms of reform, began with a bang, ended in a whimper. Oh yes, some modest steps in the direction of political reform were taken, such as commitments to invest in better voting equipment, procedures and standards for re-counting ballots in closely contested federal elections, some chastening of the media's aggressive election day exit polling and coverage techniques, and passage of some campaign finance reform initiatives. But the real wind behind the sails of reform—the wind of enthusiastic volunteers doing more than blowing hot air—this wind died down when competition ended for the major parties' Presidential nominations. It seems as if BoY enthusiasm has been replaced by EoY pessimism.[55] As Bette Midler lamented near the end of "The Rose:" "Where's everybody going? Where's everybody gone to?"[56] Yet, it sometimes helps to remember the inspiring words of Margaret Mead, the late, great anthropologist: "Never doubt that a small group of thoughtful, committed citizens can change the world; Indeed, it's the only thing that ever has."[57]

Strong people and great ideas go together. Unfortunately, it's not just strong people ("thoughtful, committed citizens") that are missing from the political reform picture as a result of 2000 and its prior political history. Great ideas are missing, too. The prevailing reform agenda is little more than a rehash of the Progressive's program of over 100 years ago.[58] We have seen, and other's have documented in detail how, in 60's parlance, this old agenda has long since been a major part of the reform problem rather than part of the solution.[59] Perhaps the 2003 California recall provided the final piece of evidence. So where is a reform agenda that can excite peoples' participation as that we saw in New Hampshire during the late winter and early spring of 2000? Let's see whether we can imagine a new agenda in our final chapter. Let's try to gather some sheaves and lumber to at least begin to build it out.

Notes

1. Reference here is to the handshake of President Clinton with then Speaker of the House Newt Gingrich, when they reportedly agreed to cooperate in pursuit of campaign finance reform.

2. Via private e-mail communication of 2/7/04.

3. Heinlein (1992), op.cit.

4. Quoted by Marlantes, Liz (2003), "Outsider Dean fires up left," *The Christian Science Monitor* (June 23), adding that "If Dean's online network grows (via another Internet service, meetup.com), it could form a grass-roots army of volunteers to knock on doors and hand out leaflets" (p.4).

5. Thus, Dick Gephardt complained of "vote-rigging on behalf of former Vermont Gov. Howard Dean" in the Moveon primary, as reported by another Internet political news letter, "The Weekly Politiker" of 6/20/2003, produced by politicsonline.com. Some other candidates also complained, although they had some opportunity to try to mobilize their supporters for the Internet primary via e-mails:

6. Franke-Ruta, Garance (2003), "Zero Sum: Why Moveon will be the real winner of its own presidential primary," *The American Prospect*, Internet edition (June 25, p.3).

7. One amendment that was adopted called for TV networks to provide time for political advertising at their lowest rates to federal candidates who abide by the rules of McCain-Feingold. Senators felt that their advertising should not have to compete with commercial advertisers for time and space—as if they were not already being marketed in ways scarcely distinguishable from the marketing of commercial products!

8. Private e-mail communication to the author during August, 2000.

9. Editorial, "The Senate Shows the Way" (Monday, April 2, 2001).

10. The quoted phrase is borrowed from David Osborne (1990), *Laboratories of Democracy*, whose book revealed how states, led by "a new breed of governor," were leading the way towards solutions of many public problems, continuing to demonstate the virtues of a federal system.

11. Walker, Adrian (2001), "The Will of the People?," *Boston Globe* (March 1, 2001).

12. As suggested by the example of another state, Minnesota, whose enactment of state campaign finance reforms including public financing precedes the recent wave of "Clean Elections" initiatives. Tony Sutton, Executive Director of the Minnesota Republican Party, reported: "not only candidates but parties take public money in Minnesota. A press release from the Campaign Finance and Public Disclosure Board revealed: For the 1999 tax year...$72,630 was distributed to the state parties..." E-mail to the "Politalk" e-forum on campaign finance reform (3/2/2001). Yet, even here, the parties' role is quite minimal. $72,630 is only 6.6% of the total public finance disbursements under the Minnesota elections statute in 1999.

13. This became quite comical at times, as when Clean Elections advocates urged that some of the Speaker's office furniture be sold.

14. This is a sharp insight of Wilhelm (1985) arising from his discussion of CFR and time.

15. As quoted by Dana Canedy in "Florida Leaders Sign Agreement for Overhaul of Election System," *The New York Times* (May 5, 2001).

16. Seelye, Katharine Q. (2001), "Little Change Forecast for Election Process," *The New York Times* (April 26).

17. U.S. Civil Rights Commission Report (2001)

18. This does not deny the need for careful selection and some training of election board workers, which political parties and/or local election authorities should be providing. Abigail Thernstrom, member of the U.S. Civil Rights Commission investigating the 2000 Florida voting disputes, stated on C-Span that "we heard a lot of bad poll worker stories." (*Washington Journal,* June 28, 2001).

19. As reported by Katherine Seelye in "Senators Hear Bitter Words on Florida Vote," *New York Times* (June 28, 2001).

20. Reference is to a 10-point set of proposals put forth by " coalition called the Pro-Democracy Campaign" over the Internet and discussed at a "Pro-Democracy Conference" in Philadelphia on July 6-8, 2001. See Seelye, Katherine (2001), "Liberals Discuss Electoral Overhaul," *New York Times* (January 21).

21. Letter from Jim Wright, Clearwater, Fla., in the *USA Today* issue of Friday, June 15, 2001.

22. "Luckily," indeed. The closeness of many of the tallies underlines how every vote counts. One local office was decided by only four votes! Two of the four questions were decided by 25-30 votes.

23. Voter "spoilage" rates in the disputed Florida counties, computed by the U.S. Civil Rights Commission, summed counts of "under"—and "over-votes"

in their numerators. "Undervotes" were those where there was no vote for President, not unusual in a race where significant numbers of people didn't care for either candidate. "Overvotes" were ones where more than one candidate was punched, which could well be the result of voter error in significant numbers of cases.

24. "According to George Carlin," June 18, 2001, as received via second-hand e-mail.

25. Quoted in Seelye, Katharine Q. (2001), "Panel Suggests Election Changes That Let States Keep Control," *New York Times* (February 5). "Let"? Aren't we a federal Republic under the Constitution?

26. Silverman, Gary (2000), "How vote ended up in a very odd state," *Financial Times* (November 9).

27. During a debate on the Report on *C-Span's Washington Journal* of June 28, 2001, Christopher Edley, Member of the Commission, stated: "I hope that the Report will galvanize action in the Congress and at the state level as well," with no mention of action at the local level even though the Commission's analysis of elections' data relied upon county and precinct-level data. And even though Abigail Thernstrom, a dissenting member of the Commission stated flatly that "there is no evidence of racial disenfranchisement in the data," we should remember that local discrimination against blacks' voting in the South was a prime impetus behind the civil rights movement and the Voting Rights Act of 1974.

28. On this and other points, see "The Case for Proportional Representation," by Robert Richie and Steven Hill. *Boston Review* (February/March, 1998). Online at www.polisci.MIT.edu/*BostonReview*. Richie and Hill are Executive Director and West Coast Director, respectively, of the Center for Voting and Democracy, a good resource on election reforms, online at www.igc.org/cvd.

29. Richie and Hill, op.cit., p.14.

30. Cambridge still fancies itself as "progressive." The City Council recently voted to lower the voting age to 17, "the first city to do so." Associated Press (March 26, 2002).

31. Unfortunately for the bill's credibility, it was introduced by Rep. Cynthia McKinney (D,GA,4th CD), who was discredited as a Congresswoman and defeated in her quest for reelection in 2002.

32. Statement included in the Center's announcement of a "Pro-Democracy Convention" in Philadelphia, June 29-July 1, 2001, found online at www.pro-democracy.com.

33. Richie and Hill, op.cit., p.6.

34. Richie and Hill, op.cit., p.9.

35. There are very many examples of this; e.g., the NJ gubernatorial primary of June 26, 2001, won by conservative Jersey City Mayor Bret Shundler on

the basis of a light turnout. Another: Congressman Stephen Lynch's "election to Congress was essentially determined in the Democratic Party primary, a contest in which 61% of 9th District (MA) voters indicated they wanted someone else to represent them" (Mickey Edwards, "Making Mass. elections more democratic," *Boston Globe*, March 30, 2002). See also "Few vote in Primaries…" *Christian Science Monitor* (March 21, 2002).

36. This is the DeFazio-Leach Study Bill, HR 57, sponsored by Rep. Peter DeFazio (D, OR) and Rep. Jim Leach (R, IA), first introduced on Nov. 15, 2000, and re-introduced on Jan. 3, 2001.

37. As reported in "Pending Legislative and Ballot Measures" by the Center for Voting and Democracy as of April 5, 2001. The National Conference of State Legislators also keeps track of state legislation on electoral reform. Electoral reform commissions have been active in several states, so those interested in this area of reform will need to follow up to find the aftermath of a wide variety of efforts. See www.ncsl.org.

38. Smith, Mary Lynn, "Roseville wants to try instant runoff election," *Minneapolis Star Tribune* (February 22, 2004).

39. See Leslie Wayne's article, "Popularity is Increasing for Balloting Outside the Box." *New York Times* (November 4, 2000).

40. Quoted by Norman Ornstein in "The Dangers of Voting Outside the Booth." *New York Times* (August 3, 2001).

41. *New York Times* (August 4, 2001).

42. *New York Times* (November 7, 2000).

43. Most people don't know that there was a 12th century "renascence"—a brief revival from the "dark ages"—that preceded the Renaissance that began in the 14th century. Will it take 200 years for us to recover from our political dark ages?

44. Dao, James (2000), "Ringing Phones, Chiming Doorbells, Stuffed E-mailboxes: The Great Voter Roundup," op.cit.

45. Committee for the Study of the American Electorate (2002), "Turnout Modestly Higher; Democrats in Deep Doo-Doo; Many Questions Emerge." News Release. Washington, D.C. (November 8).

46. Committee for the Study of the American Electorate (2002), op.cit.

47. If so, the signs may amount to a weak signal or a stillborn revival. According to Ken Weinstein, Director of the conservative Hudson Institute's Washington office, the Institute's "Project for Conservative Reform" has folded. The Committee for the Study of American Electorate (CfSAE) goes on to say that "the underlying fact remains that the electorate is…largely disengaged from politics and that…(the) percentage (disengaged) is growing."

48. "Trends in Grassroots Lobbying: Consultant Q&A," *Campaigns & Elections* (February, 1999).

49. The latter phrase is title of an August 10, 2002 report by Alexander Bolton in *The Hill*, one of the two leading newspapers for congressmen, their staffs, lobbyists and political pro's in D.C.

50. Marshall, Will (1995), "The New Citizenship: Redefining the Relationship Between Government and the Governed," *The New Democrat* (Vol.7, No.2, March/April).

51. Ibid., quotes, respectively, from the above citations.

52. Quote from the article by Bolton cited above.

53. McElvaine, Robert S. (2001), *Eve's Seed: Biology, the Sexes and the Course of History*.

54. This remains to be seen, as the centralization of power in Washington—under a Republican administration!—in response to 9/11 as well as our focus upon the Presidency, seems to suggest otherwise.

55. "BoY" and "EoY" are common abbreviations for "Beginning of Year" and "End of Year," respectively.

56. Midler, Bette and Alan Bates (1979), *The Rose*: Original Soundtrack Recording, A Mark Rydell Film. New York, N.Y.: Atlantic Recording Corporation.

57. I had the privilege of working with Margaret Mead along with a select set of others on a special project of the American Association for the Advancement of Science during the summer of our bicentennial year.

58. There is even some talk of "a new progressive era." For example, see Peter Levine's article of the latter title in the *Kettering Review* (Spring, 2001).

59. For more on this point, see Syder, Claire (1999), "Shutting the Public Out of Politics: Civic Republicanism, Professional Politics and the Eclipse of Civil Society," An occasional paper of the Kettering Foundation. Dayton, OH: The Kettering Foundation.

10.

Prescriptions—Rebuilding the American Political Community from the Ground Up

I. **Time Over Money: How People can get Involved and Make a Difference, Politically**
   A. Introduction: Time, Life and Politics
   B. Politics as a Good Cause and the Cause of Good Politics
   C. Politics as Service and the Service of Politics
   D. Politics and Technology
   E. Small Beginnings and Little Packages: Ways to Get Involved—A 'Taster's Choice' Overview.
      • Introduction: The Politics of Everyday Life
      • Local Government: Politics, like charity, begins at home
      • Local Committees of Political Parties: The traditional "vineyards" of politics
      • Political Clubs, Civic Associations and Other Groups
      • Political Campaigns: Helping your favorite candidate(s)
      • Referenda: Lots of room for initiative(s)
      • Issue Advocacy: The Politics of Good Causes
      • Bridges to Community Through Politics and to Politics Through Community: Politics in, around and through Community-Based Organizations (CBO's)
      • Use of the Internet and World-Wide Web: The digital multiplier

II. **Changes Needed to Encourage and Support People's Grass Roots' Political Participation**
      • Campaign Finance Reform: The battle continues
      • Political Parties: Not over yet
      • Decentralization and Devolution: Getting down
      • Education and Training for Citizenship: Civic empowerment for the long pull
      • Family Support Systems: "getting by with a little help from your friends" and family (and government?)

- Leadership: Sine qua non but not limited to the usual suspects.
- Changes in the Responsibilities of Elected Officials: For us, not them.
- Changes in Laws Governing Not-for-Profit Organizations: Enabling strategic alliances
- Changes in Laws Governing Electoral Politics: Making every person count
- Promotion of Political Volunteerism: "We, the people…"
- More Emphasis on "How" than on "What": Means over ends
- Media Reforms: Putting the public in (private) media
- Digital Democracy: Single digits? Surfing alone?
- Experimentation: Learning by Doing
- Introduction and Adaptation of Business Innovations in the
- Larger, Broader or Higher-level Changes Needed to Encourage and Support People's Grass Roots' Political Participation.

III. Conclusion: Revitalization, Reformation and Reintegration of the American Political Community

Executive Summary:

This book concludes with a raft of recommendations that would serve to bring about greater political equality, restore the great American majority as the owners of their political system, and reduce the influence of the currently dominant political class. In keeping with the book's emphasis on time, this summary is a shopping list with a time signature at three levels: (1) those things that we, as families and individual citizens, can readily do right now through our own choices with little investments of time and no outlays of money; (2) modest steps that take longer to effect because they involve working with others; and (3) changes in law or public policy that make take years to accomplish but that are worth working for because they'll make the system better for us all. So, in summary, here they are;

- Democratize any presumably non-political organizations of which you are a member; insist that they follow democratic procedures.
- Get involved with your local government; e.g, volunteer to join a local board, committee or commission; attend local City Council or Town Meeting(s).
- Join a local political party committee.
- Volunteer to help a political campaign.
- Join or form a local political club, book or discussion group or civic association.
- Get involved in an initiative and referendum campaign to get a public issue question on the ballot.

- Support campaign finance reforms that place a higher value on people's time than on contributors' money.

- Change the laws governing political parties so that they are treated like other private membership organizations.

- Help to democratize any political party of which you are a member; especially, push to have them provide more support for local committees and to operate more from the bottom up than the top down.

- Advocate more and better civics education for all ages but especially for the young in schools.

- Provide more encouragement and support for political participation: (1) within families; and (2) across families by providing more support of many kinds for lower income working families.

- Ask each and every candidate for political office at election time what they would do to empower you rather than themselves.

- Support changes in the laws governing not-for-profit charitable organizations of all types to allow them to participate more in the political process without endangering their tax exempt status.

- Support additional changes in election laws at the state and local levels to enable instant runoff voting, repeal of "Motor Voter" and other initiatives discussed in this chapter.

- Advocate promotion of political volunteerism by any of the several organizations that are promoting volunteerism for "good causes."

- Ask for elected representatives to pay more attention to the "how" of politics (improving the process) and less to the "what" (particular "hot button" issues).

- Insist that candidates and elected officials speak to the issue of reforming the media and push for reforms such as those noted in chapter 8, including a public Internet to promote "digital democracy."

- Support state and local experimentation with, and testing of, new public policy ideas before they are enacted nationwide.

- Improve politics and government by adapting in/to the public sector the best practices and innovations of the private sector.

- Realize of the implications of our international leadership role: We can't preach to others if we don't honor our own values.

- Push for both federal and state governments to decentralize – to transfer more power, money and responsibility from Washington and state capitals to local government.

- Provide a tax incentive for people's contributions of time as political volunteers.

- Create or enable more "space" for the self-organizing advancement of poor people.[1]

- Convene a national Constitutional convention.
- Establish a national initiative and referendum electronic voting system.

I. Time over Money: How People can get Involved and Make a Difference, Politically

A. Introduction: Time, Life, and Politics

This book has been based on two premises: that time is the genuine currency of politics as well as life in general, and that political participation is an important responsibility of the adult life of citizens in a democratic society. That is, if citizenship were realized as a responsibility rather than a right, time rather than money should become, once again, the main currency of politics and politics would become an essential aspect of adult life—like "a branch of ordinary human behavior," as Alan Ehrenhalt wrote in the August, 1998 issue of *Governing*.

As Henry Luce showed us decades ago, time is life and life is time, the signature of our mortality. Economists love the word "allocate." They focus on how people allocate, divide up, and schedule money and time. Advertisers are interested in our spending habits, so they focus on how people "spend" time as well as money. People, however, are more discriminating than most economists or advertisers give them credit for, so they often "invest" or "devote" their precious time in/to activities that generate a more lasting impact—a broader influence beyond the self, yielding satisfactions beyond a moment's pleasure. For some, political activities are among these. They can and should be so for many more who want to count for something or somebody as citizens of the oldest constitutional democracy in the world.

Since time is also the currency of our mortality, it is proper to use the adjective "precious" to mark it. In economists' terms, time is valuable as a scarce resource. We are all on limited budgets. We have a "preoccupation with time, both the scarcity of it for ordinary purposes and the common perception that events are somehow speeding up out of control."[2] As an Internet advisory on the value of time put it: "To realize the value of (even) one millisecond, ask the person who has won a silver medal in the Olympics." Even valued at minimum wage, the small increments of time that people could invest in political activity would add to a sum greater than the billion dollars or so that was spent on all federal races during the last (2000) Presidential election period.[3]

B. Politics as a Good Cause and the Cause of Good Politics

Most everybody likes to be of some service to others, even if it's just a small set of others comprised of an immediate, more intimate circle of family and close friends. How we can extend the circumference and area of our circles of service, however, is a question not easily answered. Time seems to have become our enemy. We barely can find time to spend with family and friends, let alone a wider circle for the sake of community or public life. A family cannot survive without its members working at least two full-time equivalent jobs. Then there's shopping, cleaning, personal care, kids, sports, schools or schooling, TV, etc.—seemingly so much more to do than 20 years ago! It's the proverbial "rat race" once again, with a vengeance. So you want to talk politics, even at somebody's door, after work, or around the family dinner table? Are you kidding? Who has the time?

Nevertheless, studies by the Kettering Foundation indicate that, in substantial and increasing numbers, people do find time for public service in the form of community service activities with and for a wider circle of others with shared concerns, in spite of the maddening time pressures that we all face. They do so on behalf of a variety of causes and concerns such as child-care, schools, AIDS, crime and the elderly. It is surprising and disturbing, however, how infrequently and ineffectively these activities connect, if at all, with the world of politics except indirectly and in very limited ways, as when some "non-political" event draws a large enough crowd to attract attendance by political candidates or elected officials. More studies are needed to explore how people concerned with good causes connect or fail to connect with politics.[4] Except for those reflecting on the "Christian Right," reports and articles that document the variety and extent of people's involvement with "good causes" scarcely acknowledge any interface or dovetail with political activities, let alone any active participation in such activities.[5]

Why? Why are people willing to devote valuable time to good causes and community pursuits (and some not so good; e.g., the KKK and neo-Nazis) while ignoring political activities at the same level of community? Chapter 8 suggested that the media are partly to blame. The question cannot be answered confidently without appropriate studies, yet it may helpful to pursue some additional answers. "Suggested" are just that, "suggestive," but they may at least influence the designs of studies that could provide answers once social scientists realize that there is something here that requires their attention.

One answer may lie in the legacy of "the 60s" and recognition of the fact that most of those now volunteering to serve "good causes" are the "baby boomer" generation whose identities were formed during the '60s.[6] Now that a generation has passed, there is some effective distance between us and that period. We can begin to see what was important and unimportant with the advantage that only some perspective at a distance can provide, free of the emotions that roiled the period. There has already been a great deal of writing and comment on the political legacy of the period.

What was the hallmark of the political activity that shaped the political consciousness of an entire generation raised on Dr. Spock?—"movement" politics—demonstrating or making common cause with like-minded others. This came to be viewed as either the primary or only legitimate way to make an "authentic" political statement, as conventional politics failed to provide adequate responses to Vietnam, the women's movement or the environmental movement. Of the impact of the '60s period on political parties, Shea (1999) writes:

> Failed presidencies, international frustrations, domestic turmoil, and the disruptive effects of civil rights protest, anti-Vietnam war demonstrations, and counterculture revolution pushed voters…away from the party system. Their children, today's newest voters, were socialized to be non-partisans (p.41).

Note that the non-partisan orientation is aggravated or abetted by the fact that many localities in many states have non-partisan election systems. This is unfortunate in light of studies that show that non-partisan systems decrease political participation, dampen voter turnout and weaken political parties. Unfortunately, partisanship is associated with polarization. Yet, as Mike Lynch indicated in his comments on an early draft of Chapter 3, we may need to seek the roots of political polarization within ourselves. He wrote:

> If politics is the mechanism by which a society resolves conflict, our society fails the test because it no longer teaches that (1) the majority rules, and (2) not everyone can win *all* the time. The lack of willingness to concede has led to increased polarization…[7]

Mike went on to view people's interest in "good causes" as little more than a reflection of their "self interest," but this is too limited a view bordering on cynicism, even though one could make such a case.

The willingness or desire to spend precious time on good causes is partly the non-political consequence, offshoot of or substitute for, a movement politics that made unsustained and failed attempts to change conventional politics. Perhaps the former arose out of contempt or aversion for the latter. Politically, the orientation to good causes is also a major impetus behind the "issue advocacy" politics that has demonstrated its growing power through the influence of the Christian Coalition and others.[8] As we saw in Chapter 2, however, Richard Sennett traced the roots of the decline of politics much deeper and farther back—to 19th century origins of what Christopher Lasch labeled "The Age of Narcissism." "Authentic" expressions of "feelings" replaced public debate on public issues of concern.[9] A yearning for political authenticity and truthfulness was quite apparent during the year 2000 election season, as the previous chapter indicated. The long-term factors help to explain why the decline in political participation is not peculiar to the United States even though the politics of personality, as exhibited in *People* magazine and *George*, for instance, has been more pervasive here. In fact, the search for personal authenticity and the desire to distinguish what is "real" from what is "spun," seems to be taking on new emphasis.

Unfortunately, as shown in previous chapters, better "politics as a good cause" has been taken over by "reformers" or "goo-goo's" cast in the mold of those called "progressives" a century ago. They will serve to largely destroy

American politics as a way of empowering "ordinary" people if the trends they established and the behaviors they inherited continue.

C. Politics as Service and the Service of Politics

As discussed in prior chapters, the time factor has become increasingly important with the rise of productivity and advanced telecommunications— to the point that some new labels have been coined—"The Network Economy" and "The Attention Economy." The latter, especially, highlights time as the ultimate scarce factor. For decades, the expectation has been that technology, by introducing labor-saving devices and raising productivity, would lead to a "leisure society." This has turned out to be a myth, empty dream or fond hope.

Rather, the opposite has occurred. Look at how TV has become a sink for time; indeed, so much a form of addiction that some people are now saying "Just say no; turn it off." See how the new PC computer technology, cell phones and Internet access are increasing time pressures, as people race to keep up with the rapid pace of technological change, "surf the web" and network with increasing numbers of others. The designation "Attention Economy" refers to the fact that politicians, advertisers and others wanting to get our attention find it harder and harder to do so. There are so many things demanding our attention; it seems that only increasingly extreme language, events or broadcasts do so. "So much to do; so little time in which to do it," as the saying goes. One might also add, however, "What else is new?" As popular sayings going back at least to Ben Franklin's time indicate, our culture has exhibited a near obsession with time for many generations.

Time is the #1 input to a service. For most personal services, it has ever been so. If you want to cut my hair, you need to spend time to take some care in the doing. Just putting a bowl on my head and running around it with an electric shaver won't do. Time jointly devoted is key to service quality. If I am a professor, lecturing is a service but my "productivity" may be zero if the class is asleep. On the other hand, the productivity of the teacher/student relationship may multiply if there is sufficient "quality time" spent in collegial interaction so that new insights are mutually generated. This joint, interactive and multiplicative quality is also key to successful provision of the best and most sophisticated services to business, those that are also called "producer" rather than "personal" services.[10] This quality characterizes political activity at its best, too.

So with respect to the service aspect of life; that is, one's ability to serve or be of service to, others, time is of the essence, and it is the quality of time that matters most—time devoted or invested rather than time expended or consumed. Lack of such time spells lack of sufficient care, or care-less-ness. Extra devotion to such time, by contrast, spells leadership, actual or potential, especially, the quality of leadership called "servant leadership" by Parker Palmer.[11] This is an important concept that has spread from religion to business. It is an exceptional form of leadership that needs to be introduced into politics. Note the adjective "servant" has the same root as "service."

Lack of quality time devoted to service or in the provision of services of all types is a problem of our time. The "Service Economy" appears to be a myth to those who, increasingly, find *lack* of service in stores, doctor's offices, other service establishments and, yes, from government, too. The Services Economy is paradoxical in this overall respect—a services economy that is *not*—in the area of personal services as well as some other respects. For example, elected officials increasingly emphasize their ability to provide direct "constituent" services but then fall short in their ability to provide their most important public service—better government policies via good legislation.[12] Sears, Home Depot and other outlets sell the popular idea of "do it yourself," but there are few personnel in the store to help you select the tools you need to do so.

The industrial era featured "de-skilling" of manual labor. Workers who grew up with pride of craftsmanship found themselves on assembly lines that honored the craft tradition not at all. One now has to ask whether something similar isn't affecting our new "high tech" services economy. Even while "do it yourself" is encouraged for ordinary services, some of those services that can most serve to enrich our lives are, in effect, being taken from us. Our abilities to provide them ourselves are diminished, depreciated or denied. These include singing, acting, child care, education, self-analysis, health care, environmental management and many others including, yes, the exercise of citizenship and politics. The development of the services economy has been part and parcel of the professionalization of everything.[13] As a result, our abilities to care for ourselves, our families and our communities have been quite systematically "de-skilled." In politics as in other areas of life, we have come to think that we can and should 'leave it to the experts.' Fortunately, there are some initiatives, such as those mounted by the Kettering Foundation and the Walt Whitman Center, that would help us help ourselves by building our skills in the civic and political arenas, but the accessibility, coverage and political impact of such initiatives is far too limited.[14]

D. Politics and Technology

The introduction of technology into services has aggravated these long-term trends. Provision by device is more efficient than the person with a personal touch taking time. Pretty soon we may be relying on robots—automaton-aticity. Raising the roof on a new or hurricane-damaged home is more cost-effectively performed by a well-equipped contractor than by a group of amateur, well-intended neighbors.[15] In political campaigns, campaign "technology" in the form of TV, computers and telecommunications largely supplants people working together and reaching out to others.

The myth of technology is that it empowers people—enabling more freedom by providing more time for more discretionary "leisure" activities, including involvement in community activities and volunteer services to others. The latest technology, personal computers and telecommunications of rapidly increasing speed and capacity, also reinforces the old adage "knowledge is power" by enabling nearly instant access to information and networks. The reality, however, is that advanced technologies mostly dis-empower us by subtracting people from the equations that yield services to others and depreciating our abilities to be producers of services, especially those that involve working with others. By contrast, even though most of us would not want to maintain Luddite "taboos on technology," the Amish non-reliance on technology "produces an unparalleled bootstrapping ingenuity."[16]

The implications of the replacement of people by technology are many. Most troubling, the trend is regressive. "Regressive" here means adverse to the least advantaged, not the opposite of "progressive." It is well known that the problems of people that are economically poor or otherwise disadvantaged relative to others are compounded by social disorganization and lack of access to key resources, including the Internet. The main disadvantage that prevents the poor from achieving political equality, however, is the lack of time that affects us all but afflicts the poor with a vengeance. What time is left for political participation by a person who has to work two or three jobs to survive?

The so-called "service society" is another disadvantage. The jobs it creates are predominantly poor jobs that maintain poverty (i.e., they create poor people)—jobs for people serving the rest of us at less than a living wage, where the technology is that of the mop, trays, cleaning rags, Windex and stoop labor, where the most advanced "labor saving" device is a vacuum cleaner invented 80 years ago.[17] There is no common denominator here to bring the poor together with others. The only one, in the long run, may be advanced technology. According to Bill Joy, we may all be in trouble as puny humans become an endangered species in the face of competition from advanced robots.[18] In the long run, however, as we were reminded by a great economist during the Depression years, we are all dead.

E. Small Beginnings and Little Packages: A "Taster's Choice" Overview—Ways to Get Involved

Introduction: The Politics of Everyday Life

Earlier, we saw how politics infects and affects every aspect of our lives in whatever setting we may find ourselves—families, business, church, unions, colleges and universities and other organizations. There is family politics, academic politics, politics on the job or among business(es), etc. Then there is "politics" politics. How is the latter different from any other brand?—mainly in that the stakes are higher. It's not just, or shouldn't only be, an ego game. The various forms of politics can intermingle, inform and learn from each other. Even though politics per se is an object of disdain, the fact of the matter is that many organizations in our democratic society are distinctly undemocratic. They are ruled by petty dictators, oligarchies, elites and quite undemocratic procedures. We have all seen examples, in the form of bossy "bosses" on the job, egocentric academics, bureaucrats playing position games, organizational "turf battles," et. al.[19]

Thus, three general conclusions and advisories follow:

• *First*, understanding "the politics of everyday life"—that politics is part of life and vica-versa—helps to reduce the destructive distance between people (you) and politics, so that politics can be improved and an improved politics can contribute to the betterment of the lives of yourself and your children as well as the lives of others in your community.[20]

• *Second*, everyone has a "special interest," whether they know it or not. Beware of those who talk as if they have the "public interest" more in their minds or hearts than you do.

• *Third*, we all need to look at the presumably "non-political" organizations with which we are all involved to some extent with a fresh, political set of eyes—to see whether and how they depart from basic, desirable norms of democratic governance and procedure. Even if we cannot do much to change "the system" soon or overall, we can influence the politics of our families, communities, workplaces, unions, clubs, fraternal societies, churches and other organizations that influence or express the quality of our lives. We can start by modifying the way we talk to others. Basic care, courtesy and civility are the foundation of improved civic discourse. We can also work to democratize the structure and governance of those organizations with which we are already involved.[21]

Local Government: Politics, like charity, begins at home

Local governments provide many, many opportunities for people to get involved with public issues; i.e., basically political concerns. There are numerous local boards, commissions and committees; formal, ad hoc or informal in virtually any municipality, that are either in formation or looking to fill vacancies. Meanwhile, increasingly, local elected officials are faced with empty chairs in meeting halls and council chambers. It is important for people to simply show up and pay some attention to what's going on locally. Start by attending city or town council meetings in your municipality.

We are not talking "mickey mouse" activities here. Mainly at issue is public participation in, on or before the variety of boards and commissions that have real power to make decisions that effect changes or the quality of life in their communities. These include, for example:

• Citizen advisory boards or committees on various issues established by local governing bodies;
• Local planning and zoning boards;
• Environmental, Health, Historical, recreational and other commissions bearing on quality of life issues;
• School Boards and educational committees; and
• Financial, budget and other committees.

Many people have a low view of local government—as if it focuses on petty politics and small issues like potholes and dog licenses. "Small" issues are often important because some people are very concerned about them, usually for good reason, even if they don't interest you. It hardly ever fails to be the case, however, that meetings of local councils, boards and commissions feature some significant issue(s) of real substance and import affecting entire neighborhoods or whole communities. When a local council in a historical seaport talks about the new "harbor plan" and whether or how to maintain a "working waterfront," that is a matter of substantial import. When a local planning board debates a shift to large lot ("snob") zoning, that is a matter that may affect the nature and make up of the entire community for decades to come. A very long list of examples of the matters of substance that concern local government could be prepared. If the trends towards "decentralization" or "devolution" discussed in Chapters 1 and 9 and highlighted below continue or are strengthened, the list will become longer. Thus, both needs and opportunities for citizens' involvement will multiply.

Local Committees of Political Parties: The traditional "vineyards" of politics

The easiest, most readily accessible way to get involved in politics at any time, whether or not there is a political campaign going on, is to join a local committee of a political party.[22] The second easiest way is to show up at the campaign headquarters of someone who is running for public office. The third easiest way, especially if there is not a local party committee already in existence, is to form one or to get friends and neighbors together in a political club, civic association, salon, conversation circle or discussion group.[23]

The first two ways are suggested by the fact that most political committees, party or campaign, lack people power, as we saw in Chapter 5. They are crying for volunteers and good managers of volunteers. Most local party committees are not able to fill the number of membership slots allotted to them by law; that is, the number of their active members is many less than the number allowed. Among existing memberships, moreover, one is likely to find a lot of "dead wood" in many committees—old, dyed-in-the-wool members who are no longer active, just taking up space, occupying a number of the membership slots. Thus, there is some "space" for new members in most local party committees. Nearly all such committees, moreover, are seeking new members but having trouble recruiting them.[24] Just watch out for some of the "old guard." They may be "carrying water" for some benefactors among the "powers that be."

Local political party committees have legally authorized, ongoing institutional roles and responsibilities for activities that represent the basic tasks of grass roots democracy, including voter registration and education, dissemination of political "literature," GOTV activities, political issues and more (recall Chapter 5). They also provide channels of upward mobility in politics that are open to those who become active and assume some responsibility. These include party committee memberships at higher levels—county, state and national, nominations to candidacies or positions that open up, and responsible roles in political campaigns. If someone shows up at a meeting and takes an active interest, there is a significant chance that that person can move up rapidly to become a committee officer. Alternatively, if that person were to recruit friends and neighbors to fill other committee openings, he or she could effectively transform or take over the committee.[25]

Similarly, most political campaigns will welcome volunteers and put them to work. This is especially true at the local level, where candidates run with little money. As indicated in Chapters 5 and 9, however, the growing power of money in politics, even at the local level in big cities, means that the value of people's contributions of time has been discounted or depreciated rather than appreciated. Also, campaign managers are more likely to be hired based upon their fund raising and advertising experience than on the basis of their ability to manage a volunteer network.

Volunteers are turned off by campaign managers who:

• Treat them with scarcely veiled disdain;
• Make no real effort to match talents to tasks; i.e., often have them doing busywork without any indication that the busywork has value (as in the old days of licking stamps and sealing envelopes);
• Can't provide adequate tools or materials for them to use;
• Don't make any effort to find things for them to do that make good use of their talents and availability.

So volunteers should be discriminating, not only as to the candidates they would help but also with respect to their campaign managers, else their time may be wasted and they may be turned off. Similarly, candidates need to take care in their selection of campaign managers, so that their managers are sensitive to the problems of managing volunteers. Even though they partly serve as vehicles for the politically ambitious to start up the political ladder, LPPC's need to be able to balance volunteer management and campaign pressures. Committee chairs can do this as candidates' campaign managers usually cannot, especially if they get some training in volunteer management.

Even if a local party committee does not exist, laws enabling and empowering such an organization surely do in every state, for both major and other parties. For example, note how the Reform Party organized in 19 states during 2000 and the Green Party in most states for the 2002 elections. Local party organizations are enabled by state law(s) and national party guidelines. Some state party committees provide draft bylaws and assistance to facilitate the establishment of local party committees. Some state committee members are in fact required to step in to organize or reorganize a local committee in places where the local committee has fallen into limbo or disrepair.

Some changes in party rules may be needed at both the state and national levels so that higher level party organizations would do more to help build the capacity and effectiveness of local party committees, as we saw in Chapter 5. "Soft money" donations and matching grants from state committees to locals would help, too.

Political Clubs, Civic Associations and Other Groups

The third "easiest" way to get involved—form a political committee, club, association or discussion group—is less easy than the first two but well worth the effort(s) involved because the impact can be far more significant than arm's length or indirect forms of participation like writing letters or checks.[26] Given the antipathy of many to partisan politics, some of those who want to rekindle the fires of local democracy may not want to become active in a local party committee or partisan campaign but may be willing to form a political club or civic association. There are some communities, e.g., Cambridge, MA, where the local civic association is more active and influential than party committees. There are others; e.g., Hamilton, NJ, where a local political club is much larger (partly because of the legal limits on the size of party committees) and at least as influential as its local party committee counterpart. The two types of local organization can and should be collaborators, cooperators and complements rather than competitors. Associations can be incorporated under 501(c) legal forms that allow grants funding to be accepted even though certain political activities are undertaken. See the section on "Bridges to Community" to follow.

Political Campaigns: Helping Your Favorite Candidate(s)

We have already noted that local political campaigns provide one of the easiest ways for people to get involved. Many candidates are hungry for volunteers. Most do not have a campaign headquarters (HQ). Among those that do, one can drive by and often not see anyone manning the HQ or "minding the store." This is especially the case for state and local races. If there is someone in the HQ, walk in and you'll probably be welcomed like a prodigal son or daughter and put to work. You may meet others and make new friends.[27] You'll have a chance to get to know the candidate(s) better. There is always something to be done in a campaign by volunteers. You can "make a difference," especially in state and local campaigns that are less likely (even now) to be dominated by the incestuous mix of money, media and political consultants.

Yet, as some officials in government and not-for-profit organizations have discovered, management of a volunteer network presents a great challenge. Both candidates and campaign managers can do much better than they have been doing to effect people's productive involvement in political committees or campaigns, as we saw in Chapter 4. Non-profit organizations have long since recognized that volunteer management is serious business that requires training. Why not political parties? Political "pro's" claim that volunteers are not dependable, and then use this as another excuse for not calling upon potential volunteers.[28] This sets up another vicious cycle in the political arena: People not volunteering because they are not called and not being called upon because they are not volunteering. But "dependability" depends, at least partly, upon management. So, here's another vicious cycle: Parties and candidates are less likely to take volunteer management seriously if there are few volunteers to manage, and volunteers are less likely to show up if their time is not put to good use; i.e., not well managed.

Referenda: Lots of room for initiative(s)

Ballot initiatives have often relied upon volunteers and brought some into electoral politics.[29] Some referenda; e.g., "Public Campaign" or "Clean Money" initiatives, have aimed at political system reforms that proponents have claimed would restore politics to people by reducing the influence of large private money contributions. As we observed in the previous chapter, there is (thusfar) little evidence that such initiatives have served to increase people's political participation once referenda campaigns have ended. Participation in some of these seems to have involved more people "bussed" in from the outside than people living in the area where the campaigns are being conducted. Nevertheless, referenda of all types can energize and involve people in a political process who may have been reluctant to participate in other ways.[30]

We have noted both advantages and disadvantages to referenda that need to be considered from the standpoint of political parties and the need to make our political system more democratic. Referenda serve as a safety valve. They are often initiatives of last resort reflecting, to some extent, failure of political parties and/or elected officials to adequately deal with issues that a significant proportion of the electorate believes to be important. As we saw earlier in Chapter 3, with reference to Lipow (1996), referenda are likely to be distinctly undemocratic, or just another symptom of a democratic system in decline, if they are initiated from the top down rather than the bottom up. Those who are serious about political reform in the U.S. might find a unifying common denominator in a national referendum campaign that calls upon states and the Congress to convene a Second Constitutional Convention.[31]

There are other, less sweeping, bases for "bottom up" initiative and referendum (I&R) initiatives at all levels. An I&R web page on the Internet would facilitate nationwide interactions among grass roots activists that could serve to define broad areas of consensus, well-defined priorities and appropriately worded propositions among referendum topics. A well-worded ballot initiative with a broad base of support can energize others and shake up the "powers that be." Referendum organizers, however, must also take care to prepare for follow-up, especially if a ballot initiative succeeds. Many referenda that have been won at the ballot box have lost in legislative chambers because legislators do not pass requisite legislation or authorize expenditure of appropriate monies needed to implement the initiative. This is the problem that "Clean Elections" advocates faced in Massachusetts, as noted earlier, in spite of the fact that their ballot initiative was approved by two-thirds of voters.

Issue Advocacy: The Politics of Good Causes

"Issue advocacy" overlaps "referenda" with respect to concentration on issues or causes that arouse strong feelings among many. From the standpoint of this book, however, we have been concerned with whether and how such foci advance or diminish the goals of increased participation in electoral politics and a more democratic political system. How can people translate their concern over certain issues into a political voice that is more ongoing and broader in scope than the life and gauge of a specific cause or single issue?

Focus on the question!—Issue advocacy effectively enlists the enthusiastic involvement of many who share concerns for an "issue" or "cause." The evidence is all around us, exhibited by the Christian Coalition, gun owners, "pro life" and "pro choice" advocates, and many others. Survey responses reported by Verba (1995) show that attitudes on three issues—abortion, Vietnam and prayer in the schools—animated significant political involvement on these issues but did not necessarily lead to any broader, ongoing political involvement beyond them. An exemplary exception may be the 1999 statement of the National Conference of Catholic Bishops on "Faithful Citizenship: Civic Responsibility for a New Millenium."

"Issue advocacy" has itself become an issue in campaign finance reform because of the way it has entered into closely fought election campaigns for Congress. Pollsters and campaign managers identify a "hot button" issue. They then get an organization supposedly or nominally independent of their campaign committee to sponsor "issue advocacy" ads that say, in effect, "call" candidate and/or Congressman so and so because he doesn't support you (the voter) on this issue. The use of "call" rather than "vote against" exploits a loophole in campaign finance law and regulation that some Members of Congress and reform advocates sought to close in the Bipartisan Campaign Reform Act of 2002 (hereafter, abbreviated BCRA). Recall the previous chapter.

Here is another area where the growing weakness and changing nature of political parties, noted in Chapters 5 and 9, aggravate a problem rather than provide a possible solution. Instead of playing their traditional roles of bringing people together around various issues, parties today are themselves playing the single-issue advocacy game by using "soft money" to pay for campaign ads that play on "hot-button" issues. The answer lies in restoration of parties' traditional roles (as indicated in Chapter 5). Most people realize that they can either hang together or hang separately. It is time for this realization to be acknowledged politically, especially at the community level and by political parties.

Bridges to Community: Politics In and Around CBO's

Community based organizations (CBO's) of all types need to establish more effective links with electoral politics, and vice-versa—explicitly political organizations need to establish better links with CBO's. Parties and campaigns can benefit from relationships with CBO's (and vice versa). People can more effectively exercise their concerns for "community" via participation in electoral politics, and we can be more effective participants in politics to the extent we are involved in our communities.

The main basis for better links both ways is shared concerns over public issues. These can be at any level from neighborhood all the way up to the world. CBO's are often organized to address certain concerns, such as homelessness, AIDS, children's development or child abuse, taxes, community development or the environment. Political organizations oriented to electoral politics are overwhelmingly focused on electing people to office rather than issues but they inevitably get involved with issues during the political campaign season as parties and campaigns try to address issues. To the extent that party organizations at all levels pay more attention to issues during the "off season" as well as the campaign season (as they should), the opportunities and chances for fruitful linkages with "non-political" CBO's would increase, perhaps even multiply. Likewise, this would happen to the extent that CBO's encourage their members to participate in politics. Then political organizations would be more likely, in turn, to see CBO's and their members as resources; for example, as valuable sources of intelligence on issues as well as pools of potential political volunteers. And politics would appear to be more relevant to people's lives.

There are many ways that mutually fruitful linkages could and should be forged, especially at the local level, including joint CBO/LPPC—

- Forums—on issues and/or candidates,
- Community charitable fund-raising and other worthwhile projects, such as neighborhood or environmental clean-up, or building a playground.
- Testimony or other interventions before local and/or state boards or committees on shared concerns where the organizations can make common cause together;
- Writing or speaking through media outlets on shared issues of concern; and…
- Cross memberships or officers.

One example of the latter is provided by the Institute for Community Empowerment in Chicago. Mike Lynch, one of those interviewed for Chapter 4, serves on their board. Bob Smith, another interviewee, cited other examples. Two examples of worthwhile community projects from the political side were provided by campaign volunteers during one of my campaigns for local office: (1) Spring clean-up of brush and weeds around a senior citizens' housing complex; and (2) a day of helping at the City's recycling center.

VII. Changes Needed to Encourage and Support People's Grass Roots Political Involvements and Participation

Campaign Finance Reform: The battle continues

To the extent that campaign finance reform (CFR) efforts are able to recognize and address the basic problem of politics today—that the problem is one of time more than money—reform efforts may open up new and additional ways for people to get involved in electoral politics. To the extent that they continue to treat politics as if it is just a money game or someone else's game, it will continue to be so and ways for people to "get involved" will continue to diminish.

A campaign reform program that is designed to bring people back into the political picture as producers rather than consumers, or as active, contributing citizens rather than spectators, would include the following features:

- A rulemaking procedure through which the FEC would reformulate and strengthen regulations that would require soft money to be devoted to building up local party infrastructures and promoting political participation through local committees.[32] Ensure that "party building" strengthens parties as organizations of people rather than money laundries.

- Public financing for party building activities, on a public/private matching funds' basis, to and through political parties that qualify (say, those that receive 5% of the vote in a relevant election).[33] Public financing of individual campaigns, the current focus of state CFR initiatives, should not be allowed.

- Money expenditure limits for campaigns at every level based upon minimum requirements for any candidate to be able to "get the message out." No expenditure limits, however, should be in effect for additional expenditures based upon the utilization of political volunteers or paid personnel directly utilized by campaigns or local political party committees (LPPC's) to "get the message out." In other words, "expenditures" based upon commitments of people's time would enable unlimited amounts to be spent above campaign expenditure limits based upon money only.

    [*Note that a strong assumption is being made here:* that this proviso would pass constitutional muster; i.e., would overcome state and federal Supreme Court challenges to earlier attempts to limit campaign expenditures on First Amendment "free speech" grounds. The fact that overall "expenditures" are not limited suggests that legal challenges would not succeed. Unlimited expenditures to enable the real voices of real people to be heard via real person-to-person encounters rather than just media would move politics by people to center stage and "money as speech" backstage.]

- Private soft money contributions going directly or indirectly to LPPC's or political campaigns to spend above their limits—only to the extent that such additional monies are employed to utilize and equip volunteers recruited by campaigns and/or LPCC's and/or to contribute to other local, community-based organizations that would help to identify or supply volunteers.

- Private, political soft money contributions provided to local, community-based, non-profit organizations that, in return for the contributions, would supply volunteers to local political committees.[34]

- Legislation to enable 501(c) organizations to provide money, services or volunteers to the committees of political parties, or to purchase services from them, without their tax-exempt status being jeopardized.

- Soft money also prohibited from going to state political committees unless it is to be passed through such committees to their local counterparts, with only a small percentage retained by the higher level committees, if any, for administrative overhead expenses.

- A change in the tax laws to allow:
  —Tax deductions for contributions up to $200 to political parties or campaigns (with an inflation adjustment for the limit amount);
  —A monetary equivalent value of up to $400 of political volunteers' time to be deducted by those who contribute time (the "monetary equivalent" to be based upon the minimum wage and upon time records kept by local political committees and local not-for-profit organizations that supply or utilize the volunteers in question).

These recommendations are part of a comprehensive approach to CFR that was detailed in a memo to the Business Advisory Council of the Campaign Reform Project. Notice that they also address the matter of "links" between CBO's and organizations devoted to electoral politics.

Political Parties: Not over yet.

Have political parties become dinosaurs, or could they evolve into a new species helping to bring about a political renaissance or reformation? Though many Americans may think the former, they should hope for and work towards the latter. For it is the very rare individual that can hope to "make a difference" politically by him- or her-self. The political self needs a support system, channels and venues through which he or she can be politically effective. Active, well-organized political parties provide such a system, primarily for candidates during election seasons. Traditionally or theoretically, parties provide such a system for political volunteers at any time, especially through local party committees. As indicated in Chapters 4 and 5, however, their ability to do so is far less apparent now than in the past. Thus, a number of recommendations follow.

- Political parties should be effectively de-regulated or privatized so that they are treated like private membership organizations or as political parties are treated under law in Canada.

- Campaign finance reforms and/or Federal Election Commission (FEC) rulemaking need to require that state and local party committees' use of "soft money" contributions is redirected to support local committees' political volunteer activity.[35]

- State and national party committees should do far more than they are now doing to help local committees build their memberships and capacities. Their basic orientation should be far more "bottom up" than "top down," as the interview with Mike Lynch indicated in Chapter 4.

- Parties need to reform themselves so that they are more democratic; i.e., so that party decision making relies more on rank-and-file members and less on party "bosses."

- Any public funding of electoral political activities should be limited to parties, as indicted earlier. The next round of campaign finance reform, for example, should consider providing federal funds to match a portion of the state funds that some legislatures appropriate to help finance political campaigns—but *only* the part that goes to parties rather than the campaigns of individual candidates.

- For party nomination, parties should favor candidates for elected office who have been active members of local political party committees (LPPC's) and/or local office holders for at least two years and who have also been community activists for some time.

- Party primaries should be abolished or left entirely to the discretion of a party—they are a "reform" that has served to weaken parties and increase the cost of campaigning. The adoption of IRV as suggested in the previous chapter would undercut the supposed rationale for primaries.

- The "Motor Voter" Act should be repealed. Responsibility for voter registration should lie primarily with LPPC's, local government and individuals.

- Parties should take steps, and be encouraged by any public funding to take steps, to return to their traditional role of "interest aggregators"— via issues forums, deliberative roundtables and other means that directly involve a variety of citizens in discussions on issues and party platform deliberations.

Decentralization: Getting down

One reason so many people feel they don't have any significant say over the political decisions that affect their lives is because they don't—except for a negative nay-say via vote(s) to "throw the bums out." The obvious exceptions are races for open seats but the overwhelming majority of people also have little to do here, too. The selection of candidates that become choices in the general election typically involves tiny percentages of the electorate who are politically active, and only small minorities of voters typically vote in primary elections.

This implies why decentralization is so important, so that people come to see that they have positive, meaningful roles to play in the political process. Instead of decentralization, however—moving responsibility for decisions that affect people's lives down to the local level—we see much more of an appearance of this in the form of "devolution." Devolution means responsibility for the implementation of laws enacted at some higher level has been passed down to the local level from the higher level. Often, this appears as a burden rather than a blessing to local officials who are faced with devolution as "unfunded mandates." Local officials are accountable to higher level agencies of government for the performance of "devolved" programs; for example, "low-mod" housing programs administered by "HUD"—the U.S. Department of Housing and Urban Development. Devolution, therefore, is just another manifestation of the old industrial era ("2nd Wave") control model, which insists that central mandates is the only way to ensure that "lower"-level entities behave in ways that the "higher"-level people deem to be desirable.

This old model is based on fear that backward "local yokels" can come to dominate a local government and do all sorts of socially undesirable things. This fear is not unjustified, as many, many examples of local corruption, racial discrimination, "snob zoning," election law violations, et.al. can be cited to attest. Yet, the old mandates' model ignores the lessons of both other, more recent experience and of new insights from the social sciences. As Alan Ehrenhalt, editor of *Governing: The Magazine of States and Localities*, writes: "In the first decade of the new century, the federal government is no longer the instrument of first resort when it comes to dealing with the most complex social and economic problems."[36] Rather, decentralized entities at both the state and local levels have led the way as problem-solvers and innovators in the public policy arena.

Both systems thinking and improved understanding of how people actually behave also discredit the old model. Here again, the leader has been business rather than government, as we saw in Chapter 7. Instead of standards-setting via central command, better behavior can be induced by performance benchmarking, program evaluation, revenue sharing and competitive grants. It would help us all to have a greater appreciation of what we can accomplish through our communities at the local level, and some discrimination as to areas, like education, where some higher level inducements are needed to enable or provide incentives for better results. With the latter qualifier in mind, as between decentralization and devolution, decentralization is the stronger and more desirable of the two. It means that people at the local level have full responsibility for both making and implementing laws that may affect their lives. Increasing decentralization is essential if people are to feel that they have a greater and more effective say over governmental decisions that do affect their lives. The latter, in turn, sparks people's willingness to become increasingly involved in electoral politics. People are more likely to "get involved" if they have reason to believe that their participation will count for something and they can see the fruits of their efforts.

The problem is that decentralization as a deliberate national policy has stalled at the state level with fruition of "New Federalism" efforts to move power and money out of Washington down to the states. There has not been a corresponding, deliberate or continued effort to decentralize down to the local level from either Washington or the state capitals—even though politicians of both parties like to mouth the mantra that "local government is closest to the people." One recent exception is the "Ed Flex" and other educational reforms that relegate more responsibility for education decisions to local officials. This, however, is an example of "devolution" rather than "decentralization." Legislative leaders seem to like power more than decentralized democratic decision making.[37] Fortunately, as *Governing Magazine* has documented over the past 15 years, local initiatives have kept decentralization alive by demonstrating how localities can both innovate and take increasing amounts of responsibility for programs in a variety of areas.

Thus, the most important implication of this book is that decentralization down to the local must be more aggressively and systematically pursued by both federal and state governments. Move money and power out of state capitals as well as the federal capitol. Most people are scarcely closer to their state government than to their national, perhaps even less so since the machinations of "state house politicians" are less publicized than those of Presidents and Congressmen. Also, again, people are only likely to get involved if they feel they can "make a difference." Only at the local level can we see the impacts of our efforts.

Some would respond by saying that this emphasis on local initiative reflects on lot of romantic eyewash. Not so. Recall the very unromantic, hardnosed view of "community" noted in Chapter 8. There are some "bums" that may need to be thrown out in any locality but here, too, the likelihood of seeing the need and being able to address it is greater, the closer you are to it.

Education for Citizenship: Citizens' Empowerment for the Long Pull

The decline in the quality of American democracy is a long-term trend; It's restoration requires long-term efforts in several directions. Education is one of them—the civic education of a new generation. This is one important element of an overall strategy including many others, not the whole enchilada.

The latter qualifier must be injected before continuing because American political reformers have had a tendency to see education as a primary source of hope for the transformation of American society.[38] Such hopes are naïve and misleading. The education sector is a part of the larger social/political/economic system. Faith in education as a source of system transformation amounts to hardly more than the faith we invest in the young. Our hope contains a built in contradiction. On the one hand, we see the possibility of innovation and new ideas because of the presumably greater openness and energy of a new generation. On the other hand, we design educational systems whose primary purpose is to imbue youth with our own values, goals, conventions and traditions. Let's face it: most school systems serve to drive out youth's native qualities of imagination, creativity, critical thinking, and innovation in order to prepare them to serve as functionaries in some system. We build walls for them, not open systems. Perhaps this is one reason why Pink Floyd's album *The Wall* was so popular with young listeners. "We don't need no thought control…Teacher, leave us kids alone…Ma, is it just a waste of time?…It don't mean nothin' at all…Tear down the wall"(s)![39]

Only now, with the entire world system subject to another "great transformation" is it possible to think of the educational sub-system as being a major support system for transformation. Creativity, imagination, analysis, critical thinking, enterprise, and innovation are now valued qualities, especially in the business community, so many schools are now trying to learn how to convey and develop them.[40]

It remains to be seen, however, whether qualities imbued for purposes of job-readiness will be extended to the larger realm of citizenship preparatory. Will young people learn to look for and support the importance of "creativity, imagination, analysis, critical thinking, enterprise and innovation" in politics and government as well as business and industry? Will they apply these qualities as they grapple, as citizens, with the issues of a new age? For example, will they adopt a creative as well as constructively critical stance towards existing institutions, as it becomes clear that major changes and institutional innovations are needed? Schools need to teach and encourage the application of creative and critical thinking to social, political and institutional arrangements, not just to science, math and business.

The specific need this book points to, however, is still not being met—the need for civic and political education. Young people are not being taught even the basics of how to be responsible, active citizens. They enter the world of adulthood without learning about the governance of the communities in which they have lived or may live. They do not know where to go to register to vote; they know little about political parties and how they function; most have not studied the Constitution; they have little or no familiarity with essential features of democratic political process. Many traditional courses in what used to be called "civics" have been taken out of the schools. There is great need of a nationwide effort to put civic education back in the schools and, where such courses already exist, to strengthen and enrich them.[41] An essential feature of such courses should be learning-by-doing to involve pupils in the actual political activities of their communities, such as voter registration, poll watching, public hearings, town meetings and get-out-the-vote activities.

Here again, however, what young people see in their family may be more influential than what they encounter in school. The example provided by Jedediah Purdy is marvelous:

> When a neglectful local government lets public schools languish, do you shrug in resignation or run for the local school board and, enduring vilification and harassing phone calls, spend six years working in small ways and large to improve education in your community? My mother did the second, and whatever sense of political responsibility I have I owe to that example.[42]

During the last century, many people and organizations found it necessary to establish venues for civic and political education outside of "schools"— for adults struggling to adapt to an earlier great transformation.[43] The need was not just to prepare youth but many others, too, to be effective as citizens in a changing society. Some of the 19th century models might be adapted for use in the 21st. Not only political parties but also a host of other, non-partisan organizations need to establish programs for adult civic and political education. It is more true now and will be increasingly so in the new century that "knowledge is power." The opposite may be even more to the point: Lack of knowledge means being distinctly disempowered, i.e., politically emasculated. Do you want to know the costs of *not* learning how to be an effective citizen? Add the costs of ignorance; then multiply.

Family Support Systems: "Getting by with a little help..."

Without some encouragement and support from other family members (most of whom may not participate themselves), there are very few individuals who can play an active political role. Similarly, without families receiving some support from the larger communities in which they live, family members will be hard put to participate, no matter how much money they may have, for lack of time. For families with young children, lack of affordable day care continues to be a problem even though this has been a public issue for many years. Separation and divorce impede political participation, too (as in my own case[44]) even though divorce rates have been declining. Given that nearly all of us are short of time, we may not be able to commit any of it to political activity if there is no one to "spell" us at home or watch the home front. Budgeting time for participation may be a family affair or it may not happen at all. For all the rhetoric about "family values" and "supporting families," hardly any attention has been paid to the problem of how to enable people to play their role as citizens in addition to voting.

Leadership: Sine Qua Non?

Many people seem to be waiting for the proverbial "knight on a white horse" to charge into the While House like John F. Kennedy and issue a clarion call to us to "ask not what your country can do for you but what you can do for your country." Leadership is needed to spur a transformation of the American political landscape; however, strong leadership is a double-edged sword. By focusing attention on themselves, the charisma of natural leaders like a Kennedy or a Churchill can weaken the motivation of people to self-organize to undertake grass roots initiatives. Thus, Benjamin Barber recognized the need for "facilitating leadership" to nurture a "strong democracy…Effective dictatorships require charismatic leaders. Effective democracies need great citizens. "[45]

Whether or not we introduce a new political brand or label, whether it be "facilitating," "resource person," "servant leadership" or some other, a new kind or quality of political leadership is sorely needed. What currently counts as political "leadership" is closer to private careerism than to public service. Candidates for public office say: `elect me because I want to serve you' when the truth of the matter is more likely to be 'elect me so that I can advance my career.' In other words, most candidates run to empower themselves rather than others.

This empowerment distinction is rarely expressed or understood. One reason is that our media-driven political system has no incentive to clarify basic issues so as to improve the public's understanding of what is at stake. Recall Chapter 8 on the media. We see basic issues…

—Obscured—veiled by rhetoric, vague good intentions or other sources of ambiguity; or…
—Stereotyped—posed as sharp extremes to generate controversy.

So, unlike business leadership as noted in Chapter 7, leadership in the political arena is characterized in ways that do not seem to allow any happy medium. A "leader" is someone who speaks out on the (already defined) "issues of the day." Someone who, as in the '60's, speaks the message of "Power to the People" is a populist rabble-rouser. Pinning such labels trades in the politics of fear. Even without putting people down, politicians fail us as leaders because they do not help us to confront our fears of getting involved in public life. And they fail here because they have not confronted their own fears. Palmer has pointed this out most profoundly but we don't have to dive into his deep waters in order to see it. Politicians are afraid of the media. They are afraid someone may discover skeletons in their closet, a fear that business leaders did not share earlier but that they have come to fear recently.[46] Politicians are most afraid of us—public opinion. Those distracted by such fears cannot lead. They also do not seek to empower those others that they fear—us, otherwise known as "We, the People."

There are some sources of ambiguity because a couple of grey areas are inherent in politics. One is the admixture of ambition and altruism that infects leadership types. Most candidates, myself included, have been animated by good intentions and aim to achieve public office so that they can be of some service to others. This can be called the "representation" function of public office. It is with respect to the leadership function, however, that politicians misconceive or go astray. "Leadership" is seen as "speaking out on the issues" or getting out front with a possibly controversial position. It is not seen as enabling people to better understand and/or helping them to organize so that they themselves can more effectively intervene to have an impact on issues of most concern to them. The latter should be viewed as the most important feature of leadership in a healthy democracy.

This brings us to what we can call the "What v. How" problem. Politicians, driven by polls and facing an array of unresolved "issues," emphasize what they have to do in office in order to be perceived as "doing what the voters elected me to do." The emphasis is on the "job," a la the question many voters ask: "What have you done for me today." Politicians seldom speak to process—"how" the "what" is to be accomplished. Thus, political activity too often comes to have an unethical appearance or odor about it even if there is no overt wrongdoing because it seems to be conducted as if "the end justifies the means." More to the point of "empowerment," however, most politicians have not learned a basic lesson long since learned by advanced business management and noted in Chapter 7—that leaders need to invoke, inspire and engage the active involvement of people at all levels if problems are to be solved. This is the democratic "How" that is most fundamental. Lack of attention to this in the political realm spells lack of leadership.

Thus, Barber writes that "the fairest response to such problems is *facilitating leadership*...responsible to a process rather than to specific outcomes—to the integrity of the community rather than to the needs of specific individuals."[47] There is need for political leadership training modalities and vehicles of all sorts—institutes, lectures, seminars, forums and lycea—political analogues of those that have multiplied in the worlds of business and via self-improvement/self-help advisories over the past 10-15 years. Some of these might also be similar to those that spread over the American landscape during the 19th century in response to an earlier period of economic and technological transformation.

Changes in the Responsibilities of Elected Officials: For Us, Not Them

This need for change follows directly from our discussion above of the need for new political leadership. Realistically, the latter is most likely to arise from among "them," hopefully to include some of "us" who have political ambitions. We have some reason to believe that change is possible in politicians' orientation and understanding towards their responsibilities. As indicated by Chapter 7, we have seen such transformations of leadership attitudes and practices in the American business community, once thought to be resistant to "democratizing" change. If it can happen there, it can happen in the political community as well.

Politicians and elected officials at all levels need to understand that their leadership role is not just "getting things done" for the electorate, it is…

- Helping people to help themselves or, as noted earlier, empowering people to play effective roles as active citizens rather than as just "clients" of our political system;
- Urging citizens and their colleagues in "the system" to pay attention to the non-electorate and act as leaders themselves by helping to engage and empower others—those poorly represented or not represented at all, such as children, future generations, the poor and otherwise disadvantaged.

The first admonition includes an old art, that of "community organizing." As Bob Friedman, founder of the Corporation for Enterprise Development, stated: "One person can change the world…but 500 of us have a better chance."[48]

Changes in Laws Governing Not-for-Profit Organizations: Enabling Strategic Alliances

Laws and regulations governing not-for-profit corporations need to be liberalized so that not-for-profit [primarily 501(c)(3)] organizations can play more proactive roles in the political arena. One commentator recently referred to the effect of the current legal environment for non-profits as "the big chill."[49] The lack of any substantive basis for this was noted earlier with reference to LBJ in this chapter's footnote 34.

The absurdity of this environment has been revealed in many cases, mostly notably the highly publicized case of Newt Gingrich's GOPAC activity. No wrongdoing was found after all the posturing of political actors in congressional committees and the media. The real issue here was whether a not-for-profit organization should be training a new generation of Republican political leaders. I would say unequivocally "yes" to this even if the adjective was "Democratic," "Green" or some other brand of party politics. Gingrich demonstrated true political leadership in this regard as with the "Contract for America." Those who doubt this should see the materials that GOPAC provided to participants in the "American Opportunities Workshop: Common Sense Solutions for the '90's," then adapt them to their own purposes and seek to liberalize laws and regulations regarding non-profits' involvement in political activities so that they don't get crucified the way Gingrich was.

An April 4, 2003 I.R.S. ruling pointed the way and provided some hope in this regard. The agency had revoked the tax-exempt status of the Abraham Lincoln Opportunity Foundation for paying "some of the costs of broadcasting a series of civics lectures by Mr. Gingrich." The ruling reversed the earlier decision. The implications?—"some lawyers said the decision could have far broader significance because it could permit Republicans and Democrats to set up their own charitable groups to collect tax-deductible contributions for political purposes…"[50] Thus, two consequences could emerge: (1) Some tax-exempt organizations may be better able to bridge the gap between the political and not-for-profit organizational worlds pointed to earlier; and (2) the Bipartisan Campaign Reform Act may be even less able to limit the influence of money in politics than indicated earlier, notwithstanding the Supreme Court decision.

Changes in Laws Governing Electoral Politics: Making Every Person Count

Election laws need to be liberalized in most states. The emphasis here is "states," not national. Our nation's 50 states plus Puerto Rico and protectorates provide over 50 laboratories for governmental and political experimentation, as David Osborne highlighted in his book.[51] The "commerce clause" has already been employed in heavy overtime to provide either justification or pretext(s) for national legislative solutions in many areas of concern such as crime. Changes in election laws may implicate other portions of the Constitution, such as the First and Second Amendments. There have been suits, for example, regarding both electoral redistricting and campaign activity within private shopping malls. As indicated in the previous chapter, however, the federal interest in states' electoral reforms, whether via the federal court system or the Voting Rights Act, does not necessarily or desirably translate into interventions that would "federalize" electoral politics. There have already been too many steps in this direction via the Bipartisan Campaign Reform Act (BCRA) and 2002 federal legislation in reaction to the 2000 "count" in Florida, the Help American Vote Act (HAVA).

Election laws need to be liberalized to facilitate voter registration, campaigning on private property, voting, ballot initiatives and referenda, absentee voting, electoral use of the Internet, partisan election systems and campaign finance reform, as noted earlier in the previous chapter. States should have in place legislation to enable localities to enact a variety of electoral arrangements; e.g., partisan systems, IRV and proportional representation. Then the number of "experiments" in democracy could multiply many fold—by a factor of nearly 100. Most of all states' electoral reforms need to facilitate citizens' political participation and building the capacity of political parties at the local level.

Promotion of Political Volunteerism: A Conservative Populism of "We, the People…"

One of the most notable trends of recent years is the remarkable upsurge of interest in volunteerism. It has been promoted widely at all levels but most notably via some high-profile national initiatives, including former President Bush's "Points of Light," the National Commission on Civic Renewal, Colin Powell's "America's Promise," and America On Line's "e-philanthropy." What is equally remarkable is the avoidance of politics in both the advertising and

activities these undertakings are using to promote volunteerism. The lack of
political volunteerism—that which has sustained our democracy for so long—
is hardly recognized in their diagnosis of problems, and it is totally ignored
among potential solutions.

This could have something to do with the "big chill" noted earlier; however, this cannot account for such a flagrant, puzzling oversight of political
volunteerism. The commissions in question would neither have to involve
themselves in political activity that might compromise their "501(c)" tax status
nor adopt any partisan positions in order to include political activity among
desirable outlets cited in their promotion of volunteerism. Ongoing or future
initiatives to promote volunteerism should, therefore, promote the political
variety very aggressively.

After all, increased political volunteerism would be the core of a new
populism that is as inherently genuine, yet also as basically conservative as the
great majority of the American people. This would not be the radical, in-your-
face, or in-the-streets political "activism" that has given populism a bad name
or that has given the political establishment an easy excuse to dismiss popular
involvement in politics and avoid making changes that would bring people
back into the political action picture.

More Emphasis on "HOW" than on "WHAT": Means over ends

In earlier sections, the book has repeatedly pointed to this as a generic
issue affecting the political system as a whole. It is crucial to return to it once
again to recommend what should be done. While confronting the campaign
finance issue, for example, we learned that the "HOW" corrupts the "WHAT."

The major point of a book emphasizing people's political participation can
be seen in just these terms—that if we don't reform the the process (the
HOW), then the WHAT will be corrupted and that if we do, then a lot of
WHAT people are concerned about will take care of itself. Not that one
should isolate HOW from WHAT. Some political reforms or innovations will
follow from the obvious observation that we need a greater variety of HOW-
to political tools adapted to the WHAT of a new age. In addition to voting,
"HOW" includes letter writing, ballot initiatives, petitions, public testimony,
working on campaigns, organizing or participating in political events, et. al.[52]
A rule of thumb from systems analysts is that the number of tools we need
to have at our disposal should at least match the number of goals we are trying
to pursue. A new tool that may revolutionize the "HOW" of our democracy—
to help make it more deliberative and democratic—is use of the Internet as
noted in Chapter 8.[53] Another is "public interest polling" to help us "come to
public judgement."[54]

Improving the HOW of the democratic process is essential to overcoming
the distrust, apathy and cynicism that infect our democracy. The situation is
highlighted by an old political line that used to be funny: "Politics is like
sausage; if you've seen it being made, then you don't want to eat it." Already,

a large number and proportion of people "don't want to eat it," so if we don't improve HOW it is "made," the numbers of politically alienated and *dis*-empowered people will continue to increase.

Media Reforms: Putting the Public Back Into Private Media

As indicated by Chapter 8, the complicity of the media in the decline of American democracy as a "team sport" is so significant in so many ways that whole books could be (and are) devoted to "media reforms."[55] A major recommendation, already cited in our discussion of campaign finance reform, is that free TV time for candidates and political forums be required under the new digital TV mode. Others include more aggressive promotion of both civic and investigative journalism, essential inputs to a more deliberative democracy.

More modest initiatives are underway in keeping with this book's emphasis on decentralization and creative localism. In some localities, we have already begun to see what may be a continuing reaction and response to the growing gigantism of media interests—the buying up of formerly local newspapers, radio and TV stations by media giants. In Marlboro, MA, for example, a local entrepreneur founded a new local newspaper called the *Main Street Journal*, and it has been doing well. The market for such a paper was partly revealed by complaints that are all too familiar in many other cities and towns, such as: The "local" paper (now owned by non-local interests) is…

—providing less local news coverage and more non-local coverage;
—doing little investigative journalism;
—has too little journalistic independence, etc.
—employing young reporters coming from out of town as through a revolving door. With little understanding of the locality, they work for the paper to "earn their spurs" as journalists, but by the time they know the local "turf," they leave.

We can expect to see more new, independent, locally owned and managed newspapers arising to fill local media market gaps created by media buyouts and consolidations—just as large bank mergers are creating opportunities for community banks. This line of development could be facilitated by foundations concerned with "civic journalism" if they also recognize the need to provide seed money to help new local papers get started.

Digital Democracy: Single Digits? Surfing Alone?

We found in Chapter 8 that the 'Net and 'Web have great potential to revitalize and improve American democracy. There is also potential for "same old, same old." For the positive potential to be realized, several steps need to be taken, including:

• Public information kiosks or terminals in many public locations in each town through which people can access information on government and politics at all levels, for free.

- Each registered voter to be allocated a no-cost 'Net account for access to public information and communications with public officials.
- Electronic "public interest polling," deliberation, issue forums, ballot initiatives and referenda.
- A web and Internet counterpart of public radio and television, as repeatedly recommended by one of the world's leading advocates and experts on "digital democracy."[56]
- Increased, widespread, interactive television.
- TV political debates among candidates at all levels featuring public questions and interaction, at no cost to participating candidates or viewers.
- Equipping local political committee members with hand-held data entry terminals for data entry as they canvass door-to-door.

American democracy will continue its decline if the promise of the 'Net and 'Web are lost and they turn into channels similar to those on TV.

Experimentation: Learning By Doing

Ever since John Dewey, occasional attention has been turned to "experiment" as a way to improve American democracy. Indeed, our democratic republic was viewed from the beginning, overall, as a great experiment. This attitude is thought to reflect a significant thread of authentic American character—tinkerer, inventor, experimenter—exemplified by Franklin, Edison and others. Translation from the domain of technology tinkering to experimenting with politics and government, however, amounts to a "great leap forward" that not even Dewey was not able to achieve, notwithstanding a lot of seminal thinking on the frontiers of the social science of his time.[57] Nor have others since. The concept of "experimentation" to improve our democratic system, however, may now be an idea whose time has come. There are three recent signs of this:

1. The revival of interest in Dewey and his ideas in the fields of political science and philosophy (e.g., Richard Bernstein's essay on Dewey's "Creative Democracy");[58]

2. The fact that some leading political thinkers are advocating an explicitly experimental approach to political change and public policy (re)formulation (e.g., Unger, West); and:

3. The fact that one of the year 2000 Presidential candidates, Bill Bradley, also suggested an experimental approach in some areas.

Also recognize that an experimental approach to public policy has in fact been practiced in many "soft" institutional and human-behavioral areas of concern; i.e., areas not dominated by the "hard" concerns of science and technology. These include education, employment and training, economic development, housing and urban development, and social services. The word "recognize" bears repeating because the application of experimental approaches has not been featured in the political arena. It has not even received much attention in the halls of government except among "policy wonks."

A significant step to bring experimentation to the foreground of political and policy debates, therefore, would be to make note of the fact that it's already being done; i.e., we're not talking about a new, chancy, "roll of the dice, spin of the wheel" kind of approach. We can look to see how to build on past experience, to improve and systematize existing approaches. An important aspect of this past experience is directly connected to citizens' desire for "accountability." Many programs, even if not explicitly designed as experiments, have practically (or virtually?) been "experiments" because they have been subject to performance evaluations just as if they were. Thus, a more explicit, systematic use of experimental approaches goes hand in glove with voters' desires to make government programs more accountable as well as to see that politicians not "reinvent the wheel." Or, as Peter Senge and David Osborne have said, respectively, our government can become a "learning system" characterized by "5th generation management" experimenting through "Laboratories of Democracy."

What we would be talking in this arena, however, may be politically chancy because the approach would run against the grain of politicians who like to...

- "spread the goodies around," and...
- appear to be greater than they are by introducing broad-scope legislation to "solve" big problems rather than initiatives that would experiment with potential solutions on small(er) scales. [Not to mention the likelihood that many experiments wouldn't confirm many politicians' predispositions, prejudices, preconceptions or ideological leanings of where answers to questions might be found or what solutions to problems might be best.]

It seems likely, therefore, that advocacy of more experimental approaches to public problem solving could be a credible part of the platform of politicians who, increasingly, like to say that they are "non-political." They could do so most credibly by noting that...

- There is much to be learned from past experience; we would not be "reinventing the wheel;" and...
- It is high time that we harness the engine of progress that has so enriched our nation through "hard" science to guide and/or inform the design or "reinvention" of relatively "soft" but incredibly important and expensive socio-economic policies and institutions.

Introduction and Adaptation of Business Innovations in the Political/ Governmental Arenas

Chapter 8 demonstrated that the business sector, building on advanced science and technology, has been far more progressive the than political/

governmental sector. In light of the 2002 scandals surrounding some large corporate wrongdoers, this may seem to be one of the most questionable and controversial conclusions of this book, but it is nonetheless true and the political/governmental and media careerists who dominate our politics would do well to make note and take it to heart. For here is another paradox: If they don't, the business sector will come to dominate our public life even more than political activists claim as they rail against big corporate powers.

Summary: Larger, Broader or Higher Level Changes Needed to Encourage and Support People's Grass Roots Involvement(s)

—Realization of the implications of our international leadership role: We can't preach to others if we don't honor our own values.
—Adaptations of "private" advanced business practices in the public/ political arena.
—Decentralization
—Tax incentives for investments of time (t)
—Creation/enabling of "space" for self-organizing advancement of poor people[59]
—Constitutional changes via a national Constitutional convention
—National I&R & electronic voting system(s)
—An explicit, deliberately framed and conducted *experimental approach to institutional innovation* (II).
—"Open systems architecture" applied as the driving principle for reform of the entire political system; e.g., "privatization" of political parties.

III. Conclusion: Revitalization, Reformation and Reintegration (3 R's) of the American Political Community

This book has provided 3 R's for grass roots efforts to rebuild the American political community—to:

Revitalize: By becoming the producers of our politics, we will bring back the vitality of politics by people as well as for them. We will take our system back from the "pro's." Can it be otherwise; can the "sausage" of politics even be consumed by people, let alone be good for them, if they haven't had a hand in its making and quality control?

Reform: Our political parties, campaign finance and candidate selection procedures—to ground them on grass roots political participation, of "ordinary" people's time rather than rich people's money. Promote a "conservative populism."[60]

Reintegrate: By building bridges between politics and the community-based initiatives of civic life; by oversight of the media to promote political discourse that searches for common ground and promotes the positive coming together of real people in real places; by focusing public problem solving, increasingly, at local, community levels where people can come together to address the problems of real people in real places.

It has taken our nation about 150 years to move backward from a time when politics engaged people's participation and enthusiasm as political co-producers to now, when it briefly gets our attention just before elections as consumers of a politics produced by others. This book has shown both why we, the people, need to get back in the game and how we can start to do so. Fortunately, people can be re-engaged in the political process in a variety of little ways that would add up to make a difference without everyone feeling that they have to man the barricades or sacrifice a major slice of their lives to some cause. That is why this book indeed represents a conservative populism for a great American majority that is largely conservative, in the best sense of the word. We love America; we love our families and communities; we love our flag; we love "the Republic for which it stands." We also want to make a political difference for our children even more than for ourselves. Let's do it. We do not have to let ourselves be led by self-appointed "progressives" or "reformers" who try to arouse us, as if we were victims, by the vent of their spleen against "the system" or some aspect of it. We can be the saviors of a democratic political system that is our birthright through simple but commit-ted doses of participation as "the heroes of everyday life" that most of us are or at least try to be. To repeat what Abraham Lincoln once said: "We, even we here, hold the power and bear the responsibility."[61] And you?

Notes

1. As indicated in my 1999 review of *Street Politics*.

2. Ehrenhalt, Alan (1998), "Politics and the Goulash of everyday Life," *Governing* (August).

3. For example, if 100 million people each volunteered only 4 hours a week for a month during an election season, then the time valued at a minimum wage of $5.25/hr. is worth 8.4 billion dollars.

4. On this issue, see the contrasting views of the Harwood Group, for the Kettering Foundation, expressed in "Meaningful Chaos: How People Form Relationships with Political Concerns," and my own, set forth in "Meaningless Chaos: Understanding How People Fail to Form Relationships with *Political* Concerns," in *The Good Society* (Fall, 1995).

5. One very important exception is the impressive study of voluntary political participation by Verba, et. al. (1995) noted earlier. This shows how people's involvement in various non-political organizations and "causes" provides both "civic skills" (via learning by doing) and channels for possible political involvement.

6. As earlier, Erikson's idea of identify formation figures here, too, as contingent upon the intersect of "personal history and the historical moment."

7. Marginal remarks on copy of draft returned to me.

8. See, for example, the book by Sara Diamond on "the Christian Right": *Not By Politics Alone* (New York: The Guilford Press).

9. Sennett, Richard (1977), *The Fall of Public Man*. New York: Vintage Books.

10. See Stanback, Thomas, and Peter Bearse, et.al. (1982), *Services: The New Economy*. New Jersey: Allenheld-Osmun.

11. Palmer, Parker (1990), "Leading from Within: Reflections on Spirituality and Leadership." Washington, D.C.: The Servant Leadership School.

12. Mike Lynch argues that this is "A matter of perspective. Someone else may prefer no legislation. Another constituent argues for opposite legislation." (comments on earlier draft)

13. See Illich, Ivan (1970), *De-Schooling Society* and also "Silence is a Commons," where he writes: "people cease to be able to *govern* themselves; they demand to be *managed*.", Asahi Symposium on Science and Man – The computer-managed society, Tokyo, Japan, March 21, 1982.

14. As via "Building Citizens" and "Civic Exchange" accessible via www.wwc.rutgers.edu at Rutgers, The State University, New Brunswick, NJ.

15. But for contrasting views and exceptions, see Kemmis, Daniel (1986), "Barn Building: Cooperation and the Economy of the West," *Northern Lights* (November/December), on old fashioned community barnraising efforts as a

political paradigm, and Useem, Jerry (1996), "The Virtue of Necessity" (on the Amish). *INC* Magazine (December).

16. Useem, op.cit., p.88. Not an Amish, a Luddite or even close to one, Mike Lynch says that advanced technologies serve to advance a "societal addiction" of increasing (over) reliance on technology.

17. Find the documentation of this by direct experience in Barbara Ehrenreich's *Nickel and Dimed: On (Not) Getting By in America.* New York: Henry Holt, Owl Books (2001).

18. Joy, Bill (2000), "Why the Future Doesn't Need Us," *Wired* (April).

19. For help in dealing with such impolitic people, see Larry Mullins' *Immature People with Power: How to Handle Them* [available from Actionizing, Inc., Tulsa, OK].

20. Alan Ehrenhalt. Editor of *Governing*, hit this point head on: "'Mostly, what we call politics is a goulash of everyday-life questions that force their way into the political process and demand to be dealt with...**Politics is us** (my emphasis)...The whole political system is you and me cavorting on a slightly larger stage." (Ehrenhalt, op.cit., p.8)

21. Churches, for example, whose governance may be quite *un*-democratic. See Bearse and Bruno (1998), "Church and Politics: Thoughts on Building a Community-based Politics." *Main St. Journal*, Marlboro, MA (Feb. 28).

22. In a first draft of this sentence, the adjectives "organized, high-stakes" preceded "politics." They were deleted because electoral politics is almost invariably a higher stakes game than the political games played in other settings. Academic politics, for example, is a game where those involved usually have little to lose but their egos.

23. See the *UTNE Reader* of July/August, 2002, for example, on "The Power of Talk: Create social change by starting a conversation," as well as the *UTNE* book on "salons," referenced elsewhere.

24. These are some of the findings of the National Survey of County and Local Committees of Political Parties, done specially for this book and presented earlier in Chapter 5.

25. See Robert Heinlein's book *Take Back Your Government: A Practical Handbook for the Citizen Who Wants Democracy to Work* for a lot more on to make a difference in and through work on local political party committees.

26. A political discussion group, for example, might be formed around C-Span2's "Book TV." Some readers may have seen the fine "American Presidents" and/or "American Writers" series. Also note the potential of establishing a political "salon," as indicated in the *UTNE Reader* of Sept-Oct 2000.

27. This is how I met my first wife. I walked into the Village Independent Democrats one evening and Voila!the rest was history.

28. Mike Lynch repeatedly questioned the dependability of volunteers in his

comments upon this and some other chapters. I quite understand. Volunteers' un-dependability caused me many fits during my own campaigns.

29. Lynch also remarked that this statement is "very naïve. Examine the experience of California and even MASSPIRG" (Massachusetts Public Interest Research Group). Referenda, he noted, are often driven by a "well financed minority."

30. Recall, however, the problems of signature collectors hired for money and/ or of "volunteers" imported from out of state, mentioned earlier, that have arisen in many I&R campaigns.

31. Benjamin Barber has been an advocate of national referenda, as in his book *Strong Democracy*, p.285. I have been an advocate for a Second Constitutional Convention, as noted earlier.

32. Bradley Smith, FEC Commissioner, wrote: "The idea of restricting the uses of rather than banning soft money is good" (private e-mail communication to me on 3/23/01). The 2002 BCRA has moved this issue largely down to the state level. See my testimony to the FEC on rulemaking for BCRA implementation, published in *The Ethical Spectical* of July, 2002, as well as in FEC documentation.

33. Note that "relevant" pertains to level of government. There is already a criterion—a minimum 15% of the national vote—for a party to be able to receive federal funds for its presidential election candidates. There are lower criteria at the state level to qualify parties for recognition on ballots for state contests. Unfortunately, recent "Clean Elections" or "Public Campaign" ballots initiatives have public funds going only to candidates and not to parties, unlike earlier state-level reforms like those in Minnesota.

34. According to Rep. Walter Jones (R, NC), "The political ban in Section 501(c)(3) [of the Internal Revenue Code] was inserted in 1954 by then-Senator Lyndon Johnson. This was done with a floor amendment to the Revenue Act of 1954, and absolutely no hearings or congressional record was developed on the need or reasons for the absolute ban." [Quoted in *Online Human Events* of September 27, 2002.]

35. Unfortunately, the new rules promulgated by the FEC in 2002 to implement the Bipartisan Campaign Reform Act (BCRA) do not accomplish this, any more than did the old, pre-BCRA regulations, even though state and local committees can receive soft money in amounts of up to $10,000 per contributor.

36. Quoted from "The Way We Were and Are," *Governing* (October, 2002).

37. This is reflected in remarks of Mike Lynch and observations in a book cited earlier by Dan Shea (1995).

38. Lynch's comment on this was: "They can't even convey the 3R's effectively," a sentiment with which I and many others can reluctantly agree.

39. United Kingdom: Harvest/EMI CD (1994).

40. Edward de Bono has been a leader in this direction. See his *Six Thinking Hats* (1999).

41. This is not just a matter for formal education via "civics" in schools. What about family influences, which both studies and anecdotal evidence have shown to be important? What about parental responsibility? Lynch remarked: "It's up to parents/mentors to inform them (youth)—like a rite of passage."

42. Purdy, Jedediah (1999), *For Common Things*, p.89.

43. See examples featured in David Reynold's (1995) biography *Walt Whitman's America*. Also recall Polanyi (1959), *The Great Transformation*.

44. As related in a letter to the editor of the *Gloucester Daily Times* (September, 2001).

45. Barber, Benjamin (1984), *Strong Democracy: Participatory Politics for a New Age*. Berkeley, CA: University of California Press, especially Chapter Nine: "Citizenship and Community," pp. 238-241. The "Effective" quote is from page xvii.

46. The most obvious example is Jack Welch, former CEO of General Electric.

47. Barber, 1984, p. 240.

48. Quoted in Steinbach, Carol (1999), "Pragmatic Passion: A Small Firm's Big Impact on Economic Policy," *Ford Foundation Report*. New York: Ford Foundation (Spring/Summer).

49. Paget, Karen (1999), "The Big Chill: Foundations and Political Passion." *The American Prospect* (May-June).

50. Quotes in this paragraph are from Johnston, David (2003), "Ruling May Open Financial Loophole," *New York Times*, Sunday edition (June 6, p.25).

51. Osborne, David (1990), *Laboratories of Democracy*.

52. Note what Shondra Ponder (www.friendsofliberty.com) has to say in this regard: "The reality is, most Americans DO know what's going on. The problem…is that they don't know what to do with it, or about it. What needs to happen…is that the American people need to be taught how to write letters to their congressmen (etc.)…they don't know how to do it!" (May 16, 2002).

53. For example, see Davis, Marilyn, et. al. (1997), "Features for Freedom: A Report From eVote Developers," available, along with eVote software, via www.deliberate..com. (21-22 April).

54. See Kay, Alan (1998), *Locating Consensus for Democracy: A Ten Year Experiment*. St. Augustine, FLA: Americans Talk Issues.

55. These include, for example the books on media reforms cited in Chapter 8, especially Nichols and McChesney (2000).

56. See, for example, Steve Clift's 2003), "Public Net-work." Paris: OECD E-Government Project Advisory Group (draft copy, shared by Clift via e-mail, March 11).

57. Dewey, John (1927), *The Public and its Problems* and (1922*) Human Nature and Conduct.*

58. Bernstein, Richard J. (2002), "Creative Democracy—The Task Still Before Us." New York: New School University. Based upon an article that originally appeared in Richard J. Bernstein, *Philosophical Profiles* (Philadelphia: University of Pennsylvania Press, 1986).

59. As indicated in my 1999 review of *Street Politics* (op.cit.)

60. The Hudson Institute, a conservative think-tank headquartered in Indianapolis, has been trying this through its "Project for Conservative Reform," but this emerged as little more than the activity of one person, Marshall Wittman, who fancied himself to be "The Moose," after Theodore Roosevelt's "Bull Moose" Republicanism, leading a latter day movement for T.R.-style "progressive" reforms. After Wittman left Hudson to go to work for Senator John McCain in 2002, the Project became a dead letter. But another such initiative is the "Reform Institute," whose Advisory Committee is chaired by Senator McCain. Was this established as a run-up to a potential McCain for President campaign in 2004? As indicated earlier in this book, however, those who would look for a charismatic "knight on a white horse" to lead the charge for "reform" without getting involved themselves, are inviting another potential disappointment or discredit to American democracy.

61. In his "Annual Message to Congress," December 1, 1862.

APPENDIX A

DIRECTORY OF
INTERNET POLITICAL SITES

This directory provides two features you do not usually find among other sets of "Links" provided by political websites —

(1) Descriptions of what the site offers (or doesn't).

(2) An Excel matrix of cross-references and linkage counts for every site with reference to every other, plus counts of the numbers of linkages of each site to sites not included in the Directory.

Thus, one can select a site based on both descriptive and linkage criteria.

As such, the Directory is too large to include here in print copy. Interested readers and potential users should visit the website www.politicalcommunity.us and click on "Resources" to find the Directory. Any questions regarding the site can be addressed to the author, Peter Bearse, via e-mail to: peterJ@politicalcommunity.us.

APPENDIX B

REFERENCES

Adams, Henry (1918), *The Education of Henry Adams*. Modern Library.

Ahrens, Frank (2003), "Senate Panel Approves Tougher Media Rules," *Washington Post* (June 20, p.E01).

Althusser , Louis (1999), *Machiavelli and Us*. New York: Verso.

Barber, Benjamin (1984), S*trong Democracy: Participatory Politics for a New Age*. Berkeley: University of California Press.

Barringer, Felicity (2001), "Unresolved Clash of Cultures: At Knight Ridder, Good Journalism vs. the Bottom Line." *New York Times* (June 1).

Baum, Rainer C. (1988), "Holocaust: Moral Indifference as *the* Form of Modern Evil," in: Rosenberg, Alan, and Gerald E. Myers (eds.), *Echoes from the Holocaust: Philosophical Reflections on a Dark Time*. Philadelphia: Temple University Press.

Bayat, Asef (1997) S*treet Politics: Poor People's Movements in Iran*. New York: Columbia University Press.

Bearak, Barry (2001), "This Job Is Truly Scary: The Taliban are Watching." *New York Times* (June 1).

Bearse, Peter J. (2003), "We Have Met the Enemy. He is Us," *The Ethical Spectacle* (www.spectacle.org, October, 2002).

_____ (2002), "MEMORANDUM: Propositions for Certain Aspects of Federal Election Commission(FEC) Rulemaking in re: Public Law 107-155, 107th Congress: "An Act to amend the Federal Election Campaign Act of 1971 to provide bipartisan campaign reform," in *The Ethical Spectacle* (July).

_____ (2001), Life Against Death," *The Ethical Spectacle* (www.spectacle.org, October)

_____ (1999a), "Book Review: S*treet Politics: Poor People's Move-ments in Iran." Journal of Socio-\Economics* 28 (pp.777-786).

_____ (1999b), "The Fractal Revolution," *The Ethical Spectacle* (www.spectacle.org, September).

_____ and Janet Bruno (1998), "Church and Politics: Thoughts on Building a Community-based Politics." *Main St. Journal,* Marlboro, MA (Feb. 28).

_____ (1995) "Meaningless Chaos: Understanding How People Fail to Form Relationships with *Political* Concerns," *The Good Society* (Fall)

_____(1992), "Citizen Leaders for a New Politics,." *Public Leader-ship Education: The Role of Citizen Leaders,* Dayton, OH: The Kettering Foundation in partnership with the Council on Public Policy Education (Vol. VI, November).

_____ (1987a) "Truth Isn't a Political Priority," *Gloucester Daily Times* (April 24).

_____ (1987b), "Time for a New Constitutional Convention," *Hunterdon County Democrat* (August 24).

_____ , (1987c), "Industrial Policy From the Shop Floor and the Bottom Up," *The Entrepreneurial Economy.* Washington, D.C., Corporation for Enterprise Development.

_____ (1976), "Report of the City Elections Study Panel on Par-ʼtisan and Nonpartisan Municipal Elections."Trenton, NJ: Trenton Democratic Committee.

Becker, Ernest (1965), E*scape From Evil.* NY: Macmillan.

Bell, Jeffrey (1992), *Populism and Elitism: Politics in the Age of Equality.* Washington, D.C., Regnery Gateway.

Bennis, Warren and Patricia Biederman (1997), O*rganizing Genius: The Secrets of Creative Collaboration.* Reading, MA: Addison Wesley.

Berger, Peter (1976), *Pyramids of Sacrifice.* New York: Anchor Books.

Bernstein, Richard J. (2002), "Creative Democracy – The Task Still Before Us." New York: New School University. Based upon an article that originally appeared in Richard J. Bernstein, *Philosophical Profiles* (Philadelphia: University of Pennsylvania Press, 1986).

Berry, Wendell (1996), *The Unsettling of America*. Sierra Club Books.

Boorstin, Daniel J. (1961), *The Image: A Guide to Pseudo Events in America*. New York: Vintage Books..

_____ (1973), *The Americans: The Democratic Experience*. New York: Vintage Books.

Boulding, Kenneth (1956), *The Image*. Ann Arbor, Michigan: University of Michigan Press.

Bowen, Charles (1996), *Modem Nation: The Handbook of Grassroots American Politics Online*. New York: Crown Publishing Group.

Bradley, Stephen P. & R.L. Nolan (1998), *Sense & Respond*. Cambridge, MA: Harvard Business School Press.

Brand, Stewart (2000), *The Clock of the Long Now*. New York: Basic Books.

Bronowski, Jacob (1956), *Science and Human Values*. New York: Harper Collins.

_____ (1977), A *Sense of the Future*. Cambridge, MA: MIT Press.

_____ (1976), *The Ascent of Man*. Boston: Little-Brown.

Bryan, Frank (2004), *Real Democracy*. Chicago: University of Chicago Press.

_____, and John McClaughry (1989), *The Vermont Papers: Recreating Democracy on a Human Scale*. Post Hills, Vermont: Chelsea Green Publishing Company.

Burnham, James (1943), *The Machiavellian*s. Washington, D.C.: Regnery.

Burns, Nancy, Sidney Verba and Kay Lehman Schlozman (2001), *Private Roots of Public Action: Gender, Equality and Political Action*. Cambridge, MA: Harvard University Press.

Bzdek, Jim (1999), How to Participate in Politics Effectively: A Step-by-Step Guide Every Citizen Can Use. Denver, CO: Out of print but available from the author.

Cameron, Kim (1986), "Effectiveness as Paradox: Consensus and Conflict in Conceptions of Organizational Effectiveness," 32 *Management Science* 5 (May).

Canedy, Dana (2001), "Florida Leaders Sign Agreement for Overhaul of Election System," *The New York Times* (May 5).

Cappella, Joseph N., and K.H. Jamieson (1997), *Spiral of Cynicism: The Press and the Public Good.* New York: Oxford University Press.

Carter, Bill (2001), "Survival of the Pushiest," *The New York Times Magazine* (January 28).

Case, John (1995), "The Open Book Revolution," *INC* Magazine (June).

Citizens Research Foundation (1997), "New Realities, New Thinking." Los Angeles, CA: University of Southern California (March).

Clift, Steven (2000), "Democracy is Online," *OnTheInternet* magazine. Internet Society (March/April 1998.

_____ (2000), D*emocracy is Online 2.0*, available only online via www.e-democracy.org/do.

_____ (2003), "Public Net-work." Paris: OECD E-Government Project Advisory Group (draft copy, shared by Clift via e-mail, March 11).

Coe, Fanny E. (1911), H*eroes of Everyday Life: A Reader for the Upper Grades.* Boston: Ginn and Company.

Committee for Economic Development (1999), *Investing in the People's Business: A Business Perspective on Campaign Finance Reform: A Statement on National Policy.* Washington, D.C.: Committee for Economic Development.

Committee for the Study of the American Electorate (CSAE, 1997), "Use of Media Principal Reason Campaign Costs Skyrocket." Washington. D.C.: CSAE.

_____ (2002), "Turnout Modestly Higher; Democrats in Deep Doo-Doo; Many Questions Emerge." News Release. Washington, D.C. (November 8).

Common Cause (2004), "In the FCC Rules Debate, Will Two Million Voices Trump $124 Million?" http:// www.commoncause.org.

Dahl, Robert A. (1998), *On Democracy*. New Haven: Yale University Press.

Dao, James (2000), "Ringing Phones, Chiming Doorbells, Stuffed E-mail-boxes: The Great Voter Roundup," *The New York Times* (November 7).

Davis, Marilyn, et. al. (1997), "Features for Freedom: A Report From eVote Developers," available, along with eVote software, via WWW.DELIBERATE.com. (21-22 April)

Davis, Bob (2001), *Speed is Life: Street Smart Lessons from the Front Lines of Business*. New York: Currency-Doubleday.

Davis, Richard (1999), *The Web of Politics: The Internet's Impact on the American Political System*. New York: Oxford University Press

de Bono, Edward (1985), *Six Thinking Hats*. Toronto, Canada: Key Porter Books.

DeLaney, Ann (1995), *Politics for Dummies*. Foster City, CA: IDG Books.

de Tocqueville, Alexis (1945), *Democracy in America*. New York, NY: Alfred A. Knopf, Vintage Books.

Dewey, John (1927), *The Public and its Problems*. Chicago: Swallow Press.

_____ (1922*)*, *Human Nature and Conduct*. New York: Henry Holt and Company.

Diamond, Sara (1998), *Not by Politics Alone*. New York: The Guilford Press.

Dionne, E.J. (1991), *Why Americans Hate Politics*. New York: Simon and Shuster.

Douglas, William O. (1960), *America Challenged*. Princeton, NJ: Princeton University Press.

Duncan, Dayton (1990), *Grassroots: One Year in the Life of the New Hampshire Presidential Primary*. New York: Viking.

Eco, Umberto (1986), *Faith in Fakes: Essays*. London: Secker and Warburg.

Edwards, Mickey (2002), "Making Mass. elections more democratic," *Boston Globe*, March 30).

Ehrenhalt, Alan (1998), "Politics and the Goulash of Everyday Life," *Governing* (August).

_____ (2002), "The Way We Were and Are," *Governing* (October).

Ehrenreich, Barbara (2002), N*ickeled and Dimed: On (not) Getting by in America*. New York: Henry Holt & Co., LLC, Owl Books.

Erikson, Eric (1994), *Life History and the Historical Moment.* N.Y.: W.W. Norton & Co.

Fenn, Donna (1996), "Open Book Management 101," *INC* Magazine (August).

Ferguson, Marilyn (1980), *The Aquarian Conspiracy: Personal and Social Transformation in our Time.* New York: Jeremy P. Tarcher/Putnam.

Ferguson, Niall (2003), "Overdoing Democracy," a review of Zakaria's *The Future of Freedom: Illiberal Democracy at Home and Abroad* in the *New York Times Book Review* (June 1, 2003).

Franke-Ruta, Garance (2003), "Zero Sum: Why Moveon will be the real winner of its own presidential primary," *The American Prospect*, Internet edition (June 25).

Frantzich, Stephen, and J. Sullivan (1996), *The C-SPAN Revolution.* Norman, OK: The University of Oklahoma Press.

_____ (1999), C*itizen Democracy: Political Activists in a Cynical Age.* New York: Rowman and Littlefield Publishers.

Freire, Paulo (1971), *Pedagogy of the Oppressed.* New York: Herder and Herder.

Fromm, Erich (1964), *The Heart of Man: Its Genius for Good & Evil.* NY: Harper & Row.

Gannett, Robert T., Jr. (2003), "Bowling Ninepins in Tocqueville's Township." 97 *American Political Science Review* 1 (February),

Gates, Jeff (2000), D*emocracy at Risk: Rescuing Main Street from Wall Street.* Cambridge, Massachusetts: Perseus Publishing.

Geras, Norman (1998), T*he Contract of Mutual Indifference: Political Philosophy after the Holocaust*. London and New York: Verso.

Gleick, James (1999), *Faster: The Acceleration of just about Everything*. New York: Pantheon Books.

Gordon, Robert J. (2000), "Does the "New Economy" Measure up to the Great Inventions of the Past?," NBER Working Paper No. W7833. Washington, D.C.: National Bureau of Economic Research (August).

Gozdz, Kazimierz (1995), *Community Building: Renewing Spirit & Learning in Business*. San Francisco: Sterling & Stone, New Leaders Press

Gram, David (2003), "The Price of Power," *New York Times Magazine* (May 11).

Green, John C. and D.M. Shea (eds., 1999), *The State of the Parties: The Changing Role of Contemporary American Parties*. Oxford, England: Rowman and Littlefield.

Guinness, Os (2000), *Time for Truth: Living Free in a World of Lies, Hype and Spin*. Grand Rapids, Michigan: Baker Books.

Handy, Charles (1996), *Beyond Certainty: Changing World of Organization*. Cambridge, MA: Harvard Business School Press.

_____ (1994), *The Age of Paradox*. Cambridge, MA: Harvard Business School Press.

Harwood Group (1994), "Meaningful Chaos: How People Form Relationships with Political Concerns." Dayton, OH: Kettering Foundation.

Hauerwas, Stanley (1981), A *Community of Character: Toward a Constructive Christian Social Ethic*. Notre Dame, Indiana: University of Notre Dame Press.

Vladislav, Jan (ed., 1986), *Vaclav Havel: Living in Truth*. London: Faber and Faber. See, especially, "The Power of the Powerless."

Heinlein, Robert (1992), *Take Back Your Government!: A Practical Handbook for the Private Citizen Who Wants Democracy to Work*. Riverdale, NY: Baen Publishing Enterprises.

Hesselbein, Frances, et.al. (ed.1998), *The Community of the Future*. San Francisco: Jossey-Bass & The Drucker Foundation.

Hill, Martha S. and F. Thomas Juster (1979), "Constraints and Complementarities in Time Use." Ann Arbor, Michigan: Survey Research Center, Institute for Social Research, University of Michigan.

Hoffer, Eric (1963), *The Ordeal of Change*. New York: Harper and Row.

_____ (1989), T*he True Believer*. New York: Harper Collins.

Hofstadter, Richard (1955), T*he Age of Reform*. New York: Vintage

Hughes, Robert (1993), *Culture of Complaint: A Passionate Look into the Ailing Heart of America*. New York: Warner Books.

Illich, Ivan (1970), *De-Schooling Society*. New York: Harper and Row.

_____ (1982), "Silence is a Commons," Asahi Symposium on Science and Man – The computer-managed society, Tokyo, Japan, March 21, 1982.

Ingraham, Jeson (2001), "GDA grads told to strive for community, not consumption." Newburyport, MA: *Daily News* (June 3).

Johnston, David (2003), "Ruling May Open Financial Loophole," *New York Times*, Sunday edition (June 6).

Joy, Bill (2000), "Why the Future Doesn't Need Us," *Wired* (April).

Judis, John (1997), "Below the Beltway: Goo-Goos Versus Populists," *The American Prospect*, no. 30 (January-February, 1997).

_____ (2000), "Top Down: Whatever happened to noblesse oblige," *The New Republic* (March 27)

Katz, Jon (1997), "The Digital Citizen." *Wired* magazine, no. 5.12 (December). .

Kay, Alan (1998), *Locating Consensus for Democracy*. St.Augustine, FL: Americans Talk Issues.

Keller, Ed, and Jon Berry (2004), *The Influentials*, Washington, D.C.: Institute for Politics, Democracy & the Internet, Graduate School of Political Management, The George Washington University.

Kelly, Kevin (1994), *Out of Control*. Reading, MA: Addison-Wesley Publishing

Kemmis, Daniel (1990), *Community and the Politics of Place*. Norman, OK: University of Oklahoma Press.

_____ (1986), "Barn Building: Cooperation and the Economy of the West," *Northern Lights* (November/December),

Kocian, Lisa (2000),"Locals make the…campaigns go," *Cambridge* (MA) *Chronicle* (March 1).

Kohn, Margaret (2001), "The Mauling of Public Space" in *Dissent* (Spring).

Kotler, Milton (1969), *Neighborhood Government*. New York: Bobbs Merrill.

Kruger, Eric (2001), "The Conflict of Values Between the New Republicanism and Neo-Liberalism," in Goodall, Douglas K., et.al. (2002), *The American Cultural Civil War*. New York: The Pacific Institute.

Kush, Christopher (2000), *Cybercitizen: How to use your computer to fight for all the issues you care about*. New York: St. Martin's.

Lakoff, George (1996), *Moral Politics: What Conservative Know That Liberals Don't*. Chicago: University of Chicago Press.

Lapham, Lewis (2003), "Cause for Dissent," *Harper's Magazine* (April, pp.38 and 40).

Lasch, Christopher (1995), *Revolt of the Elites and the Betrayal of Democracy*. New York: W.W. Norton & Co.

_____ (1979), *The Culture of Narcissism*. New York: W.W. Norton & Co.

_____ (1995), "Journalism, Publicity, and the Lost Art of Argument," *Kettering Review* (Spring).

Lavelle, Marianne (2003), "Gridlock," *U.S. News & World Report* (September 1)

Lears, Jackson (1981), *No Place of Grace: Antimodernism and the Transformation of American Culture, 1880-1920*. New York: Pantheon Books.

Ledeen, Michael (1999), *Michiavelli on Modern Leadership: Why Machiavelli's Iron Rules are as Timely and Important Today as Five Centuries Ago*. New York: St. Martin's Press.

Lessen, Ronnie (1988), I*ntrapreneurship*: H*ow to be an Enterprising Individual in a Successful Business*. Ashgate Publishing Company.

Levine, Peter (2001), "A New Progressive Era," *Kettering Review* (Spring).

Limbaugh, David (2001), "Moderation in all things? Not quite." *Jewish World Review* (June 6).

Lipow, Arthur (1996), *Political Parties & Democracy*. Chicago and London: Pluto Press.

Lupia, Arthur, and M.D. McCubbins (1998), *The Democratic Dilemma: Can Citizens Learn What They Need to Know?* Cambridge, U.K.: Cambridge University Press.

Mallaby, Sebastian (1999), "The New Machine Politics," *Washington Post* (November 9).

Mansfield, Jane (1980), *Beyond Adversary Democracy*. Chicago: University of Chicago Press.

Marino, Vivian (2000), "A Run for Office Can Mean a Run on Your Money," *New York Times* (Jan. 23).

Marlantes, Liz (2003), "Outsider Dean fires up left," *The Christian Science Monitor* (June 23),

Marshall, Will (1995), "The New Citizenship: Redefining the Relationship Between Government and the Governed," T*he New Democrat* (Vol.7, No.2, March/April).

Mathews, David (1994), P*olitics for People: Finding a Responsible Public Voice*. Urbana, IL: University of Illinois Press.

Maud, Ralph (2000), *What Does not Change: The Significance of Charles Olson's "The Kingfishers."* Teaneck, NJ: Fairleigh Dickenson University Press.

McElvaine, Robert S. (2001), *Eve's Seed: Biology, the Sexes and the Course of History*. New York: McGraw Hill.

McGovern, George (2003), "The Case for Liberalism," *Harper's Magazine* (December).

McKibben, Bill (2003), *Enough: Staying Human in an Engineered Age.* New York: Henry Holt & Co.

McWilliams, Wilson Carey (1969), "Political Arts and Political Sciences," in Green, Philip, and S. Levinson, op.cit. (1970).

Meyrowitz, Joshua (1985), *No Sense of Place: The Impact of Electronic Media on Social Behavior.* New York: Oxford University Press.

Misiroglu, Gina (2002), *The Handy Politics Answer Book.* Visible Ink Press.

Mitroff, Ian, and Warren Bennis (1989), *The Unreality Industry: The Deliberate Manufacturing of Falsehood and What it is Doing to our Lives.* New York: Birch Lane Press

Mitchell, Michelle (1998), *A New Kind of Party Animal: How the Young are Tearing Up the American Political Landscape.* New York: Simon and Shuster.

Morgan, Gareth (1996), *Images of Organization.* Beverly Hills, CA: Sage Publications.

Mullins, Larry (1982), *Immature People with Power: How to Handle Them.* Tulsa, OK: Actionizing, Inc..

Murchland, Bernard (1972), *The New Iconoclasm: Reflections for A Time of Transition.* New York: Doubleday.

Mutz, Diana C. (2002),"The Consequences of Cross-Cutting Networks for Political Participation" *American Journal of Political Science* (Vol.46, No.4, October, 2002).

NACL (1999), "Community Leadership: 1996-1999 Project Report." Dayton, OH: The Kettering Foundation.

(?) National Commission on Civic Renewal (1998), Report @@

Nichols, John, and Robert W. McChesney (2000), *It's the Media, Stupid!.* New York: Seven Stories Press.

Nicolis, G. and I. Progogine (1977), *Self-Organization in Non-Equilibrium Systems: From Dissipative Structures to Order Through Fluctuations.* New York, John Wiley & Sons, Wiley-Interscience.

O'Connell, Pamela LiCalzi (2001), "Mining the Minds of the Masses," *New York Times* (March 6).

Olson, Charles (1963), M*aximus Poems.* New York: Jargon.

Ornstein, Norman (2001), "The Dangers of Voting Outside the Booth." *New York Times* (August 3).

Osborne, David (1990), *Laboratories of Democracy.* New York: McGraw-Hill.

Paget, Karen (1999), "The Big Chill: Foundations and Political Passion." *The American Prospect* (May-June).

Palma, Kristi (2003), "Want 2b Friends," *Sunday Eagle-Tribune* (August 17).

Palmer, Parker (1990), "Leading from Within: Reflections on Spirituality and Leadership." Washington, D.C.: The Servant Leadership School.

Pawley, Martin (1974), *The Private Future.* New York: Random House.

Peck, M. Scott (1983), *People of the Lie: The Hope for Healing Human Evil.* NY: Simon & Shuster.

Peters, Thomas J. and R. H. Waterman (1982), *In Search for Excellence: Lessons From America's Best-Run Companies.* New York: Harper and Row.

Karl Polanyi (1957), T*he Great Transformation: The Political and Economic Origins of Our Time.* Boston: Beacon Press.

Pope, Carl (2002), "The New Patriotism: The antidote to cynicism is participation," *Sierra.* Magazine of the Sierra Club (May/June).

Potier, Beth (2003), "Groups, like people, can be intelligent…," *Harvard University Gazette* (July 17).

Price Waterhouse (1995), *The Paradox Principles: How High Performance Companies Manage Chaos, Complexity and Contradiction to achieve superior results.* New York: McGraw-Hill, (Pt. 2).

Purdy, Jedediah (1999), *For Common Things.* New York: Alfred A. Knopf.

Putnam, Robert (2000), *Bowling Alone: The Collapse and Revival of American Community*. New York: Simon and Shuster.

Quart, Alissa (2002), "A Smarter Way to Sell Ketchup," *Wired* (December). (alissa_quart@yahoo.com)

Rinehart, Stacy T. (1998), *Upside Down: The Paradox of Servant Leadership*. Colorado Springs, CO: NAVPRESS: Bringing Truth to Life.

Reynolds, David (1995), W*alt Whitman's America*. New York: Alfred A. Knopf.

Richards, Amy, and Jennifer Baumgartner (2002), *Manifesta*. New York: Farrar, Straus and Girroux.

Richie, Robert, and Steven Hill (1998), "The Case for Proportional Representation," *Boston Review* (February/March).

Riordan, William L. (1963), *Plunkitt Of Tammany Hall: A Series of Very Plain Talks on Very Practical Politics*. New York: E.P. Dutton & Co.

Rosen, Jay, and D. Merritt, Jr. (1994), "Public Journalism: Theory and Practice." Dayton, OH: the Kettering Foundation.

Salamon, Julie (2001), "A Station Pursues Both the News and the Audience," *New York Times* (October 9, 2001,

Sale, Kirkpatrick (1980), *Human Scale*. New York: Coward, McCann and Georghan.

Saletan, William (2001), "Reinventing Trust in Government," S*late* (Oct.4).

Scott, James C. (1998), *Seeing like a State*. New Haven: Yale University Press.

Seaquist, Carla (2002), "America, we need to talk – *seriously*," T*he Christian Science Monitor* (June 24).

Seelye, Katharine Q. (2001), "Little Change Forecast for Election Process," *New York Times* (April 26).

_____ (2001), "Senators Hear Bitter Words on Florida Vote," *New York Times* (June 28).

_____ (2001), "Liberals Discuss Electoral Overhaul," *New York Times* (January 21).

_____ (2001), "Panel Suggests Election Changes That Let States Keep Control," *New York Times* (February 5)

Senge, Peter M. (1990), T*he Fifth Discipline: The Art & Practice of the Learning Organization.* New York: Currency Doubleday.

_____, et.al. (1994), *The Fifth Discipline Fieldbook.* New York: Currency Doubleday.

Sennett, Richard (1977), T*he Fall of Public Man: On the Social Psychology of Capitalism.* New York: Vintage Books.

_____ (1998), *The Corrosion of Character: The Personal Consequences of Work in the New Capitalism.* New York: W.W. Norton & Co.

Scott, James C. (1998), *Seeing Like a State.* New Haven, CT: Yale University Press.

Sharpe, William and L. Wallock (1987), "From the Great Town to the Non-Place Urban Realm," in Sharp and Wallock, V*isions of the Modern City.* Baltimore, MD: Johns Hopkins University Press.

Shea, Daniel M. (1999), "The Passing of Realignment and the Advent of the 'Base-Less' Party System," American Politics Quarterly, Vol. 27, no. 1, (January), pp. 33-57.

_____ (1995), *Transforming Democracy: Legislative Campaign Committees and Political Parties.* Albany, NY: State University of New York Press.

Shuman, Michael H. (1998), *Going Local: Creating Self-Reliant Communities in a Global Age.* New York: The Free Press.

Shumpeter, Joseph A. (1942), C*apitalism, Socialism and Democracy.* New York: Harper and Row.

Silverman, Gary (2000), "How vote ended up in a very odd state," *Financial Times* (November 9).

Slaatte, H.A.(1968), T*he Pertinence of the Paradox.* New York: Humanities Press.

Slater, Philip (1970), *The Pursuit of Loneliness: American Culture at the Breaking Point*. Boston: Beacon Press.

Smith, Bradley (2000), Address to the Catholic University Law Review Symposium on "Election Law Reform," Washington, D.C. (September 23).

Snider, J.H. (2001), *Government Technology* (August 1).

Stanback, Thomas, and Peter Bearse, et.al. (1982), *Services: The New Economy*. New Jersey: Allenheld-Osmun.

Steinbach, Carol (1999), "Pragmatic Passion: A Small Firm's Big Impact on Economic Policy," *Ford Foundation Report*. New York: Ford Foundation (Spring/Summer).

Sunstein, Cass (2002), *Republic.com*. Princeton, NJ: Princeton University Press.

Syder, Claire (1999), "Shutting the Public Out of Politics: Civic Republicanism, Professional Politics and the Eclipse of Civil Society," An occasional paper of the Kettering Foundation. Dayton, OH: The Kettering Foundation.

Tebbell, John (1974), *The Media in America*. New York: New American Library.

Thelen, David (1996), *Becoming Citizens in the Age of Television*. Chicago: University of Chicago Press.

Toffler, Alvin (1980), *The Third Wave*. New York, N.Y.: William Morrow

Toulmin, Stephen (1990), *Cosmopolis: The Hidden Agenda of Modernity*. Chicago: University of Chicago Press.

Unger, Roberto Mangabeira (1998), *Democracy Realized: the progressive alternative*. New York: Verso.

_____ and Cornell West (1998), *The Future of American Progressivism*. Boston: Beacon Press.

_____ (1987), *False Necessity: Anti-Necessitarian Social Theory in the Service of Radical Democracy, Part I of Politics: A Work in Constructive Social Theory*. New York: Cambridge University Press.

United States Government, Department of Treasury (1993), *Performance Measurement: Report on a Survey of Private Sector Performance Measures.* Washington, D.C.: Financial Management Service (January).

Useem, Jerry (1996), "The Virtue of Necessity," *INC* Magazine (December).

Vargas Llosa, Mario (2001), "Why Literature"? *The New Republic* (May 14).

Verba, Sidney, Kay Lehman Schlozman & Henry E. Brady (1995), *Voice and Equality: Civic Voluntarism in American Politics.* Cambridge: Harvard University Press.

Walker, Adrian (2001), "The Will of the People?," *Boston Globe* (March 1).

Wallace, Jonathan (2001), "Minority Rule," *The Ethical Spectacle* (http://www.spectacle.org, February).

Wayne, Leslie (2000), "Popularity is Increasing for Balloting Outside the Box." *New York Times* (November 4).

Webber, Melvin (1964), *Explorations in Urban Structure.* Philadelphia:

Weiners, Brad (2002), "Making Headlines in 10,000 Point Type," *Wired* (December, p.114).

Wilhelm, Anthony (2000), *Democracy in the Digital Age: Challenges to Political Life in Cyberspace.* New York: Routledge.

Wills, Gary (1993), *Lincoln at Gettysburg: The Words That Remade America.* New York: Simon and Shuster.

Wilson, James Q. (1962), *The Amateur Democrat.* Chicago: University of Chicago Press.

Yankelovitch, Daniel (1991), *Coming to Public Judgment: Making Democracy Work in a Complex World.* Syracuse, NY: Syracuse University Press.

Zakaria, Fareed (2003), *The Future of Freedom: Illiberal Democracy at Home and Abroad.* New York: W.W. Norton.

Zuckerman, Mortimer B. (2003), "A sure-fire recipe for trouble," *U.S. News & World Report* (June 23).

We welcome comments from our readers.
Feel free to write to us at the following address:

Editorial Department
Alpha Publishing, Inc.
P.O. Box 53788
Lafayette, LA 70505

or visit our website at:

www.alphapublishingonline.com